The Orange Blossoms

50 Years of Growth in Orange County

John Sorenson, *editor*
Diann Marsh, *photo editor*

First Edition

All inquiries should be addressed to Heritage Media Corp.

ISBN: 1-886483-35-3

Library of Congress Card Catalog Number: 99-076565

Publisher: C.E. Parks

Editor-in-Chief: Lori M. Parks

Managing Editor: Betsy Baxter Blondin

Project Editor: John Sorenson

Photo Editor: Diann Marsh

Chapter Writers: Steve Donaldson, Nora Horn, Diann Marsh, Joe Osterman, John Sorenson, Doris I. Walker, John Westcott, Toby Young, Bob Ziebell

VP/National Sales Manager: Ray Spagnuolo

VP/Corporate Development: Bart Barica

CFO: Randall Peterson

Production Manager: Deborah Sherwood

Art Director: Gina Mancini

Assistant Project Editor: John Woodward

Coordinating Editors: Renee Kim, Betsy Lelja, Elizabeth Lex, Sara Rufner, Adriane Wessels

Production Staff: Jeff Caton, Brad Hartman, Dave Hermstead, Jay Kennedy, John Leyva, Barry Miller, Susie Passons, Norm Pruitt, Chris Rivera

Profile Writers: Deborah Belgum, Donna Englander, Roy Greer, Libbe S. HaLevy, Poppy Behrens, Patrick Mitchell, Trudie Mitschang, Judi Nelson, Rex Oppenheimer, Mark A. Parks, Patricia Purvis, David Seidman, Christopher Trela, Melissa Tyrrell, Holly Wagner, Jody Marquez Wood, Toby A. Young

Administration Manager: Ellen Ruby

Administration: Juan Diaz, Debbie Hunter, Majka Penner, Scott Reid, Patrick Rucker, Cory Sottek

Project Coordinators: Rex Oppenheimer, Judy Sullivan

Published by

Heritage Media Corp.

6354 Corte del Abeto, Suite B

Carlsbad, California 92009

www.heritagemedia.com

Printed by Heritage Media Corp. in the United States of America

Printed in cooperation with:

Santa Ana Historical Preservation Society

www.SantaAnaHistory.com

Orange County Historical Society

TO MARIAN BERGESON FOR HER EFFORTS IN SUPPORT OF THE HOWE-WAFFLE HOUSE

Anaheim/Orange County Visitor & Convention Bureau

ACKNOWLEDGMENTS

The Orange Blossoms: 50 Years of Growth in Orange County is the story of the county's growth in the post-World War II period. The task of compiling such a book was formidable, and the challenge was to provide coverage to all county areas. The original concept was to provide a chapter for each decade in addition to chapters for specific topics — architecture, the economic base and the institutions. The first task was to recruit the writers. The pool of talented local writers seemed to be more geographically oriented; thus the format changed.

Chapter writers, who are either Orange County residents or longtime followers of Orange County events, were encouraged to write interesting — not necessarily comprehensive — chapters. This book is not intended to be a comprehensive look at the county's history nor a chronology of all events in the county. We've chosen to include stories that illustrate the county's transformation from a rich agricultural county to a rich urban county.

Those who have never attempted to create a book cannot realize the time and effort required by all parties concerned. I wish to thank the photo editor and authors for their respective efforts.

For help with my chapter, I extend special thanks to Lori Goodrich at the A. Gary Anderson Center for Economic Research, Chapman University in Orange, who supplied much of the data for the last 20 years. She was a willing and helpful source of data and other data sources. Thanks must be given to Laura Masoner and Garden Grove Regional Branch, Orange County Public Library for the excellent collection of Orange County Progress Reports, which formed the basis of my early economic data.

Also, special thanks must be given to Earl Nickles, OCHS member, who put me in contact with Stephen Donaldson; and to librarians, Ann Harder, Santa Ana History Room, and Jane Newell, local history curator Anaheim Public Library. I also want to thank Cathy Thomas, curator of the Launer Local History Room, Fullerton Public Library, whose assistance in contacting Bob Ziebell made the North Orange County chapter possible.

A special thanks is offered to Nora Horn for the last-minute preparation of the Arts chapter and introductions to Part I and Part II. The task of editor has been a challenge, both in recruitment and coordination. Behind a book, like a boat, computer or airplane, are countless hours of effort by many working together to create a useful product. May readers reap the joy and benefits of the efforts.

by John Sorenson

Newport Beach Conference and Visitors Bureau

History Room, Santa Ana Public Library

ORANGE COUNTY
JAMBOREE
PLAYLAND
Boy Scouts of America
1953
SANTIAGO PEAK
EL 5680
LOOKOUT STATION
MODJESKA PEAK
EL 4991
LAKE ELSINORE
MODJESKA CANYON
TRABUCO CANYON
74
TRABUCO CANYON RD
EL TORO
MARINE AIR BASE
EL TORO
101
MIGUEL ROAD
ORTEGA HIGHWAY
101
BONITA LAKE
LAGUNA LAKES
MISSION
IRVINE RANCH
SAN JUAN CAPISTRANO
TO SAN DIEGO
SAN CLEMENTE
IRVINE BOWL PARK
LAGUNA BEACH
101-A
GOLF COURSE
GOLF COURSE
DOHENY BEACH
STATE PARK
STATE PARK
DANA POINT
CAPISTRANO BEACH
EMERALD BAY
SAN CLEMENTE PIER
LADDER ROCK
JETTY

Photo by Shane Giblin

INTRODUCTION

Welcome to Orange County! We are a jurisdiction that is less than 800 square miles in size, or only .5 of 1 percent of the total square mileage for the entire state of California. Yet we hold 8 percent of the state's population, which has grown over a dozen-fold from what it was 50 years ago. Our population now exceeds that of 20 states, with one out of every 100 people in the United States living in Orange County.

The economic dynamics of our county are phenomenal! Our real estate accounts for 9.5 percent of California's assessed values! And our business community constitutes 10 percent of the state's gross domestic product. This alone makes Orange County a desirable place to live. But, as the saying goes, "there's more." We have an ideal climate, three beautiful harbors, 42 miles of beaches, universities, golf courses, 32 cities, a vast network of arterial highways, freeways and toll roads and an incredibly diverse business community. This once-active agricultural area has become a major suburban complex of adjoining cities, shopping malls, amusement parks and commercial centers. Our significant growth has also allowed us to enjoy a rich cultural and ethnic diversity. And we have a vibrant history.

In 150 short years our state has risen to become the seventh largest economy in the world. On January 24, 1848, James Marshall discovered gold. The following year the "Forty-Niners" would create one of the world's largest overland migrations. By September 9, 1850, California entered into statehood, becoming our country's 31st state. As we observe our state's sesquicentennial and the new millennium, it is interesting to note that the migration and growth continue. Local history includes the Mission San Juan Capistrano founded in 1776; visits by Richard Henry Dana in 1835; the development of Anaheim Landing (1857), Newport Landing (1870), and McFadden Wharf (1888) for ocean trade vessels; breaking away from Los Angeles County in 1889; the original courthouse completed in 1901; the Balboa Pavilion built in 1905; and President Richard Nixon's birthplace in Yorba Linda that was built the year before his birth in 1913. Orange County, with its plethora of outstanding leaders, was destined for success.

In July 1966 the firms of Lowry and Associates and Engineering Science, Inc. published an innocuous little report titled "Waste Water Disposal and Reclamation for the County of Orange, California, 1966-2000." This report uncannily predicted the population growth of Orange County, including the boom years of the 70s, to an anticipated population of 3 million by the year 2000. This growth curve has made the development community in the county a very prosperous one. And why not? This is the place that most of the nation's population wants to either live in or visit.

As you leaf through the pages of *The Orange Blossoms: 50 Years of Growth in Orange County*, reflect on the joys and pains of growth and success. This is home. This is our community. This is where we work and play. This is where we are raising our families. It has enjoyed unprecedented growth. It has survived a recent financial calamity. It is resilient, dynamic and moving forward on the cutting edge into the future. It looks great. It feels great. It even has a wonderful aroma. So stop, reflect and take time to smell the "Orange Blossoms."

by John M. W. Moorlach, C.P.A., CFP, Orange County Treasurer-Tax Collector and Vice President of the California Sesquicentennial Foundation Board of Directors

PART ONE

People come to a place to live together, united by their common needs. They build homes and communities and spaces in which to do business, connected by ever-improving arteries of transportation. And when their communities achieve a confident level of comfort, they embrace the arts. The nearly three million people of Orange County share the same aspirations as those of any other community, which is why the editors of *The Orange Blossoms* have chosen to organize this first section of the book as an anthology devoted to four significant aspects of people's lives.

Part One is divided into these subjects: Arts, Architecture, Transportation and Economics. Each section was assigned to a writer who was challenged to explore the topic and uncover the interesting stories of how these common themes found their unique expressions in Orange County. Behind the dates and statistics that often overwhelm a conventional history book is a compelling narrative of the county's people, their passions and their productivity. Indeed, the sheer size and importance of the county — one out of every 100 people in the United States lives in Orange County and its economy constitutes 10 percent of California's gross domestic product — make it imperative to personalize the area's tremendous growth in order to fully appreciate the achievements of this thriving network of communities. Little more than 50 years ago the area was a quiet agricultural landscape where orange trees outnumbered inhabitants.

Today the fields are gone, replaced by homes, highways, schools and industrial parks. While some may long for the fragrance of citrus flowers, few bemoan the loss of a lifestyle where education was limited, work was difficult and livelihoods were meager. The story of Orange County's transformation is a fascinating one, from freeways to financial centers, from modest housing developments to massive centers of commerce, education and the performing arts. The people of the county made it all happen, and here are the stories of their vision and accomplishments. ■

Architecture

ARTS

TRANSPORTATION

economics

ARTS

Pride, Passion and Great Performances: The Explosive Growth of the Arts in Orange County

By Nora Horn

During the years following World War II, Orange County was a quiet backwater compared to its neighbor to the north. Its postwar population of only 200,000 was interspersed throughout small towns and cities that were surrounded by thousands of acres of citrus groves and fields of flowers and vegetables. Tranquil as life must have been, it was no magnet for the world's great artistic performers. For years if Orange County residents wanted to hear the symphony or see a great play, they had to make the tedious drive to Los Angeles, which was busy building an enviable cultural establishment.

Much has changed since the mid-20th century. Orange County's population has grown tenfold to more than two and one-half million, and the orchards have given way to industrial parks and vast subdivisions. The county has enormous pride in its economic, civic and political prowess and no patience for playing second fiddle to Los Angeles. With its economy flourishing, its population swelling and its position secure as second in size and stature in California, Orange County has the power, the population and the purse to attract and nurture the world's best artistic talent.

The brass section of the Pacific Symphony Orchestra provides dramatic music at the Orange County Performing Arts Center. *Pacific Symphony Orchestra*

Women's Clubs, formed before 1900 in most local communities, became the backbone for a variety of important cultural activities from libraries to musical and dramatic performances. *Old Courthouse Museum*

As Orange County has grown, so has its appetite for the arts and its ability to support them. From great concert halls to small community theaters, Orange County's 33 cities play host to an extraordinary range of artistic endeavors, from renowned guest artists to thriving resident companies. Each year, more than three and one-half million people pay to support museums, music, theater and dance, and it is the enthusiastic endorsement of the county's residents that has enabled the arts community to flourish. The arts form the 12th largest nongovernmental employer in Orange County, and so important are they to the life and soul of the county, that they generate direct and indirect revenues of close to $350 million every year.

The 1980s were years of dramatic growth and maturity for the arts scene in Orange County. By the mid-1990s, the power and influence of the arts were so great that the county's education, business and artistic leaders took the initiative to create an agency that would represent the arts as a cohesive community. Arts Orange County was founded in February 1995 as a non-profit arts council. It is an official arts agency of the county but receives no funding from it. The agency acts as a sponsor of programs and services designed to serve the artistic community and works to increase public awareness of the arts. Arts Orange County has the compelling mission to strengthen the life of the arts and thereby enhance the quality of life for all the people of Orange County.

Some 200 nonprofit arts organizations are active throughout the area, and the diversity of programming is dizzying. A dozen or so of these organizations are large, with budgets ranging up to $22 million, while around 20 are mid-sized. All the rest are small. The county's 12 community colleges, colleges and universities also play a part in the county's cultural life, as do the community facilities in each of the county's cities. These organizations support hundreds of artists who live and work in Orange County.

(Far left)
Charles and Ada Bowers donated their property at North Main and 20th streets in Santa Ana and their trust created Bowers Museum. The Spanish Colonial Revival building was constructed in 1934 and had its grand opening in April 1936, with Bessie Coulter as curator.
Photo by Diann Marsh

The Santa Ana High School Auditorium, built from 1935 to 1937, is well known for its exceptional acoustics. Several musical groups have regularly performed in the Moderne building.
Turville Photography
Photo by Steve Lopushinsky

(Far left)
The Imagination Celebration held each May at various locations throughout the county encourages children to develop their artistic talents. This photo was taken on Second Street in Santa Ana with the Grand Central Arts Building in the background.
Jim Gilliam, Santa Ana Arts Administrator

Each spring, members of the California Art Club come to Santa Ana to paint the historic buildings, cultural life and scenery. As participants in the Invitational Plein Air Art Exhibit, they display their completed works at a juried show at the end of the event.
Jim Gilliam, Santa Ana Arts Administrator

The result of a grand dream of many county residents, the Segerstrom Hall at the Orange County Performing Arts Center opened on September 29, 1986, with the Los Angeles Philharmonic Orchestra and soprano Leontyne Price headlining the event. *Orange County Performing Arts Center, photo by Charles McGrath*

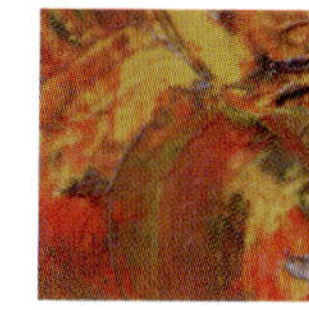

Private Initiative

Public money contributes only a tiny fraction of the revenues needed to support the county's vast artistic network. Private funding in the form of donations, memberships and fund-raising is what keeps the arts in Orange County in business, and the power of private funding is best exemplified in the creation of the Orange County Performing Arts Center. As far back as the late 60s, the performing community was eager to build a first-class facility that would do justice to its accomplishments and aspirations. The consensus was that any major arts complex must be freeway accessible, and a decade went by as site after site was rejected. Finally a direct appeal was made to the Segerstrom family.

The Segerstroms, the family who developed South Coast Plaza, trace their roots back to 1898 when their Swedish ancestors settled in Orange County. The family farmed for 50 years, acquiring land for agricultural purposes. Since 1949 they have been involved in real estate development. Believing that the arts are vital in establishing a cultural identity for Orange County, the family's substantial success enabled them to be prominent patrons of the local arts community. In keeping with their commitment, they had previously donated land for the South Coast Repertory's new theater in Costa Mesa. As part of their sizable real estate holdings, the Segerstroms owned a valuable five-acre parcel of land adjacent to South Coast Plaza. Answering the appeal for an arts site, the family agreed to donate it as the location for a new performing arts facility. In May 1979 the Segerstroms' land gift was matched with an equally generous pledge of $1 million in cash.

A major fund-raising campaign was launched, bolstered by an additional $5 million donation from the Segerstrom family and a $2 million gift from D. James Bentley. The campaign quickly accumulated $40 million in cash, and groundbreaking for the center took place in July 1983. Opening night for the Orange County Performing Arts Center was September 29, 1986, with a gala concert in the new Segerstrom Hall featuring the Los Angeles Philharmonic and soprano Leontyne Price. Henry T. Segerstrom praised the private initiative that had spurred the design and construction of the center, which he said represented the greatness of the county's ingenuity and enterprise and symbolized its pride and self-esteem. Twelve years later, the center's success inspired another generous gift of land from the Segerstrom family for the purpose of expanding the facility. The six-acre site will be devoted exclusively to the future growth of the county's arts organizations.

Orange County Performing Arts Center is one of the country's most technically advanced and acoustically innovative performance halls. Its Grand Portal is an impressive 12 stories high, while the 3,000-seat Segerstrom Theater, with its asymmetrical design and exceptional sightlines, provides an unusual sense of intimacy between the performers and the audiences. The 300-seat Founders Hall is the ideal environment for intimate concerts. Every year, the center is host to dance companies, Broadway musicals, classical musicians, and jazz and cabaret artists along with an exciting calendar of special events. Since its inception, the center has fulfilled its promise of enriching the spirit and intellect of the entire community.

Promising musicians are chosen each year by the Santa Ana Unified School District to become members of the honor orchestra, band or choir. These students were selected to be members of the orchestra in 1996.
Apple Photographers and the Santa Ana Unified School District, Coordinator Randy Coleman

Plummer Auditorium, designed by Los Angeles architect Carlton Winslow, has served as a showcase for a variety of performing groups since its dedication on January l, 1930. On the National Register of Historic Places, it is part of the Fullerton College Campus.
Turville Photography
Photo by Steve Lopushinsky

The Pacific Symphony is dedicated to education and community outreach, providing 20 different programs to serve Orange County residents. Among these are the Pacific Symphony Institute at California State University Fullerton and the Pacific Symphony Youth Orchestra at the Orange County High School of the Arts.
Pacific Symphony Orchestra

Music

Orange County's oldest music organization is the Philharmonic Society, which presents an impressive program of world-famous symphony orchestras, chamber ensembles, soloists and international folk companies. The Society's mission is to foster and promote the knowledge and appreciation of the arts, and it does so by presenting both performances and music education programs. Relying on the generosity of its patrons who include individuals, corporations, foundations and government sources, the Philharmonic Society maintains a balanced budget that enables it to be an important and progressive force in the musical life of the county. In addition to its paying performances, the Society sponsors youth programs in both public and private schools for 250,000 students from kindergarten through 12th grade. Twelve hundred volunteers work to make them possible.

The Pacific Symphony Orchestra is the resident orchestra of the Orange County Performing Arts Center, presenting a rich and varied array of musical programming and outreach activities. Each year 250,000 people attend the orchestra's more than 60 concerts of both classical and pop music. The organization is also deeply committed to the development of training orchestras and sponsors an adopt-a-musician program for schools and a competition for young artists. The orchestra performs free concerts for 24,000 students, and its programming efforts for young people have been recognized as one of the nine best music education programs in the nation.

The Pacific Chorale collaborates with the Pacific Symphony in presenting the highest-quality performances and recordings of choral masterworks. Founded in 1968, the Pacific Chorale produces its own series of choral/orchestral concerts each year and performs at the Orange County Performing Arts Center. The Chorale also performs with the Pasadena Symphony, the Long Beach Symphony, the Hollywood Bowl Orchestra, the Los Angeles Philharmonic, the Boston Symphony Orchestra, the Los Angeles Chamber Orchestra and the Ojai Festival Orchestra. Its touring schedule has taken it around the world from Belgium to Beijing with concerts in world capitals and world-class concert halls. The Chorale's achievements have been noted with a Margaret Hillis Achievement Award for Choral Excellence and the highest ranking from the California Arts Council. Pacific Chorale has four children's choruses and an active outreach program with in-school performances. Also, the Chorale can be heard on compact disc singing a cappella and contemporary works.

Orange County's oldest continuously performing arts organization is the 160-voice William Hall Master Chorale, in performance for more than 40 years. Its consistently high artistic integrity is maintained through rigorous auditions and continual training in musicianship, resulting in critical praise and international recognition. The Chorale is a founding member of the Orange County Performing Arts Center and

Internationally recognized Pacific Symphony Orchestra Director, Carl St.Clair, is one of America's foremost conductors.
Pacific Symphony Orchestra

The Pacific Symphony Orchestra was founded in 1978 and is now the third largest orchestra in California.
Pacific Symphony Orchestra

participated in the opening night concert conducted by Zubin Mehta. International tours are an important part of the Chorale's schedule, which has taken the group throughout Europe, Russia, Scandinavia, New Zealand, Australia and China. For compact disc, the William Hall Master Chorale has recorded the Rachmaninoff Vespers, Durufle's "Requiem" and Four "Motets," Benjamin Britten's "War Requiem," Igor Stravinsky's "Symphony of Psalms," and Beethoven's "Mass in C" and "Ninth Symphony" as well as "Ceremony and Carols," a collection of holiday classics.

In 1985 the vibrant and compelling Mozart Classical Orchestra was founded to bring the intimacy of chamber music to Orange County. The group focuses on works from the classical repertoire, both mainstays and rarely heard works, and since its inception has received consistently high public praise and support for the intelligence of its programs and the quality of its guest soloists. Since 1986 its musical home has been St. Andrews Church in Newport Beach while presenting other performances at the Irvine Barclay Theatre. Ticket prices are kept low to encourage the widest possible attendance.

Enthusiastic support keeps many small musical organizations flourishing throughout the county. Since 1959 the Laguna Chamber Music Society has presented an annual chamber music series and visited Orange County schools to enrich the musical education of students. Its concerts are co-presented by the Philharmonic Society and are held at the Irvine Barclay Theatre. The Aliso Viejo Symphony is a 70-member resident orchestra that performs classical, pop and Broadway music, an eclectic programming schedule designed for enlightenment and education as well as pure enjoyment. The Harmonia Baroque Players is Orange County's single professional baroque chamber ensemble, playing recorder, violin, oboe, viola da gamba, cello, lute, guitar and harpsichord. The group, which performs at the Newport Harbor Lutheran Church in Newport Beach, also plays medieval, Renaissance and contemporary pieces. Free concerts are the generous offering of the Fullerton Friends of Music, the oldest chamber music society in the county. The society invites visiting artists to perform instrumental and vocal music from the Renaissance through the 20th century.

Opera

There is enough support in the county to maintain three outstanding opera and light opera organizations. Now in its second decade, Opera Pacific, which performs at the Orange County Performing Arts Center, is the nation's 11th largest opera company. Its groundbreaking productions are studded with

Opera Pacific, the nation's 11th largest opera company, features major opera stars and musicians. The dramatic scene pictured is from *The Flying Dutchman*.
Opera Pacific

major opera stars, and its artistic team is made up of luminaries from around the world who work with the management group to present opera as a dramatic and dazzling experience. The company also produces touring productions.

The nonprofit Orange County Opera has been operating since 1976 with the support of the Orange County Department of Education and Las Campanas. Its purpose is to bring opera at affordable prices to schoolchildren, and in doing so it provides an opportunity for young professional singers to develop in a richly rewarding environment. Many Orange County Opera performers move on to international acclaim, but before they do, they make an art form available to young audiences who can then experience opera as fun and thrilling instead of intimidating and elitist. The shows are beautifully sung and convincingly acted with clear English translations and imaginative costumes and scenery.

After more than 25 years, the Fullerton Civic Light Opera is one of the largest musical theater companies in all of Southern California, and one of its best, having won more than 30 Drama-Logue and Robbie Awards. Four Broadway musicals are produced per season and are performed in Fullerton's Plummer Auditorium. The professional cast is accompanied by a full orchestra.

The Aman Folk Dancers, based in Santa Ana, showcases historic, cultural and traditional dances during its performances for both children and adults. Shown here is one of the folk dancing instruction sessions regularly held by the troop. *Jim Gilliam, Santa Ana Arts Administrator*

Dance

One of the most important members of Orange County's cultural community is Ballet Pacifica, founded in 1962 and now the area's most prominent dance troupe. Recognized for its innovation, energy and elegance, the company presents eclectic seasons of both classical and contemporary ballet. The company's concert series, priced to be as affordable as possible, is performed in the intimate Irvine Barclay Theatre. With a mission to entertain, educate and enrich the lives of its audience, Ballet Pacifica works with emerging and established choreographers and has premiered over 40 new ballets. In addition to its dance series, Ballet Pacifica presents traditional stories and imaginative ballets in its Ballet for Children Series, and every Christmas season a spectacular production of *The Nutcracker* is staged for the holidays.

In addition to the prestigious Ballet Pacifica, several smaller dance companies are active around the county. The Anaheim Ballet performs classically based ballets in contemporary presentations and features artists from such major companies as American Ballet Theater and the Bolshoi. Aspiring young dancers study under the auspices of The Company — Dance Unlimited in Garden Grove and perform a repertory of jazz and contemporary works as well as classical ballets in a professional environment. Classical ballet is showcased in Fountain Valley by the Festival Ballet Theatre, which collaborates with

The Ballet Pacifica, founded in 1962, presents both classical and contemporary ballets. Below they perform the ballet "In the Ruins." *Ballet Pacifica Photo by Mark Kirchner*

guest artists and offers narrative ballets for children. The Metropolitan Ballet Company in Los Alamitos was founded in 1989 and features a repertory of full-length classic and modern works. The company offers master classes with notable teachers and has a first-class training facility. Centered in Costa Mesa, the DeFore Foundation for the Arts offers dance training and scholarships and sponsors public performances in support of the artistic efforts of the community. In addition, other pre-professional organizations nurture the county's young dance talent.

The new 22,000-square-foot St. Joseph's Ballet building, located in the 1800 block of North Main Street in Santa Ana, was completed in October 1999. The prime focus of the organization is to allow children from all economic levels to learn to dance.
Diann Marsh

Theater

Theater both large and small entertains enthusiastic audiences all over Orange County. One of the oldest and most successful is the Laguna Playhouse, which traces its history back to 1920 when a group of local theater lovers began a thespian group that met to offer readings and performances in private homes and storefronts. Four years later The Playhouse on Ocean Avenue was built in the heart of downtown Laguna Beach. The building cost $5,000, and during the Depression it was sold to the city, which then leased it back to the players. Throughout World War II, the Laguna Playhouse did its patriotic duty, entertaining the troops and sponsoring USO dances for the soldiers. The first theater was replaced in 1969 with the Moulton Theater, built with private funds on city land on Laguna Canyon Road. Gaining professionalism and stature, the Laguna Playhouse produced increasingly high-quality works starring primarily amateur actors. By 1990 the Playhouse was transformed to full professional status, with a budget of $2 million and an annual audience of more than 100,000. Currently the Laguna Playhouse offers a subscription series that runs from September through June, a six-play season of classical and contemporary dramas, comedies and musicals and a four-play youth theater season. Special productions are also offered during the summer.

With little more to start with than talent and enthusiasm, David Emmes and Martin Benson founded the South Coast Repertory (SCR) in 1964 and have nurtured it to its current status as one of America's premier nonprofit resident theaters. Their original aim was to present world-class theater to the people of Orange County, and they have succeeded brilliantly. SCR's artistic directors have been recognized by both the Tony

Opened in 1998 in the former Barker Bros. building on North Main Street at the Santa Ana (5) Freeway in Santa Ana, the Taco Bell Discovery Science Center is a 59,000-square-foot facility filled with fun and hands-on exhibits for children and adults.
Discovery Science Center
Photo by Gene Orgami

Artist Gerald Swartz looks out of the window in his studio at the historic Santora Building on Broadway Street in Santa Ana. A wide variety of artists, including those from local colleges, have studios and galleries in the building. An open house held the first Saturday night of each month displays the artists' current works.
Diann Marsh

Ballet Pacifica performers Katherina Von Schonfeldt and Michel Gervais pose during one of the company's contemporary ballets.
Ballet Pacifica

Award and Pulitzer Prize committees. A typical season at SCR consists of 11 productions on two stages in their theater in Costa Mesa. Programs often include premieres as well as presentations of the classics and revivals of earlier successes.

The Irvine Barclay Theater is the presenting stage for world-class music, drama and dance. A season at the Barclay includes classical music luminaries, pop stars, world music, opera soloists, jazz artists, contemporary dance and productions of comedy and drama. The Barclay is the primary performance venue of the chamber music, world music and eclectic series presented by the Philharmonic Society of Orange County, Ballet Pacifica and Arpana Dance.

From Shakespeare to the alternative and avant-garde, Orange County's small theaters are consistently innovative and involved with the community. Chapman University is the site of Shakespeare Orange County, founded in 1981 and dedicated to presenting the best of the Bard, including its charming annual holiday program, A Shakespearean Christmas. The Vanguard Theatre Ensemble is theater-on-the-edge whose association of professionals redefines theater's artistic boundaries by deliberating ideas of contemporary relevance that speak to the human condition. The theater-in-the-round Alternative Repertory Theater operates out of a storefront in Santa Ana, presenting high-quality, entertaining and thought-provoking plays at affordable prices. Mystery, drama, musicals and comedy are on stage from September through May at the San Clemente Community Theater, an intimate venue at home in a 1926 house.

Museums

The Orange County museum patron can choose from a number of exceptional museums that showcase the artistic and cultural achievements of California, the Americas and the world. The Bowers Museum of Cultural Art in Santa Ana began as a gift to that city for the purpose of preserving the history of Orange County. Charles Bowers was a prosperous citrus grower and land developer who came west from Missouri in the late 19th century. He and his wife Ada were avid history buffs, and to thank the community that had been so good to them, they decided to donate a space that could showcase the history, memorabilia and archaeological artifacts of Orange County. Charles died in 1929 at the age of 87 and Ada died two years later. After their deaths, construction for the museum began on the site where their frame house had stood at 20th and Main. The Depression was a difficult time for public funding, but WPA artists were commissioned to paint ceiling murals and create interior decoration. The new Bowers Museum opened in February 1936 with a festive celebration that featured Mexican music and dance.

Over the years the Bowers enlarged the frequency and scope of its exhibits and launched an ambitious agenda of educational and community outreach programming. As the focus of the museum was enlarged to include the cultural arts and natural history of the world, in 1974 private funds were provided for an expansion. In 1988 a $12 million project added another 50,000 square feet of space. The renovation was funded by a Community Redevelopment grant. When it was completed, the Bowers emerged as a large facility designed to mount traveling art shows as well as exhibitions from the permanent collections.

Following its expansion, the museum redefined its goals. The Bowers now aims to preserve, study and exhibit the fine arts of the Americas, Africa and the Pacific. It is the only institution in the country with

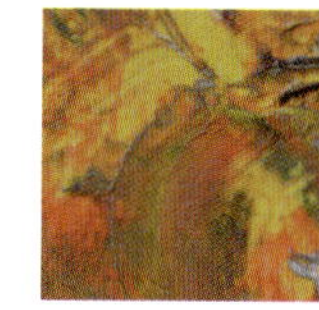

such a focus. The Bowers houses an impressive collection of historic artifacts, pre-Columbian, Native American, Oceanic and Asian art from both ancient and modern civilizations. Visitors to the Bowers are treated to an extraordinary range of special exhibits that might include musical instruments from the early Romantic period, modern art from Vietnam and ancient Colombian gold. All are designed to highlight the diversity of the human family. The quality of the Bowers collections has earned it an accreditation from the American Association of Museums, (fewer than 10 percent of American museums are so honored) a recommendation as one of the nation's must-see museums and the support of more than 4,000 members.

The oldest cultural institution in Orange County is the Laguna Art Museum. In its magnificent scenic location just steps away from the ocean, the museum focuses on California artists whose paintings, drawings, photographs and sculpture are housed in both spacious and intimate galleries. Changing exhibitions feature historical and contemporary art as well as works by new and emerging artists. As part of its commitment to share the arts with the public, the Laguna Museum is the only museum in Orange County to sponsor a gallery devoted to both sales and rental. For a nominal fee, individuals and corporations may rent artwork for display in their homes or offices.

The Orange County Museum of Art welcomes patrons to its facility in Newport Beach and to its satellite space in South Coast Plaza. The museum's permanent collection is an impressive chronicle of 20th-century California's art history from the plein air painters to the most cutting edge of contemporary art. The variety of its exhibitions and impression is rich and diversified, designed to appeal to everyone with an interest in the visual arts, from children to older adults. Throughout the year the museum offers classes for adults and children, a popular film series and lunch-hour lectures by artists, art critics and art historians.

(Far left)
Bell Rock with its grinding holes was moved from Bell Canyon to Bowers Museum in 1936. The large stone was used by American Indian women to grind acorns into meal using stone pestles.
Diann Marsh

(Top right)
One of Corona del Mar's most valuable and unsung historical treasures is the Sherman Library. Located on the grounds of the lushly landscaped Sherman Gardens, the library is devoted to the study of the history of the Pacific Southwest.
Diann Marsh
Postcard Collection

(Left)
The charm and beauty of Laguna Beach has been bringing artists to live and work in the seaside town since soon after the turn of the century. The Laguna Museum features both historical and contemporary art.
Old Courthouse Museum

(Left photos)
Orange County's oldest museum, the Mission San Juan Capistrano, was founded in 1776. In the 1890s when Charles Lummis and his Landmarks Foundation came from Los Angeles to begin the process of restoration, the buildings and courtyard were in ruins. The restoration, as well as archaeological work, is an ongoing project.
Photo by Diann Marsh

(Far right) Living history is demonstrated at the Heritage Hill Historic Park in Lake Forest. The El Toro Grammar School, a one-room schoolhouse built in 1890, is shown in the background. The Victorian Christmas and Candlelight Tours, held during the first two weekends in December, are popular events. *County of Orange*

Elementary school students frequently visit the restored courtroom, located on the top floor of the Old Orange County Courthouse at 211 W. Santa Ana Boulevard. In this photo they are role playing a court scene. *County of Orange*

Impressionism flourished in California from 1890 to 1930 as artists flocked to Southern California for the light and the landscape. Inspiration was everywhere, from the miles of breathtaking shoreline, the endless Pacific Ocean, the rolling hills and breathtaking fields of flowers. A vibrant variation of the school of American Impressionism, the California school has come into its own at the Irvine Museum, which features paintings from that period. The Irvine Museum mounts three exhibitions a year, each dedicated to a single theme and designed to present the artworks in their historical context. With the vast vistas of uninhabited land long vanished, the paintings in the Irvine Museum preserve their beauty on canvas as a tribute to the natural splendor that was California during the days when it was idealized as a reincarnation of Eden.

Smaller art centers and museums are dispersed throughout Orange County and support the arts in unusual and creative ways. The Irvine Fine Arts Center is a multi-use community facility that includes fine art galleries, an art store and photography, jewelry and ceramics studios. Classes for all ages are offered, as are year-round exhibitions. The Fullerton Museum Center presents exhibitions and educational programs devoted to history, science and art. The museum's three galleries host traveling shows and original exhibitions dedicated to contemporary topics and ideas. Focusing entirely on the work of living artists, the

The Reuben E. Lee, originally an upscale restaurant, has been converted into the Newport Harbor Nautical Museum in Newport Beach. Inspiring and authentic displays of the boating history of Orange County's oceanfront are enhanced by the atmosphere and setting. *Newport Harbor Nautical Museum*

(Far left)
The Discovery Science Center, opened in its new location on Main Street in Santa Ana in 1998, features unique state-of-the-art hands-on exhibits that bring science alive to all of those who experience the new facility.
Discovery Science Center

The Maag House, also moved to the Discovery Museum of Orange County, was originally built in 1899 by John and Katherine Maag on their Fairhaven Street ranch. The 3000-square-foot Neo-classical Revival home is presently being restored to its original beauty. The adjacent tank house and carriage barn were restored in the 1980s.
Diann Marsh

Huntington Beach Art Center presents an eclectic and comprehensive calendar of performance art, readings, dance, music, lectures, film screenings, classes and workshops.

When it comes to the arts, Orange County believes that kids count. Many of the major performing companies have extensive outreach programs for them, and two Orange County museums are dedicated to children. The Children's Museum at La Habra is housed in a restored railroad station and is a fun, hands-on museum for families with kids from infants to teen-agers. The museum offers interactive exhibits, arts and crafts and special performances. The permanent exhibits include Nature Walk, Science Station, Kids on Stage and Pre-School Play Park. Science, theater and the diversity of multicultural programming are highlighted through changing exhibits.

The Discovery Science Center in Santa Ana makes learning about science a whole lot of fun. It's so much easier to learn about complex concepts when kids can actually recline comfortably on a bed of nails, make their own animated movies or walk unscathed through a tornado. With its purpose of increasing the understanding and appreciation of science, math and technology, the center is designed to enliven the experience of education with compelling exhibits devoted to human perception, the earth, earthquakes, space exploration, computers and history's great scientists.

The Hiram Kellogg House, built in 1898, was moved from Downtown Santa Ana to the Discovery History Museum in the early 1980s and has been beautifully restored as a house museum. Children's tours, weekend open houses, birthday celebrations and special events showcase Victorian life. The museum is on Harvard Street, west of Fairview.
Diann Marsh

ARTS

From science to the symphony, the residents of Orange County have created a dynamic environment in which the arts entertain, enliven and enrich their lives. The citizens' collective commitment, both corporate and private, has made the county's explosive growth of the arts possible, and it is their ongoing passion and patronage, energy and enthusiasm that will guarantee its future brilliance. From the glittering concert halls of the established institutions to the edgy enclaves of experimental endeavors, Orange County's artists and patrons support one another in an artful adventure, free to explore and soar together.

Randy Au, one of the founders of the successful Arts Movement in Santa Ana, demonstrates his ceramics abilities at an art fair at the Santora Building.
Jim Gilliam, Santa Ana Arts Administrator

Turville Photography, photo by Steve Lopushinsky

Historic wallpapers, hand-carved woodworks, antiques and oriental rugs showcase the arts and decor popular in the 1890s. The Dr. Howe-Waffle House, a 12-room Queen Anne Victorian mansion has been authentically restored by the Santa Ana Historical Preservation Society and is available for tours and events. This photo is of the ornate polished wooden main staircase.
Diann Marsh

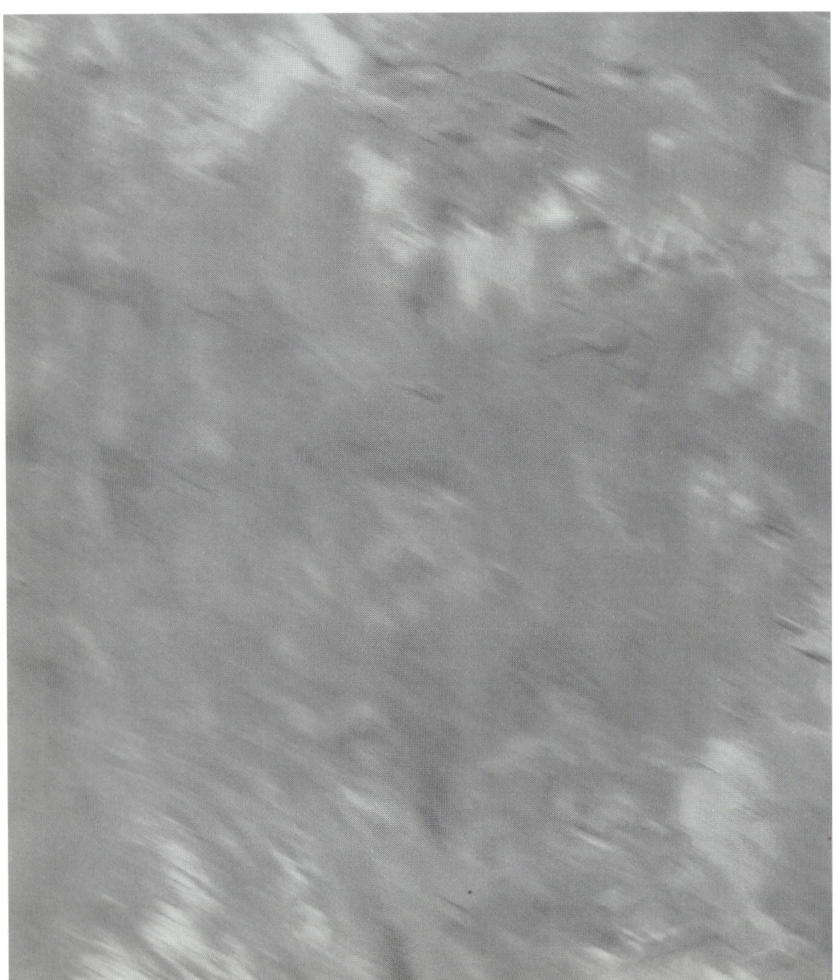

ARCHITECTURE

Orange County's Architectural Legacy

By Diann Marsh

Picture Orange County in 1945… until the 1960s, it was still possible to step outside in the evening and become inundated with the rich, pungent sweet smell of orange blossoms, as well as the tangy odors of cabbage, onions, beans, sugar beets and chili peppers. As grove after grove and field after field of Orange County's rich agricultural base were gobbled up by developers, the aromas gradually disappeared.

Orange County was an exciting place to live during World War II. The Santa Ana Army Air Base, U.S. Marine Corps Station at El Toro, U.S. Naval Air Station and Santa Ana Army Airdome had been established in the farm country southeast of Santa Ana, Costa Mesa and Tustin. A stream of cars filled with servicemen spewed from the sprawling military bases, traveled along D Street (now El Camino Real) in Tustin, turned left onto First Street and headed to downtown Santa Ana. They were among 250,000 military personnel who spent various amounts of time at Orange County military bases during and after the war years. Many of them, observing the balmy weather, palm trees, view of the mountains and accessibility to the beaches, envisioned themselves returning to live in the newly discovered land of milk and honey.

The Ranch-style houses of the early 1950s featured lots of windows, an informal floor plan, and character-defining details such as heavy shake roofs, plate glass windows and sliding doors, brick wainscotting and quaint little alcoves and bays. *Photo by Diann Marsh*

In the 1940s each town was a community by itself, separated by farms, ranches and orange groves. As a result, each town exhibited its own individual character. In Anaheim, for example, settlement was still basically confined within the boundaries of the East, West, North and South streets of the 1857 Mother Colony. After leaving those streets, the traveler was out in the country, among the orange groves and farmlands. Anaheim did have a well-developed town center, however, and a trip downtown on Saturday night was often the highlight of the family's weekly activities. Santa Ana, on the other hand, had grown dramatically during the 1920s and, by 1940, was home to 31,921 persons. In addition, soldiers came from the military bases to visit the USO or have a night on the town. The city bustled with activity.

Stable small communities such as Brea, Buena Park, Fullerton, Garden Grove, La Habra, Orange, Tustin and Laguna Beach were pleasant places to live and work. Few dreamed of the giant mushroom cloud of development that would cover the land within the next 10 to 15 years, bringing dramatic changes to the Orange County landscape.

Santa Ana, shown here in the 1950s, was the commercial center of Orange County. Stores such as Rankin's Department Store, Vandermast's and Hugh J. Lowe's Men's Furnishings handled high-quality merchandise. *Orange County Historical Society*

The farmers of Dairyland, for example, were in for unimaginable change. Established in 1955 by dairy and poultry farmers who had been forced out of Los Angeles County, the new community prohibited property sites of less than five acres. When the farmers moved to the new community, they expected to be able to stay there forever. Within 15 years almost all of the farmers were forced out to Riverside County lands near Norco and Chino. Consequently, in 1965, Dairyland changed its name to La Palma because there were no more dairies there.

From its beginnings until the 1950s, most of the county's development had occurred in the central, north and northwest regions. The southern

half was not even a gleam in the eye of the men who would eventually develop it into miles and miles of pleasant homes and tasteful shopping centers.

Each Man Has His Castle

Prosperity reigned in Orange County in the 1920s. It was said that "each man could have his castle designed in any style he wanted." Whole neighborhoods of Tudor, Spanish and Colonial Revival homes were being built in north and central Orange County. The nearby countryside was covered with a lush tapestry of picture-perfect orange, lemon, avocado and walnut groves.

During the1930s, home building virtually came to a halt as Americans experienced the Great Depression. Few homes were built as millions of Americans managed to barely survive. In 1938 and 1939 near the end of the Depression, home building slowly resumed and a trend toward modest homes, built in a single-story traditional style, developed. The nation had barely gotten back on its feet when World War II began.

As a result of the wartime constraints, most residential building ceased between 1941 and 1945. American men were away fighting the war and building supplies were scarce. The winning of the war brought a cheerfulness and enthusiasm to the country as young couples were reunited and excited about getting on with their lives.

(Far left)
Colonial Revival and Cape Cod-influenced houses were popular in the 1940s. This Colonial Revival home is symmetrical, with 6-over-6 windows on each side of the recessed front door.
Photo by Diann Marsh

(Top right)
Craftsman-influenced bungalows, built in the 1910s and 20s, provided housing for the average family in the established towns of the county and made home ownership a possibility for thousands of working people.
Photo by Diann Marsh

(Left)
Spanish Colonial Revival houses vied with Tudor Revival-designed homes for popularity in the 1920s and 30s. The red-tile-clad roofs, rustic timbers and rail on the second-floor porch, arcaded front windows, stucco cladding and a large chimney define the Spanish character of this North Santa Ana house.
Photo by Diann Marsh

One of the most popular building styles of the 1920s and 30s had a definite English Tudor influence. The steeply pitched roofs, rolled eaves, large chimneys and faux stone-decorated doors and windows evoked an English cottage atmosphere.
Photo by Diann Marsh

The Move Westward

By 1950 Orange County was beginning to show signs of the phenomenal growth that would soon burst upon the scene. In addition to the year-round balmy weather, there were several other reasons for the move westward by increasingly large numbers of people. A nationwide trend toward greater mobility gave many families an advantage never seen before in this country. Midwesterners and others envisioned a chance to make a new start in a part of the nation less restrictive and structured than their hometowns. At the same time the government increased federal expenditures, bringing the accelerated expansion of manufacturing and creating new scientific and technological opportunities. The aircraft industry, among others, brought thousands to Southern California. In addition, the nationwide banking system had moved westward, allowing Southern California to liberate itself from its dependence on Eastern capital and build its own future. Americans headed to California, looking for a new life.

Tract Housing — Fulfilling the American Dream

In the late 1930s a new phenomenon began in Orange County. Tracts of houses, each built by a single company, ushered in an entirely new concept in residential housing. Although the first tracts were small, by the mid-1950s larger and larger developments were replacing orange groves and crop lands.

In Placentia the Rev. Charles Fuller created one of the first tracts when he subdivided his 10-acre orange grove into two streets, Orange Grove and Primrose. The houses, built in 1938, were small neat Minimal Traditional homes, very similar in design. Fuller and his family lived in the Craftsman Bungalow grove house at the end of the tract. Fuller, who was the founder of the Fuller Institute in Pasadena, went on to become famous for his worldwide radio show, "The Old Fashioned Revival Hour."

One of the first tracts constructed in Orange County was built by the Rev. Charles Fuller in Placentia in 1938-39. Fuller, a Sunday School teacher at the Placentia Presbyterian Church, went on to found the Fuller Institute in Pasadena. *Photo by Diann Marsh*

Hundreds of early tract homes, built in South Santa Ana in the 1940s, provided housing for the constant flow of military families from all over the country. Such houses were small and rectangular with narrow eaves and small recessed porches. *Photo by Diann Marsh*

In Santa Ana, soon after the beginning of the war, tracts of small, square single-story houses were built as much-needed housing for newly arrived military personnel and their families.

In 1945 the first tract homes were built in Huntington Beach and they illustrate how tract home development has changed over the last 50 years. Historian Alicia Wentworth remembers the first tract because her former husband purchased one of the first homes from local builders Norton and Bailey that year. The developers had purchased 13 double lots with R-2 zoning. Each three-bedroom, one-bath house, complete with a slab for a two-car garage, sold for $4,500 to $6,000. Recently, 55 years later, one of the houses sold for over $300,000.

Soon after the war, other cities in north and central Orange County were beginning to develop tracts of houses. In Costa Mesa, for example, Mesa del Mar was built on 250 acres of the defunct Santa Ana Army Air Base. These comparatively small efforts, however, were only the tip of the iceberg. Within 15 years, huge tracts would cover most of north and central Orange County and begin to spread like a flood over south Orange County.

The Urban Pioneers of the 1950s

It was exciting to move into a new tract house in the 1950s. A spirit of camaraderie often developed among the new neighbors. A rich mixture of young families, those with older children and senior citizens populated the brand new neighborhoods. The first tract houses had few amenities and did not include fences and landscaping. This meant that the owners had to get out and meet each other to negotiate the type of fence they wanted and who was going to pay for it. Sometimes it would be a few years before all the fences and landscaping were completed. Meanwhile, the neighbors were getting acquainted because their yards were open to each other.

In addition, more people stayed at home during the day. Because most wives did not work outside the home, a mini-social life was usually part of living in a new tract. Preschools and day care centers, for the most part, were still in the future, and small children spent their days at home until they went to kindergarten.

The new houses were quite different from the homes built in Orange County between the 1860s and the 1910s. Gone were the porches, attics, basements, detached garages and second stories so familiar to the older homes of the past. During the early 1950s, some garages were still placed in the backyard, at the end of the long driveway, but by the end of the decade, most garages had moved to the front. By the 1960s a large two-car garage had been plunked down between the homeowner and the street. This could be considered a commentary on the importance of the car in people's daily lives. By the 1980s designs had changed even more as large three-car garages began to dominate the front façade of the houses.

(Far left)
Large custom homes built in the early 1950s were given the "country flavor" through the use of exposed beam ends and rafter tails and carved porch brackets. These horizontally designed Ranch houses stretched across spacious lots.
Photo by Diann Marsh

(Top right)
The Candy Lane Estates, one of many small tracts built in Garden Grove in the mid-1950s, offered its homes for $11,750, with $300 down and $300 in closing costs for a conventional loan with house payments of $94 a month. Hardwood floors, garbage disposals and kitchen hoods were part of the package.
Photo by Diann Marsh

(Left)
Contemporary in style, this typical 1950s tract house in Garden Grove featured a two-car front garage, high metal-framed sliding windows, a combination of wood and stucco siding, a recessed front door and a low-pitched roof.
Photo by Diann Marsh

In the mid-1950s the typical tract house cost between $9,500 and $12,000. Interest rates averaged 4 percent for a conventional loan with $500 down and approximately $300 in closing costs. Because many of the new homeowners had served in the military, Veteran's Administration loans, which required no down payment, were popular. For example, a veteran who joined the service in California was eligible for a Cal-Vet loan featuring no down payment and 2 percent interest. The average house payment ranged from $85 to $125, not including taxes and insurance. The typical tract home of the 1950s ranged from 1,200 to 1,600 square feet and included a living room with dining ell, three bedrooms, two baths and an eat-in kitchen. In the 1950s the new tracts were being built so fast that the telephone company could not keep up with the installation of new lines and phone service. However, doctors, nurses and a few others were given preferential treatment because of their occupations.

Most schoolchildren, and especially their mothers, will remember double sessions. The school systems could not meet the demand for new classrooms in the high-growth areas. The old schools, which had supported the population for many years, were bursting at the seams. Waiting for the new schools to be completed, students often had to attend school in two sessions, with some going from 8 a.m. to 12 p.m. and others from 1 p.m. to 5 p.m.

While these dramatic changes were taking place in north and central Orange County, the cattle still grazed in south county. While driving down Interstate 5, travelers would still see huge blankets of vegetables set out in neat rows with busy field workers tending to their needs. A few settlements, such as Old Irvine and Culver's corners, sat peacefully along the road between Santa Ana and San Juan Capistrano. Development, when it did happen, spread beyond anyone's wildest dreams. South County was in for amazing changes. By the 1980s a rich variety of tract homes, condominiums, estates and townhouses would give prospective dwellers the opportunity to find a home best suited to their needs.

New Houses in New Styles

It is hard to realize that many of Orange County's tract homes are approaching 50 years old. The National Register of Historic Places and most city historic registers give 50 years of age as the date when a building can be considered historic. The time is approaching when the historical significance of these tracts and custom homes will need to be evaluated. For this reason, it is important to add such terms as Minimal Traditional, Ranch style, Contemporary, Split Level and Neoeclectic, to the

The circular metal canopy that forms the portico of this upscale home in Santa Ana was a popular architectural feature of houses built in the late 1940s and early 1950s. Wrought iron posts support the portico. Narrow eaves and multi-paneled windows, arranged in symmetrical form, add a Colonial character to the house.
Photo by Diann Marsh

(Far right)
Although there were not many houses constructed during the Great Depression of the 1930s, a few houses designed in the Streamlined Moderne style (also called Art Deco) were built. The round "porthole" windows, rounded balcony with stylized railing, and large curved glass block windows help define the Moderne architecture.
Photo by Diann Marsh

(Above)
Narrow eaves, a small recessed porch and 6-over-6 windows are exhibited in this single-story, rectangular Minimal Traditional house. The large chimney and steeply pitched roof are reminiscent of English Tudor influence.
Photo by Diann Marsh

more familiar Victorian, Colonial Revival, Tudor, Spanish and Craftsman Bungalow styles. In addition, the thousands of people living in tract homes need to realize that tract houses possess individual characters. Well planned by developers, these houses had the conveniences and attractiveness needed to attract the potential buyer.

Included below are the major architectural styles for most tracts built in Orange County. By taking a good look at his or her home, the owner can pick out the definite characteristics that define its style and age and appreciate its special features.

Minimal Traditional Houses 1938-1949

The first tract houses were neat, understated, rectangular single-story homes called Minimal Traditional houses. The word "Traditional" was used because these early tracts reflected the form of the traditional European-influenced designs seen in the 1920s and early 30s, particularly English Tudor homes. The word "Minimal" was used because the houses generally exhibited clean lines, without the decorative detailing seen in the earlier Romantic Revival adaptations built in the 1920s.

Medium- to low-pitched gable faces, large chimneys and narrow eaves were some of the features retained from the Tudor style. These clean-lined designs featured lots of double-hung windows and a small recessed front porch. This was the only era when 4-over-4 double-hung windows, divided horizontally, were used.

Not only were families intrigued by the simple plan of these single-story houses, but many residents who had previously lived in larger two-story Victorian, Colonial Revival and Craftsman homes, also enjoyed the convenience of living on one

The multi-paned, metal-framed casement windows used in this house were popular in homes as well as industrial buildings from the 1930s to the 1960s. While most of the panes were stationary, sections could be cranked open from the inside. The horizontal lines of the chimney and windows add a Moderne touch to the appearance of this 1940s house.
Photo by Diann Marsh

(Far left)
An especially fine example of the Minimal Traditional style, this custom house in Santa Ana is capped with a low-pitched roof, narrow eaves, a slanted bay window, an unusual recessed entry with double doors and a circular medallion above.
Photo by Diann Marsh

Another type of window frequently used on Minimal Traditional houses during the 1940s was double-hung, with two horizontal panes in the top half and two in the bottom. This appears to have been the only era when this particular form of windows was used.
Photo by Diann Marsh

floor. The informal plan, in which the main rooms flowed into each other, usually featured a dining ell instead of a formal separate dining room. The kitchens were usually smaller and more convenient. Built-in cabinets revolutionized the kitchen and made better use of the space. The kitchen was still a separate room, however, and family rooms had not yet become a part of the plan. Small utility rooms featured a laundry tub and a space for the new automatic washers. The automatic dryer was still a product of the future.

Homes built at the end of the Great Depression of the 1930s, including those of fairly wealthy business owners, were usually in the Minimal Traditional style and modest in contrast to the ostentatious homes built between the 1880s and 1930s. After the country had recovered from the Depression and World War II, it was patriotic to show restraint and modesty. Lavish displays of wealth were considered in poor taste. The small, neat Minimal Traditional house reflected these trends.

The Moore Park Homes, hundreds of which were built in Anaheim and Buena Park in the early 1950s, were a good example of the Minimal Traditional style. They all had the same basic plan, which was reversed in half of the houses to create two choices. The placement of the garage also added variety to the exterior. Each house featured a small hallway, front living room with large centered fireplace, dining ell, kitchen with space for a breakfast table, three bedrooms and two baths. The Moore Park Homes, which required only a few hundred dollars as a down payment, was one of the many inexpensive tracts to provide the opportunity for young families and those who previously could not afford to become homeowners.

Minimal Traditional styles were also featured in the custom homes of the late 1930s, 40s and early 50s. These were usually designed by architects in the Monterey or Colonial Revival style. Exhibiting the same neat exterior, the custom homes, many of which were built in north Santa Ana and Fullerton, were surrounded by spacious lawns and still had the garage in the rear, at the end of a long driveway.

The Ranch House 1938-75

Called the first "true American style," the design of the Ranch house was no longer tied to European wealth and styles as most previous residential styles. The pioneers and innovators who built the country's first Ranch-style houses were risk takers and visionaries.

Made possible by the country's increasing dependence on the automobile, the Ranch-style home often featured a garage connected to the end of the house, increasing the long horizontal front façade. After the garage was moved to the front of the house, garage design became increasingly important, and it was often decorated with detailing that matched the rest of the front façade.

The Ranch style originated in the late 1930s by a handful of creative California architects, including Cliff May. The popularity of the "rambling ranch houses" grew and grew and by the mid-1950s, the style had risen to dominate the residential scene.

Ranch-style houses were usually long and narrow. This plan allowed for plenty of light for all of the rooms because of the large picture windows in the front façade and the sliding glass doors in the rear. This model has a porte cochere on the right side, with the garage in the back.
Photo by Diann Marsh

The Ranch-style home, with its horizontal emphasis, required a large lot. The rambling form of the Ranch house emphasizes the spaciousness of the yard by maximizing the façade's width.

Loosely based on early Spanish Colonial precedents of the American Southwest, the design also exhibits elements of the Craftsman- and Prairie-style homes of the past.

A departure from the very formal and Colonial Revival homes of the turn of the century, the informal plan that began with the Craftsman Bungalow was becoming even more informal. With the Ranch home came an all-important room that was first called the "lanai," but is now called the family room. By the mid-1950s, the breakfast bar, which provided an open transition from the kitchen to the family room, had become popular.

By the late 1950s, upscale tracts such as the Eichler and Cinderella homes were built. Eichler homes were very modern in design, featuring central atriums and an open floor plan. By contrast, the Cinderella homes were reminiscent of fairy tale houses, with heavy shake roofs, overhanging eaves, scalloped trim, and decorative gables and flower boxes. Some tracts, to add visual character, adorned the garage gables and rooftops with fanciful dovecotes that looked like large birdhouses.

Custom homes, long the backbone of single-family neighborhoods, were built by the hundreds during the Ranch-style period. It was quite exciting to select a lot in a custom tract, select a house design, make changes to suit your family and see the house created in front of your very eyes. Ranch-style houses were very popular with wealthy people during the 1950s and 60s. Some of these houses were huge, spreading their single-story horizontal ambiance over large lots with deep setbacks. Such fine details as ceramic tiles, spacious kitchens with fine wood cabinetry, built-in stoves and ovens, large bathrooms with built-in sinks, sliding glass doors, covered patios and huge family rooms with cozy fireplaces were innovative features of the modern home.

Split Level Homes 1955-75

The Split Level house, an adaptation of the Ranch style, rose to popularity during the late 1950s. It retained the horizontal lines, low-pitched roofs and overhanging eaves of the Ranch house, but added a two-story section interrupted at mid-height by a single-story wing. Thus, three floor levels created additional privacy within the living space.

For families who needed several types of interior spaces, the house was divided into quiet living areas, family living, service sections and sleeping quarters. The Split Level form made it possible to locate each of these on a separate level. For example, the entry, formal living room and master bedroom, bath and

(Far right top) Roy Russell, the builder of this custom home in Santa Ana, used several character-defining details in the design of this 1950s version of the Ranch style. *Photo by Diann Marsh*

(Far right bottom) The Gainsborough Homes, built in 1960 by John B. Clark, replaced a large orange grove north of 17th Street in north Tustin. *Photo by Diann Marsh*

The Cinderella homes were embellished with character-defining decoration resembling fairy tale cottages. This picturesque example is in Garden Grove. *Photo by Diann Marsh*

Orange groves disappeared from the area surrounding Tustin during the 1950s and 60s. This Ranch-style house, on the corner of 17th and El Camino Lane, was built in 1950 by Harry Taylor. *Photo by Diann Marsh*

(Far left)
A rectangular floor plan, low-pitched gabled roofs, exposed beams and rafter tails, floor-to-ceiling wood-framed sliding windows and glass-filled gables were character-defining features of the Contemporary tract homes built in the 1950s.
Photo by Diann Marsh

(Far left bottom)
A front view of the same Contemporary home, located in Garden Grove, features a recessed main entrance, wood-framed windows and a separate two-car garage.
Photo by Diann Marsh

(Top left)
The Meridith Homes tracts, built in the 1960s, were among the first tracts of two-story and split-level houses. The three-car garages demonstrate the increased importance the automobile plays in modern family life.
Photo by Diann Marsh

(Bottom left)
Designed in the manner of a Southern mansion, this custom Santa Ana home, with its two-story-high colonaded porch, was built in the 1970s.
Photo by Diann Marsh

dressing room were often located on the entry level, while the children's bedrooms and bath were on the second floor of the two-story section. The dining room, family room, kitchen and laundry room where most of the action took place was located on the lowest level, behind the garage.

Developers often offered two-story, split-level and single-story models in the same tract in an effort to attract buyers with a variety of housing needs.

Contemporary Homes 1940-Present

Most Contemporary homes were custom designed by architects and showed a sophisticated and daring attitude toward home design. Exhibited in two substyles dictated by the roof form, both flat-roofed and gabled styles were popular. Those with flat roofs are sometimes called American International, after the International style previously seen in industrial and office buildings.

The aforementioned Eichler homes were prized for their contemporary plans featuring a central atrium, clerestory windows and sliding glass doors.

Various combinations of wood, glass, brick or stone wall surfaces added drama to the Contemporary house. The exterior decoration or detail seen on previous housing styles was kept to a minimum. Landscaping and the integration of the house to the site were important to the overall ambiance of the house. In many upscale houses, the design is oriented to the view, the placement of the house on a hill or on a difficult site. Opportunities for unusual Contemporary-style houses were especially prevalent in Orange County, with its variety of hilly sites, ocean views, cliffs and canyons.

Neoeclectic Homes — A Grand Style Emerges 1965-Present

By the late 1960s, the fashions of domestic architecture were shifting backward to the Colonial, Spanish and Tudor-influenced styles. Traditional architectural shapes and detailing once again became important to the character of tract as well as custom homes.

There were, however, some big differences from the former historic styles. The garage had become a three-car monolith that commanded attention from the street. The small, recessed entry porch was usually relegated to the side, creating a sense of privacy. The rear of the house, however, blossomed into a myriad of clerestory windows, walls of glass and French doors. White-walled rooms, with open beam and two-story-high ceilings, opened into each other. Dramatic entries and staircases greet the visitor at the front door.

Orange County's new upscale tract homes were often two stories with heavy stucco exteriors and detailing. Red-clay tile

Built on the bare hills once occupied by Chandler's Horse Ranch, this Spanish Colonial Revival home was designed in one of a variety of Neoeclectic styles popular in the 1970s, 80s and 90s. *Photo by Diann Marsh*

roofs became popular, creating a sea of beige stucco topped with the red-clay tile.

For Orange County, as well as the rest of Southern California, the Neo-Spanish Colonial tract house became dominant. Huge custom homes in Neo-Tudor, Neo-French and Neo-Victorian styles can be seen marching up the hillsides of Orange Park Acres and other new areas.

The Dr. Howe-Waffle house, moved by the Santa Ana Historical Preservation Society in 1974, is a 12-room restored Queen Anne Victorian built in 1889. During the last 20 years, almost every Orange County city has established a house museum to highlight its history and architecture. *Photo by Diann Marsh*

Orange County's Historic Homes — A New Lease on Life

Meanwhile, Orange County's stock of Victorian, Craftsman and Colonial Revival houses had its own unique set of problems. As the original owners died, often leaving their homes to their children who had established themselves elsewhere, a large crop of rentals was created. As thousands of servicemen and their families arrived in Orange County during World War II, many large old houses were divided into apartments and rooming houses. In addition, financing was difficult to obtain for persons wishing to purchase old houses because a 25 percent down payment was usually required. An even worse practice, called redlining, was prevalent from the 1940s through the 1960s. Now outlawed, redlining was a policy set by banks that refused to grant loans in specific older neighborhoods.

In the late 1970s many older neighborhoods began to be revitalized as new owners, recognizing the unique charm and character of Victorian, Craftsman and Colonial Revival houses, moved in and restored the houses to their former glory. Especially helpful to these "urban pioneers" was the rise in neighborhood associations, as residents banded together to bring about positive changes.

As neighborhood after neighborhood has been revived, Orange County's historic housing stock, particularly in Orange, Santa Ana and Tustin, has become an important and recognized part of the housing scene.

These "before" and "after" photos of a house moved into the Historic French Park District to save it from demolition illustrate a success in the restoration movement that has helped revitalize Orange County's historic neighborhoods. Once used as a rooming house, it has been restored as a single-family home. *Photo by Diann Marsh*

Buildings That Touch the Skies

Orange County is resplendent with unique buildings made of glass, marble and steel, in unusual shapes. In the new age of prosperity, significant buildings continue to be built in large numbers.

In May 1979, when a press conference was held to announce the site of the new Orange County Music Center, there were those who thought the county would not be able to support the envisioned center. However, the public responded with a positive get-to-work attitude. Music guilds, formed in several cities, waged an impressive and successful campaign to raise funds to build the center on a parcel of land in Costa Mesa donated by the Segerstrom family. As a result of this public support, the Orange County Performing Arts Center has grown and prospered. The centerpiece of the large contemporary building is a magnificent sculpture of a firebird that seems to hang in midair in the entry hall.

Some of Orange County's most unusual architecture can be found at Disneyland, the dream of Walt Disney, and Knott's Berry Farm, founded by Walter Knott. Those who visited Knott's Berry Farm in the 1950s and 60s remember when it consisted of only two rows of historic wooden buildings relocated from the desert. Once visitors toured the buildings, they looked foward to sampling Mrs. Knott's famous chicken dinners. Since that time the theme park has exploded into a huge complex with a variety of restaurants and activities. The exotic, Arabian-influenced Medieval Times building was originally built to house horses. The Hollywood Wax Museum has become a fixture in Buena Park. Orange County plainly has more than its share of unusual entertainment complexes designed to ferry the public into imaginary worlds.

At the end of World War II, there were only three skyscrapers in Orange County, with one each in Santa Ana, Fullerton and Anaheim. The Xerox Building on First Street in Santa Ana is one of the county's many skyscrapers built with facades of colored glass panels during the past 20 years. *Photo by Diann Marsh*

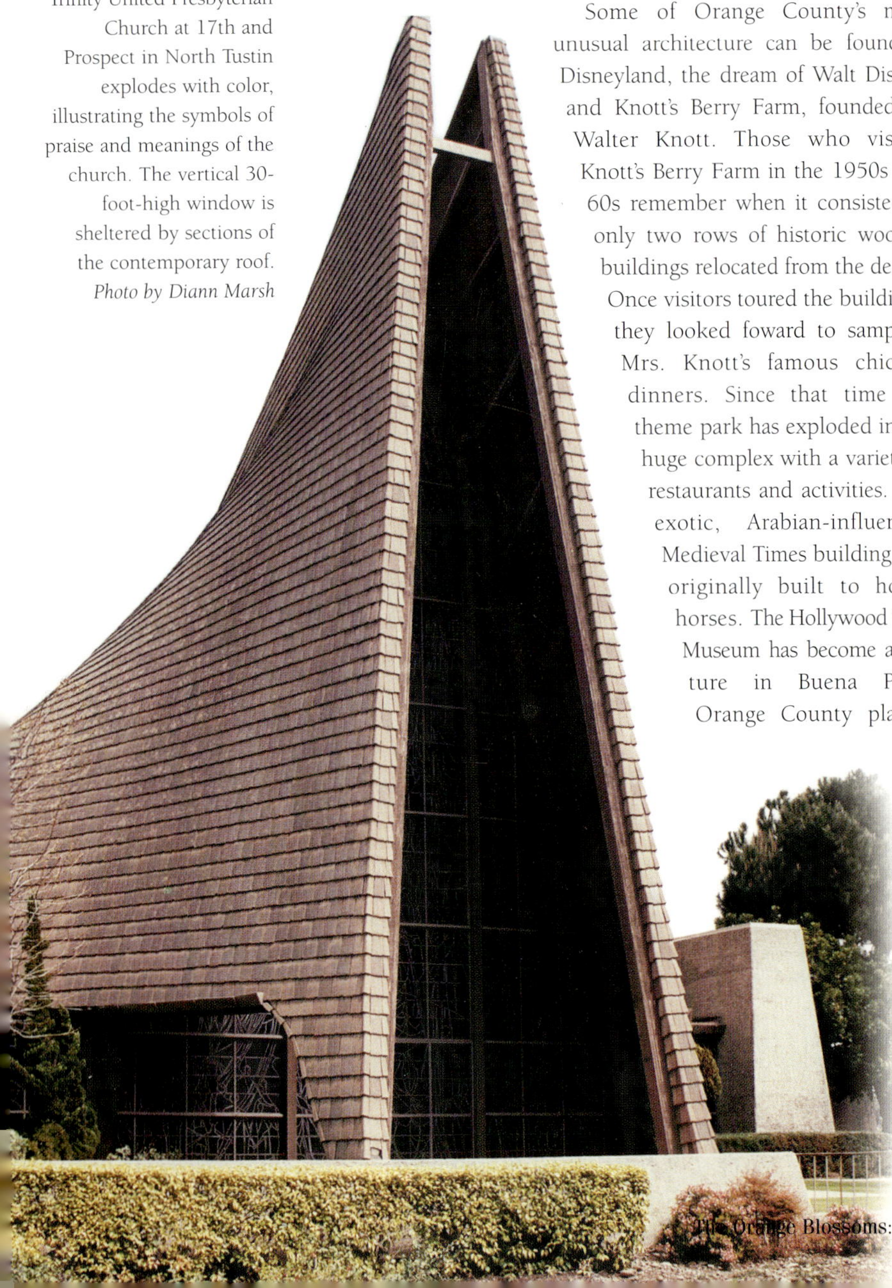

The stained-glass window in the sanctuary of the Trinity United Presbyterian Church at 17th and Prospect in North Tustin explodes with color, illustrating the symbols of praise and meanings of the church. The vertical 30-foot-high window is sheltered by sections of the contemporary roof. *Photo by Diann Marsh*

The sophistication of Orange County's churches grew from the simple wooden chapels of the 1880s and 90s to the huge contemporary cathedrals of the 1970s, 80s and 90s. Beginning in the 1920s, several congregations built large, impressive new buildings that reflected a growing civic and cultural pride within the community. Most were built in close proximity to the downtown professional and commercial core, and few had any parking facilities. This trend continued until the 1950s, when several congregations built new buildings in the suburbs, surrounded by the all-important parking lots. The new churches were convenient for those who were moving into the nearby tracts and looking for a church closer to home. Some of the new churches were very unusual in design, featuring contemporary stained-glass windows, soaring roof shapes and unusual exterior materials. A few established churches decided to remain in downtown areas to serve those who lived nearby. These same congregations were very generous in helping new churches of their denomination become established in new areas. Unfortunately, the establishment of the new churches often produced a drain on the human resources and youth of the older downtown churches.

(Far left)
The Crystal Cathedral, opened in September 1980, is a unique structure constructed of aluminum framing and glass. The Crean Tower on the left side of the building was dedicated in 1990 and features a chapel on the first floor and a carillon in the tower.
Anaheim/Orange County Visitor & Convention Bureau

One of Orange County's first high-rise condominium buildings, located in French Court in Santa Ana, was a new concept in the 1950s. Each unit features a wall of windows in the living room and a sliding glass door to an outdoor patio area.
Photo by Diann Marsh

The second movement that changed the face of religion in Orange County was the establishment of several fast-growing fundamentalist congregations during the 1970s and 80s. One of the best-known examples is the Crystal Cathedral, with its walls of glass and aluminum. It is one of the most unusual architectural religious statements.

Glass buildings, reflecting their surroundings in their surfaces of different colors, have arisen in almost all of Orange County.

Orange County's Civic Center, in downtown Santa Ana, now covers several square blocks and is occupied by more than 18,000 workers. One of the most architecturally interesting buildings is the Finance Building. It features giant 30-foot-high vertical fins attached to the building that are supposed to move with the sun in order to provide shade for the windows. Detractors say that the idea never worked. In addition to the county buildings, Santa Ana's Library, the Jail and City Hall occupy space on the Civic Center grounds. The Federal Building and State Building are large multistoried structures near the Santa Ana Boulevard entrance. The imposing new marble and glass Ronald Reagan Courthouse, accented with gold symbols, features a classicism and strength that is indicative of government buildings.

Orange County's modern skyline reveals a multitude of significant commercial and professional buildings that have been built during the past 50 years. Impressive buildings of glass and steel have been constructed in almost every section of the county, with the exception of the Santa Ana Mountains. Projections indicate that there are even more innovative and spectacular buildings in Orange County's future.

The Architects and Builders

Because of the dreams and creativity of Orange County's gifted architects and builders, thousands and thousands of beautiful homes and buildings were constructed during the prime years of the building boom.

Architect Cliff May, who is credited with changing forever the way people looked at houses, based his designs on the informal layout of the adobe courtyard. Beginning his career in 1931, he went on to design nearly 20,000 homes in several countries. Among his most significant innovations was the moving of the garage from the backyard to the front and attaching it to the house, thus enabling families to devote their backyards to entertaining and children's play. Many of May's designs were for custom renditions for special clients, but an estimated 18,000 were built for the masses using his plans.

The Hall of Records Building in the County's Civic Center in Santa Ana is one of a large complex of contemporary buildings devoted to city, county, state and federal offices.
Turville Photography
Photo by Steve Lopushinsky

William Pereira is best known for an entirely different type of architectural development. Hired by the University of California to find potential sites for a new campus in Southern California, Pereira came forth with a plan to place the campus on Irvine Company land in the San Joaquin Hills, east of Newport Bay. He also outlined the need for a master plan for the 10,000 acres surrounding the new university. Assisting the Irvine planning staff, Pereira planned a balanced community to be built in phases. Golf courses, shopping areas, parks and greenbelts would help create a complete community. In 1960 the Irvine Company commissioned Pereira to develop a master plan for the remaining 88,256 acres.

An Austrian immigrant, Richard Neutra was one of Southern California's best-known architects from the 1940s to the 1970s. Recognized for his contemporary homes featuring vast "curtain walls" of glass, his designs intimately linked distant

Custom homes by Roy Russell and Alison Honer were spacious, refined versions of the Ranch style on large lots.
Photo by Diann Marsh

landscape views with indoor space. In the 1950s Neutra and his partner, George Alexander, created the design for the fledgling Orange Coast College. Envisioning a cluster of unpretentious low-lying buildings with sunlit rooms and enclosed patios, Neutra planned informal and tranquil open spaces in which students could gather. The campus became known for its "out-doorsy" ambiance. The Robert B. Moore Theater featured a simple flat-roofed design with curving walls and flat-roofed covered walkways. Huntington Beach is proud of its Neutra-designed Central Library, begun in October 1972. Located in the midst of a 200-acre park, the building is a bold, glazed two-story pavilion sheathed in reflective glass. Sadly, Richard Neutra died just after the groundbreaking, and his son and partner, Dion, oversaw the building of the dramatic structure.

A pioneer in the development of a huge swath of Southern California, John Lusk built more than 40,000 homes and scores of shopping centers, office buildings and industrial parks. His career was characterized by his willingness to gamble his fortune on risky enterprises. For example, he built some of the first houses in Anaheim Hills, an area most felt was too far from the region's business centers to become popular for residential use. The legendary builder was also known for using his vast fortune to support many charities, especially those that helped the poor. On the educational front, he provided a $4 million grant to fund the prestigious Lusk Center for Real Estate Development at the University of Southern California.

Roy Russell, who built many fine houses in Santa Ana during the building boom of the 1950s, 60s and 70s, was known for his liberal use of fine wood cabinetry, large light-filled rooms and family living rooms oriented to the patio at the rear of the home.

Arriving in California in 1921, Alison Honer immediately began building fine custom homes in the Floral Park neighborhood in Santa Ana. Beginning with the Romantic Revivals, such as Tudor and Spanish-influenced homes, he later built many upscale, neat-appearing Minimal Traditional houses and some of the finest and largest Ranch-style homes in Orange County. In 1947 he constructed the buildings for the new campus of Santa Ana College. At the same time, he developed Honer Plaza directly across the street.

It would be impossible to mention every developer and builder who has contributed to the architecture of Orange County. They have given us towers of glass, Moderne buildings in unusual shapes, mansions in the hills, miles of tract housing on pleasant streets, and for some, a whole new way of life.

The 1926 Lovell Beach House, located in Newport Beach, is listed on the National Register of Historic Places. It was designed by famous architect Rudolph Schindler, known for his approach to a style of architecture called De Styl, which originated in Holland. *Sherman Library*

ARCHITECTURE

Until 1940 Orange County resembled a giant quilt created with shades of green and tan and an occasional town shown in the greys, white and red of streets, houses and brick buildings. When World War II began, the brown and tan of the military bases was added. It was not until the early 1950s that the quilt colors began their dramatic change. Large clusters of tract housing appeared in the north and central county first. New commercial buildings of shiny refletive glass began to dot the landscape in the early 1980s. By then undulating tracts of beige houses, many with red-tile roofs, started their march up the hills to the east and began to appear in south Orange County. Condominium and townhouse complexes brought convenient alternatives to single-family homes. From the rich detailed colors of the county's historic buildings to the shine of large reflective glass monoliths, Orange County presents an exciting and unique picture of a giant quilt with many colors.

(Below right)
Neoeclectic houses, built in the late 1990s, march up the hill on Wimbleton Street in East Orange. The large houses, fronted with triple garages and featuring dramatic two-story recessed entries, are accented with a variety of gables, roof lines, arches and massive chimneys.
Photo by Diann Marsh

(Below)
Condominiums, built in a variety of architectural styles, represent a convenient mode of living for many Orange Countians.
Photo by Diann Marsh

Homeowners in Orange, known for their efforts to restore the homes in the Old Towne Historic District, have brought new life and beauty to the historic houses in the old neighborhoods. The District is listed on the National Register of Historic Places.
Photo by Diann Marsh

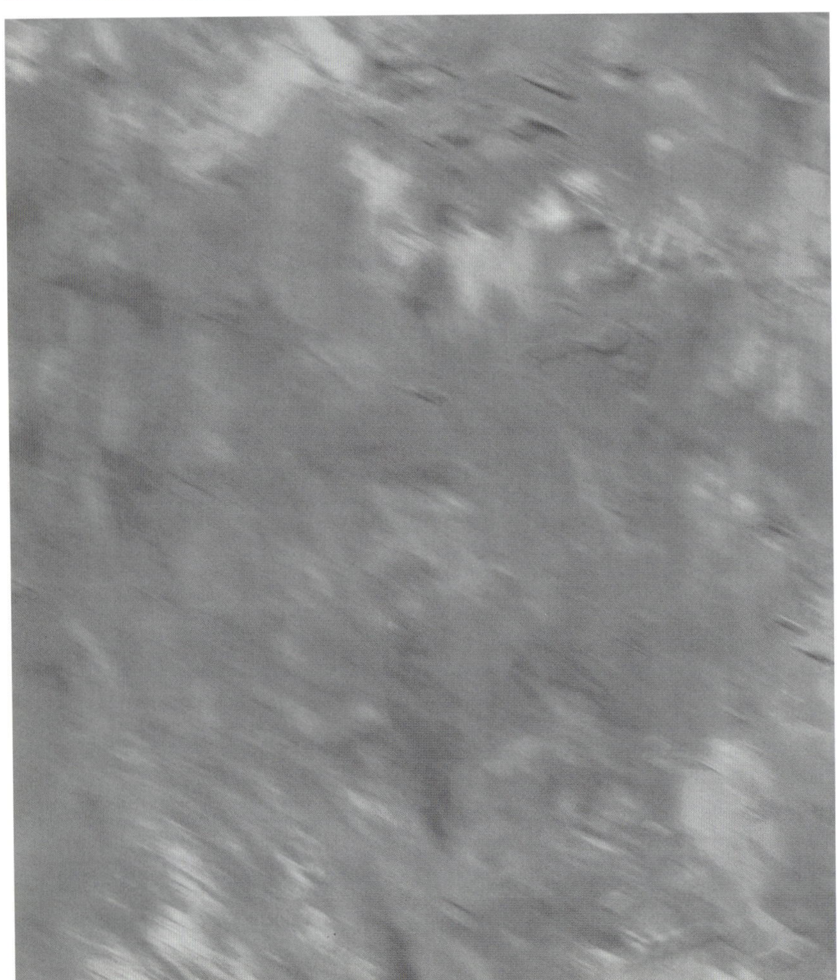

TRANSPORTATION

From World War II to the Present

By Steve Donaldson

When World War II began, Orange County transportation was comprised of many modes, both public and private. Since then, the county's transportation system has continued to grow in diversity and intensity, challenged to keep pace with a changing economy and exploding population. Statistics tell part of the story, but technological and business developments help explain the evolution of this phase of the county's infrastructure.

Highway Transportation

Between World War I and World War II the number of automobiles in Orange County grew from fewer than 10,000 to more than 100,000 vehicles. Prior to World War II, the state had completed a central highway through the county as part of the state-long route along the old Camino Real of mission times and Pacific Coast Highway along the county's beautiful ocean shoreline. By 1950 all public roads in the county had been paved to support the mature agricultural economy then present in the county. Several major freeways were built through Orange County during the 1950s and 1960s (I-5 and 405, and SR57), enhancing movement between the county and its neighbors in all directions.

(Right and inset) Santa Ana's Regional Transportation Center, completed in 1985, serves not only Amtrak and Metrolink trains, but also long-distance bus lines.
Photo by Diann Marsh

A master plan of arterial highways was developed to improve circulation within the county. Annual public expenditures for road construction and maintenance, by all agencies within the county, rose from $28 million in 1960 to $100 million in 1967. By 1968 there were 4,000 miles of streets and highways of all description, including 100 miles of express highways and freeways. Circulating throughout this network were about 600,000 passenger vehicles registered in the county and more than 2 million auto-driver trips being made each day. By the early 1960s, 84,000 vehicles were crossing the Los Angeles-Orange County border each day.

During the mid-1960s, population in the county was growing at the rate of 190 new residents per day. Automobile registration was growing by 216 vehicles per day and the highway network was growing by 360 feet per day. Despite this growth, the county ranked among the slowest of several adjacent areas in terms of average speed to and from work.

(Far right) From the 1920s to the 1970s Santa Ana was the auto center of the county, with over a dozen new- and used-car salesrooms. Monte Peters, the local De Soto and Plymouth dealer, also sold Rolls Royces.
History Room, Santa Ana Public Library

The station wagon began its reign of popularity in the 1940s. The first models featured two-toned paneled wood siding. Metal bodies introduced in the 1950s proved much safer. The 1965 Ford Fairlane shown here could be purchased brand new, with many extras, for less than $5,000.
John Sorenson

The growth in roads, motor vehicles and traffic during this period impacted the quality of life in the county. Automobiles generated 85-90 percent of the smog that Orange County shared with neighboring Los Angeles, and motor vehicle accidents injured 9,000 people and killed 175 annually. Nevertheless, automobile ownership and driving continued to increase, along with new roadways to move traffic around and through the county. Extension and expansion of the freeway system began in the 1970s and continued in the 1980s and 1990s. By 1988 Orange County freeways were handling thousands of vehicles per day. Some of these volumes were as follows: the I-5, 160,000-170,000; the Costa Mesa, 180,000; the Orange and Riverside, 210,000 each. The interchanges were even worse with 260,000 at the El Toro "Y." By 1994, the El Toro "Y" had reached 300,000 and the San Diego/Costa Mesa interchange was handling 500,000 vehicles per day. (See appendix.)

At the end of the 20th century, one of the high priorities for highway administrators and drivers alike was the expansion of the I-5 Santa Ana Freeway, dubbed "Orange County's Main Street" by modern promoters. The section south of Santa Ana, through Irvine and El Toro, including a 26-lane interchange with I-405 was completed in 1997. The latest stretch to be enlarged has been the I-5 north from its intersection with state routes 22 and 57 in Orange to state route 91 in Buena Park. This billion-dollar effort to widen and enhance the freeway used funds from a sales tax initiative passed in 1990 (Measure M) and other government sources. Its completion will likely be cause for celebration into the new millennium, just as the rail line, whose right-of-way the freeway has usurped, was over a century ago.

As the demand for more freeway capacity exceeded the resources of the public sector, the state authorized private companies to begin participating in the financing and building of toll roads. These toll roads appeared first as express and car-pool lanes on the I-91 Riverside Freeway through the north county, then as a full multi-lane highway through the coastal San Joaquin Hills. In 1998 and 1999 more toll roads were opened through the inland foothills and eastern edge of the county with more links planned and contemplated.

In addition to personal automobiles, the county highway network is also served by a number of privately and publicly owned passenger and freight carriers. Many "bus" lines began to supplement, and later to replace, rail transit lines. At the end of World War II, Pacific Electric operated four interurban motor coach routes that passed through the county carrying

In the mid-l960s this stylish Ford Mustang was available in Rangoon Red. The $2,589 price tag included many extras. In the 1940s the number of cars registered in Orange County amounted to less than 10,000. By the time this car was introduced in 1965, over 600,000 automobiles claimed the county as home.
John Sorenson

The construction of the Santa Ana (I-5) Freeway did much to change the face of Orange County. The first to be built in the county, the freeway was joined in the late 1950s and early 1960s by the 405, 22, 55 and 57 freeways, greatly improving the traffic circulation needed to meet the rapidly increasing population. *Old Courthouse Museum*

almost 6 million passengers annually. By 1968 various school and transit busses in Orange County handled about 140,000 passengers per day. Private transit services have always struggled to become or remain financially profitable. During the 1960s, despite many route additions, alterations and discontinuances, local transit companies continued to struggle.

In 1972 most of the county's private bus companies were consolidated under the Orange County Transit District (OCTD). OCTD continues to operate under its successor, Orange County Transportation Authority, now operating 376 busses over 72 routes, carrying 60,000 daily riders between 6,300 different stops. The system is steadily being upgraded and expanded. Sixteen taxi companies have evolved since World War II. In addition to passengers (in both public and private vehicles), the County's highway network accommodates a number of freight or goods vehicles. These vehicles move approximately 4 million tons of finished and waste materials annually around the county to meet the needs of the populace and industry.

Aviation

Before World War II, aviation was well established as a phenomena in Orange County by local and visiting pioneers. During the war the U.S. government found Orange County appropriate for the development of bases to support both aviation training and reconnaissance patrols. Air stations were established at no less than four sites in the county: Los Alamitos, Tustin, Santa Ana and El Toro. Following the war and later military reductions, many of the air stations later became civil and commercial aviation fields. Of these, only Santa Ana/"John Wayne" Airport attained inter-regional airline status. John Wayne was opened as Orange County Airport in September 1941 and acquired by the Army Air Corp shortly after the U.S. entry into World War II. In 1952 it was returned to the county and renamed John Wayne in 1979.

In the early 1950s, Bonanza Airlines was the first to initiate service, using DC-3s to connect Orange County with various points in Southern California and other southwestern states. In 1967, just prior to merging with other regional carriers to form Air West, Bonanza Airlines upgraded its fleet to include only jets. Air West was acquired by Howard Hughes and adopted his name

During the 1940s and 50s, various local bus lines, some with sparse service, operated in Orange County cities. In 1972 these were consolidated under the Orange County Transit District. In the 1990s, there were more than 376 busses on 72 routes operating in the county. The Orange County Transit Authority recently announced plans for further expansion. *Turville Photography Photo by Steve Lopushinsky*

The Santa Ana Army Air Base, south Santa Ana, brought thousands of newcomers to Orange County. Built on flat land that had previously been planted with beans, sugar beets and alfalfa, the base received its first training cadets in February 1942. It is now the site of Orange Coast College and the Orange County Fairgrounds.
First American Title Insurance Co.

in 1969 — a return of sorts, since he had crash-landed in a beet field near the airport while attempting a speed record 34 years earlier. The second commercial carrier in Orange County was Air California, incorporated by local entrepreneurs after national carriers could not be persuaded to provide service to Orange County. "Air Cal" inaugurated Orange County operations in January 1967, despite foggy conditions both in Orange County and San Francisco, using Lockheed "Electra" turbo-prop aircraft. Pure jet aircraft and other Bay Area destinations were added the following year. Air Cal was later acquired by American Airlines.

More national carriers serviced Orange County in the 1980s, followed by organizational changes and controversies. Commuter airlines also came and went, including Los Angeles Airways and other helicopter services, which used various non-airport parking lots around the county to provide short haul service principally to Los Angeles. Runways and terminal facilities at John Wayne Airport steadily improved. More carriers were added, with aircraft capable of maintaining excellent flying access between Orange County and the rest of the nation. Today, despite Orange County's regional airport's noise restrictions and curfews, 7 million passengers now fly in and out of Orange County annually, and two carriers provide cargo-only service on weekdays.

Of course, there persists a regional need for more airport capacity than presently exists. Many perceive the closure of El Toro Marine Corps Air Station as an opportunity with great potential for a regional airport. This has produced the predictable tension between advocates and opponents. Opponents don't want an airport in their backyards — even if such a facility has existed long before they moved in. This not-in-our-backyard argument has been used before to counter various public and private proposals for changes in land use both in Orange County and elsewhere. Nevertheless, there is increasing momentum for such conversion of the El Toro facility into a major commercial airport, but opposition from the surrounding community and other challenges must yet be overcome to attain this objective.

Shown here in 1949, a partially inflated blimp rests in one of the two giant hangars at the Lighter-Than-Air Station. The huge vessels were used to patrol the seacoast and perform rescue work during and after World War II. Each ship was equipped with a machine gun and four depth charges. The twin blimp hangars, at 171 feet in height, 1,000 feet in length and 300 feet in width, are now listed as national landmarks on the National Register of Historic Places.
Old Courthouse Museum

Helicopters operated from El Toro until they were moved to Tustin. El Toro was opened in August 1942. The base, originally built on 2,333 acres at a cost of $8 million, was closed in July 1999.
First American Title Insurance Co.

Pipelines

While most means of transportation move passengers and goods over land and above ground, pipelines move material beneath the surface. As population and economic development swelled in post-World War II Orange County, pipelines bringing water and gas and carrying away sewage kept pace. Before the war much of the county's water supply came from wells and canals, but by the later 1990s 15,000 gallons per month per

The Balboa Ferry has traveled between Balboa Island and the Balboa Peninsula since it was inaugurated by W. S. Collins in 1909. The Balboa Pavilion can be seen in the background. *Orange County Historical Society*

family came via aqueducts, reservoirs, mains and large "feeders." A feeder was the proposed water tunnel beneath the Santa Ana Mountains between south Orange County and Riverside County. Collectively the water delivery and distribution system constitutes a transportation network, which is often taken for granted by the public until the occurrence of a major failure. In the fall of 1998 the Westminster reservoir collapsed, sending its contents sweeping devastatingly through the surrounding neighborhood. In addition to these domestic water supplies, a half-billion barrels of sewage flow through a network of sewers to Orange County Sanitation District processing facilities each day.

Petroleum, too, flows through the industry's own Orange County pipeline network, first through gathering lines or "laterals" draining individual oilfields and even offshore platforms to central terminals or tank farms, and then through trunk lines, operated by various major oil companies, to their refineries in southern Los Angeles County. Most of these were developed before World War II, but since then two new crude oil pipelines have come into existence.

The first was converted from a local trunk line to connect an offshore tanker unloading facility at Huntington Beach to a refinery in Santa Fe Springs, originally owned by Wilshire Oil Company, later Gulf Oil. In the 1980s it was owned by an independent company named Golden West, and most recently it was acquired by Huntington Beach Pipeline Terminal Co., an affiliate of televangelist Pat Robertson's CENCO Refining Co.

The second pipeline was built in 1967 through Orange County to help move crude oil into California to balance supply and demand. This was the Four Corners Pipeline (4CPL), a common carrier, cutting across the north side of the county en route from the oil fields where Utah, Wyoming and Colorado abut to the Los Angeles refining area. The 4CPL moved many tanker load equivalents before being retired, divided and sold to new owners for other uses in the late 1990s. For a brief 30-year period Orange County found itself astride a pipeline facility of no particular benefit to the county. This is unlike others, which serve both national and local needs such as roads and railroads.

In addition, in 1963 a petroleum products pipeline was built by San Diego Pipeline Company, a joint venture by two of the county's railroads, utilizing rights-of-way of the parent companies. The route was from the southern Los Angeles County refining area via Norwalk through Orange County to San Diego. In 1983 when the two railroads' parent holding companies attempted to merge, they formed a new pipeline company called Santa Fe Pacific Pipeline Partners (SFPP), whose assets included many miles of petroleum products pipelines throughout the western states. The Interstate Commerce Commission (ICC) denied the parents' merger but SFPP survived. In 1996 the operating and administrative headquarters of the firm, approximately 500 employees, were relocated from Los Angeles to Orange. Then in 1998, SFPP was acquired by more diversified Kinder Morgan Energy Partners. The company still maintains both its operating headquarters and a truck-loading "bulk terminal" in the geographical center of the county itself, and moves thousands of barrels of aircraft and motor fuels daily from the Los Angeles County refineries to markets in Orange and San Diego counties.

Railroads

At the beginning of World War II, Orange County already had a well-developed railroad network, with competing carriers connecting it with the rest of the state and the nation, providing both transcontinental and local freight and passenger service. With its Pacific orientation, World War II had a profound effect upon the railroads of Orange County and the rest of the West. During the war, troop trains and materiel moved in unprecedented volume to this county's defense facilities and through the county to Pacific Fleet Navy Bases and other military camps in neighboring counties. To accommodate those record traffic levels, significant improvements were made to the county's rail tracks and signaling systems, which enhanced civilian transport needs both during and after the war.

Freight Activity. As agriculture declined in the county and industrial activity increased, especially warehousing and distribution operations, the rail freight mix in the county shifted dramatically after the war. However, the total volume remained constant at about a half-million tons per year. During the 1960s railroad freight terminating or originating in Orange County grew fourfold for the three railroad companies (AT&SF, S.P. and U.P.), from an average of 100 cars per day in 1960 to more than 400 cars per day in 1970. The railroads owned 2,300

The crew of a Pacific Electric Red Car poses in front of its vehicle. Traveling on rails, the cars served Orange County from 1904 until 1950.
First American Title Insurance Co.

In 1878 the Southern Pacific extended its line from the outskirts of Anaheim to Santa Ana. The railroad brought freight opportunities, potential landowners, tourists and a new way of communication to Orange County. It was not until 1887 that its competitor, the Sante Fe Railroad, arrived in Santa Ana.
First American Title Insurance Co.

acres of industrial land, and by adding a maze of spurs and sidings, had accumulated some 450 miles of trackage in the county. One company (S.P.) even built a new bypass or shortcut line to reach Orange County without using the congested Los Angeles terminals. In addition, increasing volumes of main line freight passed directly through the county en route to Los Angeles, San Diego, San Bernardino and points east, particularly increasing volumes of Pacific Basin intermodal traffic.

Abandonment and Reconfiguration. Although the volume of freight traffic on Orange County railroads has fluctuated with the economy, local and through freight traffic remained high on most Orange County lines through the end of the century, with between 50 and 100 trains traversing county tracks every day. Consequently, except in limited instances, closures and abandonment have been limited mostly to a mile or two. A few minor branches were eliminated due to the cessation of particular agricultural or other economic activities, or rights of way were required for other public purposes. In recent years a number of local and regional consolidations of rail operations have occurred (i.e., PE with parent SP and certain sections of PE with UP). Orange County's railroads have also been impacted by national merger activity that swept all industries during the last quarter-century, leaving the county (like the state) with fewer but stronger competitors and service by two of the greatest transportation companies in the world (Union Pacific and Burlington Northern & Santa Fe).

On July 2, 1950, the last Pacific Red Car cruised down Fourth Street in Santa Ana on its way to Los Angeles. Service was discontinued because of the widespread automobile ownership.
Old Courthouse Museum

Passenger Service and Operations. By the outbreak of World War II, interurban rail passenger services to and within Orange County had declined significantly, but did enjoy a resurgence to over 2 million passengers per year during that conflict. Following the war, the majority of those services, provided primarily by a few remnants of the Pacific Electric "Red Car" system, declined radically. Highway bus competition and substitution as well as public neglect and disinterest replaced rail services. The last passenger cars on PE's two key Orange County lines (from Los Angeles to Santa Ana and Newport Beach via separate routes) ran in the summer of 1950. Some of the old PE tracks were retained for local freight service for awhile, and other unused rights of way were preserved. However, the likelihood of their actual use for future transit purposes is uncertain. Serious attention is now being paid to the possibility of building a new light rail transit system through a high-density boot-shaped corridor in the county between Fullerton and Irvine.

Just before World War II began, Santa Fe, the only "steam" road still providing passenger service in Orange County, began introducing diesel-powered streamlined passenger trains throughout its system. The *San Diegan* was one of these new

The routes of the Pacific Electric Red Cars, as they appeared in the 1940s, stopped at many small towns and crossings to let passengers and freight on and off.
Marsh Collection

One of the Red Cars finds a final resting place at the Trolley Museum in Perris. Dedicated museum volunteers are restoring a variety of styles of trains for the education and enjoyment of the public. *First American Title Insurance Co.*

day. This action affected 700 Orange County commuters. In 1965 Santa Fe eliminated commute-hour passenger service, cutting back to three trains daily on the San Diego line. These reductions in service between Los Angeles and San Diego saw the number of passengers carried decline from a million in 1947 to half that in the early 1960s. Of the remaining passengers, half restricted their travel exclusively to the Orange County stations.

Another important Santa Fe passenger route through Orange County was through Fullerton and Santa Ana Canyon. During the war, two transcontinental trains used this route that connected Los Angeles, Chicago and intermediate points and provided a good direct long-distance rail passenger service. After the discontinuance of the "Fast Mail" in 1965, only the "Grand Canyon" used this route. In 1968 even this train was rerouted through Pasadena and the San Gabriel Valley, ending Santa Fe passenger service over its original route into the county.

streamlined trains. The "Surf Line" ran from Los Angeles through Orange County to San Diego. Throughout the state, and the company's entire service territory, the speed and comfort of Santa Fe passenger service was improved and fares were reduced. A second set of *San Diegan* equipment was added in 1941, with a lunch counter diner and a round end observation car at the rear of the train. Schedule frequency increased to five trains per day each way. Scheduled service on the "Surf Line" continued at these levels throughout the next decade, with extra trains running during the war.

The number of daily trains to and from San Diego and Los Angeles was increased to six in 1952 when two self-propelled rail diesel cars (RDCs) were introduced. The scheduled frequency of trains rose to its all-time Santa Fe high when a seventh trip was added in 1954. This was reduced back to six in 1956 when the RDCs were removed from service following a tragic wreck in Los Angeles. Eight years later, the withdrawal of the federal mail contract resulted in a reduction to four round trips per

The San Diego to Los Angeles route of Amtrak's *San Diegan* is the second most frequently traveled route in the United States. The push-pull method of operation cut down on the times needed for service because the trains did not need to be turned at the end of each route. *Diann Marsh Collection*

The National Railroad Passenger Corporation, better known as Amtrak, took over all surviving rail passenger services in Orange County and across the nation on May 1, 1971. A period followed where passenger cars and equipment inherited from the many different predecessors from around the country could be found on the trains traveling through the county as Amtrak consolidated its fleet of cars. In the mid-1970s Amtrak began introducing its standardized "Amfleet" coach and club car designs on the Los Angeles to San Diego corridor. Later this was followed by higher-capacity bi-level "California Cars." The older "streamlined" cars soon disappeared except for a few retained in private ownership and available for special trips on a charter basis.

Thanks to increasing patronage and financial support from various levels of government, frequency of passenger train service on the busy corridors through Orange County has increased to all-time high levels. By the late 1970s the Los Angeles to San Diego route had become the second-busiest Amtrak route in the United States! Reflecting this growth in demand for service, the number of daily round trips over the route has increased from four in 1976, five in 1977, six in 1978, seven in 1980 (matching Santa Fe's highest frequencies in 1915-17 and 1954-56), to eight in 1987. This growth is in response to the population growth in Southern California along the Santa Fe/Amtrak corridor, the motor fuel shortages of the 1970s, and the increased highway congestion. At the same time, all passenger services in this corridor have been revolutionized by the start of push-pull operations that reduced the service and turnaround time of the trains at each end of the run.

In Amtrak's first year, a through car was attached to one of the three daily *San Diegans*, running three days a week. This car was switched at Los Angeles to the *Coast Starlight* and traveled north through the Bay Area to the Pacific Northwest. While short-lived, this practice demonstrated that rail service to Orange County did not have to end at Union Station in Los Angeles. Heeding this lesson, in 1988 one daily *San Diegan* was extended to a new northern terminus in Santa Barbara. Later round-trip service was increased in number and even extended farther to San Luis Obispo. An 11th round trip was added to the route in 1998 with a 12th planned for the following year.

Long-distance service through northern Orange County and Santa Ana Canyon returned in 1994 when the *Southwest Chief*, running between Chicago and Los Angeles via Kansas City and the southwest, was routed this way. Also, in 1986 Amtrak rerouted its Superliner-equipped *Desert Wind*, running between Los Angeles and Chicago via Las Vegas, Colorado and Salt Lake City this way. However, this train was discontinued altogether in 1997, leaving the *Chief* the sole survivor in this category.

These Orange County rail renovations extend to the infrastructure, too. Former Santa Fe depots at Fullerton, Orange and San Juan Capistrano continue to serve rail passengers, although Santa Fe left in favor of freight offices in nearby La Mirada. The communities who own these historic depots have restored them. The depots and their restaurant operators in conjunction with Amtrak and Metrolink are providing modern commuter amenities. In addition, two new facilities have been built. The City of Anaheim constructed a small station adjacent to Anaheim Stadium in 1984. The City of Santa Ana opened its impressive Regional Transportation Center in 1985 north of the old Santa Fe station depot, which was subsequently demolished. A third new station opened in 1990 to serve Irvine and El Toro, and two more are planned for Tustin and Laguna Niguel/Mission Viejo.

The former Santa Fe Depot at Fullerton has been restored to its former beauty and is in full service as an Amtrak stop. When a coat of drab tan paint was removed, the original cream, tan, rust and blue-swirled plaster exterior was revealed. *Diann Marsh Collection*

Beginning in 1988 tracks south and east of Fullerton were rebuilt, including some sections of double track, which increased the capacity of those routes. A consortium of Southern California governments, known as the LOSSAN project, largely undertook this reconstruction with the expectation that passenger service would be improved along the route. Such improvements had been studied repeatedly over the years, encouraged by citizens who sought restoration of true commuter service to connect popular residential and employment centers.

Large groups of commuters take advantage of the station at San Juan Capistrano during the eight stops the train makes each day. The depot, constructed in the 1890s in the Spanish Colonial Revival style, was restored in the 1980s. *Diann Marsh Collection*

The Marines at El Toro unload a construction locomotive from a rail car. The photo was taken near the southwest border of El Toro Marine Base. *Old Courthouse Museum*

Under its authority Amtrak began to operate increasing levels of commuter service in Orange County and elsewhere in Southern California. In 1978 the County of Los Angeles acquired a train of 1940s-era passenger cars and engaged Amtrak to run them on a commute hour schedule through Orange County. Operating under the name *El Camino*, this experimental schedule carried an average of only 150 passengers during its first month of operation, many of which commuted to north Orange County destinations. It was discontinued after only six months. In the spring of 1990, the County of Orange undertook the next attempt on this route. This was undertaken primarily as a temporary effort to give commuters an alternative to the congested Santa Ana Freeway when expansion construction began. Amtrak provided that service with its own trains at first but later employed Metrolink equipment (even before Orange County was in its official service area).

In 1993 the County of Orange acquired title to nearly 50 miles of Santa Fe trackage in the county, including the "Surf Route" within its borders. The County opened it for operation by the Southern California Regional Railroad Authority, a consortium of regional governments familiarly known as Metrolink. This public commuter train authority began offering service on the "Orange County Line," from Los Angeles to Oceanside, in the spring of 1994. Both Santa Fe and Amtrak retained rights to operate their trains over the now publicly owned railroad.

In October 1995 regular service began over the "Inland Empire" route where 11 trains now carry 1,700 riders daily. This route was over Santa Fe trackage through Santa Ana Canyon, then over county-owned ex-Santa Fe trackage from Atwood through "South County." On September 8, 1997, Metrolink added daily service between Los Angeles and Riverside, via Fullerton. The route is over Santa Fe's north Orange County trackage currently used by three trains a day. Total daily ridership for all Metrolink lines serving Orange County is over 6,000. These commuters utilize the modern passenger services daily, saving time, expense, and fatigue when compared to the highway alternative, in "comfort, speed, and safety" as the PE used to advertise.

Over the past three decades, Amtrak patronage on the lines through Orange County has climbed steadily. Ridership on the San Diego line exceeds 50,000 patrons every day. Patronage on the Metrolink trains using the same route adds another 5,000 riders per day. During the summer, extra riders are attracted as weekend excursionists on special "Beach Trains" sponsored by the City of San Clemente or County of Riverside. Many Orange County residents use these services to make connections with transcontinental trains in Los Angeles as well as to commute to and from work. Clearly, the 1980s and 1990s have witnessed the renaissance of rail passenger service in this region. These rail corridors through Orange County have emerged as major passenger routes in the nation, with the *San Diegan* route now boasting record levels of service and patronage!

Probably the greatest single special railroad passenger movement into Orange County since World War II occurred in 1953 when 70 special passenger trains brought 50,000 Boy Scouts from all over the world to an international Jamboree held on the grounds of the Irvine Ranch overlooking Newport Harbor. Thirty-five of these trains came directly into the county over the Santa Fe. Passengers on the other 35 trains exited at S.P.'s Walnut Station and were bussed to the Jamboree site. The event included a re-enactment of the driving of the Golden Spike marking the completion of the first transcontinental railroad in 1869. This re-enactment used two 19th-century steam locomotives borrowed from Hollywood movie studios, which had to be trucked in to the (then) remote site on a hill on the ranch overlooking Upper Newport Bay where some temporary track was laid just for the exhibition.

Coincidentally, 25 years later, a company in Costa Mesa, not far from the site of this re-enactment, constructed two brand-new full-sized replica locomotives. These are now operated by the National Park Service at the Golden Spike National Historic Site in Utah. Steam locomotives had been phased out in favor of more efficient diesel-electrics on all railroads in the 1940s and 50s. A few remain for excursion purposes. This happy tradition is maintained by two museum-quality steam engines at Knott's Berry Farm.

Despite the changes over time and the changes in market orientation, Orange County's railroads remain dynamic and viable amid the changing economic conditions of the late 1990s. In addition to the growth in passenger traffic, freight traffic generates a daily average approaching 200 rail cars. A dozen different crews are required to service all of the line side customers. Admittedly, most of the former freight depots are closed, and some trackage removed, but new spurs and sidings are still being added each year. In addition, former railroad-owned real estate serves as sites for new business facilities and as routes for modern telecommunications facilities important to the county's growth in high-tech fields.

The railroads so important in the history of Orange County are partners in the county's present and will be a part of its future. However, the form of the future is not entirely clear. Proposals to build "Bullet Trains" between San Diego and Los Angeles have failed for various reasons including opposition from adjacent communities through which the proposed routes would transit. Recently, the state of California decided to build a new high-speed passenger railroad between northern and southern ends of the state — Orange County was not on the route. Regardless, the county is still "on the way" where conventional tracks still exist. Higher-speed trains have demonstrated their ability to operate over these tracks. These trains could take up permanent residence in the 21st century, along with new "people mover" concepts under consideration in some quarters.

Marine/Maritime Trade

Orange County can trace some of its earliest commerce to ocean-borne trade and transporation. Here in the 19th century, some of Orange County's earliest European settlers had arrived by sea and established a lightering (ferry barge unloading) operation to participate in coastwide trade. However, very little remained by 1940.

During World War II, one of the country's key military installations, the Seal Beach Ammunition and Net Depot, was established on Anaheim Bay. In 1942 the U.S. Navy built a harbor where barges could load and unload munitions for its vessels based or calling at Long Beach. The size of this depot has ranged from 300,000 to 400,000 acres over its lifetime. Construction of the original Navy wharf required the realignment of the existing rail and highway facilities. The Pacific Electric Railway trestle, which previously crossed the bay, was removed. The line was then relocated inland on a new elevated grade along an alignment currently followed by Pacific Coast Highway. The new wharf and its access trackage created a unique situation in Orange County where one railroad track crossed another on separate grades. In 1962 the channel was dredged to allow aircraft carrier-size vessels to use the wharf. This eliminated the need for lightering ammunition, and reduced time and costs. However, a fleet of Navy lighters is still kept on hand for transfers between harbors. In 1990 the Navy announced intention to expand the harbor and wharf substantially, but so far, the expansion has not occurred.

Although one shipment of a Saturn rocket booster has gone out over the Seal Beach Navy wharf, Orange County depends on nearby Los Angeles-Long Beach Harbor for most of its modern maritime shipping requirements. There are no commercial harbors on the county's coast, with the exception of passenger ferry services to Catalina Island from both Newport and Dana Point harbors. An offshore crude oil unloading facility at Huntington Beach was opened about 1956. In 1990 this facility gained public attention when the tanker *American Trader,* attempting to discharge Alaskan crude oil, ran over its own anchor, rupturing and spilling a large volume of cargo. This occurred just as legal trials were beginning over the *Exxon Valdez* spill in Alaska that had occurred several years before. The Huntington Beach terminal consisted of a U-shaped string of mooring buoys and a single unloading buoy connected by a subsea pipeline running to a tank farm on shore (behind the Waterfront Hilton Beach Resort). The facility continued to be used until 1995. The new owners briefly considered reactivation of the facility even as lawsuits over environmental and other damages resulting from the *American Trader* spill concluded in 1998.

A group of Boy Scouts presents the colors during the International Boy Scout Jamboree, attended by over 50,000 scouts and leaders on the Irvine Ranch in September 1953. Many came by special passenger train, embarking at Southern Pacific's Walnut Station.
Old Courthouse Museum

TRANSPORTAION

“The growth in roads, motor vehicles and traffic during this period impacted the quality of life in the county. Automobiles generated 85-90 percent of the smog that Orange County shared with neighboring Los Angeles, and motor vehicle accidents injured 9,000 people and killed 175 annually. Nevertheless, automobile ownership and driving continued to increase, along with new roadways to move traffic around and through the county.”

Turville Photography
Photo by Steve Lopushinsky

The parlor car of the Pacific Electric Red Car, (labeled “Special” because it was for the use of executive commuters), was in operation during and after World War II. It is shown here parked at the Newport Beach depot. *Charles Beecher Collection*

This popular model of the Ford Thunderbird Hardtop featured Silent-Flo ventilation that kept the interior fresh with outside air even when the windows were rolled up.

This 1965 model could be purchased for $4,486.

John Sorenson

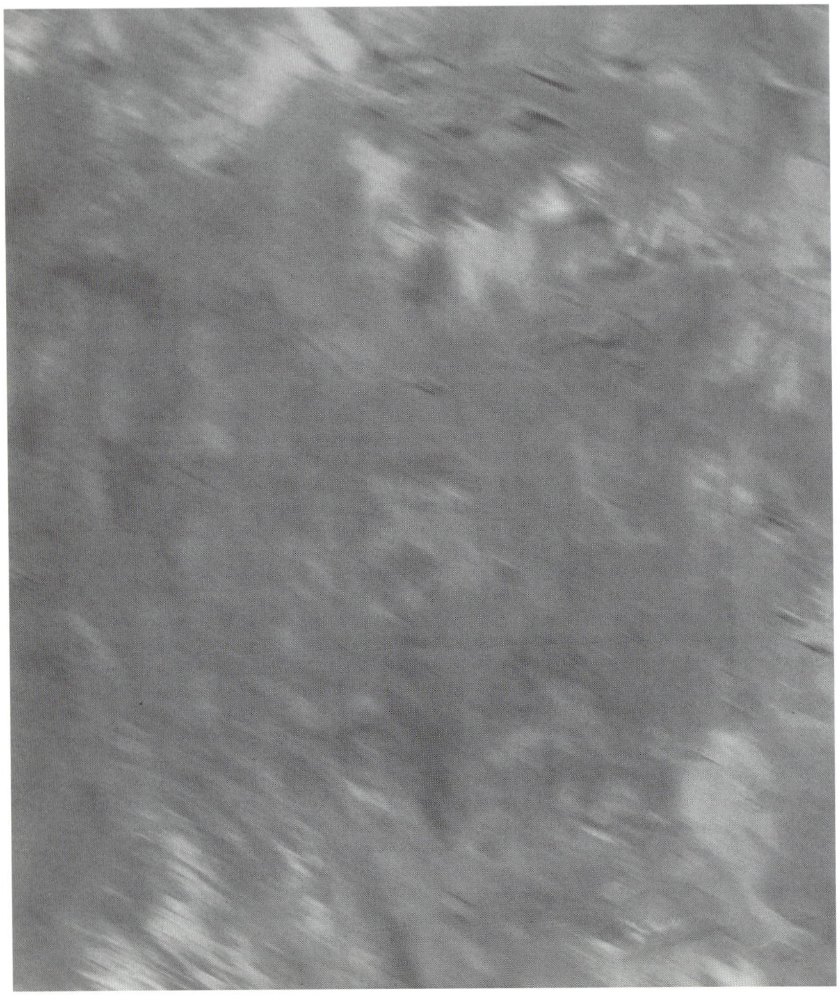

OF AMERICA
B51402981A
B97556041D

ECONOMICS

From Farm, to Factory, to Franchise

By John L. Sorenson

This is the story of the economic and employment history of Orange County as it moved from orchards and farms toward manufacturing and finally to a service-based economy at the turn of the 21st century. The story unfolds in the chapter text and tables in the appendix.

Background

The post-World War II era has brought the United States a period of economic growth unrivaled in the history of mankind. Orange County has more than shared in this prosperity. Orange County's prewar economic base was agriculture. By 1941, hard times were still the order of the day. According to Judge Robert Gardner in his book, *Bawdy Balboa*, the Great Depression began on October 28, 1929, and continued until December 7, 1941. War brought prosperity to Orange County as well as to the rest of the nation.

Agricultural Orange County had a population of 130,760 according to the 1940 Census — 97.5 percent Caucasian. The total work force numbered 48,130 and consisted primarily of traditional one-wage-earner families — the man and only the man worked and provided for the family.

The glass-encased Postmodern Xerox Building, on the north side of First Street in Santa Ana, provides an interesting contrast to the strawberry field and sales stand on the south side. *Photo by Diann Marsh*

(Far right) The white material in the rows between the orange trees was provided by the snowfall of 1949. The snow was deep enough in some areas of the county for children to make snowmen. *Old Courthouse Museum*

The woman's role was to provide for the children and maybe to teach school. Mainly, the "good jobs" were reserved for men as a matter of tradition and economic necessity. However, even in this environment of traditional values, women, youth and seniors made up at least 20 percent of the work force. Unemployment was around 6,200. This represented about 13 percent of the entire work force. Unemployment levels had remained at this level or higher for more than 10 years. Imagine a world today in which family men in their prime could say, "I haven't had a regular job since 1987 and I don't know when I will get one." No end was in sight; this was going to be the future forever.

By today's standards, the work force was not very well educated. Most people had reached the 5th grade level, but only a little over one-third of the population had a high school diploma.

The average family income was $1,650 per year with individual income being $622 per year. Even though the dollar went further, family budgeting was tight. Little money was available except for essentials. Eating out was a luxury for most and the average individual spent about 61 cents per week in restaurants.

The economy consisted of major sectors. Farming and agriculture amounted to $34 million and employed about 8,900 people. The second leading sector was oil and mineral extraction, mainly around the Fullerton and Brea areas, and amounted to $17 million. Manufacturing came in third with only $8 million. Employed in this sector were about 4,300 people, and a significant portion of manufacturing supported agriculture. The service section amounted to $16 million and employed the majority of the total work force. County government amounted to $4.5 million

Before the 1950s, agriculture dominated the Orange County economic base. Miles and miles of citrus groves, vegetable crops and cattle-grazing land provided a bucolic picture. *First American Title Insurance Co.*

Three bathing beauties representing various Orange County cities pose in front of a display at the National Orange Show in San Bernardino in 1948. The purpose of the show was to promote agriculture throughout Southern California.
Old Courthouse Museum

Those remaining at home during World War II felt strongly that it was important to do their patriotic duty. Many, wanting to show that they were "loyal Americans," became air raid wardens and plane spotters. *History Room, Santa Ana Public Library*

(Far right) The California Cadet Corps, shown here in 1949, was being trained at the Lighter-Than-Air Station near Tustin and Santa Ana. The base, converted from blimp to helicopter use, remained active until the late 1990s. *Old Courthouse Museum*

and employed 825 individuals. The total economy was $81 million. This was a simpler and poorer time in Depression-era America.

The coming of war to America in December 1941 created huge demands for everything and employment for all. The wartime period was characterized by an increased demand for food stocks and industrial goods of all kinds. The opening of major military facilities brought thousands of servicemen and their dependents to Orange County. These facilities at El Toro, Tustin, Costa Mesa, Seal Beach and Los Alamitos have left their mark on the county.

A sweet young girl poses inside the hollowed out center of a giant pumpkin at the turn of the century. Miles of fertile farming lands in Gospel Swamp, located in a vast area between Santa Ana and Huntington Beach, were noted for their remarkable vegetables such as celery, beans, sugar beets, chili peppers and pumpkins. *First American Title Insurance Co.*

However, the U.S. Congress left a greater mark on the country and the county. In 1944 the G.I. Bill of Rights was passed, granting benefits to returning veterans. This act contained four provisions. The first was the 52/20 program. The second was an education program. The third was the home loan program. Finally, there was the small business loan program. During the 10 years of its existence from 1946 to 1956, millions of veterans received benefits from one or more of its provisions.

The 52/20 program provided unemployment benefits of $20 per week for 52 weeks. The education program provided benefits ranging from $65 per month for single veterans to $90 per month for married veterans. For books and tuition $500 per year was allocated. The Federal Housing Administration (FHA) took aggressive action to make home loans available. The State of California passed the Cal-Vet Program to make low-cost loans available for returning California veterans.

In 1946 two significant legislative events occurred. The Office of Price Administration (OPA) had its price-setting authority greatly reduced. This organization had been established to control prices during the war. Both Richard Nixon and economist John Kenneth Galbraith served with this agency. With the elimination of price controls and the pent-up demand created by the war, inflation was a major issue in the late 1940s as it would also be in the late 1970s.

In addition, Congress passed the Employment Act. The purpose of this act was to assure the nation that Congress had a vested interest to ensure that the economy would generate jobs. Section 2 stated, "The Congress hereby declares that it is the continuing policy and responsibility of the Federal Government to use all practicable means… to promote maximum employment, production and purchasing power." There was to be no "Boom and Bust" economy as there had been in the 1920s and 1930s.

The Orange County Economy

The postwar period can be viewed in three parts — the postwar boom period from 1945 to 1968, the Vietnam doldrums period from 1969 to 1980, and the current period that started in 1981 and continues to this day.

Customers wait outside on the opening day of Buffum's Department Store on North Main in Santa Ana. Orange County's first upscale, modern department store, it was horizontal in design, with large plate glass windows and an open floor plan. The Yorba Room, Buffum's upscale restaurant, remained one of the county's most popular tea rooms until the store chain closed in the early 1990s. *Old Courthouse Museum*

Postwar Boom

In the late 1940s it was evident that people in large numbers were going to settle in Orange County. In June 1947 the Board of Supervisors received the Orange County Sewerage Survey, defining the required facilities needed to support the expected influx of people. Supervisor Willis Warner had a prominent role in this effort. The results of the study projected county population at 1.4 to 1.5 million by 1990. The southern part of the county was to remain undeveloped with the large ranches still intact. How realistic this assumption was is questionable. However, the large ranchers headed by James Irvine were a powerful influence in the county.

In the late 1940s inflation was a real issue; however, prices were much lower than today. Prices in the period spoke of a time when the $5 bill could be a unit of budgeting for the family. Today this unit of budgeting would have to be at least the $20 bill, but probably the $50! Examples of these price levels are easily illustrated.

When Disneyland opened, adult admission was $1 and children entered for 5 cents. In addition to admission, per capita spending inside the park was $2.73 per visitor.

In 1959 double accommodations at the three Travelodges in the county ranged from $7 to $10 per night. These motels were located in Fullerton, Anaheim and Santa Ana. Bigger and better motels were on the way. The Anaheim facility was located at 1166 Katella, three blocks from Disneyland. The one in Fullerton was located at 815 South Spadra (Harbor). Finally, the Santa Ana facility was located at 2005 North Main. Each motel averaged about 30 rooms.

In 1966 a new Mustang listed for $2,857. Other cars cost $2,000 to $4,000. While these prices were up from the previous decade, it still meant that most cars could be bought for a dollar a pound. Good hamburger could be bought on sale at three pounds for $1.

With the passage of the G.I. Bill of Rights, there was increased demand for education. Orange Coast College was established on the former grounds of the Santa Ana Army Air Base in September 1948. Santa Ana Junior College moved to a new campus at 17th and Bristol in 1949. At the time, this was orchard land on the perimeter of Santa Ana. Temporary buildings were utilized until the completion of the first building program

(Far left)
The typical tract house built in Orange County during the early 1940s was single-storied, rectangular and simple in design. The price for such a house averaged from $8,000 to $11,000. *Photo by Diann Marsh*

The Travelodge on N. Main Street in Santa Ana, built in the 1950s, is still in business today. In 1959 the standard price for a double room ranged from $7 to $10 a night. *Photo by Diann Marsh*

By 1966, convertibles with bucket seats had become popular with new car owners. The young lady in the back seat is wearing the latest capri pants. This brand-new Ford sold for less than $3,000.
John Sorenson

in 1954. Then Santa Ana had an effective campus and facilities. College enrollments for Santa Ana increased from 1,034 in 1950 to 1,938 in 1957. Similar enrollment increases occurred at Orange Coast and Fullerton. By 1955 they served 2,351 and 3,207 students respectively.

This growth in enrollment mirrored the tremendous population growth in the county in the 1950s. People needed homes and they were built in the thousands. The value of real estate loans that were granted show the growth in the construction industry during this period. Starting in 1949, $49 million in loans were issued. This number continued to grow and reached $245 million by 1954.

After the end of the Korean War in 1953, the number of yearly residential permits rocketed from about 6,000 in 1952 to 26,000 in 1955. Prior to the Korean War in 1950, 4,000 permits per year were the norm. The recession of 1957-1958 slowed the building boom. However, the year 1959 saw the return of the housing industry in all its gusto.

The new residential home stock of December 1955 had a median price of $13,460 for completed homes. However, prices were on the rise. Gone were the days of the $8,000 to $11,000 homes of the late 1940s. Housing costs were on the minds of all prospective buyers: "Better get yours before you are priced out of the market" describes the attitude of many prospective buyers.

The groundbreaking of the new campus of Santa Ana Junior College was cause for a big celebration by both students and staff in February of 1947. George Wells, holding the shovel, and builder Allison Honer, to his right, participated in the ceremony.
Old Courthouse Museum

The most popular was the three-bedroom home, with the four-bedroom not far behind. Few two-bedroom homes were offered since they did not meet the needs of the parents of baby boomers.

Homes of this period had a median square footage of 1,395. This is considerably less than many of the new homes offered for sale today. The new homes were targeted for members of the baby boom generation of the 1920s who were coming to Orange County to take advantage of the growing industrial employment.

The 1950s saw a rise in industrial employment and the decline in agricultural employment as a percentage of the county's total employment. The relative strength of each sector can be shown by the percentage of the work force employed in agriculture and in industry. In 1940 the percentages were 18.6 and 10.6

respectively. In 1950 both percentages were near equal at 13.8 and 14.6 respectively. By 1960, the percentages were 4.7 and 27.2 respectively. By 1970, agriculture represented only 3 percent of the jobs in the county while manufacturing represented 28.3 percent. In 1975 agricultural jobs comprised 1 percent of the total jobs.

The United States emerged from World War II as the industrial giant of the world and the only free world economy with a healthy manufacturing base. From 1945 to 1960 the United States was the capital goods producer to the world. Profits and wages in this sector were high. Initially, as an overflow of the greater Los Angeles basin with affordable housing and good climate, Orange County attracted some of this industry.

One great advantage industrial employment offers is the corporate structure that makes possible the growth and development of an individual worker's career. Over time, people acquired company-specific skills and knowledge that led to interesting and financially rewarding careers within a company or a sector of the manufacturing realm. This provided the upward mobility generally lacking in the agricultural field.

By July 1954 there were 365 manufacturing plants in Orange County. Most of the major companies were in Brea, Fullerton and Anaheim. Brea was home to Kirkhill Rubber and Shaffer Tools. Fullerton's industrial facilities included Beckman Instruments and Hunt Foods. But the center of industrialization was Anaheim, home to Northrop with 1,100 employees. Robertshaw and Kwikset also made Anaheim their home. Rubber Corp. in Garden Grove and Cheery Rivet in Santa Ana round out the major manufacturers of the day. These companies employed 300 to 700 people each. But bigger and better companies were on the way.

By 1961, aerospace had invaded the county, bringing good jobs, benefits, and wages and salaries to those in the industry. This was the birth of multiple-facility plants within the county that employed thousands. These organizations were so large that an individual was just a number in the employment office.

By 1955, average prices of tract and small custom houses being built in the county had increased to a range of $11,000 to $14,000. Note the separate garage in the back yard of this house on Heliotrope in Santa Ana. The garages of contemporary homes are usually in the front. *Photo by Diann Marsh*

(Far left)
The Autonetics Division of North American Rockwell Corporation located on E. Mira Loma Street in Anaheim was one of several companies that brought good jobs, good wages and benefits to thousands of new workers in Orange County in the 1960s. *First American Title Insurance Co.*

In 1949 Sears-Roebuck Store on South Main opened its doors. The store had some new features that were to become standards — its own parking lot, escalator and air-conditioning. Richard Vining remembered when he and his friends used to take the bus from Costa Mesa in the early 1950s so they could ride the county's first escalator. *History Room, Santa Ana Public Library*

The Buffalo Ranch, northeast of Corona del Mar, was a popular destination for visitors who enjoyed driving the roads of the ranch to watch the buffalo peacefully grazing. Porter's Western Store occupied the barn, while the silo was used as a food stand that sold buffalo burgers. *Orange County Historical Society*

North American located three facilities in the county, two in Anaheim and one in Fullerton. Hughes Aircraft located two facilities, one in Newport Beach and one in Fullerton. Both of these aerospace companies employed about 10,000 people each at their Orange County facilities. The balance of the companies employed 1,000 to 3,000 each and took on the feeling of major corporations. Hunt Foods and Beckman expanded their operations greatly. Ford Aeronetronics and Collins Radio located in Newport Beach. Manufacturing employment grew from 7,844 in 1950 to 47,181 in 1960.

Public Education

While manufacturing continued to grow in the 1960s, a more interesting story lies with the plight of public instruction during the decade of the 1960s. Louise Booth's book, *One to Twenty-eight, A History of Anaheim Union High School District,* illustrates this point: With the growth in schools, it is easy to realize the dynamic growth in the rest of the economy during this period.

Orange County School districts in 1940 were typically small and rural, each having only one or two elementary schools. Many teachers taught more than one grade. High school districts were separate from elementary districts. Santa Ana had the largest elementary and high school districts. Average daily attendance for both was about 3,000. These numbers were low compared to numbers after the postwar growth. The only high school and the elementary districts with average daily attendance of more than 1,000 were Anaheim, Fullerton and Santa Ana. Numerous small, rural school districts existed in the county. Some of their names have been saved as names of individual schools and others have faded into history. Here is a listing of the smallest of them all: Alamitos, Centrailia, Diamond, El Toro, Trabuco, Fountain Valley, Greenville, Katella, Loara, Olinda, Olive, Orangethrope, Paularino, San Clemente, San Joaquin, San

Chapman College (now Chapman University) purchased the old Orange Union High School buildings on Glassell Street in 1954. The school, which moved from Los Angeles, was named for benefactor C.C. Chapman of Fullerton. *Turville Photography Photo by Steve Lopushinsky*

Juan Capistrano, Serra, Silverado, Springdale and Villa Park. Some school sites are easy to place but others are quite difficult. The site of the Paularino School is now under the 55 Freeway.

Total school enrollment (K-14) went from 41,493 in 1950 to 197,939 in 1960. In comparison, between 1950 and 1960 the population of the county went from 216,224 to 703,925, proving that the schools received more than their fair share of the population increase. The following is a brief summary of the growth of junior and senior high schools in the Anaheim Union High School District.

The first postwar new building was Western Jr. High School at 501 S. Western in 1954. In 1957 this school was converted to a high school. Orangeview opened in February 1958 to replace Western as a junior high school. Enrollment increased from 1,320 in 1958 to 2,480 in 1962.

The initial Orangview campus contained 40 classrooms and an administration building totaling 76,786 square feet and was constructed for $860,000 or $11.20 per square foot. Plans for a gymnasium and cafeteria remained on the drawing board. However, the campus proved too small to accommodate the influx of students, requiring 15 Quonset huts to be moved onto the campus to provide 30 additional classrooms.

From 1959 to 1964, nine more junior and four senior high schools were opened in the district as the school-aged population exploded. The management of the limited physical plant was a major feat. Trident Jr. High began on the Orangeview campus in September 1958 as a double session and moved to its own campus in mid-October 1958. Nineteen classrooms and three portables comprised the campus. All administration functions were located in a single classroom. Orangeview in double session served as the launching point for Oxford Jr. High in the fall of 1965.

The new campus of Orange Union High School at Walnut and Shaffer streets opened its doors on May 15, 1953. *Turville Photography Photo by Steve Lopushinsky*

Trident went to double sessions when the Dale Jr. High campus failed to open on time in the fall of 1959. The projected enrollment for Dale was such that three six-period units were

A favorite weekend activity for both teenagers and adults during the 1950s and 60s was the Hot Rod Races at the Santa Ana Raceway. *First American Title Insurance Co.*

The first shipment of a polio vaccine arrived in Santa Ana in 1955. An effort was made to see that all schoolchildren were inoculated against the life-threatening and crippling disease. *Old Courthouse Museum*

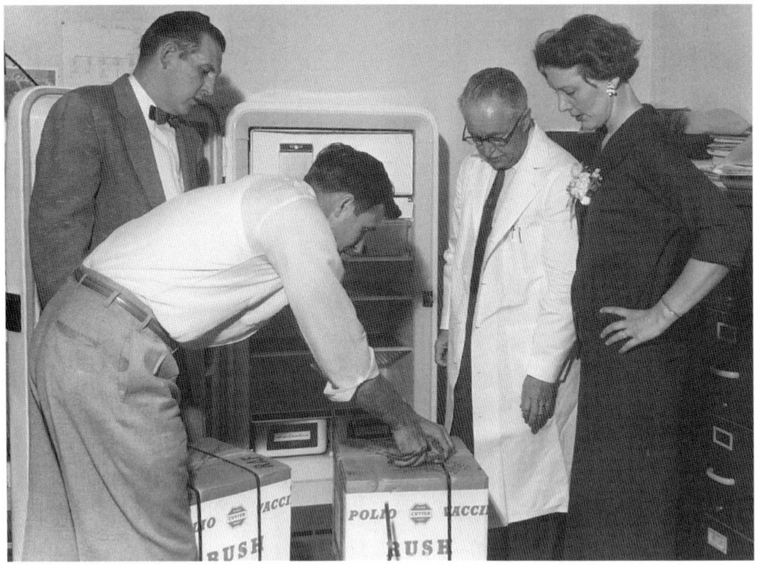

planned. This meant an 18-period day or triple sessions. Before the campus was complete, portable classrooms were moved onto campus.

Walker Jr. High opened in the fall of 1959. There were 24 teachers, only four of whom had taught before, in 18 classrooms. The floors were unfinished and no administration building, gymnasium or teacher lounges existed on campus.

Brookhurst Jr. High School started on the Western Jr. High campus in September 1956. Its new campus was ready and opened on November 12, 1956. The first year the faculty consisted of 33 non-tenured teachers. In the fall of 1961, Sycamore Jr. High started as an afternoon session on the Brookhurst campus. Each of six classes was 30 minutes in length. It was not until after Christmas that the school's new campus at 1801 E. Sycamore was ready.

For the high schools the story was much the same. Magnolia was the first to open in the fall of 1961 — somewhat incomplete and unfinished but functional. The Savanna campus remained unfinished and unusable until November 1961, so double sessions were in order. Landscaping and paving of walkways were completed after the school was in session.

Loara High School began on the campus of Magnolia in September 1962 and remained there until Christmas 1962 when it moved to its new campus at 1765 West Cerritos. The campus was once the 34-acre ranch of the Snyder family who moved to Anaheim in 1889. The faculty grew from 28 teachers to 84 teachers in three years. Kennedy High, originally named Centrailia, was organized on the Loara campus in the spring of 1964 and opened in the fall of 1964.

Richard Nixon spoke from the steps of the Old Orange County Courthouse in 1952 while on the campaign trail. This event occurred about a month after his famous "Checkers" speech in which he refused to return the gift of a cocker spaniel given to his daughters. He and Dwight D. Eisenhower won the election. *Old Courthouse Museum*

As the decade continued, the demand in education moved on to the junior colleges. In September 1966 Cypress and Golden West opened, followed by Saddleback in March 1967. This school construction was mirrored by continued residential and commercial construction, which enabled the county's population to reach 1.4 million by 1970.

A brochure advertising the latest in computers manufactured in the late 1970s illustrates the significant changes in computer systems. Pictured is a Basic/ Four system with a central processing unit (CPU) with a maximum of 128 KB memory in the center. The CPU is flanked by two 75 MB disk drive units.
John Sorenson

The Doldrums

This period, mainly the 1970s, was marked by stagnation and inflation. The sluggish economy reduced the expectations of both investors and wage earners. President Nixon created the WIN Program, Whip Inflation Now, a one-year curb on wage increases in an attempt to control inflation. To keep some of their best and brightest employees from moving on to new companies, employers created new positions and classifications to get around the WIN Program.

The balance of the 1970s was marked by a recession, followed by more inflation under President Carter. Gold and real estate prices soared as people looked for hedges against the constant upward spiral of prices and wages. Real growth was small when compared to the previous period. Investors as a whole made little gain during this period.

Two bright spots in the local economy were the aerospace and computer industries. From its beginnings in the 1950s, the aerospace industry attracted many bright and creative people to the county. In 1972 aerospace employment within the county had reached 51,200. Despite a slight decline from 1975 to 1977, the industry grew to 76,800 workers by 1980.

The beginning of the commercial computer industry dates to 1953 when IBM offered its Model 701. In 1954 it launched an aggressive sales program to sell 50 Model 650 machines — a number larger than the nation's currently installed hardware base. Eventually, over 1,000 were produced and installed, many as leased equipment. Around 1960 the Model 1401 was introduced, followed by the Model 360 four years later. Finally in 1971, the Model 370 was offered to commercial clients. These large machines carried large price tags. Many customers did not require or could not afford these large IBM machines; therefore, smaller, less costly machines were developed, creating a new industry.

In the 1960s and 1970s, the Orange County computer industry consisted of many small firms searching for their place in the market and their place "under the sun" of fame and fortune. These small companies were formed to produce computers, or computer peripherals, or components (power supplies, printed circuit boards, etc.). Due to rapid technology changes and resultant reduced product life cycles of three to five years, companies faced the problem of not being able to produce their products fast enough or not being able to sell their products at any price. Company staffing levels fluctuated greatly over the product life cycle.

Some of the major computer companies were General Automation in Anaheim and Basic-Four, Computer Automation, Microdata, and Business Systems Technology in Irvine. Burrough's Corp. had a plant in Mission Viejo. Mergers and consolidations were common events. Business Systems Technology was acquired by Memorex, which was acquired by Burrough's, which merged with Sperry Univac to become Unisys Corp. Unisys continues to have a strong presence in the county into the 21st century.

Computer hardware had limited capability by today's standards and was very costly, particularly when inflation is considered. The General Automation Price book of the era shows that a computer with 64k of memory, two floppy disks and a printer would cost about $17,000.

A unique operating system for the time that was used by several computer manufacturers was the PICK / OS developed by Richard Pick, who had a doctorate in physics and had begun

Hoag Memorial Hospital in Newport Beach was established in 1952 to fill the need for a hospital to serve the rapidly growing beach towns.
Orange County Historical Society

During the bankruptcy crisis, the entire county focused its attention on the events happening at the Hall of Administration, located at the Civic Center Plaza in Santa Ana. The Board of Supervisors' Chamber and the Supervisors' offices are located in the building. *Turville Photography Photo by Steve Lopushinsky*

working on his concepts in the 1950s. This relational database system combined an operating system (his version of DOS), a programming language (a greatly enhanced form of BASIC), a report-writing language and a terminal control language for interactive applications. In addition, a word processing and spreadsheet package was bundled with the system. Unique to the PICK system was the file structure that could store multiple levels of detail in a single record.

This PICK method for storing data provided for easier data manipulation of records compared to then traditional methods or the typical spreadsheet formats of today. Sorting and selecting records, going to other files with similar keys to get information and performing calculations were all within the report-writing language aiding greatly in meeting customer requirements. This system eventually lost out to the UNIX operating system; however, it certainly met the needs of the smaller users at the time.

The Boom Continues

With the coming of the 1980s, the economy came alive again. The problems of inflation and high interest rates were resolved over time. Early in his first term, President Reagan stated, "We will make America the investment capital of the world." Then the stock market took off like a rocket. Measured by the Dow Jones Industrial Average, investments have increased slightly over tenfold since 1981. Real income growth, while significant, has not done nearly as well.

With the Reagan defense budgets of the 1980s, employment in the local aerospace and high-tech companies grew to a peak of 96,009 in 1987. With the collapse of the Soviet Union and the Eastern Block countries at the end of the 1980s, California and Orange County experienced a dramatic, almost a free fall, decline in defense-industry jobs. California high-tech jobs fell from 716,776 in 1989 to 482,071 in 1994.

Orange County's high-tech jobs mirrored this decline, with employment levels falling from 85,700 in 1989 to 59,000 in 1994. The county's nadir was reached in 1995 at 56,100. By 1999, employment in this sector reached 63,700. Factories were

Costco is one of several new major chain stores that have recently opened stores along Garden Grove Boulevard. *Photo by Diann Marsh*

either closed or greatly reduced, individual careers were cut short and early retirement was common.

To compound the financial problems of individuals and local governments in the early 1990s, the county went into bankruptcy. During 1994, interest rates rose and bond prices fell, causing a decline in all bond funds. On December 6, 1994, county treasurer Robert Citron resigned over the collapse of the $8 billion investment pool. Initial losses were estimated at $1.5 billion. The main culprit was the use of structured notes that allowed the buyer to speculate on the direction of interest rates. Also, money was borrowed to buy additional bonds that only multiplied the losses. Not only Orange County, but many of its cities and other agencies that had invested in the pool suffered from the bankruptcy. The county reduced services, reduced personnel and sold assets in an attempt to mitigate the losses. Eventually the county officials and the brokerage houses that permitted these transactions were held responsible for the losses. Finally, these investment practices were determined to be imprudent for municipal and governmental organizations.

A 1997 survey of Orange County's largest employers shows how the county has moved from agriculture to manufacturing and finally to a service economy. Only one of the nine companies in the survey was involved in manufacturing — Boeing. In order of magnitude these companies are Disney, Boeing, Tenet Healthcare, American Stores, St. Joseph Health System, Bank America, Tricon Global Restaurants, Ralphs Grocery Company and Pacific Telesis. An entertainment company, two health care companies, two supermarket chains, a bank and a restaurant chain clearly demonstrate the importance of the service and retail industries in the present economy.

Redevelopment in the central and northern portions of the county will be a challenge for the next century. As residential structures reach their effective life span of 60 years, as defined by real estate appraisers, resources will have to be committed to rehabilitation or redevelopment. Redevelopment is currently under way in Buena Park at the Buena Park Mall and at industrial sites on Knott Avenue.

The city of Garden Grove has launched Renaissance Garden Grove. This organization is a partnership between the city, the business community, nonprofit organizations and residents. These groups, working together through the Garden Grove Community Foundation, plan to position Garden Grove to capture industrial, commercial and residential opportunities in the future. Each year, with the active support of Mayor Bruce A. Broadwater and Deputy City Manager Catherine Standiford, the foundation plans a series of events to showcase its community. The results have been gratifying to date as new construction and opportunities unfold.

By the end of the 1990s, business and employment had returned to very healthy levels. The Chapman University Economic Forecast for Orange County had projected the growth in gross domestic product to decrease in 1999 from 3.6 percent to 1.9 percent. Some of this was expected to come from a decline in exports to Asia. North American Free Trade Association exports were expected to rise. However, total international trade, exports and imports, were expected to grow at a reduced rate.

Defense spending will continue to decline. Increases in home values, after rising sharply in 1998, were expected to level off to 4.6 percent in 1999.

From now until 2003, job growth is projected to be 2.5 percent per year. Inflation is projected at 2.8 percent per year, and home values are expected to increase at 4.9 percent per year over this period.

Before:
This early view from the Garden Grove (22) Freeway shows Grand Avenue on the right and an on-ramp on the left.
Orange County Historical Society

After:
The same corner, with Grand Avenue on the right, is now occupied by Tom's Truck Center. The large five-story building in the background is the headquarters of the Orange County Register.
Photo by Diann Marsh

ECONOMICS

Like much of California, Orange County shifted from a center of agriculture to a center of industry and service in the second half of the 20th century. Fields, groves and pastures were replaced by high-rise buildings and homes for the growing population of businessmen and their families. Following the postwar boom, in which Orange County citizens welcomed prosperity and financial security, and the slump and stagnation of the 70s, the last two decades have witnessed an ebb and flow in the economic vitality of the region.

The Boeing building is located on the former site of Rockwell in Seal Beach. Boeing acquired Rockwell and McDonnell Douglas in 1996. *Photo by John Sorenson*

The Air Touch industrial complex or Sand Canyon Avenue is typical of construction in the Irvine Spectrum area during the last 10 years. *Photo by John Sorenson*

The Printronix building is typical of the new industrial construction in the Irvine Business Center. The beauty of this building is highlighted at night when the front façade is fully illuminated.
Photo by John Sorenson

PART TWO

Half a century ago, it was fairly simple to characterize Orange County: Its cities were small, its population was sparse and agriculture predominated. Today, of course, the picture is far more complicated. City boundaries became blurred as open land disappeared, the population soared to nearly three million, and farms were replaced by urban centers and suburban sprawl. While the miles of freeways and the density of the dwellings might imply a certain sameness throughout the county's nearly 800 square miles, astute observers know that diversity is what defines Orange County today. While the county's many cities may appear to blend into each other, they take great pride in their unique identities.

Part Two of *The Orange Blossoms* is devoted to an exploration of Orange County's diversity. The story of the county is divided into three main sections, each with two subsections, based on geographical location. To begin, North Orange County includes the cities of Fullerton, Brea, Placentia, Yorba Linda and others. Then, Central Orange County features an essay on the towns that began as bedroom communities of Los Angeles County, including Costa Mesa, Garden Grove, Fountain Valley, Huntington Beach, Seal Beach and Sunset Beach, along with photo essays highlighting Tustin, Orange and Santa Ana. Finally, South Orange County has been divided into the South Coast and Irvine & Saddleback Valley.

Six of the county's top historical writers were chosen to contribute to this part of the book. They wrote chapters that would captivate the interest of the reader, not necessarily to discuss every historical event in every city. The result is a lively chronicle of the character and accomplishments of the many cities whose residents have come from across the nation and around the world to contribute their talents to the exciting and dynamic place they call home. ■

A SURGE TO THE NORTH

BEACH CITIES

South Coast

IRVINE & SADDLEBACK VALLEY

Anaheim/Santa Ana

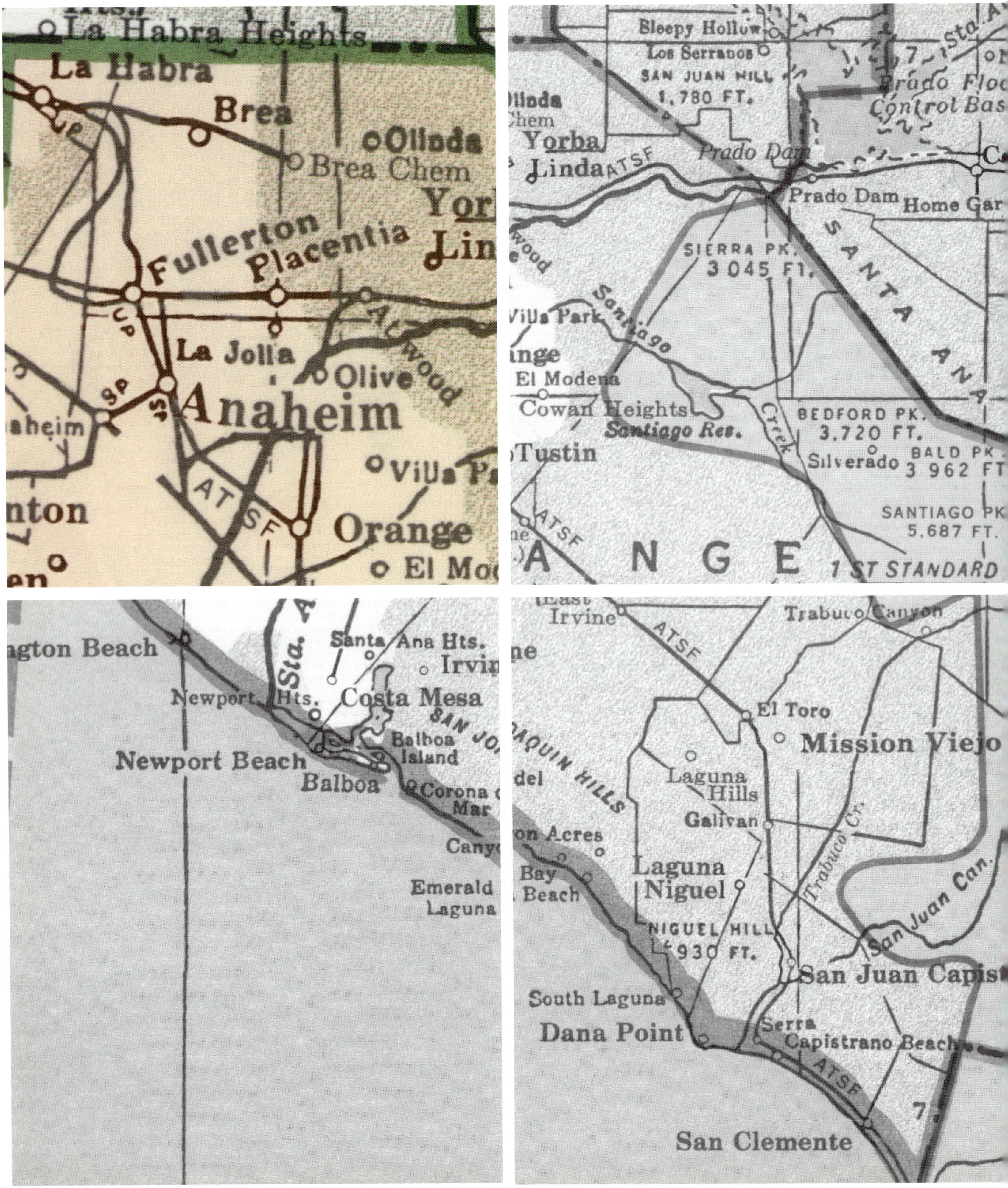
La Habra Heights
La Habra
Brea
Olinda
Brea Chem
Fullerton
Placentia
La Jolla
Olive
Atwood
Anaheim
Villa Park
Orange
El Modena
ATSF
Bleepy Hollow
Los Serranos
SAN JUAN HILL
1,780 FT.
Prado Flood Control Basin
Yorba Linda
Prado Dam
Home Gardens
SIERRA PK.
3045 FT.
SANTA ANA
Santiago
Cowan Heights
Santiago Res.
Tustin
Creek
BEDFORD PK.
3,720 FT.
Silverado
BALD PK.
3 962 FT
SANTIAGO PK
5,687 FT.
1 ST STANDARD
Santa Ana Hts.
Newport Hts.
Costa Mesa
Newport Beach
Balboa
Balboa Island
Corona del Mar
Emerald Laguna
SAN JOAQUIN HILLS
East Irvine
Trabuco Canyon
El Toro
Mission Viejo
Laguna Hills
Galivan
Laguna Niguel
NIGUEL HILL
930 FT.
Trabuco Cr.
San Juan Can.
San Juan Capistrano
South Laguna
Dana Point
Serra
Capistrano Beach
San Clemente

NORTH COUNTY

A SURGE TO THE NORTH *By Bob Ziebell*

It remained an almost pastoral scene that greeted visitors to north Orange County right after World War II. We were headed toward mid-century and still visible were orchards, two-lane roads between town sites — no freeways — and even some cattle and sheep in the hills.

But there were signs of what was to come. An unequaled surge in population had begun, a wave of growth that would cast the 50 years leading to the new millennium as an era that shaped the future of north Orange County — all of Orange County — for all of time to come.

By the numbers, here's a quick picture of the North County of 50 years ago.

Fullerton, founded in 1887 and incorporated in 1904, had seen its 1940 population of 10,422 climb to 13,958 by 1950. The city was cited in a 1956 *Architectural Forum* magazine article as forming, "... a case study of one young city's efforts to avoid the growing pains of fast haphazard development."

La Habra was founded in 1896 and subdivided into "town lots" in 1903. In January 1925 with a population of 2,100, it became a city and will celebrate its diamond anniversary early in the new millennium. The population was 2,499 in 1940 and 7,800 in 1952

One of Fullerton's best-remembered landmarks was the Pacific Electric Red Car overpass on Spadra Road (now Harbor Boulevard), constructed in 1917 and demolished in 1964. *Orange County Historical Society*

when Bill Waterson, former city building and safety director, remembers entering a city building where, "Cramped together in a one-room office were the city engineer, street superintendent, building inspector and a secretary to handle the various clerical duties for all three divisions."

Brea, known from 1903 to 1911 as Randolph, was founded as Brea in 1911 and incorporated in 1917. The population, 2,562 in 1940, had increased to 3,208 by 1950. Author Teresa Hampson in *Brea: Celebrating 75 Years* wrote, "Main Street Brea in the 1950's still seemed much like a Midwestern town."

Placentia, where a townsite map was filed in 1910, actually had its name on the books since 1879 when the school district adopted it, reportedly at the suggestion of Mrs. William McFadden. The city was incorporated in 1926 and, in 1940, had a population of about 1,600. The postwar population surge was late in hitting the community and by 1950 was only slightly greater. Historian Virginia Carpenter phrased it concisely in *Placentia, a Pleasant Place* when she wrote, "There had been a trickle of new people since World War II, then it became a flood."

Yorba Linda, founded in the ranchos of another era, gained its identity in 1909 when the Janss Investment Co. began selling land, by the acre, in an area it had named Yorba Linda. The little community quickly gained a reputation for determined independence, prompting an unidentified banker — quoted by March Butz in *Yorba Linda, its History* — to say, "If ever I saw a town haul itself up by its boot straps,

(Far right top) The Attilio and June Periotti House, listed on the National Register of Historic Places, is within the Fullerton city limits, although the family has always been linked with Placentia. *Photo by Diann Marsh*

(Far right bottom) The historic George Key Ranch, now a 12-acre County of Orange historic park, was established by George B. Key in 1893. *Photo by Diann Marsh*

(Below) The historic Yorba Cemetery, located north of the Yorba Regional Park in Yorba Linda, was established by Bernardo Yorba in 1858. *County of Orange*

Oil fields covered the hills of several North County towns beginning in the 1890s. The first Fullerton fields were discovered in 1906 when a series of gushers were brought in on the Bastenchury Ranch by Simon J. Murphy.
First American Title Insurance Co.

Yorba Linda is it." The statement was made just before 1950 when incorporation was still 17 years away.

So, there were indications of the dramatic changes to come. The influx of World War II veterans, who had enjoyed the "California Experience" while training here, initiated a pattern that would forever change the face of Orange County. But, could anyone have predicted how rapidly and with such force that change would occur?

Population Explosion

By 1960 the combined population of Fullerton, La Habra, Brea and Placentia had climbed to 105,000, an increase of more than 78,000 from 1950 totals, or about 290 percent in 10 years.

To that total, Yorba Linda, not yet a city, contributed an additional 1,198 citizens. But things were about to change in the little hamlet where Richard Nixon, 37th president of the United States, was born.

After fighting off annexation attempts by surrounding communities and surviving the disappointment of several failed attempts to bring incorporation to a vote, residents finally cast ballots on Oct. 24, 1967. The community of 11,433 (note the growth of nearly 10,000 people in seven years) officially became a city on November 2 after certification of the overwhelmingly favorable vote. The growth didn't stop there. Yorba Linda's population climbed to 28,254 by 1980, to 49,600 in 1989 and was at 60,000 plus as the new millennium dawned.

Meanwhile, the other, older communities of North County were also riding the crest of a population boom that made Orange County the fastest-growing county in the nation.

In Fullerton the U.S. Census counted 56,180 residents in 1960, a four-fold increase from 1950. That climbed to 85,987 in 1970 and the city officially topped the 100,000 mark with the 1980 census report of 102,034. That increased to 111,737 by 1990 and was estimated at 125,000 heading into the year 2000.

The building on the right is the Fullerton Road Signal Tower, shown in 1925. The orange groves and empty plots of land are now gone, replaced by houses.
First American Title Insurance Co.

(Far left)
A small 1920s Spanish Colonial Revival building was located near the entrance of the 6,000-acre Rancho Santa Ana. Sub-divided in the 1980s, it is now part of Yorba Linda.
Photo by Diann Marsh

The Yorba Linda Packing House, located on Yorba Linda Boulevard, was built by the Yorba Linda Citrus Association in the early 1930s. The building, which they occupied until the 1960s, has been rehabilitated as a commercial building.
Photo by Diann Marsh

The Charles Chapman home, built in 1904 on what is now State College Boulevard in Fullerton, featured imported Italian marble fireplaces and chandeliers, a ballroom on the third floor, seven bathrooms with imported tile, hand-painted ceilings, a two-story-high stained glass rose window and other refinements. Here it is shown when the land was being subdivided and the house was being purchased by the V.F.W. Sadly, it burned down in the 1960s.

First American Title Insurance Co.

(Far left)
New houses hug the rim of the hills of the former Rancho Santa Ana. The previously empty hills along the north side of the Riverside Freeway (91) are now covered with new development that began in the 1980s.
Photo by Diann Marsh

La Habra, Orange County's northernmost city, was founded in 1896 through the efforts of W. J. Hole. In 1975 it was honored by being designated an "All American City."
Turville Photography
Photo by Steve Lopushinsky

Brea's population in 1960 more than doubled from the 1950 population level. In 1960 the census showed 8,487 residents. By 1970 the census reported 18,447 Breans and in 1980 the number had increased to 27,100. The population currently stands at 36,000.

And in La Habra the population had exploded to 25,136 in 1960, five times the 1950 total. It increased to 41,350 in 1970 and to 45,232 in 1980. An estimated 55,100 people now reside in La Habra.

Placentia's slow growth in the 1940-50 period was followed by historian Carpenter's appropriately termed "flood" of people in the years that followed. By 1960, 5,861 residents were counted in the census — more than 4,100 greater than 1950. The 1970 census showed a population of 21,948 residing within the city limits, climbing to 35,300 in 1980, to 41,259 in 1990 and was sitting at 47,000+ with the year 2000 right around the corner.

The population growth, of course, fostered a myriad of problems for the communities of north Orange County. Where would all these people live? Where would they work? And, how would they get from one place to the other and back again?

Transportation

Railways provided the pre-1900 ties to the outside world and were the impetus for growth in the initial development of the North County. Railways continued to greatly influence North County growth in the first decades of the 20th century. Early

The Dr. George Clark House was moved from downtown Fullerton to the Arboretum on the Cal State Fullerton campus in 1972. Built in 1894-95, the house has been restored as a museum of local history, Victoriana and medicine.
Photo by Diann Marsh

The main section of the Riverside (91) Freeway follows the general path of the Santa Ana Canyon Road. The freeway opened in 1958.
Turville Photography
Photo by Steve Lopushinsky

North County residents remember well the fun of taking a date into Los Angeles via the Pacific Electric Railway.

However, the burgeoning North County population required much more in the way of links to their neighbors by the time mid-century rolled around. Those new transportation links are the ribbons of concrete Southlanders call freeways.

On the morning of July 3, 1957, the era of rapid vehicular transportation dawned in the county. This event was the opening of a 1.25-mile section of the Santa Ana (5) Freeway through Buena Park, extending from Fullerton Creek, near Artesia Avenue and the Los Angeles county line, to Orangethorpe Avenue at the Fullerton-Buena Park border.

The gates had opened and the multiple-lane roadways rapidly spread through the entire northern portion of the county.

- In September 1958 the Riverside (91) Freeway extended its route further into Orange County when the link from Magnolia Avenue to Spadra Road (Harbor Boulevard) opened. Then, on Nov. 18, 1959, traffic began moving along the extension from Spadra to Cypress Street (State College Boulevard), completing the freeway tie to Riverside County.
- The building of North County's inter-city and inter-county freeway links concluded with the Orange (57) Freeway. It happened in three stages over a three-year period from 1969 to 1972. First, the Riverside (91) Freeway to Nutwood Avenue section opened in the summer of 1969 and then the Nutwood to Imperial Highway link in June of 1970. Finally, the link to Los Angeles County through Brea came in 1972 with the opening of the Imperial to Pomona (60) Freeway section.

There were once plans for more, but high right-of-way costs through developed areas and objections from residents stymied an Imperial (perhaps to be named Nixon) Freeway route. Approved by voters, however, are plans for development of a "smart street," an improved, limited access routing for Imperial Highway. It will join Beach Boulevard in the smart street network, with perhaps more to come.

More visible to residents, however, are the massive reconstruction projects that began in the mid-1990s and will continue into the new millennium on the Santa Ana (5) and the Riverside (91) freeways. Lane additions, resurfacing, reconstructed interchanges, the addition of High Occupancy Vehicle (HOV or carpool) lanes with special "flyover" bridges at the interchanges, new bridges, overpasses and underpasses are included. The Santa Ana project, winding its way through the county from north to south, carries a price tag of about $1.1 billion. The Riverside work on an 11.5-mile stretch from the Los Angeles county line to the interchange with the Orange (57) Freeway is a $180 million effort that spans six cities — Anaheim, Buena Park, Cerritos, Fullerton, La Palma and Placentia.

The Orange (57) Freeway, which was finished in stages from 1969 to 1972, winds its way north, beginning at its intersection with the Santa Ana (5) Freeway and ending at the Foothill (210) Freeway.
Turville Photography
Photo by Steve Lopushinsky

The Orange County Transportation Authority (OCTA) and the California Department of Transportation (Caltrans) are

(Far left)
Oil vied with citrus production in Placentia in the 1920s. There are still several old packing houses located between Center and Crowther streets, near the railroad tracks.
Photo by Diann Marsh

(Top left)
The new Fullerton City Hall, built at a cost of $1,977,085, was dedicated in June 1963. The city hall staff was moved from the Spanish Colonial Revival building across the street to the east, now the police department.
First American Title Insurance Co.

Brea Boulevard, originally Pomona Avenue, was the commercial center for the residents of Brea. Early residents worked for the oil companies.
Photo by Diann Marsh

partners in the work scheduled for completion in 2000. The primary funding comes from Measure M, a half-cent sales tax approved by voters in 1990 to pay for transportation improvements.

Surface street improvements have not been left out of the equation. Fullerton constructed railroad underpasses at Euclid Street (1960, cost $800,000), Commonwealth Avenue (1962, $1.3 million) and Lemon Street (1978, $4.3 million), Gilbert Street (1987, $6 million) and has another in progress on Highland Avenue.

Roadways have been extended north and south, east and west to link the North County communities. An example is the extension of what was once known as Pioneer Avenue in Fullerton. It's now called Yorba Linda Boulevard and it extends from State College Boulevard in Fullerton to Imperial Highway in Yorba Linda and beyond, eventually connecting to the Riverside (91) Freeway in Santa Ana Canyon.

More examples include the extensions of State College Boulevard, Euclid and Gilbert streets and Placentia Avenue to provide north-south ties. Chapman Avenue has been extended eastward to link with Orangethorpe Avenue. Rose Drive and Kraemer are now through streets.

The Brea Boulevard of the 1950s was a three-lane monstrosity between Fullerton and Brea, with passing being allowed in the center lane — in both directions. Now, it's mostly four traffic lanes wide with portions divided by landscaped median.

There are more railway grade improvements on the drawing board, including Placentia's dramatic and unique proposal to place tracks below grade level through the community, running streets over the top of the rail routes. It's a study in progress. A new light rail line along Fullerton-Irvine corridor is under construction.

Thus, north countians have an easier route to travel — if it isn't too crowded. And, where do they travel to work, to shop?

Downtown Fullerton, looking south on Spadra (now Harbor) was a bustling town when this photo was taken in the 1950s. On the left is the Bank of Italy Building, designed in the Neo-classical Beaux Arts style. It recently was restored with the first floor as retail space and the second as offices.
Orange County Historical Society

Economics

Fifty years ago, North County arrivals found an economy based on citrus ranching, railroad freight operations and oil. The latter has been a sustaining commodity, to one extent or another, in all of the North County cities being discussed here. In Fullerton, oil production still accounted for about 40 percent of the city's revenue in 1950. La Habra, Brea, Placentia and Yorba Linda all enjoyed revenue derived from oil production.

But it was apparent the space and service demands of the growing population would necessitate change, and, in fact, demand a broader economic base of support.

Fullerton took action as early as 1952 with an industrial development program that fit into the city's master plan. Robert B. Clark was hired to attract industry to Fullerton. He succeeded by bringing Kimberly-Clark, Sylvania Electrical Products, Hughes Aircraft Co. and other firms such as Fender Instruments, Hunt Foods, Pacific Hawaiian and F.E. Olds Musical Instruments to the industrial base. The aforementioned April 1956 *Architectural Magazine* article credited Fullerton's success to, "careful thinking and acting from 1940 on."

And Breans were not sitting on their hands. In 1954 that city welcomed its first commercial district development outside of the downtown area — the Brea Heights Shopping Center. It was the first step to development of the North County's largest single commercial development — the Brea Mall.

Sam's Place, formerly located at 117 S. Brea Boulevard, was owned by Sam Landa. Sam was a member of a family of ranchers who settled in the Brea area soon after the turn of the century. Sam's place was popular with local residents. *Photo by Diann Marsh*

Beckman Industries, shown here in 1963 in Fullerton, was founded by noted chemist Dr. Arnold Beckman in 1935. The company produced the first spectraphotometers, helical potentiometers and other health-related medical instruments. *First American Title Insurance Co.*

On the left in this downtown Fullerton photo is the new American Savings Building, constructed in 1982 at the corner of Chapman and Harbor. *First American Title Insurance Co.*

In 1955 Brea Mayor Charles Russell and city administrator A. W. Studebaker, along with North County industrialist Arnold O. Beckman, were included in a contingent sent to the nation's capital to recruit business and industry. It worked, prompting author Hampson to comment in her book, "By 1960, Brea had been transformed from an oil and agriculture town into a growing industrial center." She also observed that the 1985 Orange County Progress Report indicated that the city's eight major industrial parks constituted more than one-tenth of all such properties in the county. And studies showed by the early 1990s, Brea's weekday population tripled into a work force of more than 100,000 people.

And what became of the mall? After the city spent $5.6 million on site preparations, according to the records, a groundbreaking was held in April of 1974. The mall opened for business in August of 1977 with the formal grand opening celebration being held Sept. 27, 1977. An $80-million renovation and expansion program at the mall was started in 1988, increasing the size of the center by 60 percent.

La Habra, Placentia, Yorba Linda, semi-rural communities by design, had become bedroom communities with sprouting commercial centers of their own. In La Habra there was Fashion

Square, recently replaced with the La Habra Marketplace. In Placentia, a commercial center was built along Yorba Linda Boulevard called La Mancha Center. In Yorba Linda, a commercial center replaced a packing plant on Yorba Linda Boulevard and businesses were rebuilt along Imperial Highway. And, while not really a commercial venture but one of significant historical importance for all time to come, and certainly a highlight of the whole north county area, The Richard M. Nixon Library and Birthplace came to Yorba Linda in July of 1990.

The library/museum, built on the site of a former school, is located at the northeast corner of Eureka Avenue and Yorba Linda Boulevard. Immediately adjacent to the library is the home where Nixon was born on Jan. 9, 1913. The remains of both Richard Nixon and his wife, the former Thelma Catherine "Pat" Ryan of Whittier, now rest at the site between the Pat Nixon Rose Garden and the home where he was born.

When the library and birthplace were dedicated, Richard and Pat Nixon joined three other presidents and their wives. This was the first time four presidents and first ladies had ever been together in one place — Ronald and Nancy Reagan, Gerald and Betty Ford, George and Barbara Bush and Richard and Pat Nixon — in the history of our nation.

The battle to locate the library in Yorba Linda had been a tough one. San Clemente, the home of the Western White House during Nixon's administration, had been in the running as the site for a long time. But, after Yorba Linda was selected, then-mayor Roland Bigonger, an acquaintance of Nixon, received a letter from the former president, which summed up his feelings about the library being located in the city of his birth. Authors Mary Ruth Erickson, James V. Granitto III and Shakunthala S. Rajan quoted from the letter in *The Yorba Legacy, A Child's History*, as follows:

"I have traveled a long road from my youth in Yorba Linda, and this project has traveled a long road back. There have been many false starts and disappointments for the library along the

The groundbreaking for the Brea Mall in April 1974 signaled a new direction for the town of Brea. The formal grand opening was held for the popular 100-acre mall on September 27, 1977.
Turville Photography
Photo by Steve Lopushinsky

(Far left top)
Brea High School, built in 1926 after the Brea-Olinda High School District broke away from the Fullerton Union High School District one year earlier, was demolished in the early 1990s. The building had been remodeled in the Moderne style following the 1933 Long Beach earthquake.
Photo by Diann Marsh

(Far left bottom)
The Richard Nixon Library, located at Yorba Linda Boulevard and Eureka Avenue was dedicated in July 1990.
Photo by Diann Marsh

(Far left bottom)
President Richard Nixon's birthplace, shown here after it was restored and became part of the Nixon Library, had special meaning to president Nixon, born here on July 9, 1913. The home in Yorba Linda provides a special insight into the early life of the former president.
Photo by Diann Marsh

(Far right top) Fullerton Junior College, founded in 1913, is the oldest continually operating community college on its original site in the state. It has continued to grow and add new programs annually. *Turville Photography Photo by Steve Lopushinsky*

Plummer Auditorium, on the campus of Fullerton High School, was dedicated in June 1930 and named for Louis E. Plummer, a prominent Fullerton superintendent of schools. It was designed by Los Angeles architect Carlton Winslow. *Turville Photography Photo by Steve Lopushinsky*

(Far right) Cal State Fullerton's first permanent campus building, opened in 1963, was McCarthy Hall. It was occupied by the letters and science departments. *First American Title Insurance Co.*

way. But the extraordinary efforts to make this project a reality have made the long wait worthwhile. Now that we have seen the kind of project it will be, we cannot imagine having it any other way or in any other place?"

The library in this "land of gracious living" is a facility for the entire nation to share. It provides yet another location for education in the north county, but it's far from being the only one to emerge in the last half-decade.

Education

The fostering of education dates back into the late rancho days in north Orange County. The Yorbas built a schoolhouse for the education of their children and those of the rancho workers. The Bastanchurys also had a school built on their ranch. Public elementary school districts date to the 1870s and the Fullerton Union High School District, which at one time took in most of north Orange County, was formed in 1893. Fullerton College is the oldest continuously operating junior college in the state. Classes began there in 1913.

But it was after 1950 and the huge influx of population, that these long-standing institutions of education began to expand. The Fullerton Union High School District, for example, opened its first campus outside of the city in 1954 with La Habra High School. Brea-Olinda High School's new $36 million, 50-acre campus opened on the hill next to the Orange (57) Freeway in 1989, touted as the first in California built without state aid or cost to local taxpayers. The money came from sale and lease of the old 40-acre high school site, now called the Brea Marketplace.

Higher education, beyond community colleges, came after 1950 and was centered in Fullerton, where the slogan, "The Education City," has been adopted.

- California State University, Fullerton — originally Orange County State College — opened classes in temporary buildings on the Sunny Hills High School campus in September 1959. There were 452 full- and part-time students and 46 employees, including 24 part-time faculty. William Langsdorf was the first president and administrative offices were on the campus at Fullerton Union High School, which moved to the school's permanent campus, a 252-acre east Fullerton site where the first permanent building, the Letters and Science Building (McCarthy Hall) opened in 1963. Earlier, in May 1962, the school got its nickname — Titans — and symbol — elephant — when elephant races were held on campus, garnering international attention. In 1999 enrollment topped 27,000 students. The area surrounding the CSUF campus is now known in some circles as "Academic Square" because of the other institutions of higher education.

• Southern California College of Optometry, founded in 1904, was the third oldest of 12 advanced schools of optometry in the United States when it came to Fullerton in 1973. The school underwent an $11-million major expansion in 1998, adding 22,000 square feet in a two-story "Academic Center." The center, dedicated to Dr. Richard Hopping and his wife Patricia, opened to its 400 students and 84 faculty on September 17, boasting the most advanced audiovisual system of any optometric training facility in the nation.

•Hope International University was known as Pacific Christian College when it moved to Fullerton from Long Beach in late 1973, starting classes with 125 employees and 325 students in the fall of the year. A school brochure correctly forecasted that the school had made an "excellent investment" when it purchased a former shopping center and the former Cal State dormitories. The university's name change came in 1998 and more accurately describes the diverse course of study offered and is more recognizable as an institution of higher learning to its foreign students.

• Western State University College of Law, the county's oldest school of law, founded in 1966, moved from Anaheim into its new headquarters, which received architectural honors in 1975. The school has graduated more than 8,000 lawyers and judges, most of who have stayed on to continue practices in Orange County. Western State also expanded its facilities just before the turn of the century, adding a new 31,000-square-foot library that more than doubled the space allotted to books while also adding a high-tech computer lab and large and small conference areas. Although scaled back from early proposals, the expansion that opened in 1998 included remodeling of the entire third floor of the existing four-story law center to provide for faculty offices, a large conference room and a tutoring center.

Meanwhile, in another major educational change, Yorba Linda Elementary School District ended its affiliation with the Fullerton Union High School district in 1989 and joined with Placentia to form the Placentia Yorba Linda Unified School District.

As all of these new things were coming to the area, it became evident some action must be taken to preserve or rebuild the old. It's called redevelopment, an often controversial political matter that has affected the north Orange County area in different ways.

(Far left top)
Located next to the Fullerton College campus on East Chapman, the Hetabrink House built in 1914 by the Hetabrink family, is a superior example of Mission Revival/ Moorish architecture.
Photo by Diann Marsh

(Far left bottom)
The former home of the C. Stanley Chapman family was donated to Cal State Fullerton by the Chapman heirs for use as the residence of its president. Originally Spanish Colonial Revival in style, the house was redesigned in a unique version of New Orleans architecture in the early 1950s.
Marsh Collection

Cal State Fullerton currently has more than 27,000 students enrolled on its 252-acre campus.
(Left) *Turville Photography*
Photo by Steve Lopushinsky
(Below)
Cal State Fullerton, Public Affairs

This pleasant single-story Colonial Revival cottage is typical of the sturdy working-class houses built for Brea residents who came to town to work in the oil industry in the 1920s. *Photo by Diann Marsh*

Redevelopment

All the cities in North County are looking at redevelopment in one form or another, La Habra is looking to revitalize La Habra Boulevard, for instance. But there are two North County communities that provide a strong counterpoints in approach. Brea is remaking its downtown and Fullerton is following a plan of restoration.

Formation of the Brea Redevelopment Agency came in 1970, but an initial downtown project proposal was defeated in an advisory referendum vote the next year. New plans began almost immediately, but some hot disputes — in and out of court — delayed firm action for nearly 20 years. In 1986 redevelopment planning for the downtown began anew, but it wasn't until 1991 that the transformation now being witnessed had its start. That year, Watt Commercial Development signed a contract to build a 50-acre commercial and town home complex at the northwest corner of Brea Boulevard and Imperial Highway and Tom Craig became a Watt partner in the commercial development — "Gateway Center."

There was more controversy, including a dispute between the redevelopment agency and the Brea Small Businessmen's Coalition that was resolved in 1992. The old buildings of downtown Brea had all but disappeared from the west side of Brea Boulevard by the end of the year. The Gateway Center has risen on the spot, and the Edwards Theater complex has been built. Redevelopment continues across the street where the old Brea Hotel has been removed.

In Fullerton, it's essentially the same old downtown — with a cleaned up face and new uses. The process of renewing Fullerton's downtown began in the early 1960s with the formation of parking districts which found public parking lots being built behind the businesses lining both sides of Spadra Road (Harbor Boulevard). It continued with formation of the Fullerton Redevelopment Agency and four project areas.

Project Area No. 1 was the Orangefair Mall.

Project Area No. 2 located in downtown Fullerton was conceived to preserve the business district by improving pedestrian traffic through installing new arcades and walkways, more efficient lighting, landscaping, better signing, "...along with additional housing and commercial improvements." The project

The Cusick House at 315 E. Amerige Avenue in Fullerton, built in 1885, is shown here in the process of being restored to its former Victorian beauty. *Photo by Diann Marsh*

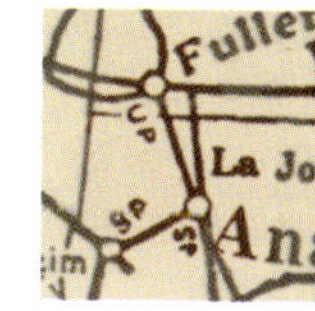

was a success except for the arcades along Harbor Boulevard, which were removed shortly after being installed in the early 1980s. Both business owners and residents objected to these arcades.

Project Area No. 3 focused on blighted areas in East Fullerton.

Project Area No. 4 concentrates on saving Fullerton's auto dealerships that contribute heavily to the cities sales tax revenue.

The seismic retrofitting of downtown buildings, most of them dating back to the early 1920s but others even older, provided for an eclectic mix of commercial businesses, antique stores and dining establishments. On the fringes of the central business district rise new housing designed to fit the mold of an earlier Fullerton where residents have easy access to the necessities of life and to transportation that can carry them about the county, into Los Angeles or to faraway places.

A major element of the downtown project was creation of the Fullerton Transportation Center and what many city officials call the hub of the city's future — as well as its past when the arrival of the railroad assured success for a fledgling community. All three of Fullerton's railroad stations have been preserved. They are as follows:

- The Pacific Electric Station (IL Ghiotto Restaurant) is on its original 1918 site on east Commonwealth Avenue at the north side of the center.
- The Union Pacific Station (The Old Spaghetti Factory) is now located at a site across Harbor and across the tracks from its original location on West Walnut Avenue. This move occurred in 1980.

This photo of downtown Fullerton taken in the 1980s shows the Harbor arcades built in the early 1980s and removed after the objection of business owners. One of the arcades can be seen along the storefronts behind the cars on the left side of the street.
First American Title Insurance Co.

Fullerton's Pacific Electric Station, built in 1918, is one of the few PE stations in the county to survive demolition. It has been rehabilitated as the IL Ghiotto Restaurant.
Turville Photography
Photo by Steve Lopushinsky

The Villa del Sol, one of downtown Fullerton's major retail, lodging and office buildings since it was built as the California Hotel in 1922, was remodeled in the 1960s to include a large addition across the front.
First American Title Insurance Co.

New industrial and commercial complexes form a chain of Postmodern buildings along the north side of La Palma Avenue and the Riverside (91) Freeway. *Turville Photography Photo by Steve Lopushinsky*

Hidden from public view is a small section of the old Cajon/Anaheim Water Company Canal, built in 1878 and lined with concrete in 1923. The last remaining section of the canal is located behind the Fire Station off La Palma. Both the canal and old Pomegranate Road beside it are being restored as a historic walking trail. *Photo by Diann Marsh*

• The Santa Fe Station, focal point of the Fullerton Railway Plaza, serves AMTRAK, Metrolink and interconnecting bus passengers. The present building constructed in 1930 replaced Fullerton's first train station built on this site in 1888.

The Brea-Fullerton contrast in redevelopment is but one look at the phenomenon that continues to grip North County and other regions. The continued effort at serving their constituents has brought honor to more than one community. Placentia, La Habra and Brea have all been proclaimed All-American cities, for example. The schools in all of the communities have been honored with Golden Bell, distinguished School or Blue Ribbon school status and other symbols of excellence in that field.

Summary

So, as we look back on the most recent half-decade in north Orange County we see the development of a community, and the start of a rebirth.

The ranch home of Susanna Bixby Bryant, owner of the 6,000-acre Rancho Santa Ana and founder and creator of the botanical gardens that graced the hills of the ranch from 1926 to the early 1950s, has been restored as a museum of Yorba Linda history. Located off of Bryant Street at the end of La Palma, it is listed on the National Register of Historic Places. *Photo by Diann Marsh*

The transportation corridors have been built and are being rebuilt. The economic base of the area was forced to change early on and it is starting to change once again through the development of different kinds. There has been a constant in the concern for education, but it, too, continues to grow and expand to meet the demands of the community at all levels.

Yes, some of the old faces have gone, but new ones have quickly filled the void. More will disappear, and they, too, will be replaced. That "almost pastoral" scene of 1950 is no longer. In its place is a north Orange County that has risen to meet the challenges of urbanization and gives every indication of continuing to do so.

The next 50 years give promise of dynamic change — high-speed rail, maybe a new airport to the south, rebuilt commercial areas, new and larger schools — many plans are already on the drawing boards.

But, it's doubtful any future half-decade will see the dramatic surge in growth and resulting changes on every level of life than that witnessed during the immediate past 50 years. ■

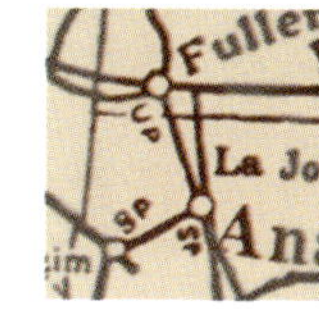

The Santa Fe Station, constructed in 1930, is one of the major Amtrak stops between Los Angeles and San Diego. Listed on the National Register of Historic Places, the building was restored by the Bushala Brothers. Painted beige several years ago, the original rich stucco colors of tan, cinnamon, grey-blue and beige were restored when the building was stripped of the newer paint.
Photo by Diann Marsh

ANAHEIM: HOW A SMALL TOWN BECAME AN ENTERTAINMENT MECCA

By John Westcott

The Old Anaheim City Hall on Lincoln Avenue was constructed in 1923 in the grand tradition of the Beaux Arts style. The ideal style for a government building or a bank, it conveyed a feeling of solidarity, stability and strong classical designs. It was demolished as part of Anaheim's Redevelopment Plan. *Anaheim Historical Society*

Used by permission from Disney Enterprises, Inc.

Jerry, "the world's most human chimpanzee," was entertainment, Anaheim style, in 1952. Jerry was part of the whimsical menagerie of Jungle Gardens, dwelling under 500 palm trees in an exotic amusement park owned by Jack Dutton. There were also a pool of alligators, colorful parrots and an elephant named "Anaheim."

No one knew it at the time, but the quiet agricultural town of Anaheim was about to become elephantine in its own way. Within a dozen years, the city was to become an entertainment mecca, with the world's most famous amusement park — light years beyond Jungle Gardens — a major league baseball team and the largest convention center this side of the Mississippi.

That was just the beginning for Anaheim, which today is on yet another growth spurt — both in population and in its entertainment industry. Construction is moving eastward at a rate that should peak at just over 400,000 in the next two decades. Disneyland is not only building its biggest expansion ever, but also hopes to shepherd the Anaheim Angels and Mighty Ducks to playoff success. The city is focusing on fixing up its "older areas" — much of which was built after the post-war boom surged in the 1950s, and by itself is larger than most of Orange County's other cities.

None of this seemed possible back in 1945, the year Jack Benny's radio show debuted its famous line, "Train leaving on Track Five for Anaheim, Azuza, and Cucamonga." National listeners had little other cause to know Anaheim then. But even as others laughed, city leaders already were planning to take on the human tsunami they knew was coming on the heels of World War II.

That wave hit much of Southern California as the returning warriors chose places to settle down, encouraged by low interest rates for housing, and a pent-up economy chomping at the bit to run on all cylinders after years of war rationing. Hundreds of thousands of servicemen already had an acquaintance with Orange County, either training at its half-dozen military bases, or returning through it after Japan's surrender.

Longtime Mayor Charles Pearson and Chamber of Commerce manager Earne Moeller wanted to make sure Anaheim benefited the most from Orange County's postwar boom. Pearson had led the city since 1936 and wouldn't end his mayoral reign until he stepped down in 1959. Moeller was chosen by the chamber to promote Anaheim as an industrial giant in the making. Roller coasters and sports franchises weren't on their minds, yet. The two leaders were joined in 1950 by Keith Murdock, first as city administrator and by 1956 as city manager.

Other nearby cities, like Fullerton and Garden Grove, were content to be bedroom communities, but not Anaheim. It began placing ads in the *Wall Street Journal* and other major publications to lure industry. Those who responded were persuaded through in-depth discussions with city and business leaders, ending with a closing pitch by Pearson.

"When I got there, the rest of Orange County's cities thought they would go broke if they took a chance on industry," Murdock said later. "But it's industry that pays the city's taxes, and it's industry that provides jobs for city residents."

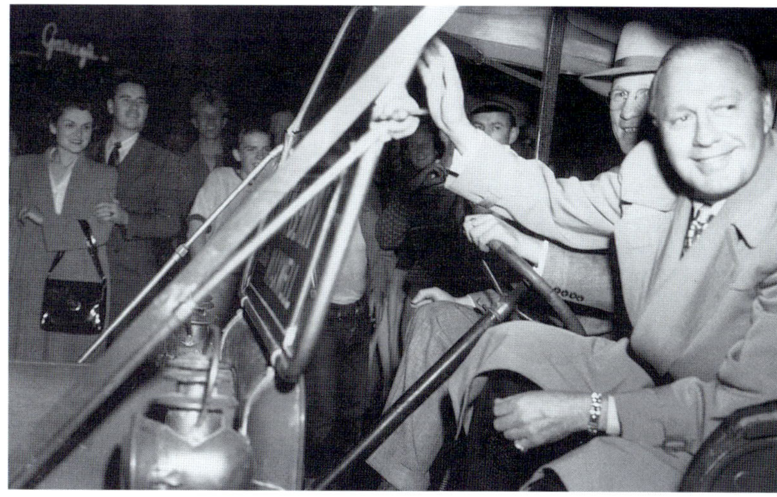

A smiling Jack Benny greets the crowds during a parade in Anaheim. *Old Courthouse Museum Society*

The SQR Store, downtown Anaheim's major department store, was founded by the Renner Family soon after the turn of the century and remained as a family-run business until the store was demolished in the early 1980s. *Anaheim Historical Society*

At the same time, the trio of city and business leaders had to sell the idea of industry to their own residents, some of whom feared a nightmare of smelly smokestacks. A campaign strove to dispel those apprehensions. The first major test was Kwikset Locks, which opened in 1948 with public tours to show how clean it was, arranged by Moeller. Later, teachers and clergymen became guests at other new firms as part of the city's "Industrial Education Days."

Citrus growers often were vocal opponents — until they saw the value of their land skyrocketing, or their trees dying of a disease called "quick decline." Land prices grew from about $2,750 an acre in 1947, to $6,000 in 1954. By the end of the 1950s, values had risen to $20,000.

Dozens of large firms received a warm welcome in Anaheim in the late 1940s and 1950s, including Robertshaw-Fulton Controls Company, the Essex Wire Company, the General Electric Company and defense giants Northrop Nortronics and Rockwell's Autonetics Electronics Systems.

Cheap land was an attraction. So was Anaheim's rapid "super stamp" system. It allowed developers to start building immediately, before submitting detailed plans. If city inspections turned up problems along the way, the developer was obliged to fix them. If developers wanted to speed up the process even more, they paid overtime to city inspectors working at night and on weekends.

Beginning in the mid-1950s and early 1960s, Anaheim's citrus groves and vegetable field crops were plowed under to make way for tract after tract of new housing. This photo was taken in 1962. *First American Title Insurance Co.*

A narrow road and the Santa Ana River meander through the Santa Ana Canyon in the 1940s. This view faces east toward Corona. *First American Title Insurance Co.*

A Dixieland band entertains the crowd at Disneyland during the late 1950s. Walt Disney's creative genius guaranteed that the theme park's guests would have a wide variety of good entertainment. *First American Title Insurance Co.*

Another advantage Anaheim leaders capitalized on was their unique city-owned electrical utility — dating back to the city's electrification in 1895 — attracting business and residential customers by passing on Edison's wholesale rates.

With the many new firms came tens of thousands of workers and their families, transforming the small agricultural community into a mid-sized metropolis in the 1950s. From a population of 14,556 in 1950, Anaheim grew at a manic pace, reaching an amazing 104,184 a decade later. The city also swelled geographically, gobbling up surrounding land in huge annexed bites: 1,493 acres in 1953, 2,700 the next year and a whopping 3,300 acres in 1955 — quadrupling the city's size in just two years.

Anaheim also took the lead in the retail side of business, opening the county's largest department store in 1955. The three-story, 200,000-square-foot Broadway soon became the nucleus of the county's first regional shopping center, Anaheim Center, later renamed Anaheim Plaza. Only a grand opening of national proportions could overshadow the Broadway's opening — and it did, just a few months before, when Disneyland opened with its huge splash.

At first, Walt Disney wanted to build his new kind of amusement park on the 18 acres he owned in Burbank. He soon saw he needed far more space. In 1953 the Stanford Research Institute pinpointed Anaheim as the ideal spot, with its relatively cheap land, central location and accessibility from the Santa Ana Freeway then working its way toward the city.

Disneyland's creation was no easy feat, even after Disney convinced Pearson and others that it would not be anything like the Pike at Long Beach or other noisy and dirty amusement parks of the time. Several sites were considered and rejected, one because it was too close to a cemetery, another after a real estate agent overheard Murdock and Disney talking about the project in a restaurant. That agent began buying up on the land and offering it to Disney at higher prices, which he duly rejected.

Anaheim's leaders saw a great opportunity in Disneyland and did everything they could to aid Disney in his quest, even after the 160-acre site of orange groves was finally found south of Ball Road. The city had to close Cerritos Avenue, which ran through it. It also had to annex the land, carefully drawing boundaries to exclude landowners who might have voted against the plan. Finally, Disney announced plans for the exciting new park in Anaheim on his national television program on April 2, 1954.

Disney also set a deadline of July 17, 1955, to open Disneyland, a deadline he stubbornly clung to despite many delays. Construction constantly hit snags. It was slowed by wet weather that later forced round-the-clock construction as July neared. After the "Rivers of America" was dug, it was filled with water — which quickly sank into the sandy soil. A clay bottom was trucked in to make it water-tight. A plumbers strike forced Disney to decide whether restrooms or drinking fountains would be ready by opening day. He chose restrooms.

Celebrants wave sparklers aboard the *Mark Twain*, Disneyland's sidewheeler. *First American Title Insurance Co.*

More than 28,000 showed up that day, though invitations had been sent only to 11,000. Broadcast live to 90 million television viewers in all its chaos, opening day was marred by traffic jams and a gas leak that closed Fantasyland. Only nine of 17 rides worked. In the sweltering heat, guests cursed the dry drinking fountains. High-heeled shoes sank in Main Street's asphalt, freshly poured that day at 6:30 a.m. A window tumbled from the upper deck of the *Mark Twain* riverboat, crashing onto a man's head. Though the man was uninjured, the press was mostly critical the next day, focusing on the many problems.

Not even "Black Sunday," as Disney called it, dampened the public's enthusiasm. Disneyland drew its first million visitors in just seven weeks. The park's first major expansion, in 1959, added new attractions, including submarines and the monorail, the first passenger-carrying system of its kind in the western hemisphere. Over the years, the guest list included presidents, movie stars and foreign leaders — but not Soviet leader Nikita Khrushchev. In 1959, at the height of the U.S-Soviet missile race, Prime Minister Nikita Khrushchev made a tour of the United States. Except for national security sites and Disneyland, Nikita was permitted to visit all requested sites. Upon learning of his denial to Disneyland, Nikita asked reporters a rhetorical question: whether Disneyland was a missile site. Personal security issues, not national security issues, prevented Nikita's visit to Disneyland. Even without Khrushchev, Anaheim now had an international presence that belied its modest size. But that, too, was growing.

Disneyland did more than attract tourists and attention to Anaheim. The Disney style, which called customers "guests" and employees "hosts" and "hostesses," was later adopted by the city as "The Anaheim Way" after it built the Anaheim Convention Center and Anaheim Stadium.

As the city's fortunes rose, the orange groves that once made Anaheim the center of Southern California's Valencia industry were shrinking. The Valencia orange's foes weren't just homes, shopping centers and tourism. A virus called "quick decline" had begun decimating local orange groves back in the 1940s. The disease reached a peak in the early 1960s, forcing growers to rip out hundreds of thousands of trees even before rapid development had a chance to uproot them.

The frenzied growth of the 1950s put a great strain on city services and schools. Anaheim Union High School was joined by Western High School in 1960, and the "union" was removed. Many new elementary schools were built to accommodate the city's rising population.

Still, Anaheim managed to keep much of its small-town charm. As many as 150,000 people lined Center Street each year to watch the city's famous Halloween Parade, a tradition dating back to 1924. The city celebrated its centennial in 1957 with small-town style, including a square dance, "Old-Fashioned Fashion Show" and beard contest. The production "Centurama" featured a cast of 1,200 residents who performed scenes from Anaheim's history nightly at La Palma Stadium.

Small-town celebrations were fine, but city and business leaders saw that a small-town government couldn't grow into the entertainment giant they now envisioned. Businesses formed the Anaheim Visitor and Convention Bureau in 1960, planting the seeds for a major convention center. Voters approved a new city charter in 1964, freeing the city of the state-imposed constraints that limited it as a general-law city. A new general plan was also adopted, along with a 4-percent hotel bed tax to help fund the planned convention center.

There was another reason to work harder at bringing more tourists to Anaheim. Despite its meteoric success, Disneyland was mostly a seasonal draw in its early years. That prompted major hotel chains to bypass Anaheim. Developer and Disney friend Jack Wrather opened the Disneyland Hotel with 100 rooms three months after the park opened. It later grew to three high-rise towers and 1,174 rooms. But the rest of the park was surrounded by a hodgepodge of small hotels and restaurants that haunted Disney and city officials.

City officials agreed that a convention center was needed, pledging $15 million to build it. The Anaheim Convention Center opened with 400,000 square feet and a space-age design. Arthur Fiedler of the Boston Pops conducted the Orange County Symphony Orchestra during its grand opening, on July 12, 1967.

The center hosted 45,000 delegates by the end of its first year, and was forced to turn others away. The facility was a money-maker for the city from the beginning. Thus began a series of expansions that put the Convention Center at 685,000 square feet by the end of the 1980s. By then it was attracting millions of delegates each year — and still turning away additional business.

Even as the convention center was still under construction, the city added yet another major league player to its entertainment base. Singing cowboy and businessman Gene Autry needed a new home for his Los Angeles Angels, an expansion team that spent the early 1960s in Wrigley Stadium, then rented from the Los Angeles Dodgers in the latter's new Chavez Ravine.

The Anaheim Convention Center opened on July 12, 1967, and became immediately successful, bringing convention-goers from all over the nation. The original 400,000-square-foot building was expanded to 685,000 square feet during the 1980s. *First American Title Insurance Co.*

Anaheim Plaza, shown here soon after its grand opening in 1955, was the first regional shopping center in Orange County. The 200,000-square-foot Broadway Department Store was the centerpiece of the mall. *First American Title Insurance Co.*

Gene Autry (left), Miss Disneyland and Mayor Sam Yorty of Los Angeles join Mayor Rex Coons to celebrate the groundbreaking of Anaheim Stadium. *First American Title Insurance Co.*

(Below far right) Anaheim Stadium, now called Edison Field, was completed in time for the for the first game between the California Angels and the San Francisco Giants on April 9, 1966. *First American Title Insurance Co.*

Jim Fregosi of the California Angels, one of the team's most well-known baseball stars, played for the team in 1967-1968. *First American Title Insurance Co.*

Even with Disneyland and the Santa Ana Freeway, Anaheim wasn't considered a favorite as a dozen cities jockeyed to be the Angels' home team. Long Beach was expected to win. But Anaheim had Walt Disney and a willingness to be flexible.

Disney sat on the Angels' advisory board and made a personal appeal to Autry. Long Beach was forced to drop out after Autry refused to rename the team the Long Beach Angels. Anaheim Mayor Rector L. "Rex" Coons was comfortable with Autry's requirement that the team's name include either "Los Angeles" or "California." He knew that Anaheim would benefit either way. So the California Angels were soon on their way.

The city found a site for a stadium near the Santa Ana River. Plans were announced in April 1964 to begin the season there in 1966, giving the city just two years to erect a new stadium. Only Del Webb's construction firm — also building the convention center — said it could handle the tight schedule. Financing was supposed to be handled jointly by the city and the county, but the county grew squeamish at the $21 million price tag. Anaheim was left to fend for itself.

In a "can-do" fashion, city leaders created a non-profit corporation to build the stadium and lease it back to the city. The move also avoided a public vote, which might have killed or delayed the deal. The $15.8 million stadium opened in time for an April 9, 1966, exhibition game with the San Francisco Giants that drew 40,735 fans. The A-frame scoreboard, 230 feet high, inspired the stadium's nickname: the Big A.

The team was a hit with the fans, but the stadium needed more than baseball and occasional rock concerts to be profitable. The city sought a professional football team, and in the meantime made up its losses with utility profits.

The city briefly hosted the Southern California Sun of the World Football League, which helped the stadium see its first profit in 1975. That league soon disbanded, so in 1978 Anaheim approached the Los Angeles Rams, a National Football League

team unhappy playing at the Los Angeles Memorial Coliseum. Anaheim offered to enlarge its stadium by 27,000 extra seats (to 70,500) by the 1980 season, spending $33 million. The city also gave the team the rights to build a parking structure, a provision that erupted into a battle in 1983 with Autry's Angels, who didn't want it. But for now, the stadium finally was a money-maker.

Many observers marveled at Anaheim's success, extraordinary for a town that even after its skyrocketing growth was still a mid-sized city. Dutton, the former Jungle Gardens owner who later became mayor, offered a facetious explanation in the early 1970s: "I always tell them that we are primarily old-timers here with our roots deep in the agricultural traditions, and maybe we are just so dumb we don't know we shouldn't be able to do these things!"

Even as Dutton spoke, Anaheim's next gem was emerging to the east: Anaheim Hills. Housing tracts were rising over Santa Ana Canyon, a former 4,200-acre cattle ranch owned by Louis E. Nohl. The land was bought in 1971 by Texaco Ventures Inc. and Anaheim Hills Inc. Over the next decade, about 15,000 people moved into the new neighborhoods. The old Bauer, Wallace and Oak Hills ranches were annexed in the mid-1980s, adding 1,300 acres to Anaheim and bringing it ever closer to the Riverside/San Bernardino border.

Even Anaheim Hills wasn't perfect. Landslides forced 40 families to evacuate in 1993, and the shifting soil continued to be a headache as the city drilled 119 wells to drain the excess groundwater. Lawsuits proliferated. But overall, Anaheim Hills proved highly desirable as it continued to grow.

Anaheim Hill's success was phenomenal, but together with the success of Disneyland and the Anaheim Convention Center, they came with a price: the dilapidation of the city's older areas. Many residents moved to the newer housing tracts as the older neighborhoods declined. The old downtown was losing customers to newer shopping areas around the city and the county. Even the old fashioned community pride that survived the early boom began to fray. Interest in the Halloween Parade dwindled in the 1970s and 1980s, and the event finally ended in 1991.

Development of the 4,200-acre Nohl Ranch east of Anaheim, began in 1971. Tract after tract of fine homes built in the area became known as Anaheim Hills.
Turville Photography
Photo by Steve Lopushinsky

As new homes began to cover the bare hills, the need for shopping centers, commercial buildings and gas stations became apparent. They, in turn, brought convenience and additional growth to Anaheim Hills.
Turville Photography
Photo by Steve Lopushinsky

City leaders began trying to revive the older neighborhoods and businesses in the early 1970s. This time, success did not come so easily.

At first, Anaheim Center and its huge Broadway drew customers away from once-bustling Lincoln Avenue and Center Street. Proposals to remedy the problem started in the 1960s. The imaginative ideas that emerged over the years included a new business and recreation area arranged around a 15-acre lake, an internationally themed center resembling Central California's Danish Solvang, and an "Avenue of Flags" on Lincoln Avenue, festooned with the banners of every state and nation.

The city settled on a more conventional approach, forming a Redevelopment Agency

The Pickwick Hotel, built in the Spanish Colonial Revival style in 1926, served as a fine hotel, bus terminal, deluxe restaurant and business establishment for many years. Listed on the National Register of Historic Places, it was demolished in the 1980s for redevelopment purposes.
Photo by Diann Marsh

(Far right)
The Masonic Lodge at 104 N. Emily Street was built by the Masons in 1913. Classically designed on the exterior, the interior featured intricate tin ceilings. It was demolished as part of the Anaheim Redevelopment Plan.
Anaheim Historical Society

Classical terra cotta trim, used on the Kraemer Building on Lincoln Avenue (shown here), was individually designed and made at the Gladding-McBean Company factory in Lincoln, California, and shipped in pieces to be reassembled on the site of the new building.
Anaheim Historical Society

in 1973 and swiftly starting its first major undertaking: Project Alpha. It rerouted and/or widened Lincoln Avenue and Anaheim and Harbor boulevards, and demolished hundreds of downtown buildings on two dozen city blocks. The program had a full head of steam when a backlash by angry residents and business owners suddenly stalled the project. The opposition grew as the city introduced Project Beta in 1975, with massive changes planned for a 2,755-acre area east of Disneyland. After vehement protests, Project Beta was abandoned.

But Project Alpha still had another major objective: a new city hall. City officials had tried for decades to replace its increasingly overcrowded 1923 City Hall. By the early 1970s, the structure built for 50 employees was crammed with 86. Another 1,400 worked in other buildings around the city. Each time the city asked voters to approve a new city hall project in 1963, 1970 and 1974, it was turned down. Finally, city officials decided instead to fund it from redevelopment money, selling off

A smiling angel decorates a fallen terra cotta capital from the Rose Marie Apartments, built in the 1920s and demolished in 1982.
Photo by Diann Marsh

land, utility profits and other sources. At last, a new $14-million City Hall was dedicated on June 24, 1980.

The battles about redevelopment weren't over yet. Land still lay vacant from Project Alpha, and anti-redevelopment groups were more organized than ever. Project Katella was proposed to improve 4,387 acres adjacent to Disneyland and eastward toward Anaheim Stadium. This time, city officials promised no structures would be torn down, but wary residents still defeated the plan through a new group called Anaheim HOME (Homeowners for Maintaining their Environment). Other anti-redevelopment groups formed, including the Anaheim Neighborhood Association, the West Anaheim Political Action Committee and the Central City Neighborhood Council.

Clashes over redevelopment led to Vision 2000, a city planning project begun in 1986 to steer Anaheim in a more peaceful direction. The recommendations that came out of citizen committees urged the city to widen major intersections, synchronize traffic signals, encourage more citizen input in city decisions, enforce drug laws and preserve historic neighborhoods.

Saving the city's past from the wrecking ball became a bigger priority, especially after the Pickwick Hotel, Anaheim Fox Theatre and other historic structures fell to redevelopment.

Heritage Square was created to preserve the 1904 Ferdinand Backs home and other relics of the city's past. The city's 1908 Carnegie Library also survived, becoming the Anaheim Museum in 1987.

As the 1980s ended, relations improved between the city and resident groups, and new businesses began to fill the empty lots. In 1992 Lincoln Village was completed, a 20-acre "urban village" mix of homes, businesses and recreational areas.

Meanwhile, Anaheim Center, which once lured customers away from downtown, eventually lost them to newer shopping malls sprouting around the county. Remodeled, enclosed and renamed Anaheim Plaza in 1973, the aging mall still had poor access from the Santa Ana Freeway and trouble attracting patrons and keeping its tenants.

The California State Teachers Retirement System bought the mall in 1984, but the decline continued as different approaches were considered and rejected. By the early 1990s Anaheim Plaza merchants advertised their empty shops as "less stress shopping" — but they were the ones enduring the stress. Finally, in 1993, bulldozers plowed through the enclosed mall built two decades before, making room for Wal-Mart, CompUSA and other discounters. As the end of the 1990s neared, sales began picking up and merchants were hopeful the remade shopping center would prosper.

A harder fix was the "glitter gulch" of hotels near Disneyland, which became more than just an eyesore — one that vexed Walt Disney until he died of cancer in 1967. The area increasingly attracted prostitution and other crime. Prostitution was so bad by the early 1980s that county judges set bail for Anaheim prostitutes at $5,000, rather than the $1,000 for those from other cities. Disney quietly began plans to deal with the surrounding clutter in the late 1980s. The firm proposed a $3 billion project to revitalize the entire area, including a second theme park called Westcot, a western counterpart to Disney's Epcot in Orlando, Florida. Westcot was to include three luxury hotels and two parking structures. But concerns grew about possible traffic and noise, and city leaders balked at the millions of dollars Disney demanded Anaheim pay for traffic and other improvements. Disney finally abandoned Westcot in 1994.

Meanwhile, city officials were seeing years of dreaming and hard work pay off in a long-sought-after major sports and

The new City Hall, on the east side of Anaheim Boulevard, was dedicated on June 24, 1980.
Turville Photography
Photo by Steve Lopushinsky

(Far left)
Anaheim's spacious new library was built at 500 W. Broadway in 1964.
First American Title Insurance Co.

Built in 1907-08 at the corner of Los Angeles Street and Broadway, the Carnegie Library became the city's personnel office in 1964 and then the Anaheim Museum in the late 1980s.
Anaheim Historical Society

The Autonetics Division of North American Rockwell Co. was one of several large corporations that made Anaheim their home in the late 1950s and 60s. *First American Title Insurance Co.*

entertainment arena. The City Council approved the planned Anaheim Arena on December 27, 1989, to be built north of Anaheim Stadium at Katella Avenue and Douglas Road. This was the home of the Phoenix Club, a German-American social club that had enjoyed the site for a quarter of a century. The club fought its eminent-domain ouster at first, but later accepted the city's offer of $8.1 million for the seven acres. The club found a new location not far away, on Sanderson Avenue, and the old clubhouse was razed.

The city acquired more land for the arena, including 17 acres leased by the county. But Anaheim had to contend with another obstacle: Santa Ana, which was racing to build an arena of its own. Anaheim rushed to a November 8, 1990, groundbreaking, and Santa Ana was forced to abandon its effort.

On June 19, 1993, singer Barry Manilow performed at the Anaheim Arena's inaugural concert. By October, the Disney-owned Mighty Ducks of Anaheim of the National Hockey League made it their home.

It started as the Anaheim Arena, soon became The Pond, then swiftly became the Arrowhead Pond of Anaheim — the result of a $1.5 million-per-year deal with the bottled-water giant that divided the extra funds among Disney, Ogden Entertainment and the city. The arena also attracted other sports teams, such as the Anaheim Piranhas of the Arena Football League and the Anaheim Splash indoor soccer team.

In its first five years, the arena sold 9.5 million tickets and held 967 events, including 99 concerts and 148 sold-out Mighty Ducks games. Yet it had lost a net of $25 million, largely due to a $126 million construction loan. Another blow was the decision of the Los Angeles Clippers to play in the Staples Arena in Los Angeles, dashing Anaheim's hopes of quickly securing a National Basketball Association team.

Meanwhile, Anaheim was experiencing mixed results with its other sports franchises. The Los Angeles Rams left in July 1995, moving to St. Louis. Gene and Jackie Autry mulled a move also, but instead sold a controlling interest in the California Angels to the Walt Disney Co. in late 1996.

Disney paid for most of the $115 million face-lift on Anaheim Stadium, including 25,000 square feet of artificial rock, waterfalls and geysers shooting as high as 90 feet. The remodeled stadium, also boasting fireworks, giant baseball bats and a gaming area for youngsters, debuted on April 1, 1998. Disney went on another spending spree after the 1998 season, signing free agent first baseman Mo Vaughn, one of baseball's elite hitters, to a six-year, $80 million contract. The team dedicated the 1999 season to the late Gene Autry, who died in late 1998.

Disney gave the refurbished stadium a new name: Edison International Field of Anaheim. It was part of a $50 million, 20-year agreement with Edison Co., the richest of many corporate

On June 19, 1993, the Anaheim Arena (now called the Arrowhead Pond) opened. It is now the location for a wide variety of professional events and is used for the Anaheim Ducks home games. *Turville Photography Photo by Steve Lopushinsky*

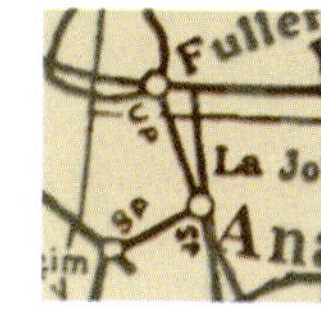

sponsorship deals struck around the nation. One Disney innovation, however, was quickly scrapped after a trial run late in the 1996 season: the Angel Wing cheerleaders and deafening sound effects that drew complaints from fans who wanted a less stimulating baseball experience.

Elsewhere, the city was working to expand its sports empire. The City Council in late 1998 approved a 30-year lease for a Gotcha Glacier indoor sports park, a huge facility planning to offer indoor surfing, skiing, snowboarding and even sky-diving. The project is the first tenant of Sportstown, a 31-acre area city officials also hope will be the home of a professional football team to replace the Rams.

Santa Ana Canyon is shown here in 1983 looking east toward Corona. The road on the far right against the hills is Santa Ana Canyon Road. The area in the left half of the photo was the 6,000-acre Bixby Bryant Ranch, Rancho Santa Ana. It has now been developed into a mixture of tract housing, commercial and industrial use and is part of the city of Yorba Linda. *First American Title Insurance Co.*

Anaheim had already undergone wrenching change since World War II — the growing pains of rapid growth and change, good luck and bad. But as the 20th century ends, the city's latest transformation is just getting started.

While most north Orange County cities were fully grown in 1999, or nearly so, Anaheim's growth rate is still soaring. Dozens of annexations have expanded the city limits to 49.7 square miles, all the way east to the county border — a width of 20 miles from the western flatlands across the rustic eastern hills.

Anaheim's population of a little more than 300,000 in 1999 is expected to top 405,000 by the time the last hills are covered, in about 2020. Those developments will include Mountain Park, 2,339 acres in Gypsum Canyon; and Cypress Canyon, 697 acres in the city's easternmost corner. The city's economic growth is headed eastward, too, as the Anaheim Canyon Business Center's 2,645 acres begin to fill. To handle all that traffic, a 24-mile, 10-lane toll road may be built through the rugged hills.

Yet, as the shining new housing tracts and businesses rise, the city also is focusing on its aging central and western areas. There are streets to be resurfaced, electrical and water utilities to be repaired or replaced, and huge blocks of blighted neighborhoods and businesses areas to be revitalized.

Redevelopment is still a major tool. The city has seven redevelopment districts: Project Alpha, the downtown effort that isn't over yet; Anaheim Plaza, including 350 acres around the county's first regional shopping center; a commercial-industrial strip including a large stretch of Anaheim Boulevard and other major streets; the Brookhurst Corridor, 316 acres along Brookhurst Street between La Palma and Orangethorpe avenues; 159 acres around Anaheim Stadium; 730-acre West Anaheim; and River Valley, set up in 1983 to fix flood hazards in a 160-acre area between the Riverside Freeway and Weir Canyon Road.

After a false start in the early 1990s with Westcot, Disneyland is going through a growth spurt of its own. Disney went back to the drawing board, as 40 of the firm's top executives and creative minds held a three-day retreat in Aspen, Colorado. They came up with California Adventures, a scaled-down $1.4 billion second theme park expected to open in 2001. Its rides and attractions will be inspired by scenery from around the state, including the Sierras, San Francisco, the beach and Hollywood. The project also includes a new hotel and shops.

The city plans to spend $560 million on neighborhoods around Disneyland, planting more trees and landscaping, putting power lines underground and refurbishing its water, sewer and electrical systems.

St. Thomas Aquinas Chapel at St. Catherine's Military School on Harbor Boulevard replaced the Victorian Second Empire building that had served Anaheim since the 1880s. *John Sorenson*

(Far right)
The Samuel Kraemer Building, at seven stories, was Anaheim's first skyscraper. It has been restored and is on the National Register of Historic Places.
Orange County Historical Society

In 1857 the Mother Colony House was the first wooden building constructed in the Anaheim Colony. It is now a museum of memorabilia from early Anaheim families.
Photo by Diann Marsh

(Below far right)
The Fred Backs Jr. House, built in 1911 on North Philadelphia Street, is a superior example of the Craftsman Bungalow style. The deep eaves and Japanese-influenced gable design, open porch, wide steps and large chimney are all details of fine design. The house is in the local Historic District and is one of seven Melrose/Backs Houses listed on the National Register of Historic Places.
Orange County Historical Society

The Frahm House, built in 1912 in the Craftsman Bungalow style, is part of the local Historic District and the Kroeger-Melrose National Register Historic District. Situated on South Olive Street, the house has been kept in immaculate condition by Jackie Frahm, the builder's granddaughter.
Orange County Historical Society

Disney's prominence in Anaheim hardly lessened as the city grew. Besides the original theme park and the California Adventures expansion, the entertainment goliath now also owns the city's two major sports teams. Disney is the city's biggest employer, landowner and producer of both property and sales tax, which makes the firm a critical partner in the Anaheim's future. Sometimes the relationship seemed to get too close, as in an annual boat party, golfing and fishing trip Disney executives once held for city officials. City Manager Jim Ruth ended the trips in 1991, fearing they gave the public the wrong impression.

In the midst of the flurry of dirt and concrete is the $1.1 billion widening of the Santa Ana Freeway. With many projects underway in 1998, central Anaheim resembled a vast, war-torn no-man's land and a motorist's nightmare. To help businesses hidden behind the carnage, Caltrans and the Orange County Transportation Authority awarded discount coupons to drivers willing to brave the narrow lanes and detours.

The latest burst in growth also left Anaheim's schools very overcrowded, forcing each of the Anaheim City School District's elementary schools to shift to year-round schedules, and even to

The Rardon House at 312 E. Broadway in the locally designated Historic District was completely restored in the 1970s. Built in the Queen Anne Victorian style, it was painted a dull white before the Rardons made it blossom with a variety of soft green and cream colors.
Orange County Historical Society

This house, built in 1912-13, was moved from South Anaheim Boulevard to Broadway many years ago. The present owners restored the Mission Revival roof features and painted it these refreshing colors. It contributes to the locally designated Historic District. *Photo by Judy Oleson*

stagger class schedules at some schools. Double sessions also became a possibility after voters rejected a $48 million school bond measure in April 1998.

School overcrowding and other problems are also impinging on the 1857 Mother Colony house, Anaheim's oldest building and symbol of its grape-growing beginnings. The landmark of the city's past is located at 414 N. West Street adjacent to Anaheim High School and on the route traveled by many students. The need for additional space at the high school and the occasional problems of the homeless sleeping underneath this structure have created public concern over the need for relocation — for the second time in its long history. It may go to a site at Center and Olive streets, or by the Anaheim Museum, or possibly to another site, or stay where it is. City officials were still wrestling with that question in the spring of 1999.

Meanwhile, other efforts to keep pieces of the city's past alive found success. In 1997 a residents group spurred the city to create a historic district around Anaheim's original boundaries: North, South, West and East streets. The city later planned to erect 30-foot-high monuments at key entrances to the district, which now includes the Mother Colony house. Anaheim has taken action to save some of its more recent history, such as the Satellite Shopland sign and other curious relics of "googie" architecture inspired by the Anaheim Convention Center's space-age design.

Anaheim thus enters the 21st century with an eye on both the future and the past. The city that boldly transformed itself after World War II from a tiny agricultural community into an entertainment center with few equals is transforming itself once again. ■

The Fred Backs Jr. Honeymoon Cottage, built in 1903, features many transoms and diamond-paned windows. Recently painted in colors appropriate to the Craftsman Bungalow style, it is listed on the National Register of Historic Places and is located in the locally designated Historic District. *Photo by Judy Oleson*

Known as an Airplane Craftsman Bungalow, this home on North Lemon Street features the smaller second story, wide low-pitched first-floor roof line, and offset front porch that gives it the "airplane" name. Built in 1911, the house is clad in specialty siding, which was quite popular during that era. *Photo by Judy Oleson*

The Bethel Baptist Church on West Broadway is one of the few old churches surviving in Anaheim. It contributes to the locally designated Historic District, is a fine example of Mission Revival/ Beaux Arts architecture.
Orange County Historical Society

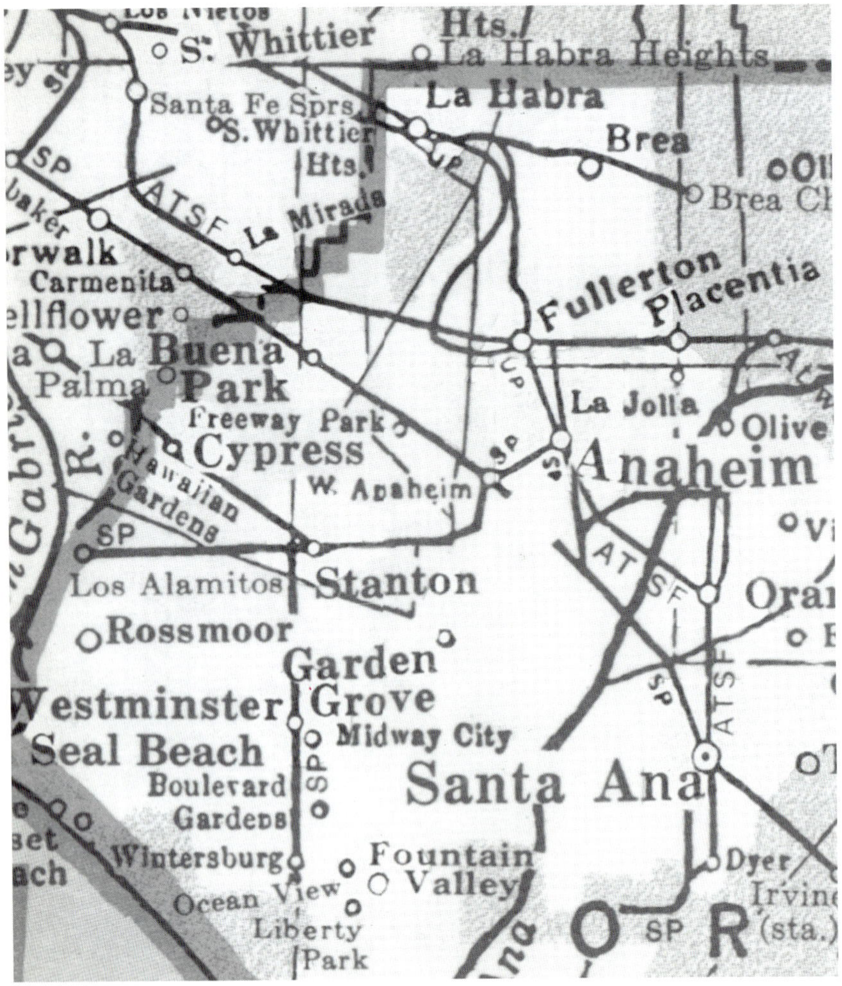
S. Whittier
La Habra Heights
La Habra
Brea
Santa Fe Sprs.
S. Whittier Hts.
ATSF
La Mirada
Olinda
Brea Chem
Carmenita
Fullerton
Placentia
La Palma
Buena Park
Freeway Park
Cypress
La Jolla
Olive
Hawaiian Gardens
W. Anaheim
Anaheim
SP
Los Alamitos
Stanton
Villa Park
Orange
Rossmoor
El Modena
Garden Grove
Westminster
Seal Beach
Midway City
Boulevard Gardens
Santa Ana
Tustin
Wintersburg
Fountain Valley
Ocean View
Liberty Park
Dyer
Irvine (sta.)
O R

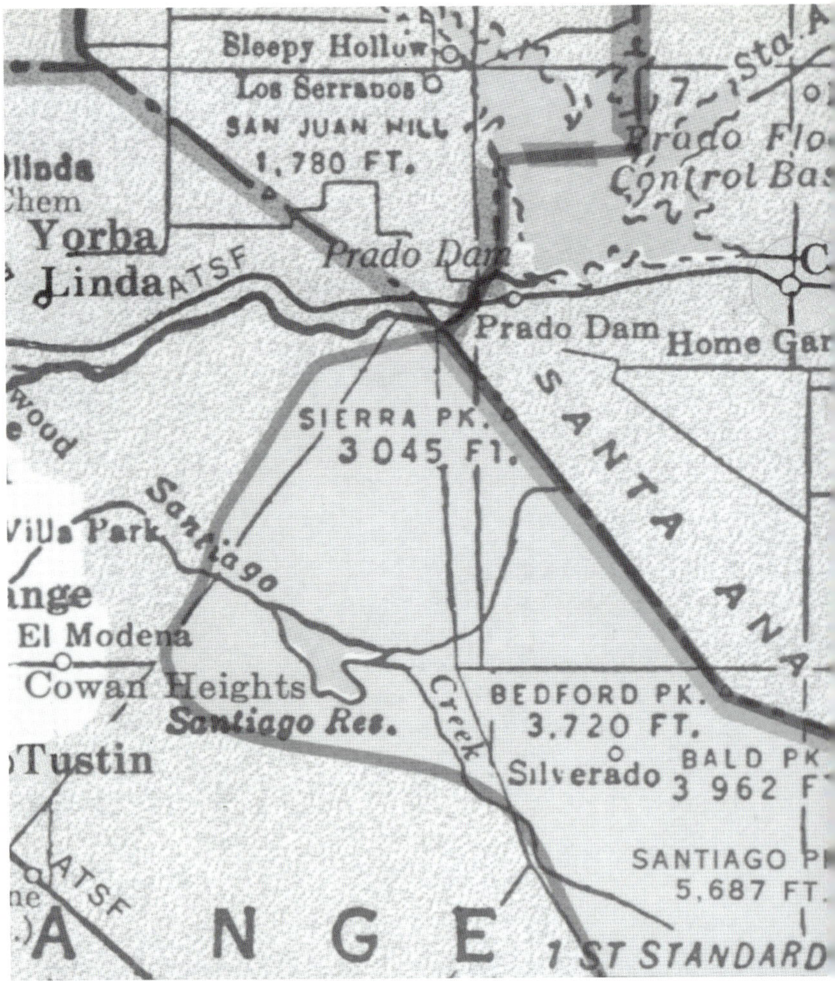
Sleepy Hollow
Los Serranos
SAN JUAN HILL 1,780 FT.
Prado Flood Control Basin
Yorba Linda
ATSF
Prado Dam
Prado Dam
Home Gar
SIERRA PK. 3045 FT.
SANTA ANA
Santiago Creek
Villa Park
Orange
El Modena
Cowan Heights
Santiago Res.
BEDFORD PK. 3,720 FT.
Silverado
BALD PK 3 962 F
Tustin
SANTIAGO P 5,687 FT.
Irvine
ATSF
A N G E
1 ST STANDARD

W. Anaheim
Anaheim
Hawaiian Gardens
SP
Los Alamitos
Stanton
Rossmoor
Garden Grove
Westminster
Seal Beach
Midway City
Boulevard Gardens
Santa Ana
Wintersburg
Fountain Valley
Ocean View
Liberty Park
Dyer
Irvine (sta.)
O R
Sta. Ana
Santa Ana Hts.
Irvine
Newport Hts.
Costa Mesa
SAN JOAQ
Newport Beach
Balboa Island
Balboa
Corona del Mar
Canyon

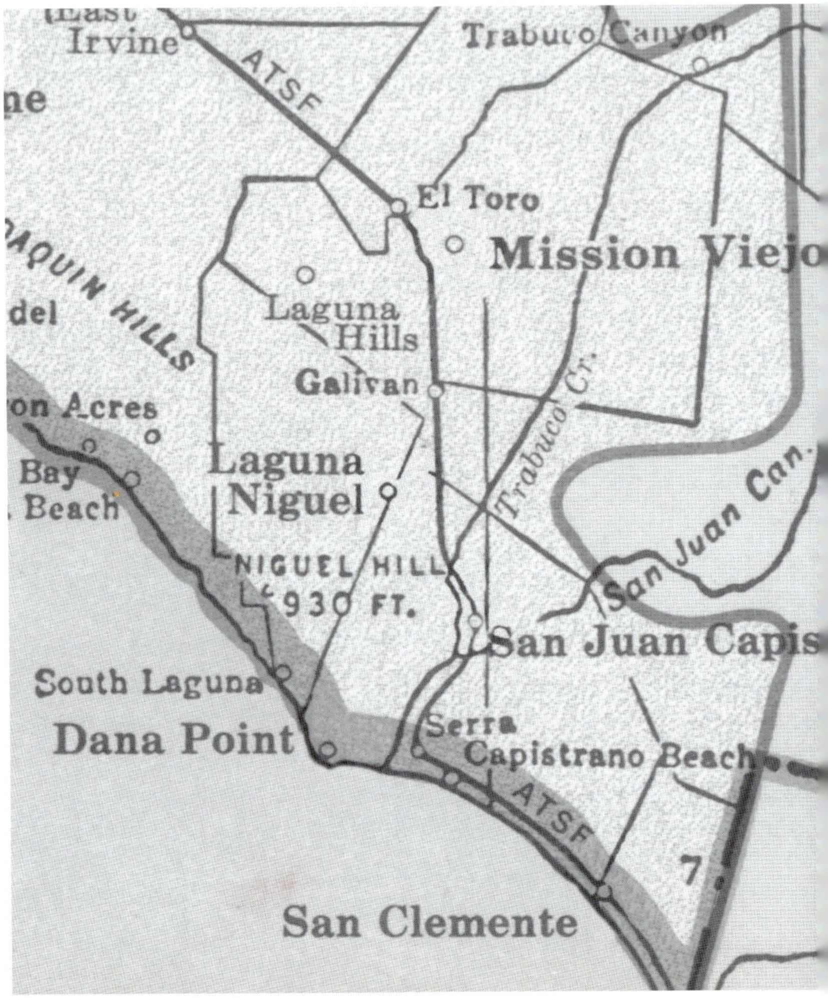
East Irvine
Trabuco Canyon
ATSF
El Toro
Mission Viejo
JOAQUIN HILLS
Laguna Hills
Galivan
Trabuco Cr.
Laguna Niguel
NIGUEL HILL 930 FT.
San Juan Can.
San Juan Capis
South Laguna
Dana Point
Serra
Capistrano Beach
ATSF
San Clemente

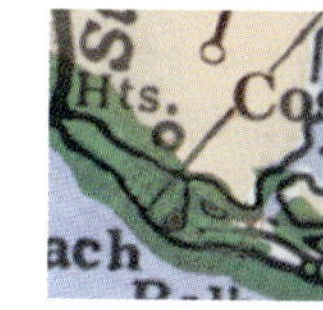

CENTRAL COUNTY

THE BEACH CITIES *By Toby Young*

If ever it could be said that out of war comes good, one could say the boom that transformed the peaceful, agricultural communities of Orange County is a good example. The county received its biggest push from World War II. Growth was inevitable but the impetus the war provided was a powerful combination of the newfound familiarity with Orange County by area military men and women; the nationwide climate of peace and prosperity at the close of the war; the postwar population explosion; and the tremendous growth of the automobile industry. Together, these factors changed the face of this portion of Orange County forever, from bedroom communities of Los Angeles County to flourishing and expanding cities in their own right. It is estimated that one-tenth of all World War II veterans located in California by the end of the war, and of that a good portion were living in Garden Grove, Westminster, Fountain Valley, Huntington Beach, Costa Mesa, Seal Beach and Sunset Beach. With Long Beach to the west, the county seat of Santa Ana to the east, and the beaches to the south, these cities were among the earliest cities to experience the dazzling transformation of Orange County.

(Far right)
Miles of bean fields once surrounded Costa Mesa and the Gospel Swamp area of Huntington Beach. Industrial parks, commercial buildings and housing tracts now cover the land.
First American Title Insurance Company

This unique revolving globe marked the location of Leisure World in Seal Beach. It is called the "Fountain of the World."
Orange County Historical Society

After World War I a building boom took place in Orange County as the servicemen returned to marry and establish homes. The architecture of the 1920s reflected the experiences of American soldiers in foreign countries. The house pictured here, located in Wilshire Square in Santa Ana, features the steeply pitched roof, gables, large windows and trim of an English Tudor house.
Photo by Diann Marsh

Ironically, a growth spurt experienced by Orange County prior to World War II was the result of a population boom after another war — World War I. Thousands of home-seekers had swarmed to California. In this boom, it was the burgeoning transportation system of the Pacific Electric trains that spurred growth into such towns as Seal Beach and Huntington Beach, whereas the post-World War II boom was fueled by the new automotive freeways that serviced the "emigrants" of the 1960s.

SAAAB Introduces Many Young Americans to Orange County

The Santa Ana Army Air Base, which was referred to as SAAAB, was an enormous training facility. Approximately 250,000 American men and women spent part of their enlistment at the base. SAAAB was a self-contained community with shopping facilities, movie theaters, libraries, churches and the like. While enlistees were stationed at the base, they became acquainted with Orange County's temperate climate, its potential for growth and generally pleasant atmosphere. They observed that unlike the crowded cities of the East, there was plenty of land for development here. When they were mustered out, many gathered up their families and headed west to cut their slice of the American dream in Orange County. Like generations of emigrants before them, they followed the sun west to the land of opportunity, in this case, Orange County.

SAAAB closed in March 1946. Most of the property that had made up SAAAB was annexed to the city of Costa Mesa in 1955.

(Far left)
Orange Coast College, founded on the former SAAAB site in September 1948, has become one of the county's most respected junior colleges.
Old Courthouse Museum

The Cinderella Homes were among the high-quality tract homes built in the 1950s in Garden Grove. They cost approximately $16,000 in 1955.
Photo by Diann Marsh

The site was divided and eventually became the Costa Mesa Civic Center, Orange Coast College and the Orange County Fairgrounds. The remaining 250 acres, which were just south of what is now Orange Coast College, were still owned by the government. They were put up for auction and purchased for the price of $4,737,610, which amounted to $19,000 an acre, by The Macco Corporation of Corona del Mar. Thus was born one of the earliest housing tracts in Orange County, Mesa del Mar. The remaining 49.5 acres were eventually purchased by the city of Costa Mesa and transformed into TeWinkle Park.

The outbreak of the Korean War in 1950 gave an additional impetus to the industrial growth of the area. Members of the 224th Infantry Regiments were again called into national service, and the war plants that had been somewhat dormant since 1945 stepped up their production once more. At the same time, new industries were being established in an ever-increasing number. By the time the Korean conflict ended in 1953, the momentum had increased. Housing tracts were springing up in Garden Grove, Westminster, Fountain Valley and Costa Mesa so fast that frequently the houses were completed months ahead of the installation of streets, sidewalks, sewers, gas and water lines, to say nothing of schools, shopping centers, churches and business buildings. In Fountain Valley, developers were too rushed to actually pull up the asparagus that had been farmed there for many years. The roots were simply ploughed under and a year later burst through foundations. One after the other, the enormous orange groves were leveled, and houses sprang up in their stead. No orange crops ever grew as rapidly as the 1950s and 1960s crops of Garden Grove houses, replacing the smell of orange blossoms with the smell of newly sawed wood.

At the same time, the automotive industry was dazzling the public with new and impressive automobiles. A generation of young men and women who had traveled to the far corners of the earth in the war effort exhibited an attitude of enthusiasm about the new mobility, an attitude unfamiliar to their parents. In Orange County this was reflected in the construction of the Santa Ana and Garden Grove freeways, which contributed tremendously to the sudden population growth of Orange County from the mid-1950s to the end of the 1960s. As new housing tracts marched from the Los Angeles border to the south, new businesses followed. No longer did Mr. America have to drive to work in Long Beach from his brand new home in Garden Grove or Fountain Valley. Now the veterans and their families could find jobs near their new homes and accessible through the new freeways traversing the area.

Costa Mesa — Goat Hill Becomes the Hub of the Harbor Area

Costa Mesa was the city that benefited most directly from the closure of SAAAB. Located on the coastal tableland above Newport Bay, the city traces its earliest history to when it was a grazing ground for cattle belonging to Mission San Juan Capistrano. During the city's "teen-age" years, the three small communities of Fairview, Paularino and Harper eventually

Newport Boulevard passed through the commercial center of Costa Mesa. This photo, taken about 1960, is looking north and features a 1957 Chevrolet, a 1950 Mercury and a 1954 Ford.
Orange County Historical Society

An aerial view of Costa Mesa and Newport Beach taken from the south shows Hoag Hospital in the foreground and Costa Mesa to the right of the freeway. *Orange County Historical Society*

blended into one town. It was named Costa Mesa in the 1920s by resident Alice Plummer, the winner of a contest to choose the city's name. At that time the business area (running along Newport and 19th Street) consisted of a bank, a drug store, a market, a grammar school, a hardware store and a garage. Everything else was farmland where crops of sweet potatoes, corn, tomatoes and strawberries were grown.

The Orange County Performing Arts Center, built on land donated by the Segerstrom family, opened to much fanfare on September 29, 1986. Featuring a wide variety of artistic events, it has more than lived up to its projections for a brilliant future. *Orange County Performing Arts Center Photo by Mike Sasso*

Despite the good intentions of Alice Plummer, Orange Countians often referred to Costa Mesa as Goat Hill because many of the poorer residents of the community raised goats. The Costa Mesa youngsters who attended Newport Harbor High School were teased about living in Goat Hill but retaliated by referring to the Newport Beach students as Mackerel Flatters after the fish cannery that thrived in Newport Beach at the time.

On June 29, 1953, Costa Mesa became one of the first cities to incorporate at the beginning of the boom years. A city seal was designed and adopted as well as the city motto, "Hub of the Harbor Area." The continuous growth of housing developments was followed shortly in 1959 by the opening of one of Orange County's first shopping centers, The Harbor Shopping Center. It was prominently located on busy Harbor Boulevard in Costa Mesa. The population boom naturally fostered an education boom and suddenly, 14 elementary schools, four middle schools and one high school flourished in Costa Mesa. In 1966 the Segerstrom family's bean fields were replaced by the South Coast Plaza Shopping Mall, one of the largest malls in California to this day.

Eventually, three major freeways cut across Costa Mesa. However, by the 1970s the city began to experience some of the problems of the unprecedented boom, and in 1973 there was a fight to save the last remaining open spaces — 257 acres of barren land between Placentia Boulevard and the Santa Ana River. To reverse the building frenzies of the 1950s and 1960s, it was decided the city would buy the open space and designate it for parks. From this action grew 26 new park sites.

South Coast Plaza, built in 1966 on agricultural property owned by the Segerstrom family, is one of the most successful malls in Southern California.
Photo by Diann Marsh

Main Street in downtown Garden Grove, shown here in the 1950s, was an important shopping center for area residents. This view looks north from Garden Grove Boulevard. *Orange County Historical Society*

(Far right) "Now & Then" Garden Grove's Main Street shopping district as it appears today — it has been revitalized with such features as trees and U. S. flags. Each year the city hosts its Strawberry Festival during Memorial Day weekend. *Photo by Diann Marsh*

As Costa Mesa became a mesh of business structures and family dwellings, local government took action to monitor noise and sight pollution. Laws were passed to limit the size and location of billboards and advertising signs. Many electric and telephone lines were placed underground. Like a teen-ager who grew too fast, the city began to mature after development slowed down. Ironically, by 1973 several of the earliest areas of business development had become candidates for redevelopment.

Located adjacent to South Coast Plaza Mall, Costa Mesa proudly shows off the internationally known Orange County Performing Arts Center that opened September 29, 1986. Where bean fields once flourished now orchestras, ballet, opera and Broadway shows entertain. Next door is the South Coast Repertory Theater, an award-winning venue of the dramatic arts.

Garden Grove — The City with No Gardens and No Groves

One of the first of the beach communities to experience the big boom was Garden Grove. Originally, the city had come into existence as the result of a general propaganda campaign in the late 1800s to encourage immigration to the West Coast. Various societies were organized to aid the arriving immigrants, including the California Immigrant Union. The union was a major influence in the development of Stearns Rancho properties, of which Garden Grove was a part. Stearns was an influential developer in Los Angeles County, particularly in the area now known as Los Alamitos, so it was logical he would continue moving into more southern territories. The city really did not come into existence at any particular date or year, nor was it deliberately established as a town. It just "grew." Eventually, Dr. Alonzo Gerry Cook named the settlement Garden Grove. He was widely criticized by others who pointed out there was neither garden nor grove in the area, but Dr. Cook optimistically replied, "We'll make it appropriate by planting trees and making it beautiful," which he proceeded to do.

The city experienced its first period of growth when the Pacific Electric Railroad came through in 1905, and buildings appeared on what is now Euclid Street and along Garden Grove Boulevard. Agriculture was the prime enterprise of the area.

The Garden Grove Post Office, located on Main Street, as it appeared in the 1940s *Orange County Historical Society*

(Far left top)
The St. Columban Catholic Church at 10851 Stanford Avenue in Garden Grove was built of brick in the 1950s.
Orange County Historical Society

(Far left bottom)
The Crystal Cathedral, begun by Dr. Robert Schuller at the Orange Drive-in Theater in the 1950s, has grown to a membership that includes thousands of worshipers. The all-glass building consists of glass panels set in aluminum frames.
Photo by Diann Marsh

Garden Grove experienced a leisurely and peaceful agrarian existence until the end of World War II when the boom hit with the force of one of the celebrated California earthquakes. Although the phrase "exploding population" did not originate in Garden Grove, it definitely described what happened. From 1950 to 1956 the population surged from 3,769 to 41,238 at the time of its incorporation. It was said that Garden Grove was the fastest growing city in the United States. In order to provide the local government with the means to govern the wildcat they suddenly had on their hands, and after three earlier unsuccessful efforts, the city incorporated on June 18, 1956.

One of the landmarks of Garden Grove to come out of the explosion was the Crystal Cathedral founded by Rev. Bob Schuller in March 1955. The beginning of Schuller's ministry was from a pulpit at the Snack bar in the Orange Drive-in. Since then his ministry has grown to worldwide outreach from his soaring Crystal Cathedral. The Cathedral is well known for its Christmas and Easter pageants. Supporters of the church are enthusiastic about the inter-denominational, psychological, social and spiritual appeal of Dr. Schuller's message.

As the growing frenzy calmed down, Garden Grove became concerned about preserving its historical past. Today, "Old Town" Garden Grove is home to the city's civic buildings and the Gem Theatre where Shakespearean plays are performed. The Stanley Ranch Museum is located nearby at Euclid and Chapman.

(Left)
For those who wanted to celebrate a special occasion, the Imperial Restaurant on Garden Grove Boulevard was one of the most popular in the county. Shown here in the 1950s, it featured French cuisine as well as fine American food.
Orange County Historical Society

Today, the only reminder of Garden Grove's farming beginnings is the annual Strawberry Festival, the largest community-sponsored event in 13 western states. The festival is held every Memorial Day weekend and attracts over 300,000 people each year.

Fountain Valley — Hometown USA

The city of Fountain Valley began as a crossroads village in an agricultural area. Even when the Orange County housing boom was exploding all around it, Fountain Valley remained calm, cool and collected until its first housing tract appeared in 1962. Then Fountain Valley sprinted from 597 citizens in 1957 to 24,321 in 1967 to 55,171 when it celebrated its 40th anniversary in 1997.

The Stanley House, owned by the Garden Grove Historical Society, represents the agrarian days of Garden Grove. A water tower, barn, post office and fire department are among the buildings that have been moved to the site and are being restored.
Photo by Diann Marsh

The Santa Ana River meanders through Orange County in this photo taken in April 1964. Fountain Valley, in the foreground, was incorporated in June 1957. *First American Title Insurance Co.*

The nine square miles of prime agricultural land that it occupied became incorporated as Fountain Valley on June 13, 1957. The name Fountain Valley was derived from the numerous underground water wells. In its early years, before becoming the "prim and proper" place it is today, it had been the site of many evangelistic meetings and was euphemistically called "Gospel Swamp."

Fountain Valley has become known for its family atmosphere and the city's chamber of commerce dubbed it "Hometown USA."

Fountain Valley is proud of several significant firsts, one of which is the election of Japanese American Jim Kanno as mayor in 1958. In Fountain Valley's formative years, Japanese farmers were prevalent. They farmed and established families and prospered but this was shattered by the "relocation" of Japanese American citizens during World War II. The citizens of Fountain Valley hoped their election of the first Japanese American mayor in the United States would help mitigate this black page in American history.

Another significant first for Fountain Valley is the fact it is the first planned city in Orange County. In 1961 members of the city council determined that the phenomenal growth of their city necessitated careful control and direction. As a result, they adopted a Master Plan of Development prior to allowing tract development to begin.

When Fountain Valley dedicated its new civic center in 1965, it was stated, "The City, through the leadership of its citizens, has and will continue to create ideal conditions in which its residents may gain knowledge, worship, reside, work, play and assist in developing a balanced community in one of the most desirable locations in Southern California." Fountain Valley continues to foster this motto to the present day.

Westminster — A Refuge from the Beginning

Westminster's founding as a temperance colony for Presbyterians was a precursor of the city's reputation as a haven for refugees from war-torn Southeast Asia. A mere 16 people incorporated the original community in 1871, but by the time it incorporated again according to modern rules and regulations in 1957, the city had boomed to a population of over 10,000. That quadrupled in the 1960s. The town was named for the Westminster Assembly of 1643, which prescribed the basic tenants of the Presbyterian Church, and around the turn of the century it was a well-known foe to intemperance.

(Far right) This Vietnamese sign on a Bank of America building on Garden Grove Boulevard reads "Chao Mung Qui Khach," which means "Welcome Valued Customer." It illustrates the diversity of nationalities present in the Garden Grove-Westminster area. *Photo by Diann Marsh*

Westminster, an early Presbyterian Community, was first incorporated in 1871. After reincorporating in 1957, the city built this new civic center. *Orange County Historical Society*

Downtown Huntington Beach, shown here in the 1950s, provided shopping for local residents and area farmers. It has grown rapidly since the city's founding in 1904. The pier, shown in the background, has attracted many visitors to the city, especially for the Fourth of July parade and celebration. This photo was taken looking south on Main Street. *Orange County Historical Society*

Like its neighboring communities, Westminster was transformed by the population explosion from a quiet and peaceful farming community to a city of wall-to-wall housing tracts with their accompanying shopping centers. At one time, the demand for public schooling outstripped the city's ability to construct the needed new schools fast enough so double sessions had to be held to accommodate the multitude of students.

In the 1970s Westminster experienced a period of prosperity, not the least of which was attributable to the new 90-acre Westminster Mall that opened with 190 shops.

It was during this period and into the 1980s that Westminster opened its doors to the fleeing refugees. The city provided shelter to Thais, Vietnamese, Koreans, Laotians and Cambodians. As a result, the city took on an entirely new demeanor with the construction of Southeast Asian businesses, restaurants and professional services. Over 550 new businesses opened in the Bolsa Avenue area, contributing heavily not only to the revenue of the city but also lending a new slant to the city's original attitude of religious freedom. A contiguous section of Westminster and Garden Grove covers the area called "Little Saigon" which has become the Southeast Asian cultural capital of the United States.

Huntington Beach — City of Expanding Horizons

Though the boom of the postwar period was tied to the growth of the automobile industry that spawned freeways throughout Orange County, the earlier growth spurt was connected to one of the first mass interurban transit systems to connect Orange County with Los Angeles County — the Pacific Electric trolleys. They were known locally as the "red cars," and Huntington Beach was one of the first Orange County cities to feel their effect.

Known during the rancho period as Shell Beach, developers came into the area and renamed it Pacific City, promoting

(Far left)
The Pacific Coast Highway opened to much fanfare in 1926 and provided an important link between the coastal cities from Oxnard to San Diego. This rather lonely early view shows the oil wells of Huntington Beach in the background. *First American Title Insurance Co.*

This view of the sea wall and oil derricks in North Huntington Beach is illustrative of the tremendous oil boom that changed the character of the city beginning in 1920. *Orange County Historical Society*

The Bolsa Chica Gun Club, located on the east side of the Bolsa Chica marshlands, was one of many gun clubs that were established in the Gospel Swamp/Huntington Beach area. Hunters from all over Southern California, especially Los Angeles, came to hunt waterfowl. Tom Talbert, a prominent Huntington Beach citizen, remembers seeing "birds by the thousands so thick in flight as to almost eclipse the sun."
First American Title Insurance Co.

Huntington Beach as a convention center and as the western counterpart to Atlantic City. The name Huntington Beach was finalized by developers when they succeeded in their efforts to attract millionaire Henry E. Huntington to extend the tracks for his trolleys into the area. Ironically, the city is now working to change its image from that of a surfer locale to a vacation destination, which is somewhat of a return to the turn-of-the-century inception.

One of Huntington Beach's yearly attractions, dating back to the postwar period, is its annual twins convention. Of course, surfing championships and a wide variety of related activities still dominate the city's national and even international reputation.

The building boom came to Huntington Beach somewhat later than to cities such as Garden Grove and Fountain Valley when a series of annexations increased the city's area of jurisdiction. Soon Huntington Beach was enjoying the residential growth experienced by its neighbors. In fact, the city grew so rapidly that at one point it was known as the fastest-growing city in the nation.

The pier area at the end of Main Street and the Pacific Coast Highway as it appears today. A new restaurant can be seen in the background. The steps and pavement were recently installed.
Photo by Diann Marsh

Huntington Beach experienced its major growth in the early 1960s with the development of Huntington Harbor, a multimillion-dollar project that turned swampland into a residential district of islands, channels and yachting facilities.

Despite its reputation as a resort, Huntington Beach has an expanding industrial area that began with the establishment of the McDonnell Douglas Aircraft Space Systems Center (now Boeing) in the early 1960s and the construction of the Edison Generating Plant in 1956. Many other businesses and industries have followed, increasing the demand for housing and shopping.

Various new facilities in Huntington Beach had their beginnings in the 1970s, including a $3 million library and a new civic center complex that was completed in 1974. In

Seal Beach City Hall, built in 1929 and renovated in 1984, is in private use today. The Administration building (clock tower) is in use today by the city. *Photo by John Sorenson*

the 1980s the city embarked on an economic development campaign that continues to this day, combining the city's natural beauty and nine miles of incomparable shoreline with a growing industrial and commercial future.

Seal Beach — The Jewel City of the Pacific Coast

Another city whose foundation was laid by the Pacific Electric Red Cars was Bay City, known today as Seal Beach because of the large number of seals who came to shore in the early days. In its first heyday, the city was a major recreational zone, complete with a Joy-Zone amusement park straight from the Panama-Pacific International Exposition in San Francisco. It was touted as The Jewel City of the Pacific Coast. However, those days ended just prior to World War II.

Uniquely, after World War II, Seal Beach received its biggest boost from the aerospace industry, which was of great interest to Americans during the presidency of John F. Kennedy. In 1963 Rockwell International Space Division in Seal Beach built the Saturn S-1 Booster, which was the second stage of the Saturn V launch for the Apollo moon shots. Not surprisingly, Rockwell was the largest employer in Seal Beach.

Another large employer in the city was the U.S. Naval Weapons Station. The successor to the Seal Beach Ammunition and Net Depot opened during World War II.The new facility was constructed in the 1960s to provide ordinance logistic support to the Naval forces operating in the eastern Pacific. In addition there is a National Wildlife Preserve within the station's borders.

Seal Beach remained a small beach town until a series of annexations doubled its land area from six square miles to a whopping 12. Building of tract homes followed immediately. Like its neighbors, Seal Beach's population zoomed from 3,553 in 1950 to 25,900 in the 1980 census. A major annexation in the 1960s was that of the retirement community of Leisure World along with the Rossmore Shopping Mall. Leisure World comprises 40 percent of the Seal Beach population. This mix of retirees with sun lovers and employees of the U.S. Naval Weapons Station gives Seal Beach an unusually diverse population.

The geography of Seal Beach brought about dramatic changes after World War II. Prior to the war, there had been a notorious campaign to rid the city of the taint of offshore gambling. Men of dubious reputations endeavored to use the tiny community as a base for taking people out to gambling ships

A lone surfer walks along the ocean near Huntington Beach. *Anaheim/Orange County Visitor & Convention Bureau*

This historic water tower in Sunset Beach was made into a state-of-the-art house in the 1980s. Note the garages and elevator at the ground level.
Photo by John Sorenson

docked offshore. The local citizens who triumphed over the mobsters vigorously opposed these efforts. However, after the war it was the oil drilling both on and offshore that caused a major controversy within the tiny community.

The city's landmark is the Seal Beach Pier. Built in 1906, the 1,864-foot pier collapsed as a result of the ravages of storms in the winter of 1983. As a demonstration of the city's pride in the pier, it was rebuilt and rededicated two years later as the result of a massive community campaign that raised $120,000 to refurbish it.

The Exception to the Rule — Sunset Beach

One town in Orange County that did not experience any building boom whatsoever, the one "city" which proves the exception to the rule, is Sunset Beach. Unlike its neighbors, Sunset Beach has no industry and has successfully fought off all efforts at redevelopment. It relishes its isolation and advertises itself as one of the world's smallest resort "towns." Sunset Beach is a one-mile strip on a 300-yard wide spit of sand, running parallel to the Pacific Ocean and connecting Huntington Beach with Seal Beach. Many people drive through and never know they were in the maverick community.

In Sunset Beach, there are no tracts of homes. Most of the housing consists of a mixture of modern homes side by side with bungalows leftover from World War II and earlier. The architecture combines shipboard chic with a sort of hobo scruffiness. A nautical theme exists throughout, especially in the 30-plus bars that comprise the most significant "industry" of the city.

As legend has it, during Prohibition, bootleggers took advantage of the remote locale to hide barrels of hooch in ramshackle cabins along the Anaheim Bay swamps. Later, this area was dredged out to create the upscale Huntington Harbor. Like many families, this part of Sunset Beach went from scalawag to upper crust in a relatively short period of time.

After World War II and especially during the booming 1960s, 70s and 80s, many attempts were made to annex Sunset Beach to Huntington Beach or to Seal Beach. But the residents have successfully warded off these efforts. The city receives its sanitation services from Seal Beach, and the Orange County Sheriff's department patrols the area, which is primarily crime-free except for alcohol abuse-related misdemeanors.

Sunset Beach has only one of three post offices in Southern California that doesn't provide delivery service. Residents pick up their mail at the post office.

Unlike other beach communities, Sunset Beach never experiences traffic jams or parking problems. Parking is so limited that all metered parking spaces are full by the time the sun rises.

Life in Sunset Beach is one of surf and sand, a mixture of the wealthy and the penniless. You might call it a motherless child, but the residents like it and intend to keep it that way.

Headed to the Future

Before World War II changed the face of Orange County, the central and coastal regions were home to people whose roots were deep in the values of agrarian America. The population of these towns was primarily Anglo-Saxon and Protestant. In the boom period of the 1950s and 1960s, the county was still predominantly ruled by those who had established themselves in the area earlier. It was known as a hotbed of conservative and ultraconservative political and social viewpoints.

However, as tracts grew and industry invaded the towns, the demographics of the area changed. Garden Grove and Westminster became home to thousands of Southeastern Asians. Fountain Valley not only welcomed the return of its Japanese citizens from the infamous internment camps, it also made one of their sons mayor of the city. Huntington Beach's character transformed from surfers to tanned businessmen. Seal Beach took on more characteristics of its elderly population from Leisure World. Even "bad boy" Sunset Beach began to rub elbows with the newly affluent neighbors across the street in Huntington Harbor.

Although the orange groves and farmers are gone, they have been replaced by a new breed of Orange Countians who are upwardly mobile, who claim a wide variety of countries as their ancestral homes and who look to a future as a time of stability, maturity and permanence. No longer do residents look over the fence to Los Angeles County for employment or for leisure activities. All their needs can be found in their own back yard.

Although each of these towns shared a similar change in fortunes from the end of World War II to the present, each has maintained its own personality and history. One might say the towns in the central beach area of Orange County resemble a family of siblings, each sharing a similar upbringing and looking somewhat alike, but each going its own way into the future.

Bill Galliene, popular general-manager of the Huntington Beach Chamber of Commerce, not only organized many of the city's major events, but also performed in them.
Old Courthouse Museum

The Santora Building on N. Broadway at 2nd Street has become a successful center for art galleries and studios. Built in 1928, the building is on the National Register of Historic Places.
Turville Photography
Photo by Steve Lopushinsky

A. The rehabilitated Grand Central Market Building recently opened as a satellite of the California State College at Fullerton campus. The new graduate student program offers opportunities for participants to have a studio in the building, show pieces in its gallery, and live in a studio apartment on the second floor. *Turville Photography, Photo by Steve Lopushinsky*

B. An art studio on the first floor of the Grand Central Market Building provides space for each student to create his or her work. *Jim Gilliam, Santa Ana Arts Coordinator*

C. The Imagination Celebration provides the opportunity for people of all ages to try their hand at various arts media. This photo was taken on 2nd Street in front of the Grand Central Market Building. *Jim Gilliam, Santa Ana Arts Coordinator*

A

B

C

The Arts Movement Brings Urban Vitality

To many of the Santa Ana residents attending, the opening of the Santora Arts Building on July 15, 1995, was like a miracle. Until 1994 the restored building had stood empty for six years. Opening night brought hundreds of people of all ages and from all over Orange County who walked the halls of the restored historic building from the basement to the second floor, admiring the wide variety of artworks. At the street level two upscale galleries, the Brand Gallery and the Arvisu Gallery, had recently opened in renovated spaces with high ceilings and shiny newly refinished hardwood floors. On the second floor were the Sasso-Cribb Photo Gallery, Randy Au's Flying Cup, and the galleries of Jean Fitz-Jones, Gerald Swartz, Sheryl Bookhout and others.

Also on the second floor David Rantz Interiors displayed the latest in home furnishings and art pieces. Everyone seemed to be having a good time as they viewed the works of art and sampled refreshments. Listed on the National Register of Historic Places, the enchanting Spanish Colonial Revival building with Cherriguesque influences exhibited fine detailing and elaborate architectural details.

The building, whose large airy rooms had been empty since its restoration in the late 1980s, had taken on a new and sparkling life that provided the energy and excitement that was to launch the fledgling arts movement in Santa Ana. Sculptor Randy Au, who helped to conduct those early tours of the unused facility for artists and others, remembers feeling the interest grow as artists began to lease space in the three-story building. These artists represented a wide variety of styles and media. Joseph Musil brought his amazing collection of beautifully detailed miniature theater sets he had created. The Rancho Santiago College District displayed the best of its student artwork in its spacious new gallery. Other artists followed until all of the studios and galleries in the spacious building were leased.

Don Cribb founded the Santa Ana Council of Arts and Culture in the mid-1980s. Possessing a vision gained from wide experience in the fields of arts and culture, Don saw great opportunities for Santa Ana to become an important center for the arts. Quoted in *Santa Ana: An Illustrated History*, he said "Santa Ana's deep historical roots, its wealth of cultural diversity, the prospects of urban vitality, and major new developments inspire a sweeping vision of our city reborn." The Council for Arts and Culture continues to play a strong role in the arts movement in the city.

Laying the groundwork for the new Artists Village, the Santa Ana City Council approved a special C3-A Zone on July 18, 1994. It allows for a variety of artist's activities such as live/work space, galleries, and photography, ceramic, pottery, glass blowing and sculpture studios in the area north of First Street between Broadway and Main streets.

In 1995 Mayor Miguel Pulido appointed 30 representatives to the Task Force for Arts and Culture. Chaired by Councilmembers Tom Lutz and Lisa Mills, the task force's assignment was to prepare a strategic plan and vision statement for arts and culture in Santa Ana. With Exective Director of the City's Community Development Agency Cynthia Nelson acting as facilitator, the group worked to establish a vision, purpose, goals and objectives for future arts and culture activities in Santa Ana.

As the arts movement, fueled by community spirit and interest, the cooperation of city officials and the affordability of the Artists Village, continued to grow, new projects and players emerged. When the city learned that California State University at Fullerton was looking for a location for a satellite campus for graduate art students, officials worked with the school to bring about the rehabilitation and use of the block-long two-story brick Grand Central Market Building. Featuring art studios, a gallery, restaurant and theatre on the first floor and studios in the basement, the 27 apartments on the second floor have been adapted as living space for graduate students. The building's historic importance had been affirmed when it was placed on the National Register of Historic Places in 1988. Mayor Miguel Pulido and President Milton Gordon of Cal State Fullerton officiated at the grand opening in February 1999. It was obvious on that day of celebration that the cooperative efforts of the City of Santa Ana and Cal State Fullerton would reap huge benefits for the city.

Open houses and events in the Artists Village have brought new customers to Santa Ana's downtown restaurants such as Trattoria Ciao and Shelly's Restaurant. Morey's Deli in the Santora and The Gypsy Den in the Grand Central Market Building now offer a variety of foods to patrons. New restaurants are making plans to open in the future.

SANTA ANA

D. The Orange County Crazies and the Pacific Symphony share space in the former United Presbyterian Church on Santa Ana Boulevard. Directed by Cherie Kerr, the Crazies give live satirical comedy performances focusing on current topics. *Photo by Diann Marsh*

E. The Palm Court, located across the street from Bowers Museum, features art galleries, a restaurant and business suites. *Photo by Diann Marsh*

F. The Whitson House and Chilton House, moved to 8th Street in Historic French Park in the mid-1980s, were among five historic homes in the neighborhood to be saved from demolition. *Photo by Diann Marsh*

G. The Topaz Cafe, an upscale restaurant located next to the Bowers Museum's courtyard, serves gourmet meals and fine wines. *Photo by Diann Marsh*

H. The Arts District has expanded across Broadway Street to the restored Empire Market building that is built in the Zigzag Moderne style. *Photo by Diann Marsh*

Bowers Museum on the corner of N. Main and 20th Street opened in 1936. The cornerstone of what is now called the Museum District, Bowers restored its original Spanish Colonial building and built a large and impressive addition in the early 1990s. The Palm Court, across Main Street, St. Joseph's Ballet, the Discovery Science Center and the Bowers Kidseum are arts-related organizations that have recently become part of the Museum District.

The success of the Santora Building, full of busy enthusiastic artists, the revival of the Grand Central Market Building with Cal State Fullerton, the spread of the arts to the Empire Market and other downtown buildings, the impressive new Ronald Reagan Federal Courthouse, and renewed community spirit in the city have brought a new sense of pride and enthusiasm for the future in Santa Ana, the county seat of Orange County.

Neighborhoods Reborn

The revitalization of Santa Ana's neighborhoods has grown in leaps and bounds during the last 15 years, backed by the interest of many new families. As an example, Stephanie Gerlach found the Historic French Park neighborhood by accident. Serving on a jury in the nearby county courthouse, she drove down the tree-lined streets of the historic district, discovering the graceful spacious Victorian, Colonial Revival and Craftsman Bungalows surviving from Santa Ana's rich past. Although there were no houses for sale that suited their needs in Historic French Park at the time, Stephanie and her husband, Bill, put their new house in Aliso Viejo up for sale and continued to look on the Internet for available properties. When a restored 1883 Italianate Victorian came up on the screen, they knew instantly that it was their "dream house," and within six weeks, became the new owners.

The Historic French Park Association held its first meeting more than 20 years ago in the living room of David and Jean Fraunfelder's house on North Spurgeon. They made plans to ask the city council to create the city's first local historic district. This was the first step in protecting the neighborhood from the rash of large three-story apartments that were replacing single-family homes in much of Orange County and allowed the association members to review plans for all restoration and building projects within the boundaries of their neighborhood.

By the early 1980s French Park was joined by Eastside, Heninger Park and the Northwest neighborhood (later divided into Floral Park, West Floral Park, Morrison Park and Jack Fisher neighborhood associations). Heninger Park, with 628 homes, became the second local historic district designated by the city council.

As the neighborhood movement began to expand and grow, other neighborhoods created their own organizations to suit their particular needs. Washington Square was unified when its residents banded together to protest the negative impact of a nearby weekly swap meet and plans for a sports arena to the south of its borders. Wilshire Square residents were brought together because they appreciated and wanted to protect the visual character of the neighborhood and the 1920s to 1960s housing stock. Saddleback View united to reduce the impact of new office towers being planned in their midst. Residents surrounding Jack Fisher Park worked together to solve parking problems connected with the park and to improve the park itself.

Christmas parties, jazz festivals, art walks, Easter egg hunts, concerts, Super Bowl parties and other social events help the neighbors to know each other, showcase the unique homes and streetscapes, and convey a special community spirit. Inspired by the improvements and hard work of the owners, tour visitors have responded with enthusiasm. Each association has its own special events that residents look forward to each year.

Comm-Link (Communication Linkages) is a citywide organization that provides a forum for representatives of all of the neighborhood associations. Monthly meetings feature speakers on pertinent topics; encourage residents to share information about their group's events; and provide communication between city officials and the neighborhoods. COP (Community Oriented Policing/ Neighborhood Watch) provides additional communication between city departments, the police force and residents.

The Housing Services Department, administrated by Pat Whitaker, has done much to facilitate and aid the improvement of the city's housing stock. Working with residents to improve their neighborhood streetscapes, members of the department meet regularly with each association board to provide support and bring new ideas to fruition.

By 1999 the number of neighborhood organizations in Santa Ana had grown to 55, each having its own individual focus. Schools, traffic issues, the preservation of historic housing and reviewing plans for new buildings are among the issues addressed by these organizations.

SANTA ANA

I. New plans for the Midtown District include the preservation of a row of impressive historic houses along Broadway. The McNeill House, built of brick in an English Tudor style, is one of the finest homes from the 1910s still surviving in Orange County. *Photo by Diann Marsh*

J. Eastside, a historic neighborhood south of First Street and east of Main Street, has a wide variety of housing styles, sizes and ages. Neighborhood advocates discovered that the large single-family homes on their streets were being demolished to make room for three-story apartment buildings. They led the fight to redesignate neighborhoods all over the city for single-family dwellings. *Photo by Diann Marsh*

K. Noted for its significant examples of Victorian, Colonial Revival and Craftsman houses, the Historic French Park District was designated as Santa Ana's first local historic district, and on May 12, 1999, was placed on the National Register of Historic Places. *Photo by Diann Marsh*

L. These students were selected for the Santa Ana Unified School District Honor Choir for 1996-97. *Santa Ana Unified School District, Randy Coleman Coordinator, Photo by Apple Photographers*

The Past Comes Alive

With over 5,000 potential historic buildings within Santa Ana's city limits, it is important to discover, evaluate and generate appreciation for the city's significant historical assets. An appreciable amount of progress has been made in this important area, but there is still much that needs to be done.

History credits Adeline Walker, the founder of the Santa Ana Historical Preservation Society, with the beginning of the historic preservation movement in the city. In 1974 she led the fight to save, move and restore the Dr. Howe-Waffle House as a house museum featuring both Victorian and medical history. Dr. Howe-Waffle, one of Orange County's first women doctors, and her husband built the 12-room Queen Anne Victorian mansion in 1889, the same year as Orange County was formed. Mrs. Walker made the restoration of the house her full-time job for the last 11 years of her life.

In 1979 Heritage Orange County, with the help of Santa Ana residents and the city, surveyed over 1,300 buildings in a designated area surrounding the downtown commercial center. A historic committee made up of those interested in Santa Ana's historic buildings reviewed the survey information and helped select the most significant buildings. The survey led to the placing of much of downtown Santa Ana on the National Register of Historic Places. Additionally, a Santa Ana Historic Register was created by the city council.

A few years later when the Santa Ana Council of Arts and Culture was formed, representatives of the Santa Ana Historical Preservation Society and the Historic French Park Association saw the need for a committee of residents to provide input to a new historic survey to be conducted by a Los Angeles-based consultant. In November 1991 Mayor Dan Young, with the blessings of the city council, appointed a representative from each of the seven historic neighborhoods and four historic organizations to the new Historic Resources Review Committee. Meeting monthly, the members photographed, researched and documented approximately 2,500 structures in the northwest section of the city. They then provided the planning department with documentation sheets on the 100 most significant buildings to be added to the 115 buildings already listed on the Santa Ana Historic Register. Finding these decisions difficult because of the richness of the resources, the committee chose 128 buildings to place on the existing register.

This task having been completed, the committee worked with the planning department to write a much-needed Historic Preservation Ordinance. The mayor and city council passed the ordinance in late 1997.

The Historic Preservation Ordinance was just the beginning, however. The members of the Historic Resources Review Committee, with support from a large group of residents and property owners, requested that the city council create a Historic Resources Commission as the official body to discuss all matters regarding historic buildings; to foster appreciation of historic properties; and to approve alterations of buildings on the Santa Ana Historic Register. In the summer of 1998 the city council took official action to create the commission. Seven residents with expertise in historic preservation fields were appointed to the newly established Historic Resources Commission. Additionally, representatives from the Planning and Redevelopment commissions were appointed to serve. With the new commission in place and a rising interest in Santa Ana's historic built environment, the future for historic preservation in the city looks promising.

Santa Ana, like every other city in Orange County, looks toward the future with a positive outlook, new ideas and expanding horizons. All of the pieces are in place for the arts movement to take wing. The Ronald Reagan Federal Courthouse has been completed. Neighborhoods are working together and the housing stock is improving. The city is beginning to recognize the importance of its impressive list of historic buildings and is embarking on an extensive historic preservation program.

With active participation and enthusiasm Santa Ana residents and elected officials are creating a revitalized city with much to be proud of.

—Diann Marsh

To learn more about Santa Ana's early history, read *Santa Ana: An Illustrated History*, published by Heritage Media Corp., sponsored by the Santa Ana Historical Preservation Society and written by Diann Marsh.

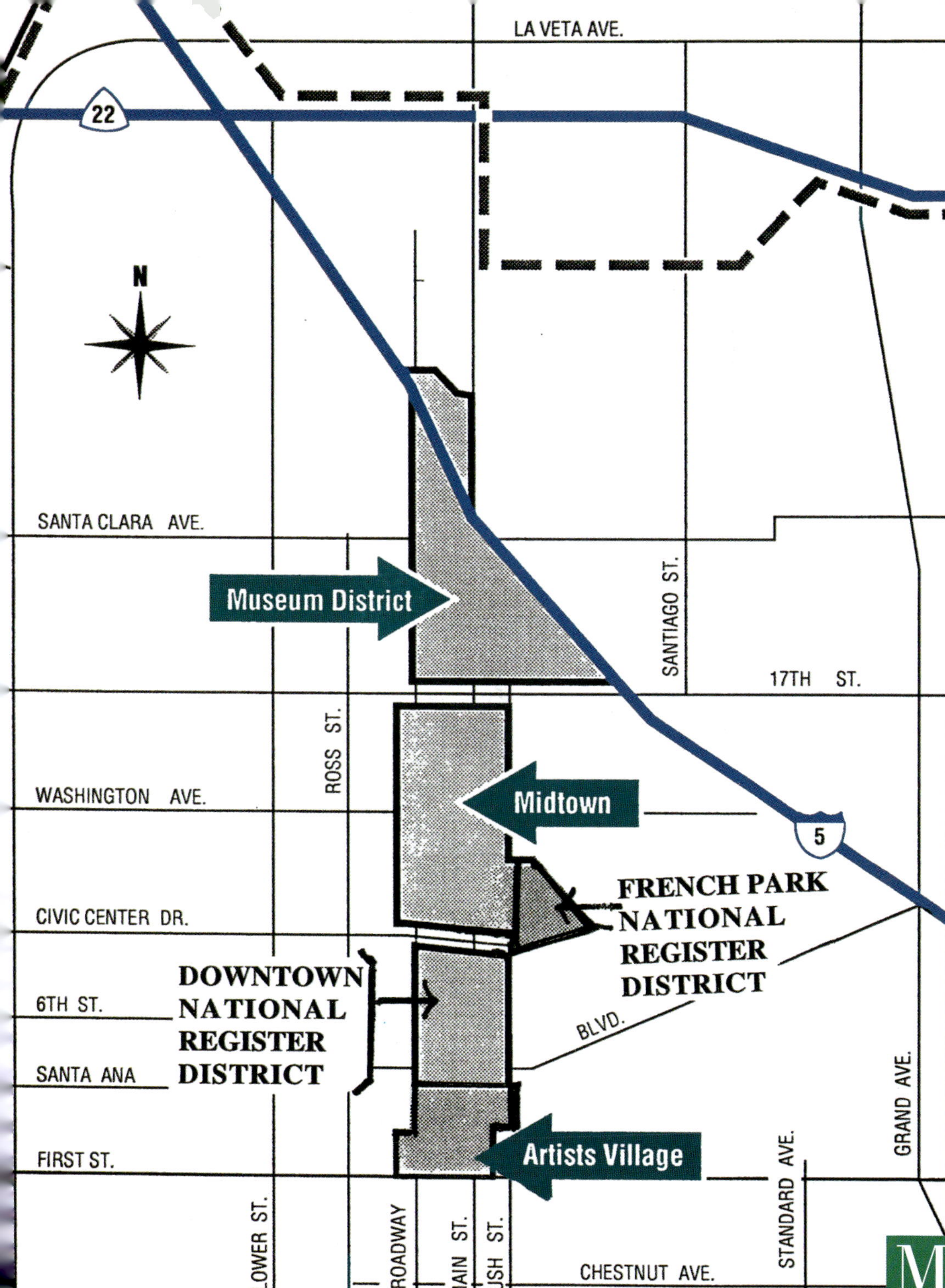

SANTA ANA

M. Within the last few years, plans have been developed for the Museum District, Midtown District and the Artists Village. Much of the Downtown Historic District is on the National Register of Historic Places. The Historic French Park District was placed on the National Register on May 12, 1999. *City of Santa Ana*

N. Floral Park, north of 17th Street and west of Broadway, had its beginnings in the 1920s. It also features superior examples of Minimal Traditional (1940s and 50s) and Ranch-style (1950s and 60s) homes. *Photo by Diann Marsh*

O. Washington Square, located between Civic Center drive and 17th Street, is a neighborhood known for its stability, neatness and tree-lined streets. Settled with single-family houses built from the 1920s to the 1960s, its active neighborhood association holds several events each year. *Photo by Diann Marsh*

P. Wilshire Square, a pleasant and inviting neighborhood of single-family homes built from the 1920s to the 1960s, is known for its many community-focused events and its cohesive organization that fosters close friendships. *Photo by Diann Marsh*

Q

SANTA ANA
FIESTA

SANTA ANA

Q. The Spurgeon Clock Tower, restored in perfect working order in the mid-1990s, represents an impressive volunteer community effort that raised over $80,000 for the restoration. The three-story Spurgeon Building, built in 1914, is listed on the National Register of Historic Places, as well as the Santa Ana Historic Register. *Photo by Diann Marsh*

R. The residents of Floral Park worked together to revitilize a neglected neighborhood park, founded by Adeline Walker several years ago. Featuring new planters, crushed granite walks, metal benches, lighting and colorful landscaping, the park has become a thing of beauty cared for by volunteers. *Photo by Diann Marsh*

S. For over 100 years Santa Ana was the commercial center of Orange County. Such stores as Rankin's Department Store, Hugh J. Lowe's Men's Furnishings and Vandermasts sold the finest in merchandise, c. 1930s.
History Room, Santa Ana Public Library

T. The pride of Santa Ana city officials, the new Ronald Reagan Federal Courthouse, featuring gold inscriptions, adds traditional importance to the revitalized downtown Santa Ana. *Turville Photography, Photo by Steve Lopushinsky*

U. Heninger Park features a variety of historic homes built from the turn of the century to the present. The neighborhood is named for Martin Heninger, who built the house pictured here as well as many others in the neighborhood.
Photo by Diann Marsh

V. The Kellogg House, moved to the Discovery Museum on Harvard Street, has an unusual floor plan and staircase modeled after a ship. The house has been completely restored as a house museum. *Photo by Diann Marsh*

W. The Historic Orange County Courthouse, completed in 1901, is a superior example of Richardson Romanesque architecture. Completely retrofitted and restored in the mid-1980s, it features a county museum and restored courtroom on the top floor. It is listed on the National Register of Historic Places.
Orange County Historical Society

The town center of Tustin, as it appeared in 1959, served the small pleasant community of Tustin and the surrounding citrus groves. The modernized Victorian-style Bank of Tustin, founded in 1888, is on the left, and the two-story brick Knights of Pythias Building is on the right. Tustin was founded in 1868 by Columbus Tustin. He laid out the streets, planted trees, established the school and post office, and worked hard to make his dream of what was originally called Tustin City come true. *Orange County Historical Society*

A. Lisa Vining poses in front of the Vanderlip House on West Main Street about 1980. Built in 1883 on a 20-acre parcel on the south side of Main Street, the rare Italianate Victorian was moved to this site to save it from being demolished when the Santa Ana and Costa Mesa freeways were being built in the 1950s. *Vining family*

B. Tustin Hardware on Main Street was built in 1912 by one of Tustin's most prominent citizens, C.E. Utt. It looks almost like it did when it was constructed. *Photo by Diann Marsh*

C. The land on which the Enderle Center was built was purchased by the Enderle family in the 1880s and developed into a productive orange grove. Harriet Enderle and her sons, Al and Wallace, presented the idea for the shopping center in 1976, and the first shop opened in May 1977. *Turville Photography, Photo by Steve Lopushinsky*

D. The two blimp hangars at the Lighter-Than-Air Base are each 1,088 feet long, 178 feet tall and 297 feet wide. This type of hangar, a marvel of construction, is the largest unsupported structure in the world. These two were built in 1942 to house the blimps that patrolled the West Coast shores but in recent years have been converted for helicopter use. *Photo by Diann Marsh*

E. The brick Knights of Pythias Building, shown here in the 1950s, is on the corner of Main and El Camino Real (originally called D Street). Built in 1925, the building housed the Knights of Pythias Lodge Hall on the second floor, with commercial businesses in the first-floor storefronts. When this photo was taken, a variety store and drug store occupied the first floor. *Marsh Collection*

F. Now owned by the First Baptist Church of Tustin, this building caused quite a stir when it was built in the 1960s. Its free form roof, described by *The American House* as the warped shell style, was a radical departure from previous standard frame and curtain wall construction. *Photo by Diann Marsh*

A

TUSTIN HARDWARE
master charge
B

CENTRE
C

D

VARIETY STORE
TUSTIN - DRUG - STORE
THE TUSTIN DRUG - STORE
E

F

G

H

I

G. The former variety store site in the Knights of Pythias building is now occupied by the Tustin Area Museum, operated by the Tustin Area Historical Society. The museum is a repository for an impressive archive of photographs, artifacts and memorabilia from Tustin and the surrounding area. *Photo by Diann Marsh*

H. Developed in 1949, El Camino Lane is a short street of custom houses at the intersection of 17th Street and Newport Boulevard. These high-quality ranch houses built in the early 1950s are good examples of the many fine houses built in the North Tustin area during that time. *Photo by Diann Marsh*

I. The Market Place/Tustin, a regional shopping complex in the Tustin Ranch area that opened in 1988, is known for its bright, cheerful colors and its monumental scale. *Turville Photography, Photo by Steve Lopushinsky*

J. One of several fine Victorian homes surviving in Old Town Tustin, this house on 3rd Street has Eastlake and Queen Anne influences. It was probably built by the Moses and Willard Chandler families in 1885. *Photo by Diann Marsh*

K. The Sherman Stevens mansion, a superior example of Queen Anne Victorian architecture, was built in 1887 for the new Mrs. Stevens, Martha Snow. The people posing in costume in front of the house are members of the Gfeller Company, the firm that restored the mansion for use as an office and built compatible office buildings on the adjoining land. The Stevens House is listed on the National Register of Historic Places. *Gfeller Company*

L. Beginning in the 1980s, the barren hills in eastern Orange County began to sprout large pretentious homes in many styles. They are a symbol of the burgeoning wealth that has emerged in Orange County in recent years. *Photo by Diann Marsh*

M. The many new developments in Tustin include the Tustin Ranch homes to the northeast of the original townsite. *Turville Photography, Photo by Steve Lopushinsky*

ORANGE

PHOTO ESSAY

The focal point of the Orange Plaza Historic District is the circular landscaped park and fountain in the center of the intersection of Glassell Street and Chapman Avenue. The park land was dedicated by the founders of the town of Orange, Andrew Glassell and A.B. Chapman, in 1871. It was not until 1886, however, that the park was developed. The first fountain, installed at that time, now rests in front of the city hall. The fountain in this 1968 photo was built in 1936.
Marsh Collection

A. Antique, collectible and gift stores now occupy much of downtown Orange. The trend began in 1962 when Emma Armen opened the first antique shop at 221 S. Glassell. This photo shows the east side of the plaza in 1982. *Photo by Diann Marsh*

B. The Neo-classical First National Bank Building on the north corner of the Plaza was designed by Morgan, Walls and Clements of Los Angeles and completed in 1928. *Photo by Diann Marsh*

C. This home on Olive Street, a part of the Old Towne Historic District, is one of the many restored houses in the Mile-square District. *Photo by Diann Marsh*

D. A ranger shows students at the Santiago Oaks Nature Center how to handle a real owl. Three hundred and fifty acres of trails, plants and wild animals are available for hiking and horseback riding. It can be reached from N. Windes Drive in West Orange. *County of Orange*

E. Watson's Drugs at 116-118 E. Chapman was founded in 1899 and is still a favorite place to have a good meal and shop. It is the oldest continuously operating business in the city. *Orange County Historical Society*

A

B

C

D

E

702
704

G

H

I

F. The Bartling House at 702-04 E. Chapman is a superior example of Spanish Colonial and Italian Revival architecture. *Photo by Diann Marsh*

G. The Sisters of St. Joseph opened the spacious and dramatic St. Joseph's Hospital in 1929. It is still in use as a hospital but is hidden behind the newer buildings of St. Joseph's and the Children's Hospital of Orange County. *Marsh Collection*

H. Santiago Canyon Community College, which opened in 1985 as part of the Rancho Santiago College District, has grown steadily since its inception. It is located at Chapman Avenue and Newport Boulevard in East Orange. *Photo by Diann Marsh*

I. Built in 1927, the Charles K. Walker Memorial Hall of the St. John's Lutheran Church serves as an auditorium and social hall for both the St. John's congregation and the St. John's Lutheran School across the street. *Photo by Diann Marsh*

J. This is one of several custom mansions now located on what was once the Chandler Horse Ranch in East Orange. *Photo by Diann Marsh*

For more information on the history of Orange, please see *Orange: The City 'Round the Plaza* by Phil Brigandi and published by Heritage Media Corporation.

J

S. Whittier
La Habra Heights
Santa Fe Sprs.
S. Whittier Hts.
La Habra
Brea
Olinda
Brea Chem
La Mirada
ATSF
Carmenita
Bellflower
La Palma
Buena Park
Fullerton
Placentia
Freeway Park
Cypress
La Jolla
Olive
Atwood
Anaheim
W. Anaheim
Hawaiian Gardens
Los Alamitos
Stanton
Villa Park
Orange
Rossmoor
El Modena
Garden Grove
Westminster
Seal Beach
Midway City
Boulevard Gardens
Santa Ana
Tustin
Wintersburg
Fountain Valley
Ocean View
Liberty Park
Dyer
Irvine (sta.)
Sleepy Hollow
Los Serranos
SAN JUAN HILL 1,780 FT.
Prado Flood Control Basin
Yorba Linda
Prado Dam
Home Gardens
SIERRA PK. 3045 FT.
SANTA ANA
Santiago
Cowan Heights
Santiago Res.
Creek
BEDFORD PK. 3,720 FT.
Silverado
BALD PK. 3 962 FT
SANTIAGO PK 5,687 FT.
ORANGE
1 ST STANDARD
Huntington Beach
Sta. Ana
Santa Ana Hts.
Irvine
Newport Hts.
Costa Mesa
SAN JOAQUIN HILLS
Newport Beach
Balboa Island
Balboa
Corona del Mar
Emerald Laguna
Mission
Laguna Hills
Galivan
Laguna Niguel
Trabuco Cr.
Bay Beach
NIGUEL HILL 930 FT.
San Juan
South Laguna
Dana Point
Serra
Capistrano
San Clemente

SOUTH COUNTY

■LATE-BLOOMING SOUTH COAST WORKS TO PRESERVE NATURAL AND HISTORIC PAST *By Doris I. Walker*

When Orange County seceded from Los Angeles in 1889, its south seacoast was a scenic stretch of barren bluffs, peopled only at a few beach breaks by fishermen and tent campers. Laguna Beach and Aliso Beach were the favorite landing places for outside visitors, who staked out the coves below the bluffs and sometimes stayed all summer. Fishing camps were the order of that day at Newport Beach and Dana Point. The Spanish-flavored remnants of old San Juan Capistrano were already luring history-oriented romantics. San Clemente was just a place the train passed through.

The first half of the 20th century would add some new inroads upon the scene. The Pacific Coast Highway would finally connect all the beach towns in 1929. By then State Route 2 (Old Highway 101) already paralleled that linkage inland, meeting the highway at Serra (later Capistrano Beach — now part of Dana Point).

The masts of many sailboats crowd the marina at Dana Point. *The Pilgrim* can be seen in the foreground. *Anaheim/Orange County Visitor & Convention Bureau*

Newport Beach had incorporated in 1906 with a burgeoning commercial wharf, and Laguna Beach had become a city in 1926, with San Clemente following two years later — just before the Great Depression would quell further financial or developmental activity throughout the area.

The earliest south county settlement, Mission San Juan Capistrano, had reached its population peak of 1,300 in 1811. However, it evolved little over the next century and a half, so that when it finally incorporated in 1961, its total population was again barely 1,300. The drive for self-rule in that isolated rural town was stimulated by the arrival of the San Diego Freeway in 1959. It brought unappreciated demolition of some historic adobe structures in its path, which awakened the populace to the loss of a rustic image and their lack of voice in the matter.

Remaining unincorporated until 1989 was the county's original Spanish anchorage that its namesake had called "the only romantic spot in California" (Bostonian Richard Henry Dana in *Two Years Before the Mast*, 1840). The boundaries initially drawn for the proposed City of Dana Point were greatly expanded by a shotgun wedding at one end and a revolt of voters at the other. Capistrano Beach to the south, denied its own cityhood by the county's Local Agency Formation Commission, was told it had to join with Dana Point in order to create one financially feasible agency. Residents of the upscale tracts to the north organized a ballot issue, then voted to secede from Laguna Niguel's plan to include their coastal area in its incorporation move. The secessionists chose instead to become the newly named Monarch Beach portion of the City of Dana Point.

The shores of Newport Bay, once populated with small wooden cabins, now feature large two-story homes. In the background is Newport Center. *Anaheim/Orange County Visitor & Convention Bureau*

(Far left)
The Mission San Juan Capistrano founded by Father Serra in 1776 was the first non-Indian settlement in what would become Orange County in 1889. It was surrounded by a small community of adobe homes, some built as early as 1794.
Photo by Diann Marsh

More than 19 miles of calm-water shoreline provide mooring facilities for millions of dollars worth of fine saltwater sportscraft.
Orange County Historical Society

Today the entire south county coastline that was once too far from any work sites to attract commuters is now an easy drive, as well as a magnet for tourists who want to experience these "classic California beach towns" — each one with a picturesque image of its own.

Newport Beach, which had labored successfully to secure a working-class small-craft harbor during the 1930s as a federal/county project, has since lured the well-heeled yacht set. Its residents generally live in pricey settings: on ocean cliffs, manmade islands and golf fairways.

Laguna Beach, with its dozens of scalloped coves, had blossomed early into the area's free-thinking art colony, isolated from most area communities by the deep canyons and gullies (such as Bluebird) that had to be filled in to solidify its coastal continuity.

At the southernmost tip of Orange County, San Clemente hung on through the Great Depression, though founder Ole Hanson's dream of creating an entirely Spanish village was necessarily modified architecturally over the lean years by the need to add development with any theme. Hanson's own handsome home, Casa Romantica, was foreclosed in 1932.

Dana Point remained aloof from local control the longest. Its few thousand residents of the mid-1900s appeared to be individuals who enjoyed the challenge of low-key living above the secluded coves. The trails to the beach were so rugged that a century before, R.H. Dana's shipmates had to toss the cowhides they traded from local ranchos over the cliffs to get them down to the visiting ships. The bay behind the point became a surfing mecca called Killer Dana when it kicked during the rough storms of winter.

The surprise attack on Pearl Harbor in 1941 stimulated national awareness of the need to strengthen the security of the entire Pacific Coast. Vast land holdings were purchased by the federal government to create military training camps, which came to be populated by troops from inland states — many of whom were destined to fall in love with the scenic moderate year-round life here. So, when discharged, they arranged to stay or to return here with their families. That fact, plus completion of the I-5 Freeway in 1960 to the county's southern border, triggered a whole new invasion of outsiders — to live or to visit.

While once rents and mortgages had been much cheaper in the south than in the north county and planned housing tracts were unknown below the mid-divide, the second half of this century has overturned those statistics. Today, along the Orange County south coast, even rustic beach cottages and small view apartments demand a high price. And while the north-central county has added world-famous theme parks that attract the world, the natural beauty, rolling terrain and multileveled vistas of the south coast lure more and more tourists who come simply to relax and bask in the sun, surf, sand — and resort hotels.

The Dana Point City Hall, shown here shortly after it was built in 1929, was designed in the Spanish Colonial style that was so popular in Southern California during that era. Considered part of the Romantic Period of the 1920s, the architecture reminded Californians of Southern California's Spanish roots.
History Room, Santa Ana Public Library

A sunny day brings out the sailboats in Newport Bay.
Anaheim/Orange County Visitor & Convention Bureau

Located on the Pacific Coast Highway in Laguna Beach, the Pottery Shack has for many years been a popular spot for visitors to purchase some of Laguna Beach's unique pottery. *Diann Marsh Collection*

A realistic mural portraying dolphins and undersea life decorates this wall in Corona del Mar. *Anaheim/Orange County Visitor & Convention Bureau*

Residents of these communities have been noteworthy and diverse. Newport has been home to such celebrities as John Wayne, for whom the county airport was named — even though he had signed the petition to keep jets out to prevent them from flying over his harborside home. Surf guitarist Dick Dale shared his ocean-front home there with his pet lion. Newport has also been home to Dick Powell, June Allison, Ray Milland and Joey Bishop. Leading entrepreneurs Dr. Arnold Beckman and Robert Flour call it home. It's also the place where mystery novelist Dean Koontz chose to build his mansion.

Laguna Beach has always had its share of well-known characters: artists and cartoonists aplenty, as well as Hollywood's Mary Pickford, Douglas Fairbanks and Bette Davis. The Hotel Laguna was a regular hangout for Hollywoodites — the likes of Greta Garbo and Errol Flynn. Drug guru Timothy Leary experienced his first arrest in Laguna, by an alert rookie police officer who later became police chief. Law professor Anita Hill chose this alluring, isolated community to write her book following the media-driven Supreme Court sexual harassment episode. Bette Midler bought a house in Crystal Cove, between Laguna and Newport and filmed her movie Beaches there.

Dana Point, the lingering surfing Shangri-La drew Hobie Alter (and his surfboards and catamarans), Bruce Brown (and his cameras) and other surfing entrepreneurs who turned it into an *Endless Summer*. Lon Chaney Jr. called Capistrano Beach home. San Clemente has been the base for rugged individuals, ranging from actor James Arness, star of "Gunsmoke," to Col. Aaron Bank, founder of the Green Berets.

Just as the repeal of Prohibition in 1933 (which had given this coast a lucrative rumrunning operation) was followed by the Great Depression, the end of World War II brought a temporary economic letdown. Newport managed to get a small revival of military patriotism in 1953 when the International Boy Scout Jamboree raised a tent city for 50,000 scouts along a road paved just for them and later named for the event — Jamboree. Ironically, the Oscar-winning World War I movie, *All Quiet on the Western Front*, had been filmed not far away in 1930.

By the late 1950s ordinary homeowners were becoming more plentiful than celebrities along the coast as housing tracts followed the freeway south. Then in 1968 international attention moved dramatically to the southernmost tip of the county when President Richard Nixon

Members of Boy Scout Troop 8 from Balboa Island proudly ride the float they constructed for the International Boy Scout Jamboree, held during the summer of 1953 on the Irvine Ranch. *Old Courthouse Museum Society*

chose that point of San Clemente for his residence and working Western White House — Casa Pacifica.

Fleets of helicopters hovered noisily over the entire area each time the Nixons commuted from Washington D.C. in Air Force One to El Toro Marine Air Station and were then air-shuttled down to San Clemente with a marine escort. Numerous signs of his presence showed up all over town. One elementary school even painted a sign on its playground welcoming the President.

The irony of Nixon's chosen property becoming an international dateline for the activities of this Republican President is the fact that the elegant Spanish mansion had been built in 1927 by Henry Hamilton Cotton. He happened to be state financial chairman of the Democratic Party and a close crony of President Franklin D. Roosevelt. So, many political fund-raising parties and gala entertainment events for international dignitaries were held at the oceanfront estate during each quite diverse administration 40 years apart.

San Clemente renamed the public street leading to the private conclave holding the chief executive's home-away-from-the-White House "Avenida El Presidente." A residential development overlooking Casa Pacifica was named Presidential Heights. The future Nixon Presidential Library was supposed to become a fixture on San Clemente's Marblehead coast, glamorously preserving the city's international fame forever. Complete architectural plans were executed, a scale model of the complex was approved by the city in 1984, and a private foundation raised pledges for $25 million to build it.

However, the project sat in limbo while the land developers debated with city officials on density limits for the rest of the property. Months of discussions brought no compromise. So when more attractive overtures from the President's birthplace of Yorba Linda were offered, the foundation acted upon them, making the library's final destination that city at the opposite inland edge of Orange County. By that time, the thrill of San Clemente's dateline had already suffered with the startling scandal of the Watergate affair that had caused California's first-born chief executive to resign in 1974.

Legend has it that Richard Nixon proposed to Pat at a viewpoint on the Dana Point Headlands, a beautiful barren promontory that has not changed much since that moment in 1940. Like the Presidential Library site, the headlands has become the object of clashing, changing and controversial development plans by the owners, city officials and citizen groups concerned with preserving some of its unique geologic prominence in a natural state within a private development.

Meanwhile, a plan that had been waiting to be launched for 20 years, delayed by the Korean War, came to fruition with construction of Dana Point Harbor from 1966 to 1971 in the very anchorage that had brought hide-trading ships like Dana's to Capistrano Bay in the early 1800s.

Richard Henry Dana immortalized the cliffs of Dana Point in his book, *Two Years Before the Mast*. Cowhides were hurled from the cliffs so they could be loaded on the boats anchored offshore. Santa Catalina Island can be seen in the distance. *Orange County Historical Society*

(Below far left) Opening in 1967, the Newport Center and Fashion Island quickly became important magnets for commercial businesses and offices, as well as upscale retail establishments. *First American Title Insurance Co.*

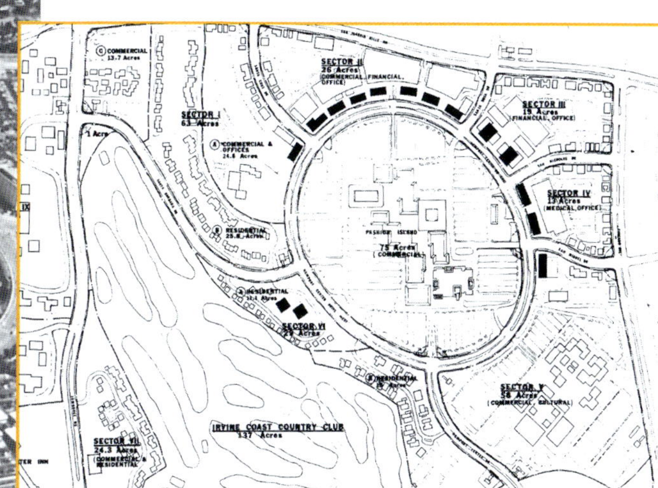

In 1965 the plan for Newport Center, with Fashion Island at its heart, was presented by the Irvine Company. The 137-acre Newport Beach Country Club is located to the southwest. *First American Title Insurance Co.*

Laguna Beach, known for its quaint cottages and colorful commercial buildings, is home to the internationally known Festival of the Arts founded in 1932.
Anaheim/Orange County Visitor & Convention Bureau

South Coast Plaza. The former farming Segerstrom family, owners of that property, would go on to donate a bean field on which to plant the Orange County Performing Arts Center. It opened in 1986, built with all private funding, and would become the cornerstone of culture in the county, soon to be surrounded by other major cultural facilities. In the new 21st century, the OCPAC itself will undergo a $100 million expansion that includes a separate concert hall. The obvious tradeoff for all this grandeur was that agriculture, once the area's mainstay, was thereby doomed and fell far behind other industries as continuing land development priorities progressed.

As tourism took the lead in the economic drama along the coast and visitors' dollars spent here began to run into the billions, major investments were logically made in hotel facilities. The Mediterranean-style Ritz-Carlton on the Dana Point oceanfront bluff tops has offered opulence since 1984 and was the first five-star resort hotel built in Southern California in more than three decades. Decorated with a rare art collection, it draws world celebrities and high-society events and has been named the "world's most romantic hotel" in a *Gourmet* magazine readership survey.

Newport Coast's recently developing multimillion-dollar mansions and top-rated hotels will be joined by a Marriott vacation club with 600 rooms, among several projected amenities. Time will tell whether this unincorporated plum piece of coast between Laguna and Newport — once a part of the Irvine cattle ranch — will be annexed to Newport Beach (or even the City of Irvine) or whether "the downcoast" will fight to become a city of its own. The 2,600-home development plan being carried out there was first proposed two decades ago with 30,000 homes. In the older part of the port city, a Newport Dunes resort hotel is expected to produce 600 rooms where once campers were the only clientele.

Other major hotels along the south coast are in the planning stages. These include a 400-room advertised "five-star-resort" in the Monarch Beach section of Dana Point next to the existing golf course. What is proposed there for the new century, though, is far more modest than the "fantasy resort" publicized during the 1980s. Then, the projected market appeared to warrant 1,000 tourist rooms, Hearst Castle architecture with a lily pond in the lobby, an ice rink in one of nine restaurants and a fountain theater. Resort hotels are also being considered in plans for the Dana Point Headlands and Treasure Island.

A refreshing touch in this massive sculpturing of the nearly virgin south coast with new deluxe hostelries is the restoration of some of the old landmark hotels. Some independent developers hope to preserve at least some of the charming historic ambiance of the area amid its obvious modern aspects.

Construction of this new small-craft harbor earned headlines of its own for several reasons: it was the first ocean marina to be pre-construction scale-model-tested and the first to have its breakwaters aligned by laser beam and its basins cofferdammed and dredged in the dry. It was also uniquely financed cooperatively by federal, state, county and private entities. This marina, plus the harbor at Newport, established the modern nautical heritage of this coast, which altogether berths about 12,000 private craft with dry storage and launching ramps for thousands more.

South Coast Plaza, built in 1967 on a land once devoted to the raising of lima beans by the Segerstrom family, became an immediate hit with shoppers who enjoyed the chic stores and wide variety of goods. At that time it was the nation's largest indoor mall.
Turville Photography Photo by Steve Lopushinsky

The oceanfront bluff tops that stretch from Newport to Oceanside had become the world's largest dry-farmed lima bean field at the turn of the century. In 1967 the northern ones grew a new amazing crop — two of the most stylish shopping oases yet seen on any coast. The Irvine Company's Newport Center included Fashion Island, an upscale mall featuring sculptures and stylish landscaping to connect the chic stores. It also developed into the area's financial center, as well as attracting medical offices, restaurants and hotels such as the Four Seasons.

In the same year, 1967, the bean fields of Costa Mesa were transformed into the nation's largest indoor shopping mall —

The 1905 Balboa Pavilion, outlined in lights, is a famous landmark now listed on the National Register of Historic Places.
Newport Beach Conference and Visitors Bureau

(Far right) The Rios Adobe, one of several approximately 200-year-old adobes still standing in the Los Rios Historic District, is in use as a private residence/ office by a member of the original family. *Photo by Diann Marsh*

The Los Rios Historic District located across the railroad tracks from the San Juan Capistrano Depot is now listed on the National Register of Historic Places. *Photo by Diann Marsh*

The ruins of the Great Stone Church on the grounds of the Mission San Juan Capistrano look much as they did in 1812 after a strong earthquake struck the then-six-year-old buildings. Recent efforts have focused on stabilizing the priceless remains. *Photo by Diann Marsh*

Known for building new mansions that decorate the bluffs within Ritz Cove and the Newport Coast, contractor Dave Busk admits he fell in love with the romantic setting and history of Dana Point. So he has directed some of his construction efforts toward restoring its first hotel, the Dana Villa that opened in 1927 at the entrance to Doheny State Beach, optimally set halfway between Los Angeles and San Diego. It was scheduled for demolition a few years ago in favor of a modern four-story motel whose funding fell through. Busk prevented its demise and lovingly re-sculptured the old Spanish-style villa to new elegance in the late 1990s while retaining its original architectural design.

In like manner, entrepreneur Dilesh Patel fell in love with the 1927 neglected and dilapidated La Casa del Camino in the heart of Laguna Beach. A Hollywood hangout in its early days, it appeared to him an opportunity waiting to happen again in the 1990s. La Casa, one of Laguna's oldest hotels, was built as a retreat for artists but now houses tourists lured by the present generation of the art colony's resident artists. Some years earlier, Hotel Laguna — originally a composite of three late 19th-century hotels moved onto one site — had undergone another revitalization to preserve its older glamour.

The 1905 Victorian Balboa Pavilion in Newport Beach, once the social center of that town, has had enough face-lifts through the decades to earn National Historic Landmark designation. Casa Romantica, the city-owned Spanish mansion built by San Clemente's founder in 1927 and companion piece to the Cotton-Nixon residence that is now privately owned, is expected to undergo intensive renovation as a cultural arts center.

Of course, a major challenge in authentic restoration of old properties is the need to replicate the original building while subtly upgrading the antiquated construction to meet current building codes.

The prime example — caught between historic eras — is the county's oldest building, Mission San Juan Capistrano, which attracts about 50,000 visitors a month. Once boasting the grandest church in the entire California mission chain, the vast stone edifice was severely damaged by a violent earthquake in 1812 — just six years after its completion. The remaining ruins, romanticized as the nesting site of migrating swallows each spring, have withstood the further weathering of two centuries fairly well. Nonetheless, they too must now meet modern seismic codes — just in case. This has led to their prolonged encasement in unsightly, reinforcing scaffolding while the necessary multimillion-dollar retrofit and restoration fund can be accumulated. The mission holds annual social mudslinging parties at which volunteers turn adobe wall resurfacing into a fiesta.

The City of San Juan Capistrano recently adopted the official motto: "Preserving the Past to Enhance the Future." However, while once it was the forced demolition of adobes in the freeway's path that bonded the residents to support incorporation, the town's main entrance from the freeway has in recent years become lined with city-approved, nondescript fast-food restaurants that challenge the historic theme. Some "rustic" commercialism has also been creeping onto Los Rios Street, a designated National Historic Neighborhood that includes some adobe buildings as old as the mission. While Capistrano preserves (and capitalizes) on its past, a remote canyon of the mission town is where NASA (TRW) chose to test the propulsion system for its advanced lunar module, an enhancement for the future.

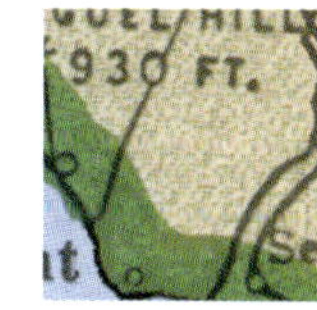

(Far left)
The County of Orange supervises 15 public beaches along Orange County's shoreline, including the Thousand Steps Beach.
County of Orange

An important tradition in Newport Beach is the famous Christmas Light Parade featuring gaily decorated boats.
Newport Beach Conference and Visitors Bureau

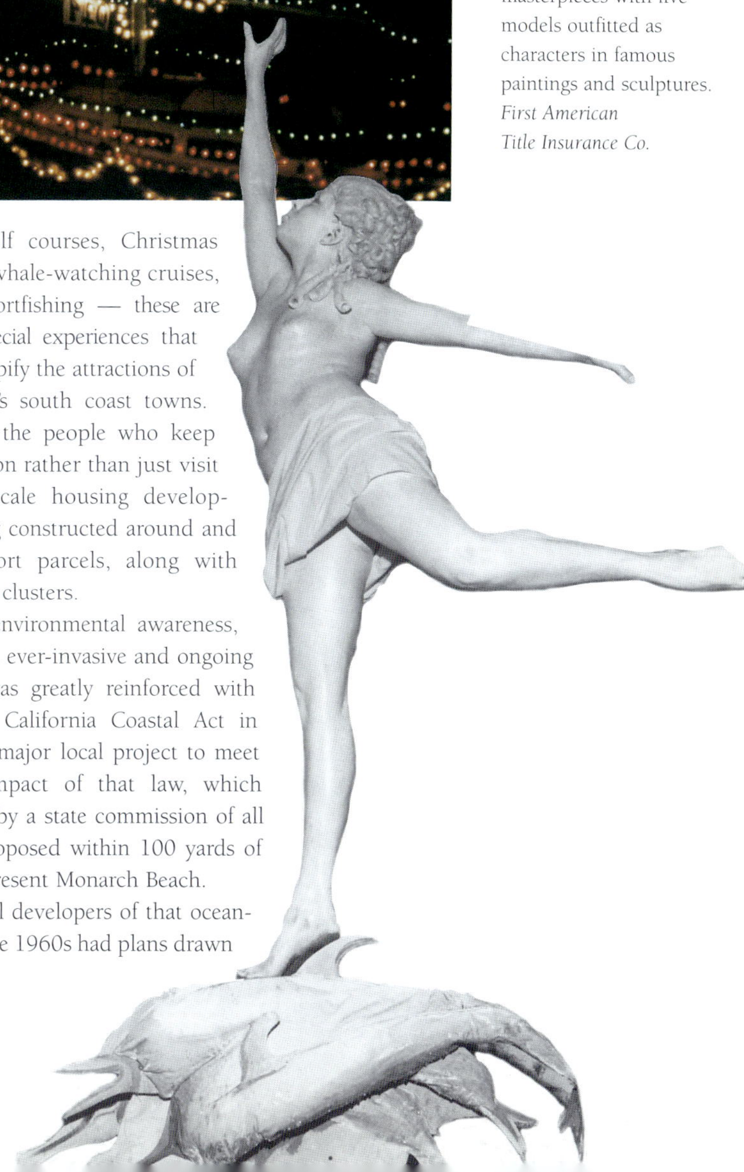

(Below)
The Pageant of the Masters, held each year in the Irvine Bowl in Laguna Beach, portrays living masterpieces with live models outfitted as characters in famous paintings and sculptures.
First American Title Insurance Co.

What separates Laguna Beach from its neighboring beach towns is its effort to keep out large commercialism. It lives instead off the smaller shops, galleries and restaurants that dot Coast Highway. City ordinances allow no buildings higher than three stories, no flashing lights or outdoor neon or animated signs, and no snack or souvenir stands. Downtown commercial operations are not allowed farther than two blocks inland from the highway, leaving the rest of the town's 10 square miles filled with a potpourri of eclectic residential architecture that delights the eye of those who probe beyond the tourist limits. The city has even appointed a "Vision Planning Committee" to consider the future.

Laguna Beach's world-famous Pageant of the Masters, where major works of art in all media are re-created with live models, has been a maturing fixture for that town since the 1930s and now draws devotees from all over the world. The cultural colony also offers three full-scale art festivals throughout the summer — brightening up the inland stretches of rugged Laguna Canyon Road. The Laguna Beach Art Museum, the county's first cultural institution founded in 1929, managed to retain its small-town character by backing out of a partially accomplished merger with the Newport Harbor Art Museum. The latter instead, by itself, came to be the Orange County Museum of Art, expanding within Newport Center in the 1990s.

Coastal golf courses, Christmas yacht parades, whale-watching cruises, surfing and sportfishing — these are some of the special experiences that have come to typify the attractions of Orange County's south coast towns. So what about the people who keep arriving to live on rather than just visit the coast? Upscale housing developments are being constructed around and within the resort parcels, along with subtle shopping clusters.

However, environmental awareness, seasoned by this ever-invasive and ongoing development, was greatly reinforced with passage of the California Coastal Act in 1974. The first major local project to meet head-on the impact of that law, which requires review by a state commission of all development proposed within 100 yards of the coast, was present Monarch Beach.

The original developers of that oceanfront parcel in the 1960s had plans drawn for a 3.5-acre recreational saltwater lake to be dug inland of Pacific Coast Highway and surrounded by a high-density resort community of homes, townhouses, apartments and a commercial center. This Sea Lake Village was to include 1,000 homes, 1,200 apartments and a massive hotel with two high-rise towers actually straddling Pacific Coast Highway. The beachfront at Salt Creek was to become a private gated community. The Orange County Planning Commission approved the entire plan.

Then, as will happen in such major enterprises, the property was sold in 1970 to AVCO Community Developers, who abandoned totally the idea of a lake. Instead, they obtained county approval to concrete-enclose natural Salt Creek, which had flowed into the ocean there for centuries. AVCO also got the county to approve the abandonment of Salt Creek Road, so that even Pacific Coast Highway could be rerouted and the oceanfront land reterraced. This provided prime ocean views for the private housing tract constructed there, while blocking the spectacular panoramic view of curving Capistrano Bay forever from the public. The company even received approval to increase its plan to 3,700 housing units.

When public outcry in the local unincorporated area was heard and concern for coastal conservation gained statewide activism, AVCO accelerated the construction activity on this parcel to around-the-clock grading, hoping to complete it before the impending election. Their plan was stopped dead, though, when voters approved the California Coastal Initiative in 1974. AVCO's grading scars remained visible from the highway for years.

The property's next owners built a modest tennis club and villas, a gated community and the Monarch Beach Golf Links on both sides of the highway. The fancy resort hotel that had been planned for decades was still in downscaled planning stages at century's end, having changed hands several more times and confronted less sympathetic city councils since Dana Point incorporated in 1989.

At the mid-1900s, "rural" Orange County had about 275 residents per square mile. In the first years of the 2000s, that number is expected to reach 4,000. The coastal land is not all urban yet, but it's difficult to define where suburbia begins. Those living in the south coast communities have become more and more concerned about being overcome by the higher density evidenced in the north, and various local petitions and initiatives appeared in the 1980s to limit or even stop growth. Both San Juan Capistrano and San Clemente have legislated housing caps, specifying the number of residences that can be built there annually. Capistrano had its recent moratorium on large commercial development earn Superior Court approval when legally tested.

In the 1990s the south coast cities joined together dramatically to fight another potential developmental hazard: an international airport proposed for the site of the decommissioned El Toro Marine Air Station. These cities find themselves within the flight path, just as Newport Beach did when John Wayne Airport was expanded in 1990.

While the early century's modest beach cottages of Laguna Beach and Balboa Island have appreciated well with the years, the ones in Crystal Cove and Treasure Island have had a different change of life of late.

When California bought Crystal Cove as a state park in 1979, it included an enclave of 45 funky little cabins that had grown up and weathered on the beach beginning in the 1920s. The composite community has earned a place on the National Register of Historic Places as the last intact example of "vernacular beach architecture."

Crystal Cove Park itself — all 3.25 miles of beachfront and 2,400 acres of coastal bluffs and canyons — was purchased from the Irvine Company for about $33 million. It has become a scenic oasis on a busy highway, allowing camping and hiking from sea level to 1,000 feet altitude. There's even a 1,000-acre underwater park with trails for snorkelers and scuba divers.

The state quietly awarded a private 60-year contract to transform "The Cottages at Crystal Cove" Cinderella-like into a high-priced luxury tourist resort — with minimal disturbance to their appealing quaintness. Longtime residents have been finally forced out, their leases extended several times as plans for the tourist trade are continually refined, contested and delayed. Already a fitness center and two of three proposed swimming

Four young boys contemplate the view of Balboa Island with its diversity of two-story beach houses and high-rise buildings. *Josephine Inslee*

The Balboa Pavilion constructed in 1905 faces Newport Bay. Originally built as a shelter where bathers could change their clothing, it now houses a restaurant and offices. *Anaheim/Orange County Visitor & Convention Bureau*

(Far left)
Newport Beach, shown here in the 1950s, has been a popular center for summer activities for over 90 years. The small boats in the foreground, including those with umbrellas, were owned by the dory fishermen who fished during the early morning and pulled their boats onto the beach to sell fresh fish to the public.
Orange County Historical Society

(Above)
The usually ideal weather of Southern California makes Newport Bay a popular location for sailing throughout the year.
Orange County Historical Society

(Far left bottom)
The Newport Dunes Resort, seen here in the 1960s, is a popular resort located in Newport Bay off Backbay Drive near Jamboree Road.
First American Title Co.

(Bottom right)
An excursion boat, middle center, heads toward the Balboa Pavilion during its tour of Newport Bay. The Balboa Ferry can be seen on the left as it heads toward Balboa Island.
Orange County Historical Society

pools have been eliminated from the resort plan. The beachfront, a restaurant, interpretive and art centers would still be open to nonguests. Now state Democrats are opposing such a private amenity within a state park; the contract was signed during the previous Republican governorship. The Coastal Commission, which still has a say, had hoped for an inexpensive hostel in the antiquated cottages.

When Treasure Island Mobile Home Park, the private community that juts out into the sea at South Laguna, was sold and its residents were evicted in 1997, the South Laguna Civic Association worked diligently to modify the city's Specific Plan governing the prime 30 acres' future. The new private development plan calls for a hotel with 225-275 rooms and a complex of 31 luxury homes. However, the matter was brought to a public referendum in April 1999 when voters approved the change to the General Plan and the developers' project. While both projects allowed a resort on the city's last coastal parcel, the plans were significantly different. The city council had scaled the original plan down from 268 residences, and the California Coastal Commission had approved both versions.

San Clemente's city beaches and Dana Point's Doheny State Beach were early additions to the public domain, donated by community founders. Capistrano Beach and Salt Creek Beach County Parks — both in Dana Point — were acquired in the 1960s. Laguna's historic oceanfront riddled with private honky-tonk concessions, bars and a dance hall in the 1950s took two failed bond elections and an array of unworkable financial plans before it was publicly acquired and remodeled into its picturesque Main Beach in 1974. The mayor parachuted out of an astronaut-piloted plane to dedicate the low-key 1,000-foot strand.

Newport's long-held public beaches are focused around two piers — at Balboa and Newport's main beach — with a state beach at Corona del Mar. San Clemente's pier of the 1920s was rebuilt in 1939 and again in 1985, while the contemporary one at neighboring Capistrano Beach weathered out in the 1960s. Laguna lost its very early piers to storms and even had to demolish the 1971 concrete Aliso Beach Pier after it was severely damaged by El Nino in 1998.

One major victory for environmental planning in the final years of the 21st century has created a contiguous "green and blue belt" of over 19,000 acres (almost 30 square miles) — with various individual parcels now combined into the South Coast Wilderness Nature Reserve. Its General Plan includes the Laguna Coast Wilderness Park and Irvine Company's Laguna Canyon parcels.

Dana Point Harbor, opened by the county in 1971, is about to undergo renovation as its 30-year private master leases are restructured. This time around it has encouraged more public input to finalize. The consensus will bring modest renovation

The unique diamond-shaped Aliso Pier, built on Aliso Beach near the town of Laguna Beach, had to be demolished shortly after it was severely damaged by a storm in 1998. *County of Orange Recreation Department*

of the existing marinas and public places, more slips for the more prevalent larger yachts and a major parking garage. The architectural theme chosen by a special revitalization task force is called "Early California Coastal."

The Orange County Marine Institute there, wishing to expand from offering merely student education to a broader base of public museum-quality marine galleries, has had these ideas squelched for potentially creating excessive traffic with a lack of expandable parking space.

That now self-supporting institution, dreamed about for decades before it actually opened in 1981, annually sends an average of 100,000 students of all ages through its onshore and sea-going labs, as well as its living history program aboard the *Pilgrim*. The brig is a re-creation of the vessel that brought Richard Henry Dana to the coast. When the classic ship became part of OCMI's anchored program, the county declared it a building and required it to install stainless steel sinks and other land amenities. It goes to sea once a year for a necessary haulout, offering impetus for a tall ship festival.

Not even Paradise is without its natural traumas. Past rainy seasons have brought landslides in various areas of the newer developed south county. Cove Road within Dana Point Harbor was closed for six years in the 1990s following an earthslide that was eventually artificially stabilized.

In 1993 a massive slide moved five houses and 40,000 cubic yards of earth and rocks down the bluffs of north San Clemente, burying Coast Highway and the railroad tracks and projecting onto part of Dana Point. It stopped traffic and trains for several months and became a controversial joint rebuilding project of the two cities, resulting in an environmental retaining wall. A similar repair became necessary somewhat farther south within San Clemente. Another mudslide onto the highway required restructuring of cliff sections in San Clemente, including the very section where the Nixon Library might have stood.

Laguna Niguel made headline news in 1998 when a 500-foot hillside supporting an expensive development slid down, destroying several houses and condominiums and bringing condemnation sentences to others. It was the seventh time there had been slides in the Niguel Summit area off Crown Valley Parkway.

Laguna Canyon Road is periodically closed in rainy weather because of floods and slides along its winding rural route. Slides in earlier decades in Laguna Beach, including ones along the filled-in areas of Bluebird Canyon, had been repaired and nearly forgotten.

Ever aware that their city's south border marks the end of Orange County and the frontier of 125,000-acre Marine Base Camp Pendleton, San Clementians watched a major brush fire cross that border in January 1976, burning 21 homes and threatening others. It even dared to roar toward Nixon's Casa Pacifica but was extinguished before reaching the former chief executive's exile estate.

That was also the year San Clemente tried for a second time to be annexed to San Diego County and assume the tax revenues of the San Onofre Nuclear Plant that had been built with controversy on the beach south of the county line in the 1960s. The secession plan failed, as did the plant in the late 1990s, when nuclear-generated electricity was declared too expensive to continue producing.

Dry 80-mph Santa Ana winds in October 1993 created a fast-moving firestorm 200 feet high in places. The flames started in the Santa Ana foothills, then leaped across Laguna Canyon Road and up to the populated ridge tops of Laguna Beach, where elegant homes had enjoyed both ocean and canyon views. The fire eventually consumed 17,000 acres, damaging or destroying 441 houses (from mansions in Emerald Bay to mobile homes at El Morro on the beach) and was one of the 10 most destructive fires in U.S. history.

However, by this century's end, three-quarters of the affected Laguna residences have been rebuilt with upgraded building codes — evidence of the will of individuals to win battles with nature in an aesthetically desirable area.

Nature, not fair or ever finished, brought predicted El Nino storms in 1997 that devastated Laguna again with slides, in which hundreds of houses and two people were lost. Then during the following year, a fire struck the downtown main street and damaged key businesses.

Thankfully, some lessons had been learned. Since the ravage of the 1993 fire in Laguna Beach, a herd of 700 goats has worked constantly to eat away potential tinderbrush, including the roots, in the hills above the city. Led by Basque shepherds, they are a flashback to old 1800s rancho times when cattle and sheep made up the major economic livelihood of the entire area. By following specially installed fences, the goats cut fire breaks in otherwise inaccessible areas and trim the brush that creeps dangerously near housing tracts.

Over-density, crowded schools, traffic congestion, natural and developmental disasters have all led to more awareness by the population as new projects have come to the drawing board over the years.

One large south county coastal property is a classic case of newly evolved community concern and action to modify a major development. The very parcel that might have held the Nixon Library in the 1970s is still in the planning and talking process as the century ends (see Appendix).

Sometimes irony adds to the drama of "progress," as in the concept of ultra-modern toll roads hurrying traffic through the county faster than freeways (that were intended to offer ultimate speed just four decades ago). These modern transportation corridors have resurrected the oldest of all the county's assets: unique prehistoric fossils from the south county's former life as sea bottom.

Most major grading in the area over the past few decades has uncovered some petrified bones of much earlier animal residents, especially rare marine mammals millions of years old. So much so, in fact, that in 1977 the Orange County Board of Supervisors enacted an ordinance requiring the presence of a paleontologist at all grading operations, with authority to halt work when a significant fossil or American Indian artifact is uncovered. The cost of the extraction of these usually museum-quality objects must be borne by the developer. Both Los Angeles and San Diego counties adopted copies of the law. In 1986 the Orange County board further decreed that all such local finds deemed relevant shall remain here rather than be taken to adjacent counties' established museums.

As plaster-encased fossils stacked up beyond the capacity of designated Orange County warehouse space, finally in 1999 a grant for preservation of the rare bones was enacted with the assistance of California State University, Fullerton. However, at century's end there was yet no public museum to display the specimens to the public — only traveling exhibits at random sites.

Among the rare fossils unearthed throughout the south coast area are the widest mix of co-deposited land and sea animal remains found anywhere and some of the most complete whale skeletons and the largest number of partial marine mammal fossils yet discovered. The extensive lengths of the toll roads have brought to light many one-of-a-kind prehistoric species, including a fossilized four-tusked walrus uncovered in San Clemente's Marblehead development.

A Bucyrus Steam Shovel, operated by Western Construction Company personnel, prepares the road bed for the 56-foot-wide main thoroughfare in Dana Point built in 1929. *History Room, Santa Ana Public Library*

Lido Isle, shown in the 1970s, has been transformed from a barren sandbar into one of Orange County's most exclusive residential areas. *Orange County Historical Society*

RICHARD HENRY DANA, JR., STATUE UNVEILING CEREMONY

Island Way and Dana Drive, Dana Point Harbor

DANA POINT HARBOR

On April 28, 1972, the Orange County Board of Supervisors and the San Juan Capistrano Historical Society unveiled a statue dedicated to Richard Henry Dana Jr. in Dana Point Harbor. This logo and wording are taken from the invitation for the event. *History Room, Santa Ana Public Library*

In some places, such as the bluffs above Newport Bay, masses of American Indian remains and artifacts thousands of years old were uncovered in the mid-1990s. American Indian residents (designated as their "most likely descendants") clashed with the developers to earn the right to rebury their ancestors with ceremony elsewhere, rather than to place them on display. In most cases the sites where these human remains had settled are now covered with new homes for modern-era inhabitants, proving that it's still "the place" to live. One major Indian village adjacent to Fashion Island is now a gated residential community.

Of the inhabitants of upscale houses built upon original burial grounds, a representative of local American Indians was quoted as saying: "When it's winter, and the doors start slamming, and they hear footsteps, they will know the ancestors are around."

Still, many of today's smallest birds and rodents in the primal stretches still left undeveloped are earning a month-to-month, decision-by-decision reprieve of their habitats because of the strength of environmental proponents.

Perhaps the most melodramatic developmental tug-of-war in county coastal history surrounds the ultimate destiny of the 121-acre Dana Point Headlands, Orange County's largest remaining prime oceanfront property. This magnificent promontory was the subject of author Richard Henry Dana's romanticized praise and was subsequently named for him over a century ago.

Ever since the 1920s, a resort has been suggested for the site, though one was never constructed. The Chandler-Sherman interests have long owned the property, but the serious subject of Headlands development did not arise until 1974. Then the county and the California Coastal Commission approved a plan for two hotels and about 800 homes, although the project was not begun before the City of Dana Point was incorporated in 1989. This brought a city planning commission and a city council into the political arena.

The first General Plan written for the new city cut the density down to somewhat over 500 homes and one 400-room hotel to be built on the Headlands. Citizen petitions to overturn the plan were submitted but declared invalid by the city attorney. However, the tables turned back when a Superior Court judge ruled they were valid, and an election to determine the plan's fate was ordered. However, the city won an appeal to knock out the petitions legally.

A Specific Plan for the Headlands, based on that General Plan, was adopted by the city council in 1994. Again, citizen petitions against its density were circulated but this time they were validated. That led to a public referendum at the November 1994 polls that overturned that Headlands Specific Plan. Next the developers sued to invalidate the referendum but lost. In 1997 the State Supreme Court refused to hear the owners' appeal against the city, upholding the referendum.

During 1997 and 1998 the city held a series of community meetings and

workshops, hoping to gain voter input for an alternate arrangement. Meanwhile, a partnership of new owners had purchased a 50-percent interest in the property, appearing on the scene with other ideas for its use. They held their own public meetings to explain their new project, which would include somewhat more than 200 homes on acreage including Dana Strand Beach. Their hotel would be a significant spa resort on the ridge site overlooking Dana Point Harbor with an adjacent commercial area. This version would leave 65 acres of open space in several separate sections.

In July 1998 the city introduced its inch-thick Headlands Specific Plan, which cut the allowable residential density to 185 homes in three bluff-top areas, along with a hotel with up to 150 rooms above Dana Strand Beach. Nearly 75 acres would remain in contiguous (largely natural) open space. A Save the Headlands group encouraged the city to change its General Plan so it would coincide with the new Headlands Specific Plan. That revision was deemed unnecessary by the city's legal counsel.

Meanwhile, the city refused to process the plan offered by the new developers, who therefore sued. During the fall of 1998 the Superior Court ruled that the city could not legally process a Specific Plan that was not in compliance with the existing General Plan. It was therefore directed to process the developers' proposal, which was compliant with the existing General Plan. Since the planning commission had already approved the Specific Plan, the city appealed the decision but was granted neither a stay nor a review of the Superior Court order.

So the city council set about rewriting its General Plan in order to modify what would be allowable on the Headlands, hoping to invalidate the owners' newly proposed development. With a stalemate in view, mediation has been suggested to suspend all legal action and close the gap between the parties.

Early in the fluctuating ideas of what should be the specific future of the Dana Point Headlands, environmentalists discovered a very tiny, endangered bird living there — the 4.5-inch-long California gnatcatcher.

Then in 1994 a second equally endangered species was found on the Headlands — the Pacific pocket mouse, also about 4 inches long. These tiny rodents are said to have lived in the immediate area for several hundred thousand years but were thought to be totally extinct since last seen anywhere in 1971. Their sandy coastal sage scrub habitat had been overtaken by development.

This is the smallest of all 19 recognized pocket mouse subspecies (named for their unusual external fur-lined cheek pockets in which to store seeds). Colonies of these hairy-footed mice obviously favor prime ocean views as much as people do. They once hid out along coastal bluffs from Los Angeles to the Mexican border but are now confined to 4 acres near the point of the Dana Point Headlands and two small spots on the Camp Pendleton Marine Base.

The political drama starring the Dana Point Headlands may continue while the fate of less than 40 unnoticing and barely noticeable remaining rodents hangs in the balance — complicating the already complicated proceedings.

In the county that made Mickey famous in the 1950s, could the Pacific pocket mouse be the millennium mouse that roars? ■

The popular Newport Pier is filled with fishermen and onlookers in this 1956 photograph. Newport Beach can be seen in the background. *Orange County Historical Society*

IRVINE & SADDLEBACK VALLEY *By Joseph Osterman*

The Mission San Juan Capistrano, founded in 1776, established the town of San Juan Capistrano, Orange County's first non-Indian settlement. Ongoing projects include the restoration and reconstruction of the original buildings. *Photo by Diann Marsh*

The "romance of the ranchos" is vividly illustrated in this painting. Some of the rancho dons lived high, precarious lives, while others worked very hard to care for their ranchos and the large group of people they supported. *• First American Title Insurance Co.*

The American Indians came into the area many thousands of years ago, and tribelets of California Indians lived in tune with nature along the creek beds from the ocean to the mountains. In 1789 the "Mission-Pueblo-Presidio" program for Alta California was spearheaded by the Junipero Serra-Gaspar de Portolá expedition. The heart of the program was the 21 missions to be established between San Diego and San Francisco Bay. The padres were given huge tracts of land on which to carry out their work.

In 1834 the Mexican government commenced its "secularization" process whereby the land was taken from the missions and made available to the local Californios. In most cases, the land, in vast acreage grants, went to men who had been of service to the government. The age of the rancho had begun.

Much has been said of and written about "the romance of the rancho." Indeed, on the surface it was a romantic time, one of rodeos (cattle roundups), recogidos (roundups of horses) and weeklong fandangos (celebrations). Still, it was a one-crop economy where "cattle was king" — a one-crop economy fraught with danger of drought. This did occur in 1862-63 when no rain fell for two years and cattle died in massive numbers. To maintain their high lifestyle, "rancheros" went to bankers and borrowed money against their lands. Even with the return of the rains, the landowners were deep in debt. Also, they faced huge legal fees in the battle to get their grants confirmed. Two decades after the drought disaster, forfeiture of the land grants occurred.

In 1997 as part of the Centennial Celebration of Irvine Park, a statue of James Irvine was unveiled. One hundred years earlier in 1897, Irvine had given 160 acres of woodlands to the County of Orange for a park. *Photo by Diann Marsh*

Arriving on the scene were capable people, in the right place at the right time — men like James Irvine, Richard O'Neill, Lewis F. Moulton and Dwight Whiting. These entrepreneurs bought up the land grants of Jose Sepulveda, Juan Forster, Julan Avila and Jose Serrano for about $2 an acre. With the exception of Whiting, who experimented with such diverse ventures as ostriches, deciduous fruits, olives and real estate, they maintained emphasis on stock-raising, cattle and sheep, and dry farming in hay, both lima and black-eyed beans, and barley.

In the midst of the rural acreage lay small towns in Irvine and El Toro. Located along the railroad, the towns contained the basic components of rural America: a general store with a post office; a one, then two-room school; a church or two; a town/community hall; the depot; a warehouse and cattle corral shipping complex; a recreation center and gathering place; and often a pool hall.

In writings about "Old" El Toro, the new phase covering the changes during the postwar era have been referred to as "a revolution of wheels and water." Water was vital to growth, and the local supply was certainly limited. The few existing water companies did not have the ability to meet the needs of the expected population explosion.

In the postwar period, one thing was paramount: There must be a water supply. The source was obvious importation via Metropolitan Water, already coming in from Hoover Dam, and the newly developed California Aqueduct. In the 1950s, pipelines, canals, storage lakes and pumping stations combined to provide the water supply.

The Irvine General Store, completed in 1912, was operated by Kate Munger, a determined woman who corresponded with James Irvine for two years, trying to convince him that a store was needed in the small settlement. The store, which was quite successful, contained a post office and had a gas pump out in front. *First American Title Insurance Co.*

Agreement on the expense involved in "subscribing" to the water was not easy. In a memoir written in the early 1980s, shortly before his death, George Whiting, son of the original Dwight, noted that, "Nellie Gail (Moulton) really had me on her list when I argued in favor of bringing Metropolitan Water to El Toro." The Moulton-Daguerre interests were among the early holdouts for the status quo, although they soon came to realize that a passing ear called for selling the land. The handwriting was on the wall. As was the case with all of the large landholdings, the Moulton-Daguerre Rancho Niguel was divided and sold to developers about 1960.

The victory of the pro-import water group ensured the destiny of the south county area. The future was determined; the destiny was locked in.

After a day of "roughing it," this group of friends posed for this 1930s photo taken on the Forster Ranch. *First American Title Insurance Co.*

The Cities and Communities

The gathering of people into communities that then grow into cities usually follows one of two patterns; there is the planned community such as Irvine, Mission Viejo, or Rancho Santa Margarita. Then there are those which, in a sense, just grow. The growth of the area from Saddleback Valley on into Irvine followed these patterns. Planning is vital for any city, and the sooner it is implemented, the better, a point illustrated by the dilemma now faced by Foothill Ranch/Portola Hills and Leisure World.

Local identities and options rank high for each community. In varying degrees each pursues its own goals, with no one formula that fits all. Community needs are guarded here as zealously as they are in the larger cities, and each has its own concerns and problems to be resolved.

Irvine

With the influx of people into the hitherto rural sections of Orange County, the first area of consideration was to bring a plethora of housing developments into governable entities through the process of incorporation. Perhaps the place to start would be Irvine. The new city was carved out of land area once a full quarter of Orange County, it was one of the movers toward incorporation and it definitely involved a plan. It provides an excellent case study of the incorporation process.

On Saturday, June 20, 1964, President Lyndon B. Johnson dedicated the site of the University of California's Irvine campus to a crowd of more than 15,000. Speaking before a friendly and respectful, but not enthusiastic audience, the Chief Executive foreshadowed the future in Orange County life when he noted that of the various frontiers to be crossed in the next decades, one of the most critical would be the frontier of city life. The President almost certainly foretold the story of things to come in the second half of the 20th century. He stated, "Just as our colleges and universities changed the future of our farm a century ago, so they can help change the future of our cities."

From the time of James Irvine's death in 1948 and until the death of his son, Myford, in 1959, a series of contentious events marked the eventual development of 17,000 acres of the "World's largest bean field." This and additional acreage became the planned city of Irvine. The battle between Joan Irvine Smith and the Board of Directors of the Irvine Foundation led to lawsuits contesting ownership and control. But paramount to the situation was prodding of the board by real estate developers and

(Far right) This apartment row in El Toro housed seasonal workers from the nearby agricultural fields. *First American Title Insurance Co.*

Irvine Boulevard, shown here in 1972, was a two-lane road lined with citrus trees. *Josephine Inslee*

When this photo was taken in 1948, most of the Irvine Ranch was still in citrus groves, vegetable row crops and cattle grazing. *First American Title Insurance Co.*

businessmen to give 1,500 acres of land to the University of California's regents to build a university, which would produce a pool of trained labor for the aerospace and high-tech industries. After a series of lawsuits and bidding wars, the joint winners moved to dissolve their partnerships. Conflicts covering four decades laid the groundwork for a final sale. The Donald Bren faction gained control in 1983 when Joan Irvine Smith sold her share of the ranch and foundation.

In 1971 the city of Irvine was voted into existence when 72 percent of eligible voters went to the polls. Some big names still opposed cityhood. The Orange County Board of Supervisors opposed incorporation, fearing the loss of the revenues from the

The Irvine Spectrum, a major commercial/retail center opened in the mid-1990s.
Turville Photography
Photo by Steve Lopushinsky

A tree-lined road led to the Sunkist Packing House in El Toro. The city has changed greatly since this photo was taken in 1969.
Josephine Inslee

Irvine Ranch. Joan Irvine Smith also opposed the concept of cityhood as, no doubt, her grandfather would have. The Irvine Company supported incorporation to prevent the land from being annexed piecemeal by neighboring cities.

Planning of the city of Irvine had begun in 1967. Planners viewed a city where people would"...work close to their homes, live in the middle, with open spaces to the north and south, anchored by the Irvine Business Center on the west and the Irvine Spectrum on the east. The focal center point would be UCI: the appeal would be a research university, a dynamic Orange County market, and a 'quality of life' in 'villages.'" An Irvine Company document, "Planning Ahead: A Periodic Publication On Issues of Interest to Residents of Irvine" proclaimed in 1997 that in only 10 years the Spectrum has become the technology hub of Southern California, an "entrepreneurial hot spot." The balance between Irvine's jobs and residences would build the city into one of the West's most vital and well-balanced communities. Progress in the future will most assuredly continue to test this bold prediction.

Along with technology, the Irvine area has become a hub of retail activities. When the gigantic Irvine Spectrum opened in the mid-1990s, it dwarfed all others in the area. Perhaps the prototype of the future, the Spectrum is a combination of retail stores, distribution depots and entertainment complexes. It also exhibits a sprawl which is quite different from the concentrated walking space of the earlier mall developments. A spread-out complex presents a problem, however, in that distance often requires alternatives in transportation. Does the future call for intra-shopping center transport — monorails, people movers, or golf-style carts? For the moment the Spectrum is the ideal, the target of the older shopping centers, now left behind.

Still another significant change in marketing in the modern era has occurred in the automobile sales business. Car dealerships were located in town, usually limited to a single brand. This limited "comparison" shopping. A logical result was the auto-mall layout featuring a variety of makes and models with a promotional emphasis on ease of comparison. Auto malls began to spring up along the freeways. Soon Irvine was bracketed by the Irvine Auto Mall on the far eastern corner of that city, right against the Lake Forest city limit. Near the western edge of Irvine, the Tustin Auto Mall went into operation.

El Toro

In spite of the explosion of housing developments, which hit the Saddleback Valley area in the late 1950s, a distinct anathema toward the name, "El Toro" occurred. The unique name of the small town that had been the center of life for the large surrounding areas of cattle ranches, farms and orchards acquired a no-man's-land status. Not one development incorporated El Toro in its title or descriptive literature. Every effort was made to divorce the project from that title. Early promoters sought to include Laguna Beach in their promotion. A tract, north of today's I-5 Freeway, and east of El Toro Road, called itself "North Laguna Beach." The tract was located some seven to nine miles inland from the craggy Laguna coast. The "Laguna" motif runs strong in south Orange County's incorporated cities of Laguna Niguel, Laguna Hills and Laguna Woods, the most recently incorporated.

Why the antipathy toward El Toro? Did it contain romantic overtones to the past "Rancho Period"? In the thoughts of the majority who voted, it conveyed an idea of the El Toro Marine Base — which is a misnomer in itself, for it is entirely on Irvine land. A consensus indicated that "El Toro" reflected the marine base, a military institution whose name as a city would lower property values.

Quonset huts on the El Toro Marine Base, shown here in 1955, were used so frequently on military bases that the building form became identified with World War II.
First American Title Insurance Co.

(Far left)
Lake Forest, built on part of the 3,568-acre Lewis Moulton Ranch, was incorporated in 1991.
Turville Photography
Photo by Steve Lopushinsky

El Toro Grammar School, which was built in 1890 and later used by St. Anthony's Catholic Church (left), and the 1891 St George's Episcopal Mission (right) are two of the restored buildings at Heritage Hill Historic Park in Lake Forest.
County of Orange

Lake Forest

Titles of real estate tracts invariably contain some degree of hyperbole and cynicism. This cynicism flourished with the name "Ponderosa Pines" attached to homes located in the 1904 Dwight Whiting eucalyptus plantation. This was one of several failed projects of that entrepreneur, which came to be known as the "gum grove" by the people of El Toro. When a tract was endowed with the fancy appellation, the amusement was hardly muted. In the mid-1980s, a letter to the editor of the *Saddleback Valley News* suggested or proposed that the new city name be "Gum Grove Gardens." The letter was not published. With much influence from the residents of manmade lake communities, Lake Forest I and II, the name Lake Forest was combined with the proposal for incorporation, and a new city was born in 1991.

The search for unique attractions has not been lost on the City of Lake Forest. The city faces another problem — the nonexistence of a city center; a focal point is a major element in the planned community. The lack of a city center confronts many emerging cities in the region. The first real estate developments were along the freeway (I-5), but the original Aliso City/El Toro, arguably the logical heart of the city, lay a mile toward the mountains along the railroad, the heart of late 19th century Southern California land booms.

Development continues to occur along the freeways. The challenge for the city is to create a civic center. This is imperative to prevent Lake Forest from becoming more than a wide spot along the freeway. The "natives" are becoming restless. Letters to the editor ask: "Where is the plan?" People seek to find a "hub" of a city, that social center, a focal point such as the town hall, or the general store, or even the pool hall, had provided in the past. El Toro Road centers are under pressure to maintain, rebuild, tear down and start anew. The dynamics of growth continue to function. The basic issues facing city governments continue but at a more rapid pace than in the past.

Mission Viejo

Mission Viejo's city plan is perhaps the best portent of the future. It originated as a planned city by the Mission Viejo Company before it was sold to Mobil Oil. The Mission Viejo Company then turned its efforts to building Rancho Santa Margarita. The Mission Viejo Master Plan was approved in 1965, a plan which called for 52 percent of the land to be devoted to residential use, 20 percent to parks, open space and recreation, 10 percent to schools and churches, and 9 percent to business properties. The estimated build-out figures for the year 2000, population 95,000 in over 33,325 homes, were nearly reached in 1999. Older malls such as Mission Viejo Mall, opened in 1979, continue to renovate, add to and change to stay in the fight for the customer dollar.

Early promotion of Mission Viejo rested heavily on "Living the Dream" on Lake Mission Viejo. Although it was clear that

Ranch hands brand cattle on the Mission Viejo Ranch in this 1963 photograph.
First American Title Insurance Co.

Mission Viejo originated as a planned community developed by the Mission Viejo Company. It was approved in 1965 and incorporated in 1988. *Turville Photography Photo by Steve Lopushinsky*

more than 30,000 homes could not all have lakeside views. In 1992 annexation of 593 acres of neighboring Aegean Hills added more space and rounded out the city boundaries. Early on, Mission Viejo has focused positive elements of community pride. The swim club, The Nadadores, contributed headlines with its development of Olympic swim champions. The still unincorporated city hosted cycling events for the 1984 Olympic games. With a national soccer team training site and a minor-league baseball team, the city has its newsworthy features.

Twenty years after the first residents of Mission Viejo moved in, the citizens voted to incorporate. On March 31, 1988, the City of Mission Viejo became the 27th city in Orange County, and the ninth largest. As with all burgeoning cities, the problems are no longer related to crops and rainfall. The age-old problems associated with people crowded into urban and suburban situations predominate. Protection and parks, building codes and regulations, gangs and landlords are the urban challenges of today.

Laguna Niguel

When the City of Laguna Niguel was incorporated in 1989, its plan called for a history of the city area, authored by Dr. Donald Decker and his wife, Mary. Typical of its genre, the booklet incorporates history of the area, the steps taken toward cityhood and a focus on its interesting components. Laguna Niguel's city limits include the building officially titled the Chet Hollifield Federal building, referred to by some as a white elephant and called "The Ziggurat" for its Middle Eastern style of architecture. The building was originally designed for the Autonetics Division of North American Rockwell Aviation.

When international developments redirected the emphasis of defense industries, the government was left with a building. As attempts by the government to sell the building proved unsuccessful, the Ziggurat became the home of a number of federal agencies and archives. Perhaps the major agency, certainly the most interesting, is the Federal Archives and Records Center. Its files include documents from the 1790s, court cases and military records. With a deep and varied information list, it has become a bonanza for citizens doing research on family trees. Still another interesting use of the Hollifield Building is its two heliports. These are used by VIPs, both national and international, headed for the not-too-distant Ritz-Carlton Hotel.

Laguna Hills

Laguna Hills was one of the latest suburban areas to incorporate but not the last. Laguna Woods and Rancho Santa Margarita incorporated in 1999, and the city of Laguna Hills had incorporated in 1996. Located on land once part of Don Juan Avila's Rancho Niguel, later part of the Moulton-Daguerre Rancho, the new city astutely annexed Laguna Hills Mall as a source of city revenue. In 1969 this mall had sprouted from the former rich bean field of Lewis F. Moulton's Rancho Niguel.

Following incorporation the city officials launched programs to focus on the unique characteristics of their city. This focus was geological in nature. Peeten Reef, extending under the entire valley, reminds us that this entire area was under water during

The peaceful roads in the back country of Orange County have been replaced by wide boulevards, parkways and cul-de-sacs. *Photo by Diann Marsh*

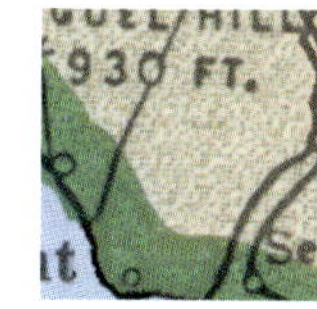

much of the geological past. It is claimed that "The Saddleback Valley is the richest area in the world in sea fossils."

On October 24, 1998, the City of Laguna Hills sponsored its first annual Festival of the Hills, a program designed to celebrate the history of the area and the city through music arts, and entertainment. Sponsors viewed 700 people in attendance at the one-day event as a successful first effort. Plans are under way to expand this program to include entertainment and learning for both adults and children. Promotion of a city's uniqueness is certainly a part of making incorporation stick, a valuable function in the building a community. Similar city-sponsored activities like the Rancho Santa Margarita Rodeo and the Victorian Christmas at Heritage Hill Park provide the necessary glue to pull the cities together.

In the 1880s, Lewis Moulton bought Don Juan Avila's Rancho Niguel. Moulton and his partner, Juan Pierre Daguerre, expanded their ranch to 22,000 acres on which they raised sheep and cattle. The ranch is now home to thousands of South County residents.
First American Title Insurance Co.

Foothill Ranch/Portola Hills

Incorporation as the alternative to being swallowed up via annexation is the major issue facing the residents of Foothill Ranch/ Portola Hills. The 18,000 residents of this planned community, happy with the peace and solitude that their community gives, are now uncertain about their future. Incorporation is under discussion but many questions remain unanswered.

Why incorporate? This fundamental question seems to have one basic answer: Control — the ability to maintain more local control of one's civic destiny. Can the community afford to incorporate? Where is the tax base? What are the unique attractions? These issues face all groups looking for the independence that incorporation brings to a community. In a sense, it is similar to the young folk leaving home to secure the blessings of one's own life. The self-support challenge can be formidable.

Foothill Ranch/Portola suffered several years ago when neighboring Lake Forest was permitted to annex areas of commercial developments that were envisioned to be in their sphere of influence. This permission, granted by Orange County officials in charge of city development, enhanced the Lake Forest tax base. In addition, this permission implies that the residential area may be the next to be annexed. The threat of annexation remains for all unincorporated communities.

Laguna Woods

The March 1999 election held in Leisure World achieved incorporation by a 432-vote margin. Laguna Woods, the only gated city of senior citizens in the entire Untied States, has 18,000 residents in a three square mile area and searches for a source of financial support for its people. The loss of Laguna Hills Mall, adjacent to its boundaries, led Laguna Woods to include potential business areas on its northern border as a possible productive tax base source. Laguna Woods restricts its residents to those 55 and older.

Still, the most significant influence in the incorporation movement was expressed clearly by its leaders. "We cannot allow the distant members of the County Board of Supervisors to dictate to us the actions to be taken in regard to the proposed international air terminal on the site of El Toro Marine Base. We are close to it, and our lives are impacted by its locations. For this one gigantic reason, we must have the autonomy that comes with the incorporation of our city."

Leisure World is an excellent example of master planning. The retirement community was founded by Ross Cortese and launched in the 1950s. He and his staff provided, in every way, for the lifestyle of the senior citizens. Still, the planners did not provide for the incorporation of Leisure World — an oversight that could be serious. Leisure World, now Laguna Woods, must wrestle with that major problem of incorporated cities, the raising of revenues needed to provide city services associated with an incorporated city.

(Far left)
The Sand Canyon Reservoir, constructed in 1942, is located between Turtle Rock and Quail Hill.
Josephine Inslee

In 1962 Ross Cortese purchased 3,568 acres of the Lewis Moulton Ranch in Laguna Hills. He built a second Leisure World, which, along with the first one in Seal Beach, is an adult residential community. The sales office opened in 1964 and featured a wide variety of housing and services, all available for those over 55 years of age.
Turville Photography
Photo by Steve Lopushinsky

The Mountain Communities

In the process of determining their own destiny are several smaller political entities. Located inland from the freeways, on Plano Trabuco in the shadow of "Old Saddleback," these canyon lands have exploded in population and have evolved into several distinct communities. Each has attracted a new generation of settlers with somewhat unique perspectives on how they want to live their lives. In October 1988 The *Saddleback Valley News* ran an "Extra on Canyon Culture" describing the various communities, their population makeup and their views on life. The extra sheds much light on the growth of each area and its particular problems both present and future.

Of course, there are the holdouts of Old Trabuco Canyon who maintain that "You don't really live in Trabuco Canyon unless you have a dirt road and a propane tank." These residents claim they enjoy the closeness and mutual support of the old days. Their view of "flatlanders" is that they don't understand the lifestyle: "They rent or buy here, and then they complain about the roosters crowing." The Trabuco residents have two primary concerns: an oft-threatened widening of Live Oak Canyon Road and 200 proposed homes in Saddleback Meadows at El Toro and Live Oak Canyon Roads, both of which they vehemently oppose.

Arden, the Helena Modjeska Historic House and Gardens, is set among a 14.4-acre park of woodland in the foothills of the Santa Ana Mountains. The house is historically significant for its associations with Madame Modjeska, Poland's famous Shakespearean actress, and Stanford White, well-known New York architect. Modjeska lived here from 1888 to 1906. The house and grounds are now being restored as a county historic park. *Photo by Diann Marsh*

Coto de Caza, located in Gobernadora Canyon, is a unique gated community for over 9,000 residents. *First American Title Insurance Co.*

Approximately 2,000 "Trailblazers" live in Las Flores, a community much in tune with environmental issues. Its people plan to leave 600 of its 1,000 acres as open space. Even in the midst of a building boom, Las Flores folks still see deer and coyotes on a regular basis. Still, this post-1994 development faces a dearth of recreational facilities and parking, situations that must be addressed.

Recreation and parking also pose problems for a number of other small communities that comprises the Plano Trabuco. Dove Canyon, Robinson Ranch and Trabuco Highlands must deal with the common problems of population and space requirements and the retention of local control of their space.

After the sale of the Mission Viejo project to Phillip Morris, the O'Neill family interests headed by Anthony Moiso moved up on the Plano Trabuco to build Rancho Santa Margarita, creating a 5,000-acre community for 18,000 family-oriented people. The community achieved cityhood in the November 1999 election. In celebration the first city council meeting was held on New Year's Day. The goal of this multi-use community is to allow the bulk of the residents to live, work and shop in their own community. Rancho Santa Margarita residents enjoy a business-supportive community, and one resident in all probability speaks for the people when he notes, "...like we are in our own little valley. People have the same focus — kids, education and sports."

Home for approximately 9,000 people residing in the rustic luxury of what used to be Gobernadora Canyon is Coto de Caza. This gated community to which residents return after their day at work provides a "hunt club" environment for their recreational amenities. This community and others in these mountains wrestle with the problems of incorporation — affordability and control — and security via police protection.

Growth in Schools

There is little doubt that one of the most evident "explosions" in the south Orange County area can be seen in the schools. Gone are the one- and two-room schools that provided basic education for the kids of small rural communities and the "union" high school districts that provided a secondary education for a small, albeit ever-growing high school population over the years.

The Irvine United School District (IUSD) is an example of the growth experienced by all the south county school districts in the last 30 years. IUSD was formed in June 1972, and by 1973 had six schools and 7,500 students. In 1998, IUSD had 31 schools and 22,500 students with plans to open five new schools in the next five years, including Northwood High. These new schools would provide facilities for approximately 5,200 students. Northwood will join the other three "regular and two "special" high schools in the district. University High was opened in 1971, Irvine in 1978, and Woodbridge in 1980. In the 1980s SELF and San Joaquin were opened for students with special needs. In 1979 Irvine Valley Junior College was opened as part of Saddleback College.

In July 1954 a Civil Air Patrol plane crashed in the bean field near Ocean View (part of Huntington Beach). Thousands of acres of bean fields once covered Irvine land, now covered with tracts of houses.
Old Courthouse Museum

Programs need to go beyond the classroom, such as Irvine's Science/Nature program, "Exploring Ecosystems at Limestone Canyon," for seventh graders. Tours of Heritage Hill Park in Lake Forest and its "Living History" program as well as students spending a morning in a one-room school are examples of educational enrichment experiences available to the suburban school child of today. It is a far cry from the single teacher school of the past to the current approximate pupil/teacher ratio of one to 30 today.

Building programs and financing problems have been eased by the formation of Community Facility Districts (CFD) more widely known as Mello-Roos legislation where purchasers of new homes pay school taxes. The premise is "New growth pays for its share of school needs." Also factored into the facility equation is the meeting of state-mandated class sizes in primary grades.

The Infrastructure: Roads and Airports

In the beginning, there was the Santa Ana Freeway, later called I-5, which came to Santa Ana then moved on to San Diego. The I-5 was followed by I-405, the San Diego Freeway, which swung through the coastal areas then joined with the Santa Ana at the corner of the Irvine and Moulton Ranches on its way to the south. This junction is known as the "El Toro 'Y' " — an infamous point of congestion. For about 20 years, highway building went into a hiatus.

Eventually, the increasing population load in the south county led to a renewed effort to build the San Joaquin Toll Road through the hills behind the beach city. This resulted in the toll road concept. With the concept established, a plethora of toll roads came into existence. The Portola Parkway linked the homes of Rancho Santa Margarita and other hillside communities with the workplaces in the county and into Los Angeles County. The extension of Jamboree Road in Tustin into the Santiago Canyon makes trips to Irvine Park and Lake and the historic Madame Helena Modjeska home much more accessible.

In response to the call for an easier route from the Inland Empire, a location of affordable housing, toll-road Routes 133 and 241 were built. They move from the San Diego Freeway at Sand Canyon over the hills and valleys of the Santa Ana Mountains to connect with The Riverside Freeway, US 91, near Weir Canyon and Green River. Thus the commuter can, at a modest price, move into south county from homes as distant as Elsinore and Temecula. To complete Route 133, another toll road, State Route 261 was developed to funnel workers from the Inland Empire into the Irvine industrial complexes. The eastern leg was opened in October 1998 and the western leg in March 1999.

In January 1999 another segment of the Foothill Transportation Corridor, 241, opened to the Oso Parkway in Mission Viejo. The ultimate plan, scheduled for completion in 2003, is to extend the corridor to a connection with the I-5 Freeway in the San Onofre area at the Orange and San Diego County border. Each section of the corridor calls for resolution of conflicts between transportation advocates and environmentalists; the basic issue is providing corridors, essentially underpasses, for wildlife.

Still the story of transportation remains rather basic: People are continuing to come to the south county, either to live or to work. The infrastructure will follow, making previously inaccessible areas open for all to benefit.

This reproduction of the original entrance to Irvine Regional Park was built as part of the celebration of the park's centennial year in 1997.
Photo by Diann Marsh

El Toro — the Airport

Perhaps the single common bond tying communities and groups in the south county area is the El Toro Marine Base. Viewpoints range widely about what to do with it since its closure in July 1999.

One proposal is to build a major air terminal for freight and passengers, an Orange County International Air Terminal, on the land. The objections range widely, from pure and simple safety to plain old noise pollution. However many, including Los Angeles Mayor Richard Riordan, see the economic benefits of such a plan. But virtually everyone agrees that the name El Toro has to go!

Another proposed plan for use of the facility, when vacated, includes an expanded jail facility. This is also the target of virulent protest.

Most recently, the eight cities of the Anti-Airport Confederation continued to push for its own proposal for the future utilization of the huge facility. In 1998 Measure D was approved by local voters and is known as The Irvine Millennium Plan. This Plan strongly urged that the proposed air terminal and the jail be replaced by the following: "A research and technology facility, an arts district, and an entertainment/sports complex surrounding a central park." It could be assumed, perhaps, that the existing base golf course would remain as a part of the entertainment/sports complex.

Preservation

With the oncoming population rush under way in the south county, there came a period of destruction of anything deemed old in the minds of developers and residents alike. In the late 1950s the Santa Fe Railroad streamlined its operations in the area, and the traditional depots at El Toro and Irvine joined many others along the railroad as outmoded, in-the-way, no longer usable and fit only for the wrecking ball. Almost overnight, the depots were gone.

A similar fate awaited the unique octagonal Community Hall in El Toro. The hall, with its redwood siding, was razed even though a pioneer family reportedly had offered five acres of land for the landmark's relocation.

In the 1970s, however, a new spirit of preservation and restoration swept the area. Historical societies began to form, their major goals being to preserve a glimmer of the past, the heritage of an area. Governmental bodies became more interested and historical commissions were formed to promote the operations of the various groups.

Founded in 1974, the Saddleback Area Historical Society worked for a decade to get Heritage Hill up and going. The next decade was spent in working out the details of the park's operation. Heritage Hill Park initially consisted of two buildings, the original El Toro one-room schoolhouse (1890), and St. George's Episcopal Mission (1891), both representative of the past, which the society deemed worth saving. A county park, it stands as a memorial to a time gone by. Soon after, the Harvey Bennett ranch house (1908) was deeded to the county and the building moved to Heritage Hill. The society hopes to add another building, the pioneer Raymond Prothero, Sr. family home to those already on display. Without the help of government, private businesses, and interested people over many years, these valuable assets would not be here for all to enjoy.

(Far right) The Craftsman-style Bennett ranch house, originally located at 2nd Street and Cherry Avenue in El Toro, was moved to Heritage Hill in the 1970s. Built in 1908 by prominent local ranchers Harvey and Frances Bennett, it has been restored as a house museum to allow the public to see how a typical south county farm family lived.
Photo by Diann Marsh

The Serrano Adobe, the centerpiece of Heritage Hill Heritage Park in El Toro, was built about 1863 by Don Jose Serrano. It was the second of five adobes built on his 10,688-acre rancho. It is now a California State Landmark.
Photo by Diann Marsh

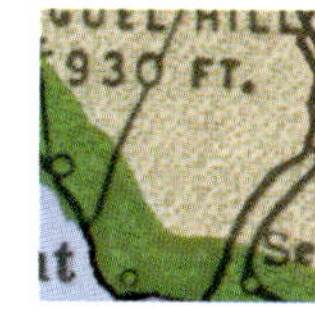

In Irvine, preservationists move forward with plans to make a historical museum site of the old Irvine home ranch. Tustin's people have their eye on the acquisition of one of the two gigantic hangars, reportedly the largest wooden buildings in the United States. Located in the Irvine-Tustin boundary area, this unique and historic building may be the home of the Tustin Area Historical Museum now that the Marine Corps helicopters have departed.

The preservation movement remains strong. A truism supported by the City of Lake Forest and used on T-shirts for incorporation day said it best: "Remember the past; prepare for the future!" Every year special programs and events are held to support history and preservation, including Acorn Day in O'Neill Park, Victorian Christmas at Heritage Hill and special days at the Modjeska House. The job is ongoing.

Retaining and displaying aspects of an area's past culture take on a variety of forms — art being one of them. Joan Irvine Smith, who sponsored and funded the Irvine Museum in large part by herself, wrote, "...environment, especially land and water, nurtured and sustained a rare quality of life." Paintings of a century ago illustrate this quality. The Irvine Museum is open to the public, utilized extensively by school groups, and is a collection of California landscapes of the Impressionist period dating from the 1890s through the 1930s. The collection does much to retain a spirit of the past. Without a doubt, the museum of art, along with other elements of parks, exhibits and programs, combine to provide a launching pad for students to move forward in all areas of man's story, past, present and future.

In 1884 Dwight Whiting purchased the Serrano Adobe and most of the old rancho. His son, George Whiting, improved the adobe in 1932 by adding a dining room, master bedroom and kitchen. The parlor shown here was part of the original adobe.
County of Orange

The Foothill Ranch subdivision, located northeast of Lake Forest next to the Whiting Ranch Wilderness Park, is one of several groups of homes in Saddleback Valley.
Turville Photography
Photo by Steve Lopushinsky

(Far left)
The Irvine Blacksmith Shop served the farmers of the Irvine Ranch from the time it was built in 1908 until the 1980s. Part of the Old Town Irvine Project in East Irvine, the building is now a restaurant and retains much of its original rustic character.
Photo by Diann Marsh

The stage building at Irvine Park is one of a complex of Craftsman-style buildings that have been restored and are on the National Register of Historic Places.
Photo by Diann Marsh

BIOGRAPHIES OF WRITERS

JOHN L. SORENSON

Editor and Writer

John Sorenson's father was a sailor and professional yachtsman who spent his life on the sea. John's interest in history stems from the stories his father told him of growing up in pre-World War I Norway, a world far removed from today, and then of his tales at sea. History and adventure came alive in John's household in San Pedro where he was born and raised.

His first loves are naval architecture and history, stemming from the days he sailed with his father. He has come to admire the history of Orange County for its dramatic growth over time. Each stage of growth has its own story to tell.

John has his degree in economics from UCLA and was employed in the local computer industry. He then moved on to aerospace as a computer programmer. He has belonged to the Orange County Historical Society for 24 years and has been a board member for the last five years. He recently joined the Santa Ana Historical Preservation Society to further pursue his interest in historic homes. His previous writing efforts include an article about naval ballistics and armor penetration formulas, a series of articles condensed from the works of Terry Stephenson for the OCHS *Courier*, and a 1940 map restoration and information project.

DIANN MARSH

Photo Editor and Writer

Diann Marsh has loved history and historic buildings since she was a child. She and her husband, Robert, recently moved from an 1883 restored home in Santa Ana to Galena, Illinois, where they bought another Victorian house to restore. Diann and Robert have seven grown children and 10 grandchildren.

An avid preservationist, Diann has served on the boards of several historical organizations including the Historic French Park Association, Santa Ana Historical Preservation Society and the Orange County Historic Commission.

Her specialty is historical architecture. She has conducted architectural surveys in 15 cities and prepared the applications to place more than 400 buildings on the National Register of Historic Places, and she has written architectural style guides for several cities.

In addition to her historical research and writing, Diann draws detailed pen and ink illustrations and paints in watercolor and mixed media. It's no surprise that her favorite subjects are Victorian homes.

Diann has written several books and articles on historic preservation and architecture and authored *Santa Ana: An Illustrated History, Corona: The Circle City* and *Huntington Beach: The Gem of the South Coast.*

STEVE DONALDSON

Steve Donaldson was raised and educated in Southern California. Transportation has been both avocation and vocation for Steve, including summer employment in railroad operations, a college education in transportation management and administration, and an early career in petroleum transport. Now retired in the San Francisco Bay Area, Steve has authored several articles and two books on Orange County railroads.

NORA HORN

Nora Horn is a lifelong resident of Los Angelés with a longtime interest in history and the arts. She earned her bachelor's degree in history from the University of California, Los Angeles. Her professional portfolio includes many years as a promotional writer for retail, fashion, architectural and corporate clients. She is a free-lance writer who has been a regular contributor to Heritage Media since 1998. She lives with her husband and son in the Silver Lake neighborhood of Los Angeles.

JOE OSTERMAN

Joe Osterman has had a lifelong passion for California history. He was born in Santa Ana in 1921 and spent his childhood in El Toro, where his father ran the general store. After earning a bachelor's degree in history and his teaching credentials from USC, he taught history, English, basketball and golf at El Rancho High School from 1952 until his retirement in 1991. He is the author of three books and numerous articles and essays that deal with the "old" El Toro of the first half of the 20th century. He lives with his wife, Edra, in Whittier.

DORIS I. WALKER

Doris I. Walker is the author of several books, including *Home Port for Romance*, the history of Dana Point and Capistrano Bay, and *Sections of Orange*, the official Orange County centennial history. Walker has earned nearly 100 communications awards, including Best Historical Book and Best Historical Articles from the National Federation of Press Women. She teaches California history classes for adults, is an appointee to the Orange County Historical Commission and is listed in the Millennium Edition of *Who's Who in the World*.

JOHN WESTCOTT

John Westcott has been a reporter for the *Orange County Register* for 18 years and currently writes about local history for the newspaper's Millennium Project. In 1990 he authored the book, *Anaheim, City of Dreams*. He has a bachelor's degree in history from the University of California, Riverside, and a master's degree in journalism from the University of California, Berkeley.

TOBY YOUNG

Toby Young has been an Orange Countian since 1982 and makes her home in an Old Towne Orange 1908 house. She has been a writer for Heritage Media Corp. since 1996, writing business profiles for books on the cities of Orange, Huntington Beach, Newport Beach, Corona and Ontario. She also writes life stories for individuals and gives speeches about the importance of life stories in maintaining family histories.

BOB ZIEBELL

Bob Ziebell is a journalist and author who continues to work as an editor with Orange County Register's community newspapers. He wrote *An Anniversary Album*, a 75th anniversary publication of the *Daily Star Progress*, and *Fullerton*, a pictorial history produced under the auspices of the Fullerton Museum Center.

BUILDING A GREATER ORANGE COUNTY

Orange County electricians, interior designers, and real estate development and construction industries shape tomorrow's skyline, providing and improving working and living space for area residents.

Turville Photography
Photo by Steve Lopushinsky

CB RICHARD ELLIS

CB Richard Ellis is the leading diversified commercial real estate services firm in the world. The company has a rich history spanning back to the beginning of the century, when the company's roots sprang from the debris of the 1906 San Francisco earthquake. In 1906, five months after the great quake laid waste to large portions of the city, Colbert Coldwell and two associates borrowed $10,000 to capitalize a venture into the real estate brokerage business and used their new enterprise to help in the process of rebuilding the city.

Beginning in the 1920s the company began establishing offices in Southern California in response to burgeoning demand. By the 1960s Orange County became a viable location for a company office. During the decade from 1951 to 1961, Orange County's population had trebled to 783,000, with continued

THE "NEW" CB RICHARD ELLIS IS CONSIDERED THE LARGEST VERTICALLY INTEGRATED COMMERCIAL REAL ESTATE SERVICES FIRM IN THE WORLD.

rapid growth predicted for the balance of the decade. The Irvine Company, the major landholder in Orange County, appointed the company as its commercial property leasing agent. The population boom, coupled with The Irvine Company appointment, provided the justification for an office to be situated in Orange County. John Parker, then manager of the company's Wilshire office, was selected to manage the new office.

The first Orange County office opened in Santa Ana in 1961. The following year, in 1962, the office was moved to Newport Beach with a staff of 18. The Newport Beach Office became the 17th location for the company in 15 cities spanning California and Arizona. The office was situated at the corner of MacArthur Boulevard and Pacific Coast Highway, adjacent to what is today the Newport Beach main public library. Behind its parking lot at the rear of the building was a wire fence, beyond which was only rangeland and Irvine cattle.

The CB Richard Ellis Anaheim office
Photo by David Melton © 1999

In 1989 the commercial real estate group split from the residential group to form a separate company, CB Commercial Real Estate Group. In November of 1996 CB Commercial completed an initial public offering and now trades on the New York stock exchange under the symbol CBG.

In August 1997 CB Commercial merged with the Newport Beach-based property and asset-management giant, Koll Real Estate Services. CB Richard Ellis was created in 1998 when REI Limited, the holding company for all Richard Ellis operations outside of the United Kingdom was acquired. In July 1998 CB Richard Ellis acquired London-based Hillier Parker May & Rowden. In the United Kingdom, CB Richard Ellis now operates as CB Hillier Parker. As a result of these acquisitions, the "new" CB Richard Ellis is considered the largest vertically integrated commercial real estate services firm in the world, with annual revenues of over $1 billion in 1998. These strategic moves have created a company which can offer the "one-stop-shopping" service that clients now demand.

Commercial real estate is driven by successful personal and business relationships. CB Richard Ellis takes that notion a step further. It becomes its client's partner. Through seamless working relationships

The CB Richard Ellis Newport Beach office on Jamboree Road

and a thorough understanding of their objectives, it helps clients capture the greater market opportunities. The focus is no longer on closing the transaction. Instead, it is on the synergies gained

Whether a client has one property or a portfolio of multinational locations, CB Richard Ellis' offerings scale to meet individual client needs.

by working collaboratively to foresee what lies ahead and what course to follow. The company's focus is on the results that work best.

With offices in cities around the world, CB Richard Ellis combines global reach with localized knowledge. Whether a client just has one property or a portfolio of multinational locations, the company's offerings scale to meet individual client needs. No matter how complex that need may be, CB Richard Ellis provides a custom mix of products and services that deliver significant, measurable returns.

The company's proprietary data network gives CB Richard Ellis instant access to the local and global market knowledge that its clients need. It also enables the company to build cross-functional teams to work collaboratively on projects. With real-time access to state-of-the-art information systems, the company's

professionals are empowered to support clients in achieving their own business goals.

Today, CB Richard Ellis has nearly 10,000 employees worldwide. CB Richard Ellis serves real estate owners, investors and occupiers through more than 230 principal offices in more than 30 countries. CB Richard Ellis currently has two offices in

In addition to brokerage services, the Orange County offices provide property management, corporate services, investment banking, investment management, capital markets, appraisal/valuation, research and consulting.

Orange County. The Newport Beach office is located in a mid-rise building at the intersection of Jamboree and Bristol, overlooking Newport Beach's scenic back bay. The Anaheim office has recently relocated to a new mid-rise building at the intersection of Katella and Howell and is adjacent to the Edison International Field and The Anaheim Pond.

CB Richard Ellis offers a comprehensive array of commercial real estate services, and specializes in meeting all the commercial real estate needs of its clients. In addition to brokerage services, the Orange County offices provide property management, corporate services, investment banking, investment management, capital markets, appraisal/valuation, research and consulting.

DPS PLASTERING, INC.

Behind the DPS shield stands an almost 20-year commitment to quality and tradition. DPS Plastering, Inc. in Santa Ana, has evolved since its founding in 1980 from a traditional plastering company to one that utilizes the latest technology. This evolution has closely mirrored what has been happening to Orange County over the years. What was once the remnant of a Spanish-influenced farming and ranching region has become not only a population mecca, but a hotbed of technology as well.

DPS has helped the look of Orange County evolve from its historic mission or ranch style into a contemporary community ready to enter the new millennium. When David Schutte first started the company, he relied on skills learned from his time spent as both an apprentice and journeyman with various large plastering contractors. One of his early jobs included a historical restoration of the First Christian Church in San Juan Capistrano. DPS used finishes that were applied back in the mid-1900s and re-created arch designs to complete the restoration. DPS used systems, designs and finishes that were originally applied to the buildings. Other early projects included the *Kelley Blue Book* building in Irvine and the Coto de Casa Club House in Coto de Casa.

The recession of the 1980s was tough for the country and for DPS; but even though growth was slow, it was steady. The company relied on its reputation for high-quality work to increase its business. And as the company grew, it looked for bigger and better jobs. During this time, it took on several public works projects, including the Costa Mesa and Los Aliso water districts.

The Foothill Ranch Regal Theater work-in-progress demonstrates a combination of conventional lath and plaster with foam cornice and balustrade system.

The historic building style that is indicative of Orange County easily lent itself to DPS's style of plastering. The look of traditional plaster is still very popular in the Southland, and the company continues to do jobs that maintain the historic appearance. But an influx of technology-based companies has led to a general modernization of the area. As the style changed, DPS diversified its skills to include new methods. "Working on the old-style buildings vs. newer, more modern buildings is like night and day. The work is completely different, so we need to maintain very diverse abilities," explains Schutte.

While the company works on mostly large, commercial projects, it also does some work for the residential market. The company has worked on a variety of building types:

Community Christian Church in San Juan Capistrano is a 12-year-old historical restoration that highlights balanced detail work and shows off the simplicity and authenticity of the San Juan Capistrano style.

- Historical restorations: San Juan Church and the Whittier Gymnasium
- Churches: Capistrano Christian Church and St. Timothy's, Fr Solano R.S.M.
- Institutional: Tustin Medical Center, Fountain Valley Library and San Clemente Hospital
- Clubhouses: Mission Viejo, Tustin Ranch and Coyote Hills
- Hotels: Candlewood, Extended Stay America and Westminster Inn
- Residential: Hunter's Ridge, Pelican Point and Ritz Cove
- Celebrity Houses: Barry Bonds, Michael Chang and Lenny Dykstra
- Restaurants: Spago, Wolfgang Puck and Macaroni Grill
- Schools: Irvine Valley, Montessori Irvine and Saddleback Valley
- Retail: Edwards Cinemas, The Home Depot, Walgreens and Wal-Mart, Stater Brothers, Vons

In 1995 DPS added a new technology to its repertoire — external insulation foam systems (EIFS). This system involves applying an acrylic coating over foam for external walls. EIFS is more flexible, which allows buildings using this system to better withstand earthquakes. It includes expansion joints to safeguard against earth movement, sonic activity and other stresses. It also provides more insulation and greater longevity. And since the color is integral to the coating, the color is more consistent than with standard plaster.

In general, when DPS is working on an older-looking building, it utilizes standard plastering techniques. But as EIFS becomes more popular, more uses are being found for it. It is beginning to be used on historical restoration work as well. The foam is being shaped into traditional forms that simulate historical building profiles. Since EIFS is a fairly new technology, DPS is working with architects, designers and others in the industry to ensure the system is used to its fullest potential and creates the most value for the building industry.

In addition to the company's concern for providing the best possible product to clients, it is also concerned about its employees. The company has been working with Cal-OSHA, other general contractors and scaffolding contractors to continually develop and implement safety programs. DPS has developed its own fall-prevention program, created a daily job-safety checklist and organized joint safety meetings with general contractors.

DPS is also concerned about and involved in its community. The company has sponsored events at a children's museum, sponsors Christian international aid organizations and contributes to the Veterans of Foreign Wars.

The 21st century inspires Dave Schutte. He believes that advanced technology and communications, cutting-edge safety programs and automation will be key for companies to continue to prosper. This belief motivates him to keep his company as contemporary as possible. DPS has fully computerized most functions — everything from correspondence to plans to estimating.

DPS has earned a reputation for quality. This reputation has fueled demand for its services throughout the state. In fact, demand for its services have come from as far away as Sacramento and San Francisco, where it has worked on churches and restaurants. DPS is currently considering opening an office in that area.

In the future, DPS plans to pursue bigger and better jobs and further develop the new EIFS technology. The company is constantly trying to use the latest technology to its fullest potential and hopes to find ways to even better maximize the system.

The modern lines of the Tustin Ranch Club House show the contemporary side of DPS' work.

GLENN R. JOHNSON SCALE MODELS

With some glue, plastic, paint, tools and hard work, Glenn R. Johnson built a childhood hobby into a career. Johnson received his first model kit when he was about 9 years old, and was hooked. He built cars, then airplanes. He read model-building magazines to learn all he could. Eventually he built an entire model town.

A miniature version of John Wayne Airport is among the notable Orange County landmarks GRJ Scale Models has built.

After graduating from high school, he enrolled as an architecture student at Fullerton College. When an assignment required the class to build a model of one of their designs, the other students groaned; Johnson couldn't wait. A competition was set up among the entries, with a group of local architects serving as judges. Johnson's model won hands-down. Soon after, he saw an advertisement for a model shop in Santa Monica. He visited the shop and got a part-time job there. "It was great. I could actually make money building models," says Johnson. "And it was the best education I could have gotten."

He started work at age 19 creating maps and other architectural artwork. But when his employer went out of business two years later, he rented a small workspace in Orange and started his own business doing what he had always wanted to do: build models.

In the early days of Glenn R. Johnson Scale Models, Johnson operated pretty much on his own, his mother pitching in with the bookkeeping and his father occasionally helping build models on weekends. When Johnson got really busy with building projects, he would hire people temporarily. About 10 years after starting the company he hired his first permanent, full-time employee. Now a thriving corporation with 25 full-time employees, Glenn R. Johnson Scale Models may be the largest model shop in Southern California.

When the company was contracted to make a model that was too big to fit in the original Chapman facility, GRJ Scale Models moved to a 1,200-square-foot space on Collins. As the company kept growing, it continued renting more workspace in the area. In 1979 the company purchased the 6,000-square-foot facility on Chapman where it presently resides.

The artists at Glenn R. Johnson Scale Models created the entire Newport Beach coast in miniature — from topographically correct polyurethane foam mountains to tiny filter foam trees and rippled Plexiglas water.

GRJ's scale model of the Irvine Spectrum is accurate in every respect — right down to the storefront signs and palm trees.

The company works on 25 to 30 projects at a time, in various stages of development. The majority of the work comes from architectural and trade show firms. The firms supply auto-CAD drawings, which Johnson converts to more simplified shop drawings that the company's artists will use for their models. A laser cutter uses a computerized program that allows it to cut any kind of shape with a laser beam.

Then comes the fascinating task of building, painting and detailing each miniature creation. The company's 22 artists are highly specialized — a few build topographic maps, one operates the topographical cutting machinery, several artists' sole job is to make miniature trees and the others are involved in various levels of building and detailing the models. Some trees are made of air filter foam; others are prefabricated cast metal stems with steel wool added. The buildings are made of Plexiglas with laser-printed windows and detailing. Water is rippled Plexiglas (like the kind used in shower doors) painted varying shades of blue to create the illusion of depth. The company buys tiny cars and people by the hundreds.

Johnson has traditionally worked 80 hours a week or more, and is proud of his hands-on role. "I work in the shop every day. To me that's the way a business should be, because most people start a business because they do something really well. Pretty soon, they're in the office doing all the paperwork, trying to hire someone to do the job well."

The company has built a vast variety of models including the Los Angeles International Airport Air Traffic Control Tower, the John Wayne Airport Terminal Building, Childrens Hospital of Orange County, the World Trade Center in Long Beach, the Irvine Spectrum Entertainment Center and the Ritz-Carlton in Naples, Florida — all just inches high. GRJ has even built the Lake Elsinore Baseball Park and the entire Newport Coast. The artists have built numerous models of housing developments for use by real estate sales offices. They have built a Tyrannosaurus Rex and an MRI machine for trade shows, and have created models for courtroom re-enactments. And when a client asked for half of a real working toilet, Johnson found a saw that could cut one in two. The success of the business, says Johnson, has been their willingness to please clients and take on any project, no matter how unusual. "I never say no," he explains. The company also provides service, relocation and repair of the models as clients request.

One of the most important jobs came in the early 1990s, just when the company was reeling from the effects of the recession. That's when GRJ Scale Models was asked to build the interior of Disney Concert Hall. Each audience member in the stunning model is individually detailed, and at 10 x 15 x 12 feet high, it is the largest model the company has created.

GRJ Scale Models makes it a point to stay at the forefront of technology. The company is very proud of a new lighting technique it has pioneered. The artists vacuum-form a piece of clear plastic to the topographical model so the land is actually made of a clear plastic shell. Then they paint it with translucent colors. "It looks like a regular topo map until you turn the lights on under it," says Johnson. With breathtaking results, the model actually lights up from below, allowing different areas of the map to be spotlighted and viewed as needed. Ever the innovator, the company is always looking for ways to use its old models. GRJ recently donated some old models to the fire department for use as training props.

Two of the company's biggest developments have been the arrival of Johnson's daughters, Heather and Heidi. Heidi has served as office manager since the mid-1990s; Heather joined the company as its first director of marketing in 1999.

As the company looks toward the future, it plans to maintain its edge by keeping up with technology and going out of its way to please clients. Johnson is pleased with the current staff of artists and plans to keep scaling back his own hectic schedule to a modest 60 hours a week. That will give him time to spend with his family and pursue his other hobby — collecting and restoring his collection of classic cars — full-sized ones.

ICI DEVELOPMENT COMPANY

When fresh landscaping, state-of-the-art architecture and vital new retail shops replace a run-down shopping center, it provides more than a cosmetic change to the property. It brings a social, commercial and fiscal rebirth to a city and its surrounding community. ICI Development Company has made this kind of transformation its mission for the past two decades. The fact that ICI has remained so successful amid the ups and downs of the real estate development industry stems from the company's extraordinarily strong leadership and unique way of doing business.

It all started in 1977 when R. Scott Bell began his career as a realtor with Grubb & Ellis, one of the largest commercial real estate firms in the country. A graduate of California State University, Fresno and MBA fellow at the University of Santa Clara, Bell was honored as Grubb & Ellis' Rookie of the Year. Even bigger accomplishments would soon be in store.

Bell's vision of creating a regional development firm was realized when he met Leo David of Leo's Stereo in 1980. Amid the booming real estate market of the time, the two men forged a partnership that formed the strong cornerstone of ICI. David capitalized ICI in 1981. In 1984, Dan Wojkowski, a highly successful banker at Union Bank, joined the firm as chief financial officer. Bell, David and Wojkowski all remain principals of ICI today.

ICI's strong capital foundation provided a powerful advantage over leveraged developers, many of which have long since gone out of business. But money wasn't the only factor that set the new company apart. The firm based its dealings on a steadfast corporate philosophy: on any project, the most important thing to be built is consensus. This philosophy earned ICI its strong reputation for forging successful partnerships between the developer, the city and the surrounding community. ICI's projects involve such varied details as acquiring individual parcels, renegotiating leases, signing on tenants, and designing and building the site. ICI works with a pool of highly experienced architects and contractors to provide the right design for each project. Rather than a more typical "one-size-fits-all" approach to development, ICI is convinced that its more individualized design-build process better serves the needs of its customers and the community.

R. Scott Bell

"There are two things that set ICI apart," according to Bell. "One, we are very entrepreneurial, which means being innovative and highly responsive. That's something we hear often from the cities and the communities we work with. Two, most of our competitors have to partner with a Real Estate Investment Trust (REIT) or other investors. We don't. Not only are we well capitalized, but on most projects, we're working with our own money and have a very substantial credit line."

The company quickly began making a name for itself in Orange County by converting unprofitable, often dilapidated community problems into well-designed, thriving retail centers and sales tax generators for those cities. In fact ICI has developed an impressive list of 51 retail centers throughout California — from Orange County to Modesto.

One of ICI's most notable achievements is its transformation of Santa Ana's Bristol Marketplace. Originally occupied by the 350,000-square-foot Honor Plaza Shopping Center, what was once Orange County's largest shopping center had deteriorated badly by the 1980s. ICI acquired the property in 1990 and began transforming the site into a first-class retail center featuring a HomeBase, Montgomery Ward, Ralphs and Sav-On Drugs. But the change to the property and the community didn't stop there. In 1994 ICI made an innovative proposal to the Santa Ana Unified School District, suggesting they make use of California's new "Space Saver" school program,

(Far left)
Leo David

Dan Wojkowski

which encourages schools to partner with commercial ventures in providing new facilities. It was a radical change, but the proposal was so strong the city agreed. The school that now shares the Bristol Marketplace site became one of the first Space Saver campuses in the state.

Similarly ICI's development of the Harbor Center in Costa Mesa greatly benefited that community. What had been the city's largest retail center when it opened in the 1950s had a high vacancy rate by the 1970s and had a seldom-used rear parking lot that was an eyesore during the day and a crime-ridden nuisance after dark. Although the city and numerous other developers had made efforts to acquire the site, none of the attempts had succeeded. ICI acquired ownership of the entire site in 1999 and signed on such high-profile tenants as Home Depot, Albertson's and T.J. Maxx, putting this area on its way to becoming a state-of-the-art center for local residents and shoppers from across the county, as well as a significant tax generator for the city of Costa Mesa.

ICI's other successful projects include Santa Ana's Centre on Seventeenth, Modesto Scenic Place and Modesto Central Valley Plaza, Platt Village in West Hills and Brea Union Plaza.

Like many other industries, the real estate business has been affected by technological changes. The Internet now allows access to virtually all the pertinent information about a proposed project — from market demographics to community history to pertinent local agencies and annual average rainfall. While the technological advancements have offered ICI easy access to facts, they ironically make it more challenging to maintain a competitive edge, as everyone has access to the same data. Not surprisingly, ICI easily rose to the challenge.

ICI's ability to keep up with technological advancements is matched by its ability to stay at the forefront of environmental and community factors that affect business. In an industry in which issues such as traffic and noise impacts have become critical factors in a project's approval and success, ICI has earned a reputation for forging partnerships between all parties involved.

Although ICI works throughout the state, it remains firmly rooted in Orange County. "Orange County is not only a wonderful place to do business, it's our home," says Bell. He is active in a number of community and charitable organizations, from AYSO soccer to serving on the board of directors of the Salvation Army of Orange County.

Twenty years after its inception, ICI has no plans of slowing down. Committed to its mission of forging strong relationships and creating state-of-the-art retail centers, ICI enjoys an unmatched reputation as it continues to look toward its future successes — no doubt many communities will find new life and increased revenues as a result.

REEL LUMBER SERVICE

Southern California contractors, cabinetmakers and fine craftsmen seeking quality hardwood count on Reel Lumber Service to fulfill their needs. Family-owned and -operated since 1932, the Anaheim-based company offers Orange County's largest selection of domestic and exotic hardwoods, plywood, moldings such as baseboards and crowns, as well as custom milling.

The Reel family, whose roots go back as far as the Revolutionary War, includes a spy for the Colonies deported to Australia by the British, a Nebraska state senator, a provisioner who sold corn to the Confederates before joining the Union army and several suffragettes. In 1928 company founder E.G. Reel moved from Nebraska to Southern California, where he worked for a hardwood lumber company. When the Depression forced that company to declare bankruptcy, Reel went into business for himself. As credit manager, he knew which customers paid their accounts promptly and was able to secure their business. He opened Reel Lumber on Slauson in Los Angeles and within a year moved to a larger location in east Los Angeles on 63rd and Hooper. At the time, Orange County consisted of a few small towns and a lot of open space.

E.G. operated Reel Lumber Service as a wholesale brokerage, taking orders from customers and buying materials on a need-to-order basis. The yard stocked only limited amounts of hardwood lumber. E.G. — who believed that wearing a tie was a symbol of success and always wore one, even while cutting wood — never advertised, relying on word-of-mouth to fuel his company's expansion. Los Angeles-area movie studios such as Paramount and Columbia were among his early clients.

By World War II Reel Lumber was well established. E.G.'s sons joined him in the company — Donald in 1949 and Gilbert in 1950. Business remained steady during Los Angeles' construction-boom years, when the company employed between 12 and 20 people and attracted a constant flow of customers seeking quality hardwood. Still a wholesaler, Reel Lumber sold to manufacturers, furniture builders, stores and retail hardwood outlets, which would resaw and resurface the wood before selling it.

E.G. passed away in 1968, and his sons took over the business at that time. In an unusual move for a wholesaler, they established a small will-call area. If someone wanted oak for

Reel Lumber Service's two-acre Anaheim yard stocks more than one million board feet of domestic and foreign hardwoods.

cabinets or furniture, for example, an employee would pull out a load of lumber and let the customer personally pick through the lumber. This proved important because the quality, color and wood grain of each piece varies. Hardwoods are used in exposed areas of houses, so it's important for the pieces to conform. Allowing clients to select their own wood gave Reel Lumber Service a definite edge over its competitors.

When fire destroyed the Los Angeles yard in 1976, Reel Lumber Service relocated to East Santa Ana Street, near downtown Anaheim. Orange County was experiencing tremendous growth in new-home construction, and to take advantage of the expanding market, Reel Lumber increased the number of hardwood species it carried and added hardwood plywood and moldings. The company also turned a small area next to the mill into a will-call building where customers could buy finished lumber as they would at a retail lumberyard.

The company grew rapidly. In 1982 Don and Gil opened a mill on the property that offered full-service milling for Reel Lumber Service customers as well as other lumberyards throughout Southern California. Inventory expanded to include hardwood moldings such as baseboards, crowns, chair rails and plant-ons in a variety of woods and designs. In 1986 the company acquired an established lumber outlet on Chicago Avenue in Riverside, California, and when will-call outgrew its space at the mill in 1989, it was moved into an 18,000-square-foot facility on N. Kraemer Boulevard in Anaheim.

Today the company stocks over one million board feet of domestic and foreign hardwoods and 400 different moldings, and it maintains a fleet of trucks that make deliveries anywhere in Southern California. It can provide any hardwood from oak, cherry and maple to exotics such as jelutong and cocobolo. The computerized mill can custom-run almost any detail according to the customer's drawing. In addition, the Riverside store caters to wood carvers, offering space to groups that wish to hold classes, and stocks woodworking tools, books, and a complete line of stains and finishes.

This family business continues to thrive as a third generation emerges. E.G.'s granddaughter, Shirley Reel, heads the company as CEO; her husband Jim Cadwell and her sister Linda and brother-in-law Don Clark are also integral parts of the company. Don and Gil, though semiretired, still drop in regularly to offer advice.

Shirley Reel attributes the company's continued success to the excellence of its employees. Between 60 and 80 people work at the company's various locations. The business of hardwood lumber is complex, as hardwood is managed by a different system of measurement and grading than other woods. Employees must be trained entirely on the job. Jim Cadwell estimates that it takes two years for each new hire to fully understand the business. He considers all employees as highly trained professionals.

The demand for quality hardwood products in Orange County remains constant year-round as contractors create new communities and homeowners upgrade their homes. Business continues to expand, and the family knows that E.G.'s legacy of Reel Lumber Service will continue through the generations to come.

The 18,000-square-foot Kraemer Boulevard will-call building for Anaheim's Reel Lumber Service

STANDARD PACIFIC

Drive through Orange County, and you'll pass mile after mile of beautiful homes in idyllic, planned neighborhoods and lush, gated communities. Chances are many of these homes you've admired were built by a single company — Standard Pacific. For more than 30 years, Standard Pacific has been a leader in the homebuilding industry, both in Southern California and throughout the southwest. Despite the tremendous changes in the housing industry over the past four decades, Standard Pacific has maintained a strong stable presence and has retained a position of industry leadership.

In the early days of the company, Standard Pacific established solid relationships with land developers like The Irvine Company, placing itself in a leadership position as real estate was being developed. The company kept a sharp focus, making a commitment to building private residences rather than branching into the commercial or public domain. The strategy paid off. Standard Pacific enjoyed early success and went public, its shares first being traded on the New York Stock Exchange in 1977.

Standard Pacific began to expand once it established a solid footing in Orange County. The company opened offices in Northern California and San Diego in 1971 and in Ventura in 1972. It expanded into Texas in 1978, opening an office in Houston. Satellites in Dallas and Austin opened in 1981 and 1992 respectively. The late 1990s saw Standard Pacific expanding into the thriving Phoenix, Arizona area.

Standard Pacific has a tradition of excellence in choosing the finest locations for homes that blend the warmth of day-to-day family living with grand-scale design and appointments. *©1998 Jeffrey Aron Photography*

As Standard Pacific has expanded, the company has created a decentralized operating structure. Local management teams in each of the company's markets maintain strong, long-term relationships that provide access to land and other resources critical to sustained success. With constant communication among local team members and with design consultants, subcontractors and homebuyers, Standard Pacific is able to deliver a top-quality product. An uncompromising inspection process maintains quality control at every level and at every stage of construction.

Dedication to customer satisfaction is a matter of company pride and personal integrity.

Standard Pacific builds a wide variety of housing, ranging from single family homes ideal for young and growing families to spacious estate residences. Each community location is specifically selected for its lifestyle advantages, including proximity to schools, recreation, shopping and employment — all the essentials for family-oriented living.

The architectural design of the homes tends to be in keeping with current styles, yet of a timeless quality. Standard Pacific offers the most modern of amenities and uses the most updated, refined designs and construction methods. It strives to use the highest-quality building materials and craftsmanship available. The fact that many Standard Pacific employees live in homes created by the company is a testimonial to the high quality of construction each employee aims for.

Currently employing a staff of 693 home-building professionals, Standard Pacific has constructed more than 36,000 homes over the years and is one of the nation's largest and most successful publicly owned home-building companies. In 1998 Standard Pacific reached record annual revenues of nearly $760 million, up $175 million from 1997. The company has garnered many industry honors for its community planning, product design, marketing and advertising efforts.

Recent years have seen strong company growth. In 1998 Standard Pacific acquired a seasoned management team and an inventory of existing projects to establish a division in Phoenix, Arizona. As an extension of its homebuilding activities, the company has also established a mortgage company to provide home loans for its homebuyers.

Despite its strong and wide-ranging presence in the industry, Standard Pacific maintains the atmosphere of a small company dedicated to its people. In fact, the company credits its success to its employees and often promotes from within. Prospective staff members are attracted by the stability and longevity of its employment record and the stability of company itself; many Standard Pacific employees have been with the company for several years.

Like the solid, timeless quality of its housing designs, Standard Pacific favors a steadfast, traditional approach to company management as well as community outreach. The company believes in being active and supportive in the community it serves.

As Standard Pacific looks toward the future, it is poised to embark on a number of exciting new building projects in Northern and Southern California, Texas and the Phoenix metro area. Whether a moderately priced home or a luxury estate, each new Standard Pacific home, like the thousands that preceded it, will be built in the most desirable locations with the same solid quality and timeless style that have made Standard Pacific a known and respected name in the homebuilding industry.

Through the years, families can feel the special difference in a Standard Pacific home.

Attention to detail is the key to exquisite architecture and high-quality construction.

T&B PLANNING CONSULTANTS, INC.

T&B Principals (seated left to right) James Greco, Doug Boyd, Barry Burnell, (standing left to right) Firouz Ghaboussi and Russ Garcia draw on complementary yet varied talents and more than 95 years of combined experience.

A journey of a thousand miles begins with a single step. If that first step, however, is just a few degrees off course, the traveler can end up miles from the intended destination.

Successful land development is no exception to this rule. Miscalculations in the beginning of a project can result in huge errors only discovered later, when correcting them is very costly and difficult. The use of an expert land planner from the outset is crucial. Vibrant communities result from a planning consultant's high-quality, front-end work.

One premier planning firm esteemed for its high quality is T&B Planning Consultants. The firm, founded in 1974 by Lou Turrini and Bob Brink, originally designed and processed the land where many Orange County residents now live, work, play and shop. Many of T&B's early designs have become dynamic Orange County and Southern California communities. A vast portion of Laguna Niguel arose from T&B's Colinas de Capistrano project. The Irvine Ranch communities of Westpark, Northwood and Northpark resulted in part from the company's efforts. Today, T&B is the lead design, documentation and processing firm for the new community of Talega in San Clemente, very likely one of the last major planned communities in Orange County.

T&B serves all of Southern California — and other areas of the western United States — from offices in San Diego and Santa Ana. The nationally renowned company is recognized for its multidisciplinary approach to planning, design and environmental analysis. As a pure planning firm, T&B provides a wide range of services related to producing "developable" projects. These services include design, site evaluation, master planning, land planning, "urban-infill" and "transit-oriented" design, planning and environmental documentation and processing.

The firm's five owner/principals — Doug Boyd, Barry Burnell, James Greco, Firouz Ghaboussi and Russ Garcia — draw on more than 95 years of combined professional experience. Their varied but complementary backgrounds make the company as a whole stronger. All five have worked as a team at T&B for most of their planning careers, bringing a unique continuity to the firm's vision and creative energy. This enduring relationship enhances the ability of these talented professionals to tap all of their experiences effectively. Through their efforts, T&B's projects are consistently accepted by approving agencies, communities and the marketplace.

While widely acclaimed for its role as a traditional planning consultant, T&B's aesthetic and physical design elements make it truly distinctive. The firm has been praised for wedding the

The 3,510-acre Talega project's Master Plan, Illustrative Site Plan and its Village Center's multifamily and commercial areas, its public plaza & Village Green and the extensive project's 18-hole golf course with scenic "Nob Hill"

architect's creativity with the engineer's practicality: T&B creates appealing designs that work.

For a plan to work today, it must be more than functional. Environmental and community issues often have a major influence on project design. Because of its experience, creativity and dedication to research, T&B can anticipate problems and design plans that mitigate many of these concerns. The T&B approach transforms potential physical and environmental obstacles into opportunities to preserve resources while promoting efficient and economically feasible design.

THE FIRM'S FIVE OWNER/PRINCIPALS — DOUG BOYD, BARRY BURNELL, JAMES GRECO, FIROUZ GHABOUSSI AND RUSS GARCIA — DRAW ON MORE THAN 95 YEARS OF COMBINED PROFESSIONAL EXPERIENCE. THEIR VARIED BUT COMPLEMENTARY BACKGROUNDS MAKE THE COMPANY AS A WHOLE STRONGER.

The Talega project demonstrates this approach. Confronted with inefficient and costly existing entitlement, Talega turned to T&B for a dramatic design solution and creative entitlement documentation. T&B's design creates a new sustainable community that meets or exceeds the city of San Clemente's and the developers' high design standards while drastically reducing grading quantities and preserving all the developable area. The Talega design features 4,500 homes of varied size and type, a vibrant town center village, a professional 18-hole golf course, a 1,172-acre nature conservancy, three parks with an extensive trail system, 80 acres devoted to job-creating office and industrial uses and an elementary school.

T&B has also demonstrated unsurpassed expertise in its ability to fashion plans that aid and enhance the eventual transformation of large tracts of land from their current use. Owners of entities such as dairy farms, landfills and mining quarries have had the vision to recognize that their current or planned uses, though often long-term, will not be maintained permanently. They have retained T&B to design the initial use so that it not only efficiently yields current resources but also will facilitate the site's future conversion and development to generate the highest environmental and monetary value.

Gold Medal Merit Award Winner Rio Vista West's Illustrative Land Use Plan and Perspective

An example of T&B's virtuosity in such planning, Rio Vista West, was a winner of the prestigious Gold Nugget Merit Award. It was designed and processed for CalMat Properties Company in San Diego to replace a 95-acre Mission Valley resource extraction operation. This mixed-use, transit-oriented project features residential products, a much-needed power center, an office complex, a transit hub and a series of public places that provide passive and active open space amenities for residents and employees. The city of San Diego has recognized T&B's innovative approach by designating another similar project, the Carroll Canyon Master Plan, as a "Transit-Oriented Design" (TOD) demonstration project.

These award-winning projects and the company's superb national reputation have resulted in T&B being retained by an impressive list of diverse clients. Among those in Orange County and Southern California that have sought out the company's expertise include Brookfield, Catellus, Genstar, The Irvine Company, Kaufman & Broad, Lennar Homes, Lewis Homes, Pardee Construction Company, Pulte Home Corporation, Standard Pacific, Walgreen Company and Valencia Company.

T&B has performed varied services for many diverse clients, both large and small. It has done master planning for such atypical sites as cemeteries, high schools, landfills and dairies. Private landowners, who have long maintained large pieces of family-owned land, have trusted T&B's pure planning talents, singleness of purpose and tradition of excellence to inform them and help them make the best decisions on current and future use of their land.

Personal attention is a T&B hallmark. The company has carefully controlled its growth to continue to allow one of the firm's principals to personally direct each project.

With its devotion to quality, efficiency and creativity, T&B has helped ensure the successful planning, design and entitlement of over 100,000 acres of land. The company's well-conceived and dedicated approach has left its countless clients happy that they chose to take the first step of their land development journey with T&B Planning Consultants.

THE ROBERT MAYER CORPORATION

What started as one man remodeling houses has grown into the thriving corporation behind Orange County's newest and most outstanding coastline resort — The Waterfront — as well as a major player in the revitalization of Huntington Beach. The journey that brought The Robert Mayer Corporation to its current status is a long and fascinating one.

Robert Mayer founded his own construction firm in 1955.

Robert ("Bob") Mayer began his career at a construction firm in 1948 where he worked as a draftsman, eventually becoming general manager. After seven years of working for someone else, Mayer decided it was time to go into business for himself, and he started Mayer Construction Company in Downey in 1955. Because he lacked capital, he had to start with small jobs. "I'd remodel a kitchen, or build a room addition," recalls Mayer. "It didn't take any money — you got paid as fast as you did the work." Before long Mayer had the means to buy his first piece of property and build his first duplex rental building, which was quickly followed by a four-unit building and then a 10-unit building. The Southland was full of open land and housing demand was high. Stick by stick, unit by unit, Mayer began to build apartment buildings by the score. The construction company grew quickly, and by the 1960s had become the largest apartment builder in Southern California. The company has financed and developed more than 25,000 residential units, setting numerous home-building records.

Steve Bone became company president in 1986, ushering in a new era of development.

The company built its first hotel in 1970, founding the Ambassador Inn chain of hotels throughout California, Arizona and Nevada. Mayer Construction employed about 1,000 people by the early 1970s; 500 in the building division and 500 in the hotel division.

By 1980 Mayer had enjoyed a 32-year career, 25 of which had been as a business owner. It was time to retire — or so he thought. Mayer sold the company in 1980 and went into semi-retirement. But the same tireless work ethic that made Mayer Construction such a success wouldn't let him rest. Just a few years after selling his company, he started The Robert Mayer Corporation in Newport Beach.

He surrounded himself with top-notch executives. Steve Bone, a graduate of Columbia Law School, joined The Robert Mayer Corporation in 1986, ushering in a new era of development. He serves as company president and as Mayer's partner in the development of The Waterfront project. Robert ("R.J.") Mayer Jr. joined his father in the company in 1997 and now serves as the company's senior vice president.

The company's main focus since 1986 has been The Waterfront resort complex. The 50-acre beachfront location in Huntington Beach is the only large resort along the coastline for 25 miles in either direction — and the city's first and only luxury resort. This makes it a focal point for tourism, business conferences and social events. The 300-room Hilton Waterfront Hotel, developed, owned and operated by the company, is the first of three hotels that are planned for the resort.

The second hotel will have 520 rooms and will reflect the graceful, Andalusian Spanish style of architecture — reminiscent of California's "Golden Age" — lending a relaxed elegance to the shoreline. Most of the guestrooms provide dramatic ocean views. The 15-acre, four-story hotel features four ocean-view courtyards with a 52,000-square-foot ocean-view conference center, two restaurants, two tennis courts, a shopping arcade, a 25,000-square-foot destination spa and a pedestrian overpass to the beach.

More plans are underway for the expansion of The Waterfront project, including the eventual addition of a 250-room third hotel which will be located between the two hotels and a gated luxury residential community. The luxury Waterfront resort will become a focal point for Orange County and the surrounding Southern California area as residents make use of its banquet rooms, restaurants and shops.

In addition to the Waterfront project, The Robert Mayer Corporation maintains an active development program to identify and develop new commercial, residential and gaming opportunities. For example, the company developed, owns and operates the Key Largo Casino and Hotel on Flamingo Road in Las Vegas. It also has residential communities and commercial centers under development in the Coachella Valley in Rancho Mirage and Palm Desert.

The company's principals have managed to stay very active outside their work for the company. Mayer cofounded Metro Bank, which was purchased by Comerica Bank in 1996, and is currently involved in a new bank — Prime Bank — as cofounder and director. He also chaired the committee and raised funds to rebuild the Huntington Beach Pier in the early 1990s. Company President Bone is active in a number of Orange County organizations. He is founding cochairman of the Orange County Tourism Council, founding chairman of the Orange County Film Commission and the Huntington Beach Conference and Visitors Bureau, and serves on the Orange County Business Council board of directors and the Orange County Cancer Education and Research Foundation board of directors.

This commitment to quality growth and service to the community, combined with a distinguished residential and commercial portfolio and the experience of four decades in the industry, provides The Robert Mayer Corporation a solid foundation on which to build. As a result, The Robert Mayer Corporation is leading its industry into a bright future of highly successful development.

The Waterfront, Huntington Beach's first and only luxury resort, will have three hotels, a gated luxury residential community, an ocean-view conference center, several tennis courts, two restaurants, a spa, a shopping arcade and a pedestrian overpass to the beach. Pictured here is the 520-room Hilton Grand Coast Resort, scheduled to open in 2001.

The Hilton Grand Coast Resort will feature graceful Andalusian Spanish-style architecture reminiscent of California's "Golden Age." Reflected here is the hotel's porte cochere.

VINTAGE DESIGN

Buying a home is always an exciting experience, but it can also be a stressful one, especially if the house is being newly built. Making the decision to buy is the easy part. Seeing the project through to completion is much more difficult, especially when there are so many choices. There are flooring and window coverings to select, then cabinets and doors, countertops, lighting fixtures and appliances. The list goes on and on. Even after weeks of searching and researching, it's easy to become overwhelmed — unless of course you turn to professionals that can help you step by step through the entire selection process. Vintage Design does exactly that.

Located in Yorba Linda, Vintage Design is a full-service design center that works with both the buyer and the new community home builder to assure mistake-free choices when finishing a new home. With its floor covering and options management service staffed with certified, professional designers, the company is committed to providing its customers with quality materials that are competitively priced; unparalleled product styles to chose from; and experienced, qualified craftsmen that will complete the job to the buyer's satisfaction. And best of all, Vintage Design provides one-stop shopping. Everything needed to custom-finish homes to the individual lifestyle of its owners can be found under one roof in a beautiful and relaxed environment.

Vintage Design is the creation of Timothy Buckley. Born and raised in Orange County, Tim grew up in the family business. His father, Tom, owned Crest Floors and Plastics, and saw to it that each of his children spent their summers mastering a different position in the company. From working on the showroom floor to learning accounts payable or being out in the field, he taught them everything they needed to know. Tim had a genuine love for the business right from the start. When his brother, Mike, bought the company from their father in 1980, it became Suncrest Interiors, and Tim became vice president of operations, a position he held until 1986 when he decided to open Vintage Design on his own.

Vintage Design showroom in Yorba Linda
Photo by Smith Photography

Vintage Design helps new owners custom-finish homes to fit their individual lifestyles.

Tim's passion for what he does is evident the moment you hear him talk about Vintage Design. "Our philosophy is simple," he says with a proud smile. "We focus on service and teamwork, and we build long-term relationships by doing exactly what we say we're going to do. I think that's a pretty solid basis to operate on." Building strong partnerships with his vendors is also one of Tim's top priorities. It is those reliable ties that allows Vintage Design to offer its customers all grades, levels and styles of a particular product or design concept so that there is something to fit every need as well as every budget. That's a lot to offer considering the company works with a list of 15 to 17 new home builders of homes ranging between $139,000 and $1.8 million. Contracted to do every house in a new community, with a workload of 30 to 40 communities at any given time, Vintage Design seeks not to be the biggest, but simply the best at what it does.

Teamwork is also important to Tim. He believes that an excellent management team and a great staff of dedicated employees have been integral to the success of his business. "If you have good people who believe in the philosophy of the company," he states, "if they walk the walk and talk the talk, you're bound to be successful." Vintage Design Vice President Jaimi Julian believes that Team Vintage is composed of a talented and knowledgeable group of professionals that takes great pride in what they do. In order to insure that high standards of service, excellence, and teamwork are maintained, Vintage Design offers prompt scheduling with a three to five day turnaround, and has an in-house labor

(Far left)
Vintage Design offers a fabulous array of choices in all grades, levels and styles of a particular product or design concept.
Photo by Smith Photography

The end result is a custom-finished home that the new owners are sure to enjoy.

department with computerized billing procedures, a 1-Day Customer Service Response Management Team, full-time field superintendents and sales liasions and A.S.I.D. Qualified design consultants.

The first step of the selection process begins when a new home buyer meets with a design consultant at one of the Vintage Design showrooms. (The main showroom is located at the 17,000-square-foot corporate facility in Yorba Linda, while a 3,200-square-foot showroom is located in Irvine.) "Our designers are very professional and knowledgeable," says Julian. "Without being high-pressure, they take buyers through a most stressful time and educate them so that they come away from the process knowing more about their options, and knowing that the designers really care." Once a house is released to them by the builder, Vintage Design's expert installers go to work, and take pride in completing a project without ever missing a closing date.

Options are endless at Vintage Design, with all looks and styles from modern to traditional. A customer's choice of window coverings includes everything from decorator blinds and shutters to custom draperies, while countertop choices include ceramic tile, corian, tumbled stone, granite slab and granite tile in an exciting range of colors. Floor coverings offered include all levels, grades and styles of carpeting from many of the leading U.S. manufacturers, and hardwood floors (prefinished or unfinished) available in plank, parquet or herringbone designs that can be customized with exquisite borders, medallions, or personalized designs created by the customer and hand inlaid by professional craftsmen. Choices for fireplace surrounds abound as well in styles of pre-cast concrete, stone, brick, marble, tile, granite or wood that make for beautiful custom mantles. Additionally, Vintage Design offers a fabulous array of choices in doors, windows, lighting and plumbing fixtures, tub enclosures and wardrobe doors. Customers also have choices in finish carpentry. They can choose everything from standard to bull-nose corners, upgraded baseboards, door frames, window casements and ledges.

Without a doubt, Vintage Design has earned a reputation for integrity and fairness in the industry. And with a company philosophy that is strongly service-oriented, it has become a leader in its field. So with a track record like that, what are Tim Buckley's plans for the future? "I'd like to see us continue to improve all facets of our operations," he says. "I'm also looking to expand to San Diego, Phoenix and Las Vegas." There's no doubt about it — Tim Buckley will do just that.

(Far left)
The Yorba Linda showroom lets owners see a variety of design concepts in order to help them make their choices.
Photo by Smith Photography

Floor coverings offered include all levels, grades and styles of carpeting from many of the leading U.S. manufacturers.
Photo by Smith Photography

BRIGGS ELECTRIC, INC.

After World War II ended and America and her allies emerged victorious over European and Asian forces, the U.S. economy began an unprecedented growth surge fueled by entrepreneurs from around the country. Among them was S.E. Briggs, founder of S.E. Briggs & Sons in 1946. Conceived in the garage of Briggs' home in Newport Beach, the electrical contracting concern would go on to become Briggs Electric Inc. by the early 1970s, when the elder Briggs sold the company to his son Bob Briggs and Tom Perry.

Founded on the principle "Deliver excellence, and clients will keep coming back," Briggs Electric has emerged as a business-in-progress that is one of Irvine's most enduring corporate citizens. Serving the commercial and industrial building markets, Briggs Electric provides installation, wiring, lighting and electrical system services for both new and remodeled structures. Together with its Carson City, Nevada-based office, which serves the greater Reno area, the full-service electrical contractor caters primarily to the West Coast region, with the majority of its clients in Orange and Los Angeles counties, though San Bernardino and Riverside counties also make up its market share.

Sensitive to current economic conditions and extremely competitive, the Southern California electrical industry has seen many companies come and go. However, Briggs Electric maintains a steady customer base and consistent revenue stream due to its quality service, a company hallmark. Its reputation is cemented by value-added service features, including fast-track design programs that ensure the shortest possible construction time, and a value-engineering process that provides the most versatile electrical systems at a competitive price.

The workforce of Briggs is composed of a carefully selected group of electricians, project managers and office administrators. The company's exceptional work performance speaks volumes about its commitment to service excellence; bidding opportunities for new projects in Southern California rarely go without consideration of Briggs Electric. Still, the contractor takes nothing for granted and continues to treat each new project as if it were the first.

Among Briggs Electric's many projects, which range from commercial buildings and parking structures to medical facilities to manufacturing plants to interior improvements, are: Hoag Hospital, Newport Beach; Tustin Market Place, Tustin; Irvine Spectrum Center, Irvine; Irvine Medical Office Building, Irvine; Rainforest Café, South Coast Plaza and Ontario Mills Mall; and many others.

The link between good corporate citizenship and the well-being of the surrounding community isn't taken lightly by Briggs. The contractor supports the local police association and firefighters, the local Boys/Girls Club and various athletic events, such as health-improvement and -research walkathons. It also sponsors employees as participants in community-based charitable events.

Briggs Electric, Inc. continues to make history in Orange County with its visionary approach to business and its commitment to the highest ideals of customer service. Its contribution to the corporate community of Southern California has proved integral to the region's designation as one of the country's most vibrant state economies.

Briggs Electric Inc.'s first company vehicle, c. 1949

BRINDERSON COMPANIES

This is a technological age. What was science fiction yesterday is reality today. Machinery and equipment accomplish tasks so immense they seem to dwarf human endeavors. Brinderson, builder of some of the world's most advanced technological structures and processes, affirms the stature and significance of the individual — Brinderson is built on people. The company knows people are the key to quality, and quality is the key to success.

Chairman and CEO Gary L. Brinderson, who founded the company in 1965, had a vision of quality. As a teenager, he had worked for a local contractor. The contractor was successful, but the quality of the work and the people were not at a level that Gary equated with success.

Brinderson knew that the way to produce the highest quality was to employ the best people. That meant doing the most difficult work. In construction, as in many trades and professions, the best people are often drawn to the most challenging, complex tasks. The firm focused on technically ambitious work involved with complicated processes.

It went on to build the most elaborate processes for hospitals, industrial plants, water filtration systems, power plants, nuclear facilities, oil refineries, army ammunition plants, ports, submarine bases and many other enterprises. Brinderson has been responsible for many of the most prominent construction projects in the United States.

One of the country's largest and most prominent engineering and construction companies, Brinderson has completed projects valued at more than $3 billion. The company has completed projects of global proportions, such as the world's largest desalting plant in Yuma, Arizona, with a total project value of $400 million. Brinderson also completed work on more than 600 million gallons of water filtration systems in North America — 10 percent of the entire water supply. The company's Orange County projects include a partnership on the San Joaquin Hills Transportation Corridor and as general contractor for the Yorba Linda Feeder Power Plant. Brinderson has also built more than $1 billion of power and refinery work.

The firm's clients are now mostly *Fortune* 100 companies. Although it will still work on a project-by-project basis, Brinderson is now much more likely to form alliances, as it has with five *Fortune* 50 clients.

In these alliances both parties have a commitment to each other. Brinderson becomes the exclusive engineer and constructor. The client represents not just a project, but a relationship. That relationship is based on quality and performance; competition is stiff and performance must be high. Brinderson continues to deliver cost reduction and improvement. The company integrates with the client and becomes part of the client's goals and objectives. Brinderson has completed more than 500 projects under the five alliances.

Because Brinderson works in such a technically demanding field, where the level of responsibility is immense and the margin for error is virtually zero, safety is a major concern. The company sees safety as the most important objective. It also considers safety to be a management process: If a company can manage safety effectively, it can manage any process successfully.

The national average for OSHA-recordable incidents (the criteria used to measure accidents) is 11 per 200,000 hours of labor. Brinderson's record is 1.6. The company has exceeded one million safe work hours. Everything at Brinderson starts with safety — and finishes safely.

Gary Brinderson likes to say, "In this business we only have one thing, and that's client satisfaction." Brinderson has built its reputation for satisfying the most demanding clients by exceeding their expectations on the most difficult jobs in the world.

Brinderson performing a heavy lift of a process column for ARCO at its L.A. refinery

(Far left)
New coal-fired power plant built by Brinderson in upstate New York

CONTROL ELECTRIX

A cogeneration plant exemplifies some of Control Electrix's high-tech talents.

Ever since Paul and JoAnne Greenwell founded Control Electrix on a rainy February day in 1987, the firm has been ready to respond to clients' needs, 24 hours a day, seven days a week, rain or shine.

In the beginning, Control Electrix's office was composed of a phone on the floor of an empty bedroom in the Greenwell's Orange County home. JoAnne would take invoices to work early in the morning and type them up at her job. She remembers when providing service 24 hours a day, seven days a week, meant Paul answering calls at 2:00 a.m.

Control's first customer, Hillcrest Beverly Oil Company, familiar with Paul's technical expertise and solid work ethic, had encouraged him to start his own company. Hillcrest not only became Control's first customer but referred many others as well.

The firm's earliest jobs were primarily at oil production facilities. A slowdown in the oil business spurred Control's move into other areas of industrial electrical work. The company's efforts were hailed by its clients, and the list of referred customers expanded to include companies in the chemical, steel, food and container industries. It wasn't long before Control had established itself as a quality electrical contractor, able to perform the most technical services.

Today, no job is too large or elaborate for the Anaheim company. Control's dedicated and capable crew gets the job done on time and within budget, whether it's installing the process control and lighting for a Clorox production line; designing and building a 12,000-volt line for Unocal; traveling to Morocco to install a fire protection system for Voice of America, or to Chile to perform an electrical installation for Inland Container; or designing and installing a line that turns out 750,000 Hot Pockets a day for Chef America.

With its full-service design and build capabilities, Control Electrix can turn rough plans into engineered, schematic drawings and complete the project to the highest standards.

Now Control's sterling reputation in the industrial field has attracted the attention of the commercial market. Demand for the company's services has escalated, and Control Electrix has planned substantial growth to meet its commitment to this market segment.

With the industrial base waning in Southern California, Control's emphasis on the commercial market makes sense for the company — and its new clients. The firm's high-tech expertise in designing, engineering, installing and maintaining the most complex electrical projects provides an extra level of assurance to contractors, engineers and developers. They can now call on the first-class craftsmanship and proven performance of Control Electrix to handle all their electrical needs for office buildings or other commercial projects.

Taking care of customers' needs, Control has come a long way since it was just a phone on the floor of an empty bedroom. The company has operated from its own 9,000-square-foot building since 1994.

What hasn't changed from the very beginning is the firm's dedication to its clients. The company still services Hillcrest Beverly Oil, its very first customer, and has retained an impressive 80 to 90 percent of all its clients. Control Electrix has the well-earned reputation of giving customers guaranteed, positive results. As Paul Greenwell puts it, "The reason for our success is plain and simple — we take care of our customers."

GOLDEN GATE CONCRETE CUTTING

Cinderella's House at Disney's Magic Kingdom serves as a backdrop for Golden Gate Concrete Cutting company vehicles, parked just outside the gates while the contractor completes a project.

Hardly could Robert F. Huie III have known that the opportunity to work on one of the country's most enduring landmark structures back in 1982 would inspire him to explore his entrepreneurial instincts. That, however, is the lore of Huie's Golden Gate Concrete Cutting, a full-service, concrete-cutting-and-removal contractor serving the Southern California market.

From 1982 to 1985, Huie, along with a host of other Dillingham Construction workers, plied his pavement-carving skills to complete the removal and replacement of the massive deck of San Francisco's famed Golden Gate Bridge. No easy task for the faint-of-heart or the weak-handed, the painstaking yet successful project is probably the most oft-mentioned job on Huie's résumé — for good reason. His company is steadily solidifying its reputation as one of Orange County's most promising businesses.

Founded by Huie in 1989 in Irvine, California, Golden Gate Concrete Cutting relocated to Tustin at the start of 1999. An Orange County native, Huie uprooted the business to lessen the commuting distance from his home in nearby Lake Forest. The sole proprietorship with the landmark-inspired name is among the thousands of small- to middle-market companies that form the very foundation of the state's economic base. Offering slab-sawing, wall-sawing, hand-sawing, architectural-sawing and core-drilling services 24 hours a day, Golden Gate is the culmination of Huie's more than 20 years of experience in the construction industry.

Dedicated to providing state-of-the-art trucks, equipment and professional operators at a competitive rate, the contractor serves the residential, commercial and industrial markets, the bulk of its contracts deriving from industrial assignments. Though cutting and removing concrete isn't the most glamorous of endeavors, Golden Gate Concrete Cutting has taken on projects for some of the most famous institutions in the country. Past projects in which Golden Gate has participated include the University of California at Irvine Residence Halls, the Richard M. Nixon Historical Library in Yorba Linda, California State University Los Angeles Simpson Tower seismic retrofit and Disneyland's Mainstreet Parade route.

In addition to its memorable work with a national monument and the home of the venerable Mickey Mouse, Golden Gate Concrete Cutting also serves hotels, hospitals, grocery stores, restaurants, factories and highway projects, among countless other concerns.

According to Huie, Golden Gate Concrete Cutting is distinguished from its competitors by its unwavering commitment to thorough, clean and timely service. It is this quality service that enables the company to assist clients from as far south as the Tijuana border to those located in the northern region of the state. The contractor joined the California Building Industry Association (CBIA) in 1998, affirming Huie's commitment to strengthening the company's ties to the construction industry while enhancing its marketability to current and potential customers.

Having gone from a one-man operation to a family-run organization with six to eight employees — and counting — during its first 10 years, Golden Gate Concrete Cutting is by any measure a small company. Size, however, does not deter the contractor from taking a big-business approach to the market. In its pursuit of growth through premium service, Golden Gate aims to extend its reach in the region's construction industry. According to Huie, the company's mission is to set the standard for concrete cutting and removal in Southern California. With a name that is synonymous with longevity and faultless workmanship and more than 20 years of experience in the construction industry, Golden Gate Concrete Cutting may not only set the standard for its industry peers, it may well raise the bar for the competition in the years to come.

IMPACT INTERIOR DESIGN, INC.

Pat Yeiser (center) formed Impact Interior Design with son Mark Burkhardt (left) and daughter Debra Porter (right). ©1999 *Bright Light Photography*

Impact's commercial interior designs include South Coast Plaza's flagship couture store for Gianni Versace.

Impact Interior Design, Inc. was founded in February 1996 by Pat Yeiser, a leader in the interior design community. It was no wonder her new company enjoyed tremendous success right from the beginning; it was built on a solid foundation. Yeiser's award-winning reputation spans three decades, garnering both local and national recognition for her innovative design concepts and her strong partnerships with both builders and architects.

As a successful entrepreneur, Yeiser has always been ahead of her time. She has maintained an active commitment to the industry and community. Yeiser has been instrumental in raising funds to develop Children's Hospital of Orange County (CHOC). She has written numerous newspaper and textbook articles for the industry and has frequently served as keynote speaker at various events. She was one of the nation's 20 industry professionals selected by *Builder Magazine* to attend a prestigious management workshop in Japan, serving as the group's only woman and sole representative of the interior design industry. Most recently, Yeiser received personal recognition for her contributions after the Deane Brothers were recognized by *Builder Magazine* as one of "The 100 Most Influential in the Industry."

On the forefront of Orange County's booming housing growth of the 70s and 80s, Yeiser started her career with Deane Brothers, then the nation's leading developer of innovative home-building concepts such as the famous "Garden Kitchen" design and on-site design studios for buyers' optional selections. During this time, Yeiser was building a strong reputation in the building industry and establishing herself as an innovative interior designer in her own right.

In 1975 Yeiser cofounded Yeiser/Garland & Associates, working with leading developers designing model homes. Within two years, it was the West Coast's fastest-growing design firm. The firm's creativity led the building industry to create the first master-planned communities in Southern California, including Huntington Beach, Mission Viejo, Laguna Niguel, Lake Forest, Irvine, Yorba Linda, Big Canyon and Diamond Bar.

Although Yeiser/Garland became one of the nation's top four interior design companies and continued to win several more awards for design, the company was not exempted from the housing industry's recession of the early 90s. The company was closed in 1994.

Impact is known for its distinctive, luxurious interiors. ©1998 *John R. Bare Photography*

Yeiser's new company, Impact Interior Design, capitalized on her intimate knowledge of the building industry from cost and budgeting to materials. To achieve the strength that would allow her firm to diversify, Yeiser joined forces with the most gifted designers she knew — her son, Mark Burkhardt, and her daughter, Debra Porter. In the new company — Impact Interior Design — they have expanded their designs into new challenges that include retail stores, super yachts and private jet airplanes.

Looking back at the many successes of Yeiser and the Impact designers, they look forward to meeting the changing needs of the housing industry. While the company plans to expand and increase its exposure in the hotel industry and the senior housing markets, it remains committed to the model home merchandising that it does so well.

Impact Interior Design, Inc. strives to keep its designs original, never losing the vision of turning its client's dreams and aspirations into reality.

J.L. HARE ASSOCIATES, INC.

One of Orange County's most prominent claims to fame has consistently been its phenomenal growth. Since 1950 the county's population has grown incredibly — more than 1,200 percent! This influx of new residents has led to a booming building industry — both for residential and industrial development.

Along with this building boom come the complexities of planning and arranging all the details that are inherent with large projects. This is where Jackie Hare comes in. Hare worked for the Mission Viejo Company from 1972 until the company's construction division was dissolved in 1988. There, she was responsible for all building permit processing and Department of Real Estate Reports. It wasn't uncommon to have six construction starts and six sales starts each month. And none of this would happen if Hare and her department didn't get the necessary permits on time.

When the division was dissolved, Hare decided to go it alone and become a consultant. Her company, J.L. Hare Associates, Inc., performs basically the same functions she did for her previous employer, but now it works for the entire Orange County building industry. Work initially came easy since her fellow former employees spread out to new companies, many of which didn't have a person who fulfilled her duties. "My first three months, I had 1,000 permits to pull and needed help. My daughters and husband helped initially. I began hiring a full-time staff and opened the Tustin office about a year later," Hare explains.

The company specializes in development processing and governmental relations for both small and large builders/developers for residential and commercial projects. It develops an overall strategy and timetable for each project, and coordinates all activities between the agencies, construction staff and professional consultants. It provides overall project management of the permit process from grading to final occupancy permits.

For the typical project, the company will do an initial study and prepare a comprehensive permit schedule. It then prepares, in coordination with the design team, the permit applications and submits the application package with the required documents and monitors the plan checks for any needed corrections. Processing corrections are coordinated with each agency and final approvals are garnered. Finally, the permits are issued.

J.L. Hare Associates specialties include: building permits; conditional use permits; feasibility reports; grading permits; health department approvals; fire department approvals; infrastructure permits; sign permits; site plan approvals; tenant occupancy permits; and tract maps. Projects have included major retail centers, golf courses, hotels, industrial complexes, universities and large residential tract developments.

To make sure her company keeps current, Hare has developed a computer system that helps streamline projects. "With this system, we have incorporated all of the fees for the area cities and counties. When clients come to us and need information on what their total fees will be, we can easily get that for them," she adds. The company has also been working hard to keep up with the current trend of online permit processing in the cities that are now offering it.

(Far left)
Jackie Hare
Photo by Lia Photography

The staff of J.L. Hare Associates, Inc. assembles at Soka University of America job site in Aliso Viejo. Kneeling in front (left to right): Jeff Salisbury, Phil Coughlin, Joseph Lambert. Standing (left to right): Jennifer Crocker, Jackie Hare, Holly Sandler, Peggy Martin
Photo by Lia Photography

What sets this company apart from others that perform similar tasks is the vast experience and knowledge of Hare and her employees and the close working relationship the company has developed with government agencies. Part of Hare's duties at the Mission Viejo Company included being the company representative at Building Industry Association (BIA) codes and standards committees and the County of Orange Processing Task Force. In this capacity, she not only helped establish local standards, but she was able to increase her knowledge of the building industry and forge crucial relationships with many on the "approval-side" of the industry. This is one of the main keys to J.L. Hare Associates' success. She is now active in the BIA of Southern California, the National Association of Industrial and Office Properties, and the International Conference of Building Officials, and serves on local governmental affairs committees for the BIA, among others. Knowing and respecting the system and the people involved in that system are major factors in establishing and maintaining long-term relationships. And that is what makes J.L. Hare Associates, Inc. unique.

K. HOVNANIAN COMPANIES, INC.

Cruise along the scenic Pacific Coast Highway, take a tour of the city of Irvine's master-planned communities or drive down some of Orange County's quiet residential streets. Chances are, some of the homes you encounter are the handiwork of K. Hovnanian Companies, a Newport Beach-based builder that provides high quality and extensive choice to Southern California homeowners.

K. Hovnanian "Winchester"

For more than 40 years, K. Hovnanian — one of the country's leading home builders — has built and sold a wide variety of home designs, from a young couple's first entry-level condominium to luxury single-family homes in planned communities in New Jersey, Pennsylvania, North Carolina, Virginia, Florida and California.

Founded by Ara and Kevork Hovnanian, K. Hovnanian started as a family operation dedicated to the art of architecture, quality design and value. Since that time, the company has grown considerably, but its core philosophy has never changed.

Although its parent company, Hovnanian Enterprises Inc., is currently a large, publicly held corporation, the Hovnanian family still controls over 60 percent of its stock. The result is that clients receive the best of both worlds — the credibility and dependability of a large public corporation and the care and attention to detail of a family operation.

The company's commitment to quality, integrity and an unparalleled level of personal service continues to be its benchmark. Today, K. Hovnanian offers nearly a half century of home-building experience, expertise in all phases of design and style, and a diverse range of additional services, including mortgage financing and title services, and developing and managing income-producing properties.

K. Hovnanian understands that each "dream" home is different. For that reason, its designers create a vast array of sizes and styles to choose from. Garden-style condominiums, townhomes, patio homes and large single-family structures include whatever the customer needs: one bedroom or five, one-car garage or a four-car garage, a tenth of an acre or six acres, vaulted or flat ceilings, family rooms, libraries, basements or home offices — whatever the customer desires, K. Hovnanian strives to deliver.

While rich in tradition, K. Hovnanian homes incorporate the latest design ideas from across the country to ensure that each home will be appealing even as lifestyles change. Additionally, as a national builder, the company is able to blend leading-edge design concepts from different regions of the United States and introduce those amalgams to the local market for architectural plans that are fresh, new and accommodating.

Kevork Hovnanian (left) and Ara Hovnanian (right)

(Far right) K. Hovnanian "Saratoga"

LA JOLLA PACIFIC, LTD.

In a county famous for its planned communities, La Jolla Pacific, Ltd. is building a reputation for taking care of things that don't go according to plan.

Don Neff founded Neff and Associates in 1993, and incorporated as La Jolla Pacific in 1995 after discovering that a construction-defect litigation upsurge followed on the heels of the Orange County building booms of the 1970s and 1980s. As Neff found his services as an expert defense witness in increasing demand, he saw how many of the defects that led to litigation could be prevented.

He developed the company's trademarked Shark Repellent® system to help builders photographically document the quality of their construction. The "zero defect service" helps monitor subcontractors and report errors for correction before they have a chance to lead to costly construction-defect litigation.

Most of the time, the litigation "sharks" need water. Water damage is the leading and most preventable cause of construction-defect litigation. La Jolla Pacific's professionals do frequent on-site inspections documenting key structural elements like framing and concrete; installation of electrical, plumbing and HVAC systems; sheet metal, drywall, insulation, fire stops, sound attenuation, finish grading and drainage. They pay special attention to the elements that make homes watertight — window flashing, lath installation and roofing.

La Jolla Pacific's experts produce a complete, layer-by-layer photographic record of single structures or entire tracts, noting the date, time and exact location where each photo was taken. In the best case they are the ounce of prevention that spares builders costly cures later on. In less favorable circumstances, they can help builders reduce legal liability with forensic testing and expert testimony.

The La Jolla Pacific team — (left to right) Chip Sparks, Ron Travers, Tammi Mueller, Alaynia Smith, Don Neff, Cassie Cherry and Mark Buberl (not pictured: Chu Lai)

Don and Chip documenting proper installation of window flashing

Since customer service breakdowns are a common spur to litigation, La Jolla Pacific helps builders develop plans for headache-free transfers to homeowner associations. This can include educating customer service representatives and improving their communication with the construction superintendents responsible for resolving problems.

The company's custom homeowner association manuals detail everything from association structure, procedures and responsibilities to maintenance schedules and instructions to keep common areas in peak condition. This education component helps increase occupant ownership of maintenance responsibilities.

Before starting the company, Neff was an officer of several investment, development and home construction companies in California. This business experience followed completion of a master's degree at Harvard University.

The La Jolla Pacific team comprises over 80 years of experience in development, general building and landscape contracting, project management, field superintendent work and weatherproofing. Senior Associate Ron Travers, AIA, has 40 years of experience as an architect and is licensed in eight Western states. He has participated in all phases of the litigation process from testing, analysis, discovery, depositions and pretrial preparations to testifying in court. Senior Associate Chip Sparks has nearly 30 years of experience in design, processing and construction. He has overseen construction of more than 2,000 homes. Associate Mark Buberl is a licensed landscape contractor with 16 years of experience in the trade. He is also a licensed pest-control applicator and certified arborist.

In a county where rapid growth has been the hallmark for the past 50 years, not every project is perfect. When the failure of a home or other structure ends in litigation, legal and construction professionals know they can weather the worst if Don Neff and his staff at La Jolla Pacific are on their side.

BUSINESS & FINANCE

Banks, credit unions and financial service companies provide a financial foundation for a host of Orange County companies.

MARINE AIR FEDERAL CREDIT UNION

Since 1962 Marine Air Federal Credit Union (MAFCU) has been reaching out to new horizons. During that time, MAFCU has been led by the desire to provide a special breed of service for a growing family of credit union members. Originally designed to encourage saving, solve troop indebtedness and allow United States military personnel to borrow money at a low interest rate, MAFCU has become a full-service financial institution with over 20,000 members from both military and civilian life. That's substantially more than the original seven members, all Marine Corps personnel, who formed the credit union in February of 1962 at the Marine Corps Air Station El Toro.

The MAFCU seed was planted in 1961, when Sergeant Major Arthur L. Summers was assigned to MCAS El Toro. The Third Wing Commander expressed his concern to Summers about the indebtedness of the troops stationed at El Toro, and asked him to help find a solution to the growing, ongoing problem. During discussions with other Sergeants Major at the base, the subject of a credit union arose. The concept seemed ideal for providing service personnel with a way to save money, so Summers approached the local civilian credit union about adding the marines to its roster. The request was denied. After consulting with the California Credit Union League and discovering how a credit union functioned, the marines decided to start their own.

Seven Sergeants Major stationed at MCAS El Toro held a special meeting on February 8, 1962. Each paid $5 for a share in the credit union, plus a 25 cent membership fee, and El Toro Marine Federal Credit Union (later renamed Marine Air Federal Credit Union) was born. Initially the credit union operated on a volunteer basis, and limited hours (Monday through Friday, 11 a.m. to 1 p.m. and 4:30 p.m. to 6:00 p.m.) made it easy for credit union "employees" to work a shift.

MAFCU's first office, located inside the old station hospital (1962)

The first ETMFCU office was located in a nurse's station in Building 64, the old station hospital. On the initial day of operation, the credit union took in $69 in deposits. One week later, the credit union made its first loan of $200. The credit union concept of having every member buy a share and become a part of the credit union into which they deposit money may have been new, but it caught on quickly with the military personnel.

"The object of the credit union is first to promote thrift, then secondly to make money available for low interest loans," stated an article in the *Flight Jacket* newspaper (the weekly paper of MCAS El Toro) when the credit union first opened. The credit union delivered on that mission, because by mid-April, ETMFCU had $30,000 in assets and 700 members. The credit union also had made 90 loans. The credit union concept was working well for the marines. Personal savings of military members began to increase, and MCAS personnel were learning financial management while decreasing their indebtedness. And with low interest loans (maximum amount of $750) available for everything from automobiles to home furnishings, marines were borrowing, but borrowing wisely. By the end of 1962, $200,000 had been loaned and deposits were more than $100,000.

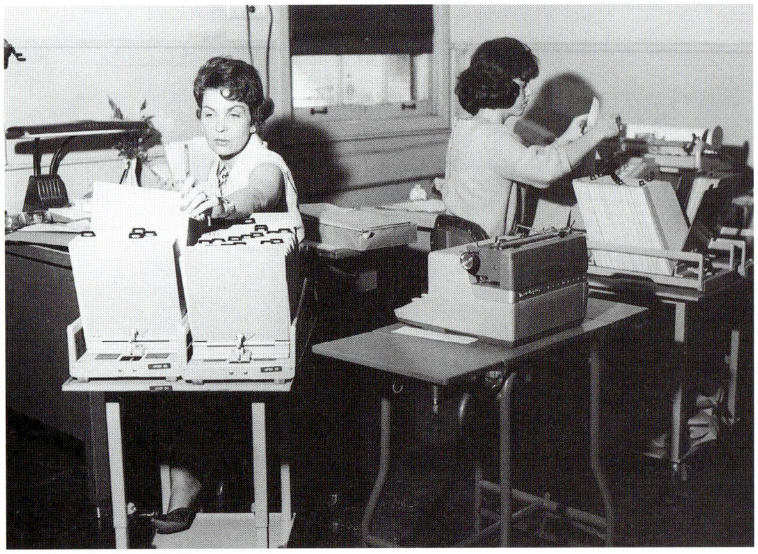

In 1965 the office expanded into the dependent's clinic. *U.S. Marine Corps*

In March 1963 ETMFCU assets had reached $200,000. By July, that amount had reached $350,000 and loans totaled $500,000. July also saw the 2,000th member sign up with the credit union.

In December the credit union began to add selected services for its members, including a Christmas savings program as well as payroll check cashing. This sounds like a small addition in service; however, cashing your payroll check was a major accomplishment during this time. The base was surrounded by orange groves and strawberry fields. Check cashing services were scarce. Adding this service gave the marines the opportunity not only to join the credit union right then, but it made it easier for marines already members to make loan payments or add to their savings account.

Two years after cofounding ETMFCU, Sergeant Major Summers retired from active duty in the Marines so he could devote all his time to running the credit union, which had just signed its 3,000th member. In April 1964 the credit union moved into a new, larger office in the dependent's clinic to better handle the influx of new business. By July the credit union had 4,000 members and assets topped the $1 million mark. According to an article in the July 10, 1964 edition of the *Flight Jacket*, "the credit union has helped more than 1,100 members in the purchase of washing machines, TV sets, furniture, automobiles, and just about every other type of necessity and comfort to make life a little more pleasant."

By now, the credit union was open from 9 a.m. to 3 p.m. Monday through Friday. Due to popular demand, a branch location was opened at MCAS Tustin. The credit union certainly was successful, because by February 1965, barely three years after opening, the credit union numbered over 4,500 members. Assets stood at $1.6 million, and over 6,200 loans had been made for a total of almost $5.5 million. Just three months later, those figures had climbed to 7,000 members with assets over $2 million — a remarkable feat given the newness of the credit union concept to the military.

Groundbreaking of new building, November 1967
U.S. Marine Corps

MAFCU (c. 1971)
Photo by Gordon Lundene

Credit union membership and assets continued to climb, so in November of 1967, the credit union broke ground on a new building. In February 1969 ETMFCU moved to its new location, which offered 5,500 square feet of office space (more than double the previous office) with four teller windows, a loan interview booth, information counter, a committee room, conference center and a lounge. Eighteen employees were needed to run the credit union, which now had assets of $4 million and over 11,000 members.

Throughout the 1960s the credit union had posted consistent growth in membership and assets, and with the approach of a new decade it showed no sign of slowing down. The focus of ETMFCU remained true to the original vision of counseling young people on their money problems. The credit union offered hands-on lessons in thrift, and provided many marines with positive experiences within the savings and loan world.

The start of the 1970s saw ETMFCU assets grow to over $5 million. In 1971 savings grew at a greater rate than loans, the first time in the history of the credit union that this had been achieved. Later that year, ETMFCU merged with MCAS Yuma Federal Credit Union Arizona, creating the need for a name change. Now serving two Marine Corps Air Stations in California and one in Arizona, the name Marine Air Federal Credit Union seemed a natural.

The late 70s saw a number of firsts for Marine Air FCU. In October of 1975 MAFCU became one of first credit unions to offer a share draft (checking) program, and in July of 1977 MAFCU was one of the first credit unions to be accepted by VISA USA to issue Visa Credit Cards. Rapid computer postings and a readout system for instant display of credit union accounts were added in the mid-70s, enabling the credit union to provide customers with faster, more efficient service. MAFCU saw tremendous growth numbers — more than double those of five years prior. The hours of operation also increased at all branches to better accommodate members' schedules.

Once membership reached 15,000, MAFCU knew something had to be done to handle the continuous influx of membership business, so a new wing of the credit union building was added in 1977. That same year, a new branch was created in the city of Yuma, Arizona (Branch 03), and the following year a new California branch office in the city of Orange (Branch 04) was added. Orange County was growing, but so was Yuma County, Arizona. The MCAS Yuma (Branch 02) began construction on a new office in 1978, and the Yuma Army Proving Grounds Credit Union merged with MAFCU later that same year.

By the end of 1978 membership had topped 16,000, and assets reached $27 million. The figures continued to climb throughout the 1980s and into the 90s, when assets topped $100 million, membership hovered around 20,000, and loans totaled $825 million since the formation of the credit union, most to Marine personnel and their families. That speaks volumes about the credit union's desire to assist marines with their financial matters, and its dedication to providing the best service and programs possible.

Originally formed solely to help marines, the MAFCU began adding select small companies to its roster, and now welcomes hundreds of companies and tens of thousands of employees throughout Southern California and Yuma, Arizona, to its many branch offices. In Orange County, select employee groups from companies based in Laguna Hills, Santa Ana, Irvine, Costa Mesa, El Toro, Orange, Tustin, Fountain Valley, Lake Forest, Huntington Beach, Brea, Dana Point, Westminster, San Juan Capistrano and other cities are eligible to use the resources of MAFCU. In 1988 the merger of Auto Pro Federal Credit Union, South Coast Medical Center Federal Credit Union, and Mobile Homeowners Federal Credit Union opened the door for their members to have the benefits of a full-service financial institution.

MAFCU Tustin branch (1990s)

MAFCU (c. 1971)

Through the years, Arthur Summers has remained president of the MAFCU. He was present when the first credit union office opened, and when the El Toro Marine Corps based closed in 1999. But the closing of the base did not mean the end of the Marine Air Federal Credit Union. Administrative offices remain in the area, as well as branch offices in Orange, Lake Forest, Laguna Beach, Miramar (where the most of the troops were transferred) and Yuma, Arizona. Membership in MAFCU is a lifetime benefit — no matter where a member goes or what they choose to do with the rest of their lives the MAFCU will always be there to help serve his or her financial needs.

MAFCU SERVICES & PRODUCTS

The mission of the Marine Air Federal Credit Union is to provide members with the advantage of a sound, well-managed, full-service financial institution. The MAFCU is a member-owned financial cooperative organized not for profit, but for service to its members. Essentially, members pool their savings and lend them to each other. Joining is very simple — just a minimum deposit of $25 and a one-time membership fee of $5. Once membership is established, a remarkable portfolio of financial services is available to meet the growing and changing needs of MAFCU members.

Basic banking services are just the start for MAFCU members, although members can bank safely knowing that savings accounts are federally insured up to $100,000 by the National Credit Union Administration. There is additional insurance on balances up to $250,000 through the American Share Insurance, the nation's largest private deposit insurer. Special Life Savings

MCAS Tustin branch (1990s)

Insured Accounts are available, as are money management accounts, certificate accounts, IRAs and IRA certificate accounts, and various checking accounts. ATM cards allow instant access to MAFCU accounts at over 100,000 ATM locations worldwide, including the Armed Forces Financial Network, Plus System, Star System, The Exchange, Visa and American Express.

MAFCU, Yuma, Arizona

For those members who go on deployment for six months or more and share a joint account with a spouse, MAFCU maintains a special deployment account to help arrange finances during that period of time. A special sub-account is established with automatic transfers for a specified amount from the joint account.

Financial counseling has always been an important part of the MAFCU. Credit Union personnel are always available to deal with everything from issues of credit to balancing a checkbook. Borrowing money is a financial reality of life, and MAFCU can help members borrow for the right reasons, for the proper length of time and at the best possible interest rates.

The credit union can provide real estate loans for first and second trust deeds, home equity and new construction loans, mobile home loans and a wide variety of consumer loans. For auto loans, the credit union offers several value added options for the purchase of a vehicle. The 100 percent financing option makes car ownership easier than ever, and the Mechanical Breakdown Insurance program provides peace of mind no matter what make or model of vehicle is purchased.

Owned by its members and managed by a board of directors elected from the membership, the credit union has always been interested in "helping you help yourself." MAFCU strives to assist members with money problems — not to entice them into indebtedness. This was MAFCU's philosophy in the 60s, and it will continue to be the watchword as MAFCU strives to provide members with the best credit union possible.

MAFCU founder Arthur L. Summers

THE FIRST AMERICAN FINANCIAL CORPORATION

The First American Financial Corporation is part of the fabric upon which the Orange County tapestry is woven. Founded on the same day, the company has grown along with the county over the decades to include ventures of global proportions.

Founder C.E. Parker

First American traces its history back to August 1, 1889. That day, Orange County separated from Los Angeles County, and two title abstract companies were founded. Anticipating the split, the companies sent researchers to the Los Angeles County archives to seek records for what was to become the developed Orange County. A staff of six people was put to work for six days a week, manually transcribing all of the documents relating to the founding of the new county.

In 1894 Charles Edward "C.E." Parker merged the two abstract companies to form Orange County Title Company, the forerunner of First American. The abstract companies created voluminous property research files for people who wanted to buy or clear title to a property. Back then, it was not unusual for searches to include Spanish and Mexican land grants. Some documents dated back as far as 1834 and some had to be translated from Spanish. The mammoth project took two years and set a company standard of staunch accuracy — in the 110 years since, only one error has been discovered in those original records.

Although the abstract method was the standard in the East, swift development in the West led to a shorthand procedure, the title search, that assembled a list of relevant documents into a small, manageable file detailing only encumbrances on a property. The practice, driven by rapid growth, is the West Coast standard today and one that has helped First American make inroads in other parts of the world. Removing attorneys and solicitors from the mechanics of the real estate purchasing process enabled the company to deliver with the speed that was so important given the county's boom cycles.

The company has nurtured development in Orange County, from its own $3,500 headquarters first constructed in Santa Ana in 1901, to some of the county's largest projects for its major employers. Throughout its history, First American and its predecessors have guaranteed keystones of Orange County, including the county's first stone courthouse and the modern one in use today; Disneyland; and many of the county's seaside resort communities, including San Clemente, Dana Point and Capistrano Beach.

Development of Southern California brought buyers, speculators and investors to the county and fueled the need for First American's services. The family business was growing with C.E. Parker still at the helm, his son George A. Parker and son-in-law L. Rex Kennedy in key positions along with Harvey Gardner, who soon became the company's second president.

To build its business, Orange County Title Company took a more personal approach to sales and service. In the 1920s the company had one salesman, John Lutz. His idea of researching prospective clients and marketing the company's escrow services to potential clients was a new concept that took off.

Orange County Title Co., pictured in 1902, spawned an empire.

The state insurance commissioner granted title insurance powers to Orange County Title Company in 1924, opening new avenues for business. Orange County Title Company began providing title insurance policies exclusively in 1928 and has been building its business in that arena ever since. When C.E. Parker died in 1930, Gardner, George Parker and Rex Kennedy took the reins. Gardner resigned as president in 1943, leaving George Parker in command. Kennedy's son, Don "D.P." Kennedy, joined the company as associate counsel in 1948.

During the 1950s Orange County Title hired Dick Othmer away from a competitor. He would revolutionize the way the company — and ultimately the industry — viewed the title process. Until that time, title companies were more of a passive partner in transactions; they churned out research and insured transactions after the parties sorted out the details. Othmer's idea was to be more proactive on the title-processing end of the business. The company was the first to handle both title and escrow, removing obstacles to subdivision transactions.

In an effort to strengthen the company and position it for growth, beginning in 1957 the company initiated an aggressive expansion and acquisition policy, and in 1960 it took the First American name. The name change was strategic in several ways. When the company bought smaller companies in Ventura, Riverside and San Bernardino counties, it was clear that Orange County Title Company had outgrown its name.

The First American Financial Corporation moved into its new headquarters in 1999.

First American aggressively expanded its network of title offices by assimilating smaller companies all over the nation. That network now encompasses more than 500 offices and an extensive network of agents in the United States and abroad.

The company made its initial public stock offering in 1964. By 1968 expansion had led to so much growth that The First American Financial Corporation was formed as a general holding company for First American Title Insurance Company, First American Trust Company and all their sister companies.

During the late 1970s and early 80s the company was forced into debt as it fended off three hostile takeover attempts in rapid succession. In each case First American had to buy out the raiders, leaving the company to climb out on its profits. The same spirit and family leadership that founded the company saw it through those challenging times. Parker S. Kennedy, D.P.'s son, joined the company in 1977. He became president of First American Title in 1989 and president of The First American Financial Corporation in 1993. He has been at the helm ever since, with D.P. remaining as the company's chairman.

In 1998 the company's revenues reached nearly $3 billion. First American is the largest title insurer in the world, with a 90 percent market share in Canada. Today, The First American Financial Corporation, through its family of companies, is the leading provider of business information and related products and services. Its primary subsidiaries include First American Title Insurance Co., First American Real Estate Information Services, Inc., First American Home Buyers Protection Corp., First American Capital Management and, exclusively in Southern California, First American Trust Company and First Security Thrift Company. In addition, the company recently established its Consumer Information and Services division.

Chairman D.P. Kennedy and President Parker S. Kennedy (seated)

First American remains loyal to its home community and recently constructed a new headquarters in the city it has called home for more than a century. The company broke ground July 30, 1998, on a new 210,000-square-foot facility at MacArthur Boulevard and State Route 55 in Santa Ana. The unique design melds contemporary California style with traditional Jeffersonian architecture for a distinctive look that will ensure First American's presence in the community for future generations.

So intertwined are the Parker and Kennedy families with Orange County that what began as a collection of family photos has become a countywide resource archive of historical photos. The library is open one day a week and arranges to provide photos for display and reproduction for historical purposes.

The company continues to support the community through service and donations to the South Coast Repertory Theater, Bowers Museum, Orange County Performing Arts Center, Orange County Business Committee for the Arts and Chapman University. The company also supports the Orangewood Children's Foundation and its Business Mentor Program.

ORANGE COUNTY TEACHERS FEDERAL CREDIT UNION

The middle of the Great Depression might not seem like the best time to start a business, but for an organization formed to help people, it was the perfect time. Orange County Teachers Federal Credit Union (OCTFCU) was founded in 1934, when 126 school employees pooled $1,200 and established a financial institution to help improve each other's lives.

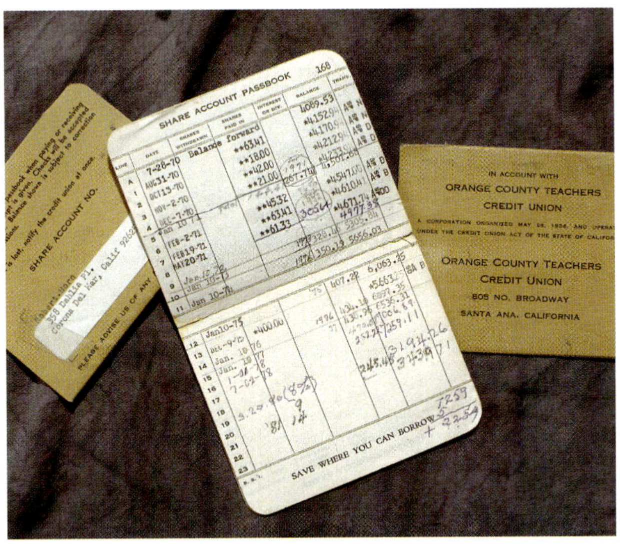

Serving Members through the generations — passbooks of original Member Robert Horn, his daughter Perdita Meyers and granddaughter Paula Meyers

OCTFCU continues its tradition of serving Members through the generations. The Hass family: Erma Lee, Ervin, Michelle, Desi, Sean and Connor, together, have over 58 years of Membership.

Initially one Santa Ana High School teacher — Harry Jackson — managed OCTFCU from the back office of World Travel in Santa Ana. Founded on the "people helping people" credit union philosophy that still exists today, OCTFCU served its Members by offering competitive rates and terms on loans and savings. From that day forward, OCTFCU has served generations of Members, providing them a full range of financial services.

"The Little White House," as the credit union was affectionately known, provided financial safety and security for Members. From its modest beginnings, what set the credit union apart from other financial institutions was the common bond among Members — a bond that is still felt when walking into an OCTFCU branch today.

Although its original Membership qualifications have expanded since its inception, OCTFCU has remained the Orange County *Teachers* Federal Credit Union to pay tribute to its heritage and the people who play such an integral part in shaping the lives of children in Orange County. OCTFCU works side by side with the Department of Education, educators and Member groups to better meet the needs of Members in the educational community.

Like all credit unions, OCTFCU is a Member-owned, not-for-profit financial cooperative and is able to pay back earnings directly to its Member-owners in the form of higher savings rates and lower loan rates.

As shareholders in their financial institution, Members have the opportunity to elect their board of directors. The board consists of Members, who are experienced professionals, who act as unpaid volunteers and work countless hours to make decisions

"The Little White House"

in the best interest of the Membership. The board's first priority has always been to provide Members exceptional service delivered by caring employees, or "teammembers," as they are commonly known at the credit union.

As its name indicates, Orange County Teachers Federal Credit Union has strong ties with the educational community and the individuals that dedicate their lives to education.

Through the board's direction and leadership, OCTFCU has evolved into one of the most financially solid credit unions in the nation. With service always at the heart of OCTFCU's goal to make Members' lives better, it has grown into the eighth-largest credit union in the United States and the largest educational credit union overall. As a democratic organization, OCTFCU's Members each have a voice to ensure the products and services offered at their credit union are a reflection of the needs of the Membership. Whether they are saving for their children's education, buying a new car or home or planning for retirement, Members have a variety of options for all of their financial needs.

Although the credit union has expanded its operations throughout Orange County, its Santa Ana headquarters stands at the same Broadway location where the "Little White House" first became a landmark in the Orange County community. In 1999 OCTFCU's Membership grew to more than 200,000 Members. It accommodated the continuous increase in its Membership by adding branches throughout Orange County. Currently, OCTFCU has eleven branches where Members can receive one-on-one personal service with OCTFCU teammembers, while taking care of all their financial needs.

In keeping with their goal of exceeding Members' service expectations, OCTFCU has successfully combined service with technology. Through OCTFCU'S Express Services, Members can access their accounts and perform a variety of transactions at over 100 Automated Teller Machines (ATMs) located throughout the greater Orange County area, through TellerPhone, its 24-hour automated telephone transaction service, and its online banking system, located on its Web site.

In addition to its branch and ATM locations, OCTFCU's presence is also felt throughout Orange County as it plays an active role in the local community. The credit union supports many community and educational programs as a way to give back to the community and people it serves. Each year, OCTFCU sponsors the Orange County Department of Education's Teachers of the Year Awards and the Academic Pentathlon. In addition, OCTFCU funds and administers annual scholarship programs, such as its Member Education Awards and Worthy Student Awards.

As Orange County Teachers Federal Credit Union continues to serve its Members through the generations, it will identify ways to meet the changing needs of the Membership in the 21st century. The credit union will put new technology to work for its Members while continuing the tradition of personalized service that has become the hallmark of OCTFCU. With service as its primary goal and a not-for-profit philosophy as its basis, OCTFCU is people helping people — freely — democratically — to improve each other's lives.

OCTFCU Members share a common bond as well as part ownership of their credit union.

WELLS FARGO BANK

Most people are familiar with Wells Fargo's stagecoach logo. It has been a source of pride to the company since 1852 when, because of the gold rush, a quarter of a million people swarmed into California. It was during this population explosion that Henry Wells and William G. Fargo, Eastern businessmen who had helped found the American Express Company, realized the need for a place where gold could be exchanged and miners could get loans. To fill this need, they formed the first banking and express office in San Francisco.

This early financial organization served the community as both an express office and a money exchange institution at a time when the stagecoach was the only link between Western towns and the rest of the country. The stagecoach had a reputation for reliability — an important image then and one the company maintains today.

W.H. Spurgeon, Wells Fargo Agent, Santa Ana, California — 1879-1888

Wells Fargo was such a success story that it prompted 19th century journalist Samuel Bowles to write, "A billiard saloon, a restaurant and a Wells & Fargo office are the first three elements of a Pacific Coast mining town." The economic boom stimulated by the gold rush was great for a while, but hard times were just around the corner. On Friday, February 13, 1855, they arrived with a thud — a financial panic forced the San Francisco office to close its doors for three days while the bank converted gold dust and gold bars into legal tender and gold coins. But other branches of Wells Fargo stood firm and met every customer's demand, allowing the company to weather "Black Friday."

By autumn 1855 Wells Fargo had 55 agencies and its reputation for "coming through," symbolized by the stagecoach, continued to develop. The company's success at that time was often based simply on its ability to do the job a little better or faster than expected. Agents were known, too, for community service, sponsoring civic festivities and collecting funds for disaster relief.

Wells Fargo was also one of the earliest integrated companies, hiring people of all nationalities. London Luff, an African-American employed as a messenger, was well known for his reliability. And William Robinson, an African-American leader in his hometown of Stockton, California, worked for the company for 40 years. Jose Estudillo was a Wells Fargo agent and treasurer for the bank in San Diego County in 1870. There were also more than 160 women who held positions as agents throughout the company's western territory, a rarity during the 19th century.

By the early 1900s the company had created a spectacular financial and mercantile distribution system, and in 1905 Wells Fargo merged with Nevada National Bank of San Francisco.

California and Oregon Stage Company carries Wells Fargo & Co. and the U.S. Mail.

By World War I 35,000 employees served the country through 10,000 offices over 80,000 miles of railroad routes. Then came World War II, which transformed the nation and the banking industry. Before that, Wells Fargo had been a commercial bank specializing in lending to businesses. But now it borrowed an idea from the retail world and opened small branches throughout California. Accessibility spurred further growth, but the sign of the stagecoach still stood for friendly, helpful neighborhood bankers.

In the 1880s Dr. Fuller's Drug Store in Tustin, California, was also the Wells Fargo & Company Express office as well as the local telegraph office.

In the 1960s Wells Fargo headed along the road at a full gallop, determined to bring better banking to its customers. In 1967 it introduced Stagecoach Checks featuring pictures of a Western scene. And soon after came a wide array of products and services including charge cards and automatic paycheck deposits. The company was also one of the first to introduce the "One-Line" service method which guided customers to teller windows in the fastest way possible. And, always on the lookout for new technology, in 1995 Wells Fargo became the first bank whose customers could view accounts online. Later, more Internet functions were added, and now Wells Fargo leads the nation in online customers.

Personal service, new products and reliability were the mainstays of the Wells Fargo name. But mergers were also a big part of the company's growth. In 1986 Wells Fargo stunned the banking community when overnight it doubled in size by purchasing Crocker Banks. Not even the stock market's 500-point drop on October 19, 1987 could slow the company's momentum as it continued to purchase financial properties throughout California. In 1996 Wells Fargo & Company merged with First Interstate Bancorp completing the biggest bank merger for that time in U.S. history. Then in 1998 Wells Fargo combined with Norwest, creating the nation's seventh-largest bank holding company in terms of assets.

Today customer service "with a capital C" is the guiding principle at all facilities, according to company literature. Dick Kovacevich, chief executive officer, believes Wells Fargo should stay close to its customers, "...understanding their needs, and providing professional, personalized and timely service." According to Well Fargo management, people make the difference. The talented team members, as employees are called, "... care about each other, care about their customers, care about their communities and care about their company."

At Wells Fargo's Private Client Services office in Orange County, personalized service is practiced every day. Founded in 1984, this specialized office of Wells Fargo offers retail and business customers a breadth of financial services including trust, brokerage and investment management as well as private banking. "Run it like you own it," is a company policy which insures that those in charge manage customer's money as if it were their own. "Yet still," says Regional Manager John Evans, "we have the full resources of a large, successful company behind us."

This regional office further emphasizes customer service by ensuring clients have direct access to an assigned bank officer, financial consultant, and portfolio manager or trust administrator as needed. Management believes in the company directive, which states, "We deliver products, services and information when, where and how the customer wants them." And community involvement is as important today as in the past. In Orange County, for example, bank contributions and grants totaled more than $360,000 in 1998 and the Private Client Services Office has twice been given the prestigious Orange County Business Committee for the Arts award for its volunteer efforts.

So Wells Fargo has come full circle, continuing to offer the dependability and reliability that its stagecoach logo denotes while still making sure that customer service is provided the "old-fashioned" way. But advanced technology is also a top priority in today's financial world. As Chairman of the Board Paul Hazen says, "Stagecoaches, telegraphs, telephones, computers, the Internet — whatever technology provides better service, we're going to find a way to use it."

EAGLE COMMUNITY CREDIT UNION

It was during the Great Depression that credit unions emerged with a motto sure to succeed in hard times, "People Helping People." These new financial cooperatives could offer value-oriented savings and lending programs to its members because they did not operate for profit. A pioneer in the industry, Eagle Community Credit Union, then known as Orange County Postal Credit Union, was established in 1937. Its original charter aimed to provide affordable financial services for postal and federal employees as well as their families.

Young members receive a warm welcome.
Photo by Lia Photography

From modest beginnings in Santa Ana, it has now grown to include the counties of Riverside, San Bernardino, San Diego and portions of Los Angeles. Eagle Community Credit Union has also expanded membership to include other select groups of companies seeking to offer the added value of credit union membership to their employees.

In business over 60 years, the credit union offers stability to its members and prides itself on personalized service and convenience. Featuring 24-hour a day telephone and computer services and an extensive network of ATMs, it offers members a variety of financial products in addition to traditional lending and savings programs. Members also qualify for free financial planning, AD&D insurance, discounts to theme parks and wholesale-warehouse memberships.

Eagle Community Credit Union leads the way in offering special services to children, teens and seniors. Its Circus Club account helps children to learn the habit of saving money and teens as young as 13 are allowed ATM cards and checking accounts. "We believe in a family-oriented approach to savings," says marketing manager Kirsten Sanchez. "We look to draw lifetime memberships by building a solid relationship with our young members."

With $135 million in assets and deposits insured up to $350,000, including combined coverage from both the National Credit Union Administration and private share insurance, members, young and old, are assured peace of mind. "A credit union has to meet rigorous financial criteria to qualify for this private share insurance" notes Sanchez, "and we're proud to offer it."

Even with the distinction of being one of the largest credit unions in Orange County, Eagle Community Credit Union is not resting on its laurels. Its objective is to grow in assets and membership while seeking to become the financial institution of choice for members. Future plans are to expand offerings of value-priced financial products while still maintaining a commitment to personal attention and service.

And it is that personal approach which motivates employees and pleases members. "Credit unions were built on the concept of people helping people," says president & CEO Joy Lawrence. "Actually, the members own the credit union and we work for them," she adds. So, to keep the focus on individual attention and service, those who submit comments on the credit union's quality surveys receive a personal response directly from her.

Community involvement is another way the credit union provides service. Active in local chambers of commerce, it also supports nonprofit agencies and awards scholarships to graduating high school students.

Placing the highest priority on personal attention and sound business practices, Eagle Community Credit Union intends to keep the promise of its mission statement, "...to provide the highest quality products and services while insuring stability and financial growth for members." Committed to these goals, it expects the next 60 years to be full of excitement and phenomenal growth.

Members financing with the credit union have a lot to smile about.
Photo by Lia Photography

MANUFACTURING & DISTRIBUTION

In addition to producing exceptional goods for individuals and industry, Orange County manufacturing and distribution companies provide employment for area residents.

SOUTHERN COUNTIES OIL COMPANY

The history of Southern Counties Oil Company is the tale of a small agricultural supply company that rose to be the largest independent petroleum distributor in California and one of the largest in the western United States. Southern Counties was also the first American company to do business in the former Soviet republic of Georgia.

Southern Counties: A company that values its customers, employees and community. A firm that has contributed not only to the quality of life in Orange County, but to world stability. A story of the courage and vision of the Greinke family.

Frank H. Greinke joined Standard Oil of California (now Chevron USA) in 1952. Beginning as a mail boy, he worked his way up through the ranks, first in accounting and then in sales. It was in his position as sales engineer, when he was counseling independent distributors, that Frank realized he could do much better on his own. Bitten by the entrepreneurial bug, and with confidence in his ability to make it happen, he resigned from Standard Oil in 1965.

Standard Oil also had confidence in Greinke's ability. When they heard he was going to do a deal with Texaco, they avoided having Frank as a competitor by making it possible for him to buy their Signal Oil consigneeship in Tustin, California.

The company Greinke bought, Motor Fuels Ltd., had been founded in 1930 as L.L. Hood. In the 35 years since the company had been established, its customer base and Orange County on the whole remained primarily agricultural. The city of Tustin, where the company was then located, had just one stoplight and a population of only 14,000.

Greko "minimart" and Gas Station in Tbilisi, Republic of Georgia

Eduard Shevardnadze, president of the Republic of Georgia (left) and Frank H. Greinke, the republic's first Citizen of The Year

Greinke named his new company Tri-County Transportation and continued to serve the farmers and fruit growers of the rural region. It provided petroleum products for farm machinery, such as the Irvine Company's tractors and wind machines. It also supplied the Orange County government.

In 1969 Chevron sold Signal Oil, for which Southern Counties was a consignee, to Exxon. After about nine months under the new ownership, Greinke's company, then called Greinke Petroleum, decided to take the bold and liberating step of becoming an independent distributor.

With the completion of the freeway and the continued growth of Los Angeles spilling over into Orange County, farms and orange groves were sprouting new suburbs. The favorable living conditions and economic opportunity attracted more business and development. Soon people were pouring into the area; growth was on everyone's mind and the word "boom" was on everybody's lips.

Greinke Petroleum, renamed Southern Counties Oil Company in 1976, grew along with Orange County, but the company's success didn't just happen because it rode the wave of development. A wave's power can provide an exhilarating lift, but it can also prove dangerous. Losing balance, making bad decisions and taking wrong turns have wiped out many.

Entrepreneurial visionaries and hard-working contrarians, Southern Counties introduced innovations like the Cardlock

Frank H. Greinke (left) and Frank P. Greinke, still behind the wheel

24-hour automated commercial fueling station and expanded into fleet-fueling and home heating oil when other companies were pulling out of these markets. Southern Counties Oil made the right decisions at the right time. It did so because of brilliant leadership and an acute awareness of the marketplace.

Time and again when market conditions or government regulations have presented problems, the company has approached them as challenges. Southern Counties Oil has found opportunity where other companies have discovered difficulties.

While the oil business is often associated with riches, the term "gusher" has its counterpart — the "dry hole." The industry has always been risky. The OPEC crisis of 1974 was the worst thing that could happen to an independent; there was no guaranteed supply. Southern Counties Oil Company's solid relationships with suppliers and its reputation in the industry, coupled with its innovative methods, let it figure a way around the shortage and create opportunity out of chaos. The company actually expanded from the latter part of 1974 through 75. During another world shortage in 1979, Southern Counties expanded again, at a time when most other companies were shrinking.

Frank H. Greinke's oldest son, Frank P. Greinke, worked at the company as a kid in the 1960s. When he was just 13, he would drive a truck off-road to service farm accounts, leaving his bike in a field. He officially joined the company when he graduated from high school in 1972.

In 1989 Frank P. Greinke became president and chief executive officer of Southern Counties Oil Company. He became part owner in 1991 and through a carefully executed plan assumed full ownership in 1995.

The transition from one generation to the next was a challenge. The Greinkes, always prepared to rise to a challenge, met this one with characteristic success. A long-term plan provided for the change to happen over time and permitted all parties to be ready for their new roles.

Frank, the father, has passed along his secret for success: a customer-oriented, innovative approach that exceeds expectations. Frank, the son, with exceptional organizational skills, a knowledge of what the company wants to accomplish and an insightful vision of where the market might go, has continued to lead Southern Counties Oil to even greater success. The company experienced more growth in the first 10 years of his presidency than in the previous 20 years.

When Frank P. Greinke assumed full ownership, his father assumed the dual title of ambassador/founder. Southern Counties Oil is one company that needs an ambassador more than most.

By 1991 reforming communists were increasingly visiting the United States on fact-finding missions about capitalism. The Greinkes had a friend in the international engineering business who would sometimes bring groups of communists to look at Southern Counties Oil. One day he brought the new Ukranian Republic's president and seven members of the country's congress to observe the company's automated Cardlock operation. The visit was reported by a local paper.

Soon the Greinkes received a call from some Russian communists. They wanted to know why the Greinkes were doing business with the Ukrainians and not the Russians? In reality Southern Counties Oil was only hosting some communist groups interested in seeing the automated facilities. It wasn't doing business with any of them.

Cardlock Fuels Station, La Mirada, California

Southern Counties Oil Company's corporate headquarters in Orange, California

That was about to change. The Russians invited the Greinkes to come to Russia to discuss business opportunities. After the first trip in August of 1991, just two weeks after the coup attempt, Southern Counties Oil began working on a project to construct gas stations in Russia. After a year and a half it had to abandon the project when the regime in St. Petersburg changed.

It was on a side trip to the Republic of Georgia that things changed again. Southern Counties Oil became the first American company to do business in Georgia, which was the first breakaway republic from the former Soviet Union. The company built the first Western-style gas station in the country. Southern Counties Oil followed that with several stations and an office, from which it imports and exports product.

Southern Counties' operations in Georgia have been only slightly profitable, while the frustrations have been immense and frequent. The transition from communism to capitalism requires more than freedom. There is much to learn. The command economy did not have accounts receivable or a cost of inventory. There were no checks, no credit cards — no credit. In fact, the country is largely ignorant of credit. Often they don't pay and have no intention of paying. Southern Counties, which firmly believes in ethics in business, has had to remain small while trying to patiently teach the Georgians a new way of doing business.

The motivation for doing business in the former communist country isn't profit. The Greinkes believe a free world is a better world. Success for these countries means jobs for workers, and food and products for the people. The Greinkes are on a humanitarian mission doing what they do best: succeeding in business.

When Frank H. Greinke bought a house in Georgia, the government wanted to retain ownership of the land. Greinke, a firm believer in individual property rights, wouldn't let the issue, or Georgia's president, Eduard Shevardnadze, rest. He implored Shevardnadze, the former Soviet foreign minister, to maintain control through taxation and relinquish property rights to the individual. Surprising everyone but Greinke, the president relented. They changed the policy and Frank bought the house and the land.

Gas stations and personal property rights are not all that the Greinkes have brought to the former communist nation. Whenever Southern Counties Oil ships lubricants to Georgia, half the containers are full of medicines, samples donated by American doctors. Because of the primitive economic situation in the country, there are virtually no lights on the roads. Greinke brought over road reflectors, the first in eastern Europe. When headlights would hit the reflectors in the black Georgian night, the reflections were so bright that the locals joked that planes would mistake them for landing lights on an airport runway.

The Republic of Georgia made Frank H. Greinke an honorary citizen. They then named him the republic's first citizen of the year.

The Greinkes' political involvement began at home. Frank H. Greinke served on eight local or regional commissions, was president of both the local chamber of commerce and Lions Club, and trustee for two medical research societies and two colleges. He was on the Tustin City Council and was then elected mayor. Greinke was instrumental in creating Irvine Valley College and in negotiating the development agreement with the Irvine Company for Tustin Marketplace — one of the most successful developments in Southern California.

Frank P. Greinke is also a past president of the Tustin Chamber of Commerce. During the time between the two

Greinke Petroleum in Tustin, California, (c. 1965)

Fleet Fuels at work, providing convenient on-site fueling

Greinkes' tenure in office, goals changed. Ironically, while Frank H. campaigned to bring more traffic into Tustin to help create development; when the younger Greinke served, 10 years later, one of his objectives as president was to control traffic.

Southern Counties Oil Company gives to many charitable causes. One of the younger Greinke's favorite projects is Mary's Kitchen, which provides meals for the homeless and indigent. All charities supported by Southern Counties must meet a standard: at least 85 percent of funds must directly support the constituents, not administrative costs. The company formed an employee committee to identify the best way to use funds allocated for donation.

Southern Counties Oil Company has had a remarkable history. The company's future looks to be even more spectacular. In 1988 it moved its headquarters to Orange, where it occupies more than three acres, with a 50,000-square-foot office and warehouse. It operates from facilities in seven Western states and serves California, Arizona, Nevada, Washington, Oregon, Utah and New Mexico.

A wholesale supply company, Southern Counties Oil is now an integrated marketing company comprising five different companies: Southern Counties Lubricants, Fleet Fuels, Pacific Northwest Energy Company, Total Energy Products and Cardlock Fuels.

It is one of the nation's top 10 distributors of refined lubricants for Chevron, Shell and Unocal; it provides mobile on-site diesel fueling for fleet vehicles; it furnishes home heating oil to the Pacific Northwest; it is a trading company shipping through pipelines, trading with other traders and supplying independent gas stations; Cardlock Fuels is believed to have been the first of the commercial cardlock, automated-fueling facilities. It is the industry leader.

Family is very important to the Greinkes. A third generation has stepped in to learn the business and lend a hand. Frank P. Greinke's children, Steven, who works in operations for Cardlock Fuels, and Cindy, who works in the legal department, have joined the company, much to the delight of their grandfather and father.

Frank H. Greinke has been awarded countless plaques in recognition of his assistance to numerous causes. Other people might put the plaques in a public place to show them off. Frank put them in the garage. He is content to go into his garage at night and look at them himself. They remind him of the experiences, the service that earned the plaque. He is pleased to have accomplished something of value, to have helped others.

Frank P. Greinke also has his share of awards. He is very active in the community through organizations such as the Young Presidents Organization (YPO). When he first came to work at Southern Counties Oil, Frank and his father still drove the trucks. A bookkeeper made up the company's third employee. Now, when he is addressing employee groups, vision meetings or the annual Christmas party, and he sees the families of Southern Counties Oil Company's more than 320 employees, he thinks, "because of our desire to have a successful company, good lives have been created, and that's a really satisfying thing."

As Frank H. Greinke says, "The company's Christmas party's gone from chili & beans and hot dogs in a warehouse in Tustin, to a full-dress party at the Hilton. We always want to keep that chili & beans flavor, but it's neat to see a truck driver in a tuxedo!"

No matter which of the many suits or hats the Greinkes have worn building Southern Counties Oil Company, they've been comfortable: succeeding and helping others to succeed.

A Pacific Northwest Energy Company service vehicle

ROBINSON PHARMA

Robinson Pharma has not only been making vitamins, it appears to have been taking vitamins as well. The company, which began in 1989 as a small distributor of dietary supplements to the Southeast Asian market, has grown to become a major, full-service contract manufacturer of vitamins and other supplements, serving customers worldwide. Robinson Pharma's growth has been a direct result of its unwavering commitment to excellence, its ability to efficiently cut costs without sacrificing quality and its dedication to superb customer service.

The company's story begins with one man's vision and perseverance. Tuong Nguyen, the firm's founder, immigrated to the United States from Vietnam in 1984. Nguyen had graduated from university with his civil engineering degree in 1975, just five days before the communist takeover of Vietnam.

Nguyen worked as an engineer for some time, but his entrepreneurial spirit eventually led him into the world of business, and in 1979 he started a company that manufactured animal food. Although running one's own business was wrought with problems, Tuong had always been able to form good relationships with friends and associates. That, and his skill at providing excellent products at a reasonable cost, allowed Tuong not only to survive, but to thrive and become very successful.

In spite of his success, Nguyen, guided by the desire to secure a better future for his family, decided to leave Vietnam and come to the United States. Once in this country, Tuong Nguyen had to struggle with a new language and culture as he tried his hand at business. A combination of good fortune and good friends led him to open a wholesale pharmacy and become a small distributor of dietary supplements.

A man of vision and courage, Tuong believed that Robinson Pharma could compete effectively as a manufacturer of dietary supplements. The firm would have to start small. Nevertheless, Tuong Nguyen was sure that with a dedication to quality, and by using his entrepreneurial skills to lower costs, Robinson Pharma could succeed.

Beginning with just one machine, the Orange County firm started manufacturing in 1990. Concentrating on the export market and producing small orders, the new manufacturer began building a reputation for superb customer service. Continued customer satisfaction translated into many referrals. The firm grew steadily, adding machines and employees, as it expanded into additional markets in the Pacific Rim and Eastern Europe. In 1991, the company was licensed by the Food and Drug Administration to manufacture over-the-counter and prescription drugs for export.

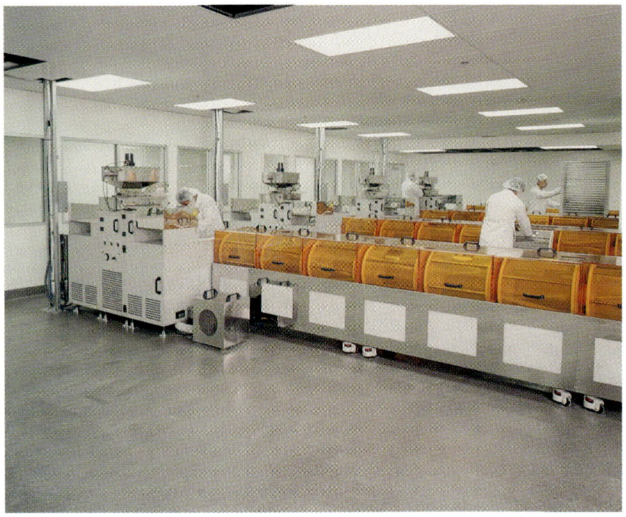

Manufacturing soft gelatin capsules

With its credentials established overseas, Robinson Pharma turned its attention to the U.S. market. The company soon distinguished itself in the domestic marketplace through its remarkable commitment to customer service. If a client just needed one emergency run, the company was willing to customize production and create a schedule to satisfy the customer. If it could be done, Robinson Pharma would do it.

Today, the company manufactures several forms of dietary supplements. The firm produces over eight billion nutritional and pharmaceutical tablets, capsules and soft gelatin capsules annually. The manufacture of soft gelatin capsules marks Robinson Pharma as a forward-thinking industry leader willing to invest in new technology to provide its clients with more manufacturing options.

Robinson Pharma's main facility in Santa Ana, California

In addition to soft gelatin capsules, Robinson Pharma can manufacture tablets with clear coating, color coating and enteric coating in a multitude of shapes and sizes. The firm's formulation expertise can provide customers with products such as instant-release tablets, sustained-release tablets, sublingual tablets and chewable tablets. Two-piece capsules and powders are other solid-dosage forms produced by Robinson Pharma's laboratories and production facilities. The company's packaging options include bottles, blister packs and packets.

Robinson Pharma's technical experts will formulate products to satisfy specific customer needs. The company can manufacture supplements based on a client's proprietary formula, which is held in strictest confidence, or they can create dietary supplements, such as vitamins or multivitamins, based on nonproprietary formulas. The company can also create pilot batches and conduct analytical testing. In addition, the firm offers value-added services, such as package design, label copy, label production, shipping, warehousing and special handling of customer-furnished materials.

With a keen eye toward intelligent growth and continually improved customer service, the company has always reinvested capital in new laboratory and production equipment. In June 1999 Robinson Pharma expanded into its new 112,000-square-foot building in Santa Ana. The addition of this impressive state-of-the-art facility increases the company's administrative, production and laboratory facilities to a total of 174,000 square feet.

Tuong Nguyen is a man of great vision. In 1990, when he first began manufacturing dietary supplements, he acquired a 3,500-square-foot space. Some friends and family members teased that he only had one machine surrounded by so much empty room. Nguyen believed his dedication to quality and the ability to keep prices low would make the business successful; he was confident that the company would soon need even larger facilities. Within one year the new firm moved into a 7,000-square-foot space, doubling in size, and it wasn't long before the successful company had expanded to 16,000 square feet.

Now, with Robinson Pharma's 174,000 square feet, Tuong Nguyen can already envision the need to expand. He expects that the company, which grew from $500,000 in its first year to $25 million within one decade, will do $60 million in the year 2000, and that Robinson Pharma will hit the $100 million mark by 2001, at which time it will most likely go public. While these are projections, they are not idle boasts. The company's track record confirms Tuong Nguyen's vision.

Tableting Machine

Pharma's growth has been impressive. The company's equally impressive expectations of future growth are in large part fueled by pervasive customer demand for the company's services.

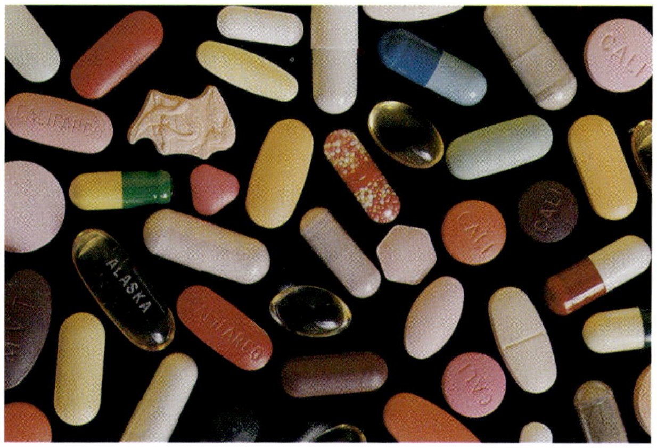

Tablets, capsules and soft-gelatin capsules come in many colors, shapes and sizes.

Robinson Pharma has maintained an unswerving dedication to providing the best customer service possible. It is the only way it can succeed.

Contract manufacturing is a customer-driven business. Everything is made to order. Products must meet rigid technical specifications. Customers impose extremely demanding delivery schedules. Robinson Pharma has succeeded by doing everything possible to accommodate its customers.

The company prides itself on its "sudden service," defined by rapid response on quotations, quick turnaround on pilot runs and short lead-times for full production runs. Robinson Pharma has grown because it can satisfy customer demands and perform at a level that exceeds expectations. Its pricing is extremely competitive due to the high volume of business, sophisticated equipment, and the dedication and skill of the Robinson Pharma team.

Members of senior management at Robinson Pharma are all well-respected industry leaders in their areas of expertise, which include technology, quality, manufacturing, purchasing, marketing, sales, management and operations.

Robinson Pharma has demonstrated great flexibility in its ability to meet the needs of customers. Being flexible is also a key to its own growth. The company is moving forward, always striving to identify more opportunities for diversification. The firm's commitment to the new soft-gelatin technology represents solid confidence in its abilities and signals a possible expansion beyond dietary supplements. Soft-gelatin technology can be used in the manufacture of many items including dietary supplements, over-the-counter and prescription medicines, cosmetics and a variety of other products.

A coating machine

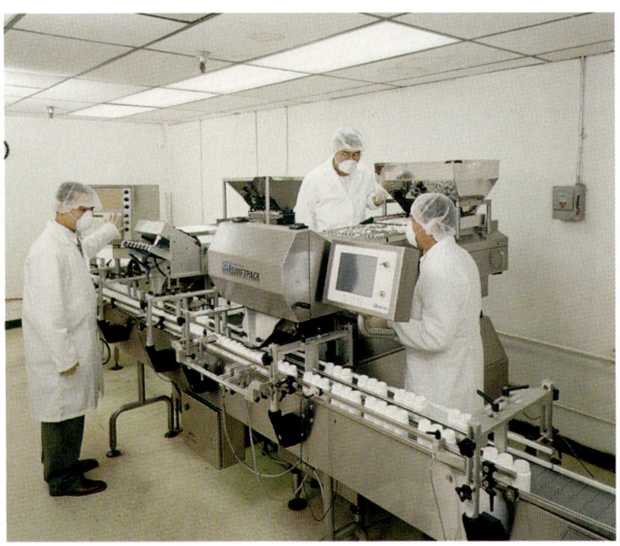

Workers maintain quality on the packaging line.

An encapsulating machine

Many companies may value a commitment to customer service and satisfaction, but in the field of contract manufacturing it is essential. A contract manufacturer doesn't control its own destiny. It can't manufacture a product and try various means of marketing it. Rather than attracting customers to a product, a contract manufacturer must attract customers with its reputation and actual performance.

In this business, the customer literally comes first. Without customers there are no products, since items are custom manufactured for the client. The only way to maintain efficiency and succeed at contract manufacturing, as Robinson Pharma has, is to retain clients. The firm has grown because its performance remains exemplary. The reputation that precedes it reflects a company that values its customers as the driving force in its business. With its can-do attitude and capabilities, it seeks to form partnerships with clients to pursue the mutual goals of success, satisfaction and pride of performance.

DON MIGUEL MEXICAN FOODS, INC.

Every day, millions of Americans face the age-old challenge. What's for dinner? For the better part of the last century, Don Miguel Mexican Foods, Inc. has provided the answer.

Founded (as Alex Foods) in 1908 and built upon a commitment to quality, Don Miguel is an Orange County success story. The past nine decades have seen the Anaheim-based company rise from a simple tamale pushcart to a small, family-owned business to one of America's leading manufacturers of premium prepared foods.

The initial manufacturing plant was built in 1926 adjacent to the residence of the company founder, Alex Morales Sr., and by 1940 the company had well-established direct store delivery routes throughout Southern California. After World War II, Alex Morales Jr. became president of the company and built a brand new, state-of-the-art food production facility on a 2.5-acre site in Anaheim.

The 1970s saw the company's first major acquisition of XLNT Mexican Food and sales expanded outside of California. In the 1980s the acquisitions of Piñata Mexican Foods and Don Miguel Foods firmly set the foundation for the company's future growth.

In the early 1990s the company purchased the Mexican Holiday brand of dinners and entrees and Lucca stuffed pastas and sauces. These were closely followed by the acquisition of the El Charrito line of frozen dinners, entrees and burritos.

In 1995 the combined companies emerged as Don Miguel Mexican Foods, Inc., and rededicated itself to satisfying America's appetite for great tasting food. Generations of experience in the food industry have allowed Don Miguel Mexican Foods, Inc. to become an industry leader in product innovation. In 1996 the company launched their Lean Ole! product line of

98 percent fat free Mexican foods, which became an instant success with health-conscious Americans.

To keep up with increasing demand, Don Miguel opened a second production facility in Dallas, Texas, but the corporate headquarters remains in Anaheim. Today the product lines include El Charrito Dinners, Entrees, and Burritos; Don Miguel Burritos and Chimichangas; Lean Ole! Enchilada Dinners, Entrees, and Burritos; XLNT Chili con Carne and Tamales; and Piñata Tortillas and Burritos. Last year Don Miguel made dinner, lunch, and snacks for over 60 million people!

Don Miguel proudly supports the community by sponsoring various Little League baseball and soccer teams, and is an active supporter of programs at California State University, Fullerton and the university's advancement foundation. The Olive Crest Abused Children's Foundation also continues to be a special interest.

BOATSWAIN'S LOCKER, INC.

Some companies are not content to drift along a familiar course; when they sense a shift in the wind, they seize the opportunity to change direction and sail to the head of their field. That's just how Boatswain's Locker Inc. charted its course to success.

The story of Boatswain's Locker began in 1939 when the Orange County coast remained largely undeveloped. Captain John Reckman opened a boatyard in Newport Beach, naming it "Boatswain's Locker" after a boat officer's equipment-storage locker. As the local boating industry flourished, the boatyard became a familiar and trusted sight along the shoreline.

Besides servicing boats, the company began selling engines and parts in the 1960s and 70s. Boatswain's opened a store in Seal Beach in 1960 and a warehouse in its present Costa Mesa location in the mid 1970s. Ed Gribble and Hank Hill led the company as its prime shareholders and officers, steering it slowly away from service and toward a sales emphasis.

In 1982 Ed Gribble's son Dan, along with two other managers, bought half the business. Gribble, who had earned degrees in mechanical engineering, naval architecture and business, was well-qualified for his new role. By 1986, as the company's new sole owner, Dan Gribble decided to sharpen the company's focus. Boatswain's sold the boatyard and stopped selling to the public, instead concentrating on the wholesale distribution and sales of smaller marine engines (in the 10 to 500 horsepower range) primarily used in pleasure craft. Boatswain's would sell the premier brands like Yanmar, Crusader and Mercruiser that dominate the market. Gribble consolidated the business, closing the retail stores and moving operations into the Costa Mesa location.

Boatswain's Locker as it is today. To the left are sales, marketing, administrative offices as well as parts warehousing; to the right, engine service, prep and warehousing.

The change was radical. Private customers, accustomed to seeing the familiar boatyard as they cruised up the coast, could no longer take their boats there to be fixed. With the coastal presence gone and the customer base shifted, some people thought Boatswain's had gone out of business. But that was far from the case, as the industry was soon to discover.

To advertise its new incarnation, the company sent out mailings and press releases, visited yacht clubs and put on service seminars. It was important to let customers know that the company was still in business and that its top-flight power products were still available. Part of the strategy was to build grassroots demand and then funnel the sales through Boatswain's emerging dealer network.

After initially struggling like a startup, the newly configured company broke even in 1989. Rob Apted, as general manager, became a minority shareholder instrumental in the success of the company's new plans. Determined to succeed, Gribble set a new goal in 1994: within three years, he vowed, the company would become the No. 1 marine engine distributor in its niche in the southwest United States. The company met its goal, becoming so successful that it quickly outgrew its Costa Mesa headquarters and expanded into the warehouse next door.

Primary to the success of the company is its technical support of its products through the dealerships. Its highly trained staff answers questions and provides service and training to the dealers. The relationship works both ways, with dealers often solving problems for Boatswain's. Strong relationships with suppliers have also been vital. Most instrumental was the association with Yanmar Diesel Engine Company, and more recently the company is enjoying the success of QuickParts, a new parts-delivery system it has developed with Mercury Marine.

Technological advancements have played a major role in the development of the company's products and delivery systems. For instance, technological changes to metallurgy,

After extensive testing in Mag Bay, Mexico, Boatswain's Locker President Dan Gribble (center) is rewarded with a good day's catch.

fuel injection systems and electronic controls have resulted in diesel engines that are smaller, lighter, cleaner burning and more powerful than they used to be. The Environmental Protection Agency, the Air Resources Board and other regulating agencies have indirectly brought about many such changes. Like the automobile industry, the boating industry is moving away from carbureted gasoline engines in favor of electronically fuel-injected models. Boatswain's has benefited from these changes by distributing industry-leading brands. For example, when Santa Barbara Air Quality Management District was repowering boats in its harbor to earn emissions credits, Yanmar diesel engines, distributed by Boatswain's, were among the few that qualified for the standards. It was a terrific sales opportunity that Boatswain's seized.

View of the original Boatswain's shipyard as it looked in the early 1960s

Increasingly Boatswain's uses new computer technology for its distribution system. The company is in the process of converting to a new pilot software system. The state-of-the-art system — developed with Mercury Marine and Prophet 21 Wholesale, a distribution software company — allows the company to efficiently monitor and control inventory while improving delivery and adding to the bottom line. The company plans to institute an Internet commerce program that will allow dealers to order parts with the click of a mouse, automatically printing the order in Boatswain's parts warehouse. Boatswain's salespeople, freed from having to take catalog orders, will become even greater resources to dealers.

Boatswain's stays very active in the boating community, maintaining high visibility for itself and support for the industry. It sponsors *Start Me Up* and *Alliance*, both sportfishing boats, at various events and tournaments. The company maintains a presence at boating rendezvous and shows including the Long Beach, San Diego and Northern California boat shows. The company puts on seminars and donates raffle prizes for boating-related events. Boatswain's is a sponsor of local sports teams and the Balboa Yacht Club Junior Sailing Program and has participated

Boatswain's Locker installation specialist repowers with what was, in the early 1960s, the state-of-the-art marine engine.

in programs that involve underprivileged and handicapped children in boating activities.

Boatswain's future plans include moving into higher horsepower engines — up to 1,000 hp — which are mostly used in yachts. In addition to serving dealerships and boat builders, Boatswain's also works in the military and commercial industries as a subcontractor, providing products to Navy SEALS, offshore oil drilling companies, the Mexican government, the Coast Guard and more. Quite often the company will partner with its customers to build and test boats with a variety of propulsion systems. This is not only a strategic move, but one that is especially interesting for Gribble, given his naval architect background. The company looks forward to expanding its military and commercial business.

The company, which does about 70 percent of its business in California, plans to expand further, possibly opening other distribution centers. Gribble would also like to open a school to train marine engine mechanics and to train its retailing clients to utilize computers, manage inventories and provide better customer service. Boatswain's future plans are ambitious and far-reaching, but considering how far it has come since its early days, there seems no limit to the potential of this seaworthy company.

Boatswain's showroom and parts counter

3 DAY BLINDS

3 Day Blinds had its modest beginnings in 1978 as a furniture store in Laguna Hills. At the time, draperies were still the favorite window coverings of America, but mini blinds were beginning to emerge as a functional alternative. Ed Ulyate, the company's founder, soon realized that he could produce mini blinds faster and cheaper than the major window covering manufacturers of the time. In order to offer less expensive mini blinds to his customers, he began manufacturing them in the back of his store.

Business continued to boom since 3 Day Blinds was the only window coverings company able to manufacture and deliver products within three days from the date ordered (vs. as long as five weeks, the standard at that time within the industry). Within a short time, Ulyate had opened over 80 3 Day Blinds stores, and there appeared to be no end in sight to the company's growth.

In 1989 a number of major changes occurred that continued to drive the company forward. The founder decided to retire from the business and sold 3 Day Blinds to an investment group. Art Schumann was appointed president and chief executive officer and Roger O'Brien was named executive vice president and chief financial officer.

3 Day Blinds expanded its custom-manufactured line to include several different product categories, including 1-inch aluminum mini blinds, vertical blinds, 1-inch and 2-inch wood blinds, Virtual Wood™ blinds, 2-inch PVC blinds, cellular and pleated shades, as well as carrying Simply Sheers drapery and Hunter Douglas products. The new management team emphasized improving overall product quality. At the same time, management continued its expansion program, opening 40 more stores in Arizona, California and Nevada.

Cellular Soft Shades add dimensions of style and comfort to any home. Customers can choose from translucent fabrics that allow soft, diffused light into rooms, or room-darkening fabric for the utmost in light control.

The richness of natural wood, beautifully finished, enhances any room. 3 Day Blinds manufactures custom wood blinds in 1-inch and 2-inch slat sizes.

Under Schumann's direction, the company also implemented a number of major changes in operational procedures to ensure the high quality and consistency throughout all 3 Day Blinds stores. These included an intensive sales training program which is recognized today as one of the best in the industry, and the implementation of a computerized point-of-sale system to ensure all orders are downloaded quickly and accurately to the manufacturing floor.

The mini blind soon outsold the cumbersome curtain. The blind's clean lines and unique union of function and fashion led to higher demand and consequently a larger market for 3 Day Blinds. Simultaneous with this increased demand for blinds, a demand arose for more versatile and aesthetically pleasing blinds. Vinyl vertical blinds emerged as the successors to standard mini blinds, offering more stylistic options because they could be embossed or made to resemble fabric.

Wood blinds also revolutionized the window covering industry. A wide, horizontal slat, and natural, versatile colors and texture made wood blinds one of the fastest-growing forms of window coverings. Equally notable are cellular shades, which, crafted from heavy polyester, possess a distinctive, honeycomb-like structure.

Vertical blinds produce a winning combination of function and fashion. A gorgeous selection of colors and styles lets customers create the fashion look they want.

These shades are admired for their varying degrees of opacity, as well as their powerful insulation capability.

In 1997 3 Day Blinds began to open a series of 3 Day Blinds Superstores. These Superstores are three to five times larger than the traditional retail outlets and are located in more-prominent shopping areas. Instead of merely displaying blinds on a wall, these showrooms feature professionally decorated room displays that offer customers an opportunity to view window coverings in the equivalent of a miniature model home. These impressive 3 Day Blinds Superstores have set a new standard for the retail window covering industry.

The expansion of 3 Day Blinds continues and is moving eastward. In February 1999 the company acquired the Habitat Wallpaper & Blinds chain in the Midwest, and 3 Day Blinds Superstores can now be found as far east as Ohio.

A uniquely differentiating service that separates 3 Day Blinds from its competition is its Shop at Home services. A design consultant will come to a home and take measurements, provide samples and install the blinds as well as offer design expertise.

The management team at 3 Day Blinds has made the company an integral and essential part of the Orange County community. As a business, the management of 3 Day Blinds has received several nominations for Entrepreneur of the Year, an award granted annually by local business people of Orange County. In addition to its business success, 3 Day Blinds is appreciated in Orange County for its community outreach and contributions. The company has established an ongoing relationship with the Children's Hospital of Orange County through its support and sponsorship of the hospital's 5K CHOC Walk each October. This event, which raises money for hospital research, is attended by more than 10,000 people.

3 Day Blinds also demonstrates its concern for children with its unique Child Safety Program, which includes the distribution of thousands of free child-safety kits each year. These kits have been designed by 3 Day Blinds to quickly and easily modify older window coverings to be safer for children. They are distributed free of charge throughout the company's network of showrooms.

From small beginnings here in Orange County, a nationwide retailer and manufacturer has evolved and will continue to grow in the years ahead. 3 Day Blinds continues to serve the needs of its friends and neighbors in Orange County and throughout the country.

New to 3 Day Blinds is Simply Sheers drapery. The Pinch Pleat drapery is the most common type of drapery available today that works well in formal or casual settings.

BAL SEAL ENGINEERING COMPANY, INC.

The story of Bal Seal Engineering Company, Inc. is the story of invention. To paraphrase a familiar saying, invention is necessity's child — and the founding of Bal Seal illustrates this adage. It was the 1950s, during the infancy of the space program, when Pete Balsells, Sr. (then an evening engineering instructor at the University of Dayton in Ohio) identified the need for a new kind of seal that could withstand extremely low temperatures in outer space.

A native of Barcelona, Spain, Balsells was a gifted young scientist who was determined to succeed not only in his academic pursuits but in business as well. Identifying the puzzle was simple; solving it was not. Working with his wife, Joan, also a talented engineer, Balsells spent the next seven years developing a means to do so.

Balsells' professional work at the time involved developing new fire extinguisher technology. In 1958 Balsells and his wife moved to California to expand the fire extinguisher business into the western United States. Still at work on his seal, Balsells applied the work he had done on the fire extinguishers and experimented with a relatively new material called Teflon®. Once Balsells perfected his canted, spring-loaded design, he sent it out to have the seal fabricated. The idea was so good that the fabrication company immediately copied the idea and became Balsells' first competitor. Undaunted, Balsells purchased a lathe and learned to manufacture his invention in his own garage. In 1962 Balsells' seal gave flight to John Glenn's Atlas Rocket, a new industry was born and Bal Seal Engineering Company Inc. was headed toward a bright future.

But the story of Bal Seal Engineering is not just the story of one invention; it is the story of a company that made invention its product, means of growth and way of conducting business.

Still working at another company by day, the entrepreneurial Balsells worked from 5:30 to 10:30 p.m. and on weekends to fill orders. He and his wife soon began to hire students to help, working out of their living room and garage in Santa Fe Springs.

BUT THE STORY OF BAL SEAL ENGINEERING IS NOT JUST THE STORY OF ONE INVENTION; IT IS THE STORY OF A COMPANY THAT MADE INVENTION ITS PRODUCT, MEANS OF GROWTH AND WAY OF CONDUCTING BUSINESS.

Balsells was an engineer, not a salesman. As such, his first sale was predictably tough to close. But once the company's product proved successful, it quickly expanded from the space industry to the aircraft industry, and then just about every type of enterprise imaginable. Bal Seal Engineering had or could develop a component that would improve the

Sleek, state-of-the art architecture provides the setting for Bal Seal's new 125,000-square-foot headquarters in Foothill Ranch.

performance of any product that needed to seal liquids, gases and powders at high or low temperature. Working with hundreds of customers, Bal Seal Engineering created hundreds of types of seals and applications. Bal Seal products are used in hundreds of applications from dental instruments and pacemakers to espresso machines, gas pumps and even tattooing equipment. Ever the innovator, Balsells found many ways to reinvent his own creation — his company now holds approximately 50 active U.S. patents and over 70 active foreign patents on seals, gaskets and spring releases.

Soon after the company started in the Balsells' home, neighbors complained and the operations moved to a small Quonset rented for $40 a month. Finally, in 1965, the company was making enough money to pay Balsells a salary; he quit his day job and devoted his full attention to Bal Seal Engineering. It remained a characteristically family business, with the Balsells children helping their mother with the office work, and Balsells himself doing sales in the morning, engineering in the afternoon and continuing to work late into the evening.

In 1975, with approximately 30 student employees working out of two Quonsets, the company moved to a 24,000-square-foot facility in Santa Ana. Just a year later, during some high-temperature testing, a fire ignited. About 70 percent of the new facility burned, setting the company back three years. Toiling by candlelight and flashlight, with many workers relocated to the Balsells' living room, the dedicated team quite literally reinvented Bal Seal Engineering.

The company grew stronger, enjoying about a 30-percent growth rate per year. Then, in 1993, with a degree in business management under his belt, Peter Balsells, Jr. took the reins as COO and ushered in a new era of success. Balsells set to work discovering why sales levels were not growing as fast as the work force was growing. Applying a new business model based on the "Theory of Constraints" (TOC), Balsells and his new production manager identified a bottleneck in production and implemented a new production methodology in the context of an entirely new manufacturing business paradigm. As a result, production increased, overtime work decreased and profits doubled in a single year. Having successfully reinvented the way the company conducted operations, Peter Balsells, Jr. eventually became company president, allowing his father to concentrate on developing new products and be company chairman.

The engineering firm opened a sales office in The Netherlands in 1994, expanding its customer base in Europe and Asia. In 1998, with 250 workers operating out of two separate buildings, the company built a new facility in Foothill Ranch, nestled at the base of the beautiful Cleveland National Forest mountains. The scenic location was the inspiration of Balsells, an avid hiker. The bold design of the building itself was the vision of Balsells' son-in-law, Jonathan Stillman, who was the company's president from 1991 to 1996. Working with a local architect,

In the early days, Bal Seal Engineering operated out of this modest Quonset.

Stillman directed the sleek, modern building to flow from a shimmering circle symbolic of the seals that the company creates. The new facility is 125,000 square feet, with the possibility of expanding to 200,000 square feet. The company that seemed to be continually on the move since its inception was ready to settle down.

Bal Seal has won numerous awards for its products and its outstanding business practices. The company takes particular pride in two of these awards. In 1998 Arthur Andersen Inc. and *Business Finance Magazine* awarded the company the Vision Award for Excellence in Business Performance Reporting, in recognition of Bal Seal's application of TOC. In

BAL SEAL HAS WON NUMEROUS AWARDS FOR ITS PRODUCTS AND ITS OUTSTANDING BUSINESS PRACTICES.

1999 the Employers Group recognized Bal Seal with its Best Practices Award for "introducing human resource programs that influence business success." Among these programs were TOC-based restructuring, flexible schedules, a 401(k) program, onsite language instruction, a new compensation system, 125 cafeteria plan, employee incentive programs, and new vacation and education policies.

The company maintains a dedication to education and has always employed student workers. It holds biweekly, in-house courses in English and Spanish and operates a program to pay for the continuing education of employees. The Balsells family funds four fellowships in engineering for students pursuing postgraduate degrees at the University of California, Irvine. The company also participates in a statewide engineering council that sets University of California policy for coursework and student programs in engineering.

The future promises great things for Bal Seal Engineering. It plans to continue to grow and expand worldwide. And of course, it plans to keep inventing new products — and no doubt, reinventing itself — to meet its customers' needs.

BONERT'S SLICE OF PIE

With their tender, flaky crusts and fresh fillings made from scratch, Bonert's pies taste homemade and old-fashioned — but the history of Bonert's Slice of Pie is a totally modern success story. Bonert's Slice of Pie began in 1993 when its CEO, Michael Bonert, sensed an unmet need: homemade-quality pies that could be mass-produced and distributed. It was a proposition that required building a high-tech business around a low-tech product.

Bonert's prides itself on the high quality of its home-style pies. *Photo by Lia Photography*

But though the company was new and its enterprise was challenging, Bonert's was determined to succeed. In the beginning the company gathered a small number of personnel experienced in pie manufacturing, design of labels, logos, brochures, sales and marketing. They knew that there was a need in the marketplace and they had plenty of ideas and concepts.

The new company rented a vacant and previously run tortilla factory on Adams Street in the Enterprise zone of Santa Ana, where its employees set about creating a line of 40 classic home-style fruit and cream pies. To start, they used basic equipment like large kettles that steam hundreds of pounds of fruit, machines that could create rack after rack of picture-perfect crusts, ovens that could bake pies and freezers to freeze and store the pies. From the beginning the company emphasized quality, selecting only the freshest and best quality ingredients, including Dutch cocoa for its chocolate crème pies, fresh egg whites for its meringues and crisp apples delivered daily for its apple pies.

Bonert's fruit pie fillings are prepared from scratch. *Photo by Lia Photography*

Bonert's quality, innovative packaging strategies, reasonable prices and 100 percent delivery guarantee made its products desirable. Soon it was selling its first truckloads of pies to blue-chip grocery stores, primarily in Southern California and in the Midwest.

In its first year, Bonert's topped sales expectations and quickly set its sights on improving and expanding. To attract new business and solid relations with established customers, Bonert's offered truckload specials and customized labels.

When Bonert's pie sales began to take off nationwide, the company expanded its pie line to grow its business. In 1994 it

IN 1997, 1998, 1999 AND 2000 BONERT'S PIES WON THE RECOGNITION OF THE AMERICAN PIE COUNCIL, WHICH JUDGED SEVERAL OF BONERT'S PIES THE BEST IN THE NATION.

added no-sugar-added pies and gourmet 9-inch pies. In 1995 it added new flavors such as peach pineapple and key lime and in 1996 premiered its home-style cream pies. Gourmet French lattice twists and a new line of 5-inch pies were added in 1998, followed by its latest 12-inch upscale pies in 1999. The company now offers over 350 varieties of raw, frozen or thaw-and-serve baked pies to grocery chains and the food service industry throughout the continental United States and Hawaii.

In 1997, 1998, 1999 and 2000 Bonert's pies won the recognition of the American Pie council, which judged several of Bonert's pies the best in the nation. All together the company has won 18 such awards, for its apple, pumpkin, lemon meringue, apricot-pineapple, strawberry-rhubarb and peach pies.

From the beginning, Bonert's faced the challenge of seasonality inherent in the industry. Pie sales peak at Thanksgiving and remain relatively slow the rest of the year. The experienced Bonert's team met the challenge by finding ways to work more efficiently year-round. Careful planning led to a well-coordinated manufacturing schedule that allows for early buildup of seasonal inventories during nonpeak periods.

A carefully maintained production schedule allows Bonert's to meet seasonal demands for pies.
Photo by Lia Photography

BONERT'S CREDITS MUCH OF ITS SUCCESS TO THE QUALITY OF ITS WORK FORCE, WHICH SEEMS TO TAKE TO HEART THE SLOGAN PRINTED ON THE FACTORY FLOOR: "QUALITY BEGINS WITH ME."

Bonert's has continued to expand and modernize since its early days of success. It made a habit of replacing existing equipment with bigger, state-of-the-art equipment, automated machinery that makes entire pies — from crust to filling — and sends them down a conveyor belt in a fraction of the time it took using traditional machinery manned by several workers.

Illustrating its strong commitment to its employees, Bonert's concluded that increasing automation did not require staff reductions and the company focused on using workers more efficiently to meet increasing sales. By 1998 Bonert's employed triple the number it had just five years earlier. Moreover, the company has created a management team and workforce that has a combined 400 years of bakery experience.

Bonert's credits much of its success to the quality of its work force, which seems to take to heart the slogan printed on the factory floor: "Quality begins with me."

Bonert's progressive corporate profile includes an active commitment to community. The company has not forgotten that the city of Santa Ana helped it by providing guidance on the complicated new business-permitting process, assistance with Enterprise Zone tax credits and more. As Bonert's grew and prospered, it shared its success with the community. Bonert's makes an effort to hire Santa Ana residents, who account for nearly 80 percent of Bonert's workforce. Company management serves on a city commission. In 1999 Bonert's took a leadership role in the community's efforts to obtain Federal Empowerment Zone designation, which is designed to improve neighborhoods and provide training and job opportunities for its residents. The company has made donations to a number of charitable organizations, including food banks, churches and the City of Hope.

Bonert's also maintains an aggressive recycling program — including everything from metal cans to cardboard cartons.

Bonert's is keeping an eye continuously focused on the future. It is continually expanding its facilities and equipment. The company is installing a new computer system that will improve inventory, production scheduling, logistics tracking and general communications with vendors, customers and brokers. But still, at the core of Bonert's progressive plans is its continued commitment to old-fashioned customer service and creating the finest pies it can make.

HINES NURSERIES

From its modest beginnings in 1920, Hines Nurseries has grown to be one of the largest wholesale growers and distributors of ornamental plants in the nation. At the company's 437-acre site in Irvine, California, expert horticulturists raise more than 18 million plants per year. These include more than 1,600 varieties of woody shrubs, perennials, annuals, holiday plants and topiaries.

Considered a showplace of horticultural technology, Hines is a hub of constant activity. With the aid of lights and a full-time night crew, custom-designed trucks are loaded around the clock as plants are expertly packed to reach their destination locally and across the country. The company maintains a competitive edge by ensuring that plants and shrubs arrive at their destination when they are needed, in the healthiest possible condition for display and sale.

Hines Nurseries is a national leader in the horticultural industry, focusing on a commitment to quality.

Over the years, Hines Nurseries built its excellent reputation within the nursery industry by specializing in ornamental shrubs such as *rhaphiolepis*, *hibiscus* and *bougainvillea*. And though plants such as *Nandina domestica* 'Gulf Stream' and *Rhaphiolepis indica* 'Hines Dark Leaf' Bay Breeze™ are still very popular with consumers, Hines is always looking to develop new varieties to add to the product mix. This focus on growing new strains has yielded 26 patents and many new varieties for people to enjoy.

Consistent quality is evident in the beauty of the growing grounds in Irvine, California.

Flowering plants such as marigolds, petunias and ivy geraniums are also part of the booming business at Hines these days. Recognizing the increased demand for bright splashes of color in home landscaping, the company has a growth strategy that involves acquiring facilities already selling color material to the large home centers and mass merchandisers. With eight operations in California, Oregon, Pennsylvania, South Carolina and Texas, Hines continues to look for quality acquisitions that will stimulate future growth.

Diversity of product has greatly contributed to the success of the company, too. Hines recently purchased Sun Gro Horticulture Inc. and added peat moss to its product mix. Harvested from bogs in Canada and Oregon, this garden staple accounts for approximately 36 percent of overall sales, and customers include greenhouse growers, vegetable farmers and golf course developers.

Hines also uses new marketing concepts to increase customer satisfaction and sales. One such innovation spawned the Patio Tropics® line of green goods. These lush, vibrantly colored plants are prepotted in attractive containers and provide the end user with a convenient decorative item for patio or poolside.

The development and use of the latest growing and technological techniques is another way in which Hines Nurseries leads the field. It pioneered the use of drip irrigation systems on containers and was one of the first to use innovative equipment like the bottom-heated mist beds that keep plant roots warm, facilitate rooting and speed growth. The nursery also utilizes a 1.5-million-gallon reservoir to continuously capture and recycle irrigation water. This reduced water use by 35 percent, and Hines was recognized by the California State Association of Water Districts for its efficient water-use practices.

By remaining on the forefront of technological development, paying attention to the buying habits of customers and landscaping trends, broadening its marketing base and acquiring new suppliers, Hines stays ahead of the growing game and remains a leader in the field.

While continually working to maintain industry leadership, Hines Nurseries is equally committed to being a good neighbor by contributing to worthy causes within the community. A partial list of beneficiaries to which it donates either money, time or plant material includes: Ronald McDonald House, The Orange County Academic Decathlon, Irvine Temporary Housing, Habitat for Humanity, Memorial Garden at the Santa Ana Zoo, Irvine Senior Foundation and numerous schools and institutions in the local community.

The company is also proud of its quality and team-oriented business practices. In 1994 Hines received a Sterling Award of Orange County for its "Commitment to Quality." This award is sponsored by a consortium of Orange County companies and organizations and modeled after the U.S. Commerce Department's annual Malcolm Baldrige National Quality Awards. Hines Nurseries won in the large manufacturing category for quality programs that have, according to award organizers, "done an exceptionally good job of communicating its vision, mission, goals, objectives and strategies throughout the organization."

Hines won the award in part because its leadership team rates quality as a top priority. It has built a partnership with customers and employees that encourages and recognizes input toward the goal of improving products and services. In fact, Hines bases its employee compensation plan on quality, safety, productivity, housekeeping and team development. To further ensure quality results, many employees receive up to 80 hours of specialized training every year through the company's corporate training program.

But employees are not the only ones with a say in how plants are grown at the nursery. Customers contribute too, as "customer councils" are periodically brought in to provide input on what constitutes the best plant. This information guides new product development, shapes Hines' product mix and helps management write the standards by which the product is grown.

"We have established standards for our products and programs that constantly measure them," explains western region vice president Bud Summers. "Plants are biological units, not widgets, and we track each one back to its growing field." The goal is to produce a perfect plant, and Summers believes this tracking system provides employees with "opportunities for improvement." By starting with this goal and working backward to improve methods, Hines is able to grow the "best of the best."

Management's goal at Hines is to become the most respected and recognized name in the lawn and garden industry. Hines is committed to its effort to be a model employer that provides a safe work environment where employees can work collaboratively, grow professionally and contribute — and be appreciated for their contributions. The company's motto reflects the commitment to quality apparent in all the lush green plants as well as the satisfied faces of employees and customers: "Hines, where all that we value keeps growing: people, plants, profits, and a new and brighter future for the lawn and garden industry."

Nandina 'Gulf Stream,' a Hines-patented variety, has gained popularity with nurseries and gardeners everywhere for its compact shape and autumn color.

INDEPENDENT FORGE COMPANY

There weren't many women — let alone minority women — at the top of the aluminum forging industry in 1975. But that didn't stop Rosemary Ruiz, president and cofounder of Independent Forge Company. Ruiz had started her first job at a local foundry 17 years earlier. On her first day of work, Ruiz did not think she would like it, but she soon grew to love the heat, the precision and the variety of tasks involved in aluminum forging. She worked hard, learned all she could and was soon promoted to a lead position on the production floor. Ruiz also forged a very important friendship with two coworkers — Erma Linda Diaz and Kwok Ming Wong — who would become vice presidents and cofounders of Independent Forge.

As Ruiz trained and supervised other workers, she watched as time after time, younger, less experienced men were promoted above her. In 1975 she was still making $3.75 an hour — about a fourth the salary of the lead person who replaced her. Convinced they would never advance further in the company, Ruiz, Diaz and Wong made a decision: they would start their own company. "We didn't want to look back at 60, 70 years old and regret that we hadn't tried it," says Ruiz.

Rosemary Ruiz, Kwok Ming Wong and Erma Linda Diaz, founders of the aptly named Independent Forge Company

Ruiz told her supervisor she needed a few hours off work to attend a small business conference. Soon the employer caught wind of Ruiz, Diaz and Wong's plans, all three were fired and Independent Forge was born. They pooled their combined life savings of $30,000, rented a facility in Orange and bought a single press.

Ruiz never regretted attending that seminar, for it taught her an important lesson about business: no matter how small or new a business is, it needs an accountant and an attorney. Even though Ruiz, Diaz and Wong did not draw salaries for three years, they employed an accountant and an attorney from the beginning.

The three entrepreneurs had a company and a rented facility — they even had former coworkers who wanted to work for them. Unfortunately there was no work to do. For months Ruiz telephoned and went door to door begging companies to let Independent bid on jobs, but no one was willing to risk working with the unproven company. "Only through the grace of God did we survive with no money and no experience in business or sales," says Ruiz.

During these lean days, the company survived by taking on low-paying surplus work for other local foundries. Though these proved to be hard times for the company, they were very rewarding as well for Ruiz and her colleagues. "You're very grateful for what God gives you. You appreciate it. It also made us take a very good, hard look at money — that money isn't everything," she recalls. This thinking led to a simple, steadfast philosophy that has guided Independent Forge to this day.

The company's first break, several months after its founding, came from Boeing. The regional sales representative took pity on the fledgling company and began to send request for quotation forms (RFQs) so Independent could begin bidding on projects. But before long the RFQs stopped coming. When Ruiz called to ask why, the sales representative said he was no longer allowed to send RFQs to Independent because of the new company's financial straits. He referred her to Boeing's head of finance. Ruiz admitted that the company had no money. But, she said, they did have credit lines with tool makers and with a raw materials supplier. Ruiz's explanation met with silence. Finally, Ruiz asked, "Have you ever been broke? Someone gave you a chance didn't they?" The RFQs began rolling in again.

Air-powered sanding guns are used to repair imperfections in newly forged parts.
Photo by Lia Photography

Independent was on its feet, but still shaky — making ends meet by subcontracting for other foundries. The company's next big break came several years later, when a visiting representative from Northrop Grumman Corporation recognized some of Northrop's parts on the production floor. He asked how much the other foundry was paying Independent to make the parts and promised Ruiz the next bid. Soon after, Independent received a contract from Northrop. Assuming a clerical error had resulted in an incorrect sales figure, Ruiz called him to explain that there were "too many zeros." He assured her the figure was correct: $1 million.

Independent was able to buy a second press and an oven, and Ruiz, Diaz and Wong collected their first paychecks. Several years later, Independent was able to purchase the rented facility.

Wong left the company in 1985, but Ruiz and Diaz continue to lead the now 50-employee-strong work force in creating aluminum-forged pieces — like doors, engine mounts and brackets — used primarily in commercial airplanes like the 737, 757 and 767. Independent's products are also used in bicycles, jet skis and other items.

Independent is proud of its employees' loyalty; the average worker has been with the company for about 15 years. Independent offers benefits, regular pay increases, bonuses, profit sharing and safety incentives. And, says Ruiz, the company always tries to promote from within. Despite fluctuations in workload, the company is proud that it has never had to lay off an employee because of lack of work.

The company has garnered considerable recognition, including the U.S. Small Business Administration's Small Business Subcontractor of the Year award. Ruiz has been named the city of Orange's Small Business Minority Woman of the Year, and she and Diaz have received Pioneering Women awards from the National Association of Women in Business.

Independent applies its simple, homespun philosophy to its community involvement as well. It sponsors local sports teams, volunteers at the area's Oktoberfest and has also sponsored a local art and music festival. The company has also been involved in the United Way.

Although Independent has made great strides since its precarious first days, it prefers to remain small, maintaining a strong commitment to its work and its employees. Whereas local competitors have up to 15 to 30 presses, Independent still has just three. The company was not computerized until 1997 and did not hire a human resources coordinator until 1998. "You can only eat so much. You can only drive one new car at a time," reasons Ruiz.

Nonetheless, Independent looks forward to expanding and improving in the future. It is poised to begin working directly for the U. S. government and has set its sights on expanding into the airbus industry. The company plans to expand into other areas of the country and would like to add a fourth press. Above all, as Ruiz and Diaz look forward to retirement, they are preparing a new generation of workers to take their places at the head of the very aptly named Independent Forge Company.

Press operators forge aluminum parts in fires blazing as hot as 700° F.
Photo by Lia Photography

RADIAN AUDIO ENGINEERING, INC.

His love for music and a desire to hear music reproduced as clearly as possible prompted Richard Kontrimas to found Radian Audio Engineering in 1988. As a leading designer and manufacturer of premium-quality loudspeaker components, high-powered woofers, stage and front-of-house systems, and replacement diaphragms, the company has earned a reputation for industry excellence.

(Far right) Radian's manufacturing manager inspects product workmanship on the assembly line.

Dr. Kontrimas, holding a 15" coaxial that is ready for placement into a speaker cabinet

When Kontrimas began Radian, he started by hiring a team of experienced industry professionals to get the company off the ground. Plans came together quickly, and within a matter of months, product was designed, manufactured and ready to ship. By 1989 Radian was an international company producing a line of coaxial loudspeakers, compression drivers and premium replacement diaphragms for JBL, TAD, Altec, Emilar and Radian compression drivers.

Radian's loudspeakers are primarily used in top-quality professional audio installations, such as the one for the 1996 Summer Olympic Games in Atlanta. They were also selected for use inside the sound system at the Three Tenors concert at Dodger Stadium in Los Angeles, and at several of the annual "A Taste of Orange County" events as well as the Long Beach Jazz festival in 1998. In addition, many recording engineers insist on using Radian products in their studios as well as in their home stereo systems.

Radian speakers were used at the 1998 Long Beach Jazz Festival, featuring famous jazz pianist David Benoit.

One of the keys to Radian's success is the technology it uses to manufacture compression driver diaphragms. Diaphragms are dome-shaped structures similar to the human eardrum. They are designed to vibrate in an electromagnetic circuit, which in turn creates sound. Radian begins with a flat wafer, then forms it into a diaphragm — the heart of a compression driver. Diaphragms require precision manufacturing to aerospace tolerances, within 1/1000 of an inch. Long before they ever leave the Radian facility, all of Radian's diaphragms undergo rigid testing under various pressures and temperatures to ensure excellence and consistency.

In addition to diaphragms, Radian manufactures coaxial speakers which consist of two speaker components joined together to create a full-range loudspeaker. These special speakers have an extremely wide frequency response, from 35 to 20,000 cycles per second. They come in a variety of sizes and power ranges and are designed for use in recording studios and high-level playback applications.

Radian loudspeakers have a reputation for reliability. All speakers are quality-tested in the Radian "torture chamber," a soundproof box that can hold several speakers at one time. To test them, Radian engineers play the speakers at 80 percent of full-rated power to weed out any deemed less than perfect. Speakers that pass inspection are then retested by computer for appropriate frequency response.

"Professional performance and reliability are not accidents that happen, but are deliberately engineered into every Radian product," says Kontrimas. "Our advanced designs utilize superior bonding technology and space-age metallurgy techniques — standard items in all Radian products."

With high-profile clients like the All-American Sport Park, Caesars Palace, Bally's, Beau Rivage and the Hawaiian Convention Center, Radian is continually being called upon to meet the demands of today's high-tech sound systems. In July 1998 Radian went global at the Festival

Opole in Poland — its coaxial loudspeakers and compression drivers were the transducers of choice for the stage monitors at the 35th annual event, which was attended by more than 16,000 people.

Radian supplied the stage monitors during one of Pope John Paul II's visits to Poland.

One of the newest products in the Radian line is the RPX-108P, a small personal-type stage monitor. The monitor is constructed of 13-ply Baltic birch and coated with a tough new coating that Radian calls Duradian. This new finish is waterproof, scratchproof and designed to reduce box resonance. Other innovations include the premiere of the new RCX series, which is designed to meet the needs of fixed-installation applications such as churches, auditoriums, and nightclubs. A full range of configurations is offered, including 8", 12" and 15" full-range systems, as well as single and dual 15" and 18" subwoofer systems. Radian also introduced the new 512/2BK Coaxial 12", a high-performance component intended for applications that require very high audio quality in large listening spaces with high ceilings. The component is already being used at Bally's and Caesars in Las Vegas, and in other large venues.

In 1998 Radian was honored with a RPX112 nomination by *Live Sound International* magazine for the company's Monitor Wedge Loudspeaker, which came shortly after the product debuted on the market. "It was an honor to have been nominated in December, since the product was only introduced in March," said Kontrimas.

Radian employs a highly skilled labor force to maintain the high-level technology and quality its customers have come to expect. The company is constantly expanding and updating its product manufacturing process, and quality control is consistently at the forefront of the company's manufacturing process.

Over the years, Radian's customer base has continued to expand. Today, Radian loudspeakers are installed in stadiums, churches, convention centers, university auditoriums, corporate presentation rooms, amusement parks, nightclubs, concert halls, and recording and television studios. Radian loudspeakers are also utilized on tours by some of the largest sound companies in the music industry. In addition, many original equipment manufacturers trust Radian enough to put their brand name on Radian components for their own products.

Radian's reputation for technological excellence and superior performance has set an industry standard that is unparalleled. The company's commitment to quality, reliability and value, combined with the uncompromising focus of its visionary founder and CEO, have made Radian one of the most respected loudspeaker manufacturers in the world today.

Model RCX-215, 15" coaxial and a 15" subwoofer in a single cabinet

TOLAR MANUFACTURING COMPANY, INC.

When transit riders seek relief from the sun or inclement weather, many of them duck into bus shelters created by Tolar Manufacturing Company, Inc. From design to fabrication and often installation, this Placentia-based company provides attractive, low-maintenance shelters for train stations, bus stops, shopping malls, college campuses and community transit centers.

As one of North America's top manufacturers of transit shelters and related street furniture, Tolar Manufacturing's products can be found locally in Los Angeles, San Diego, Ventura, San Bernardino mountain resorts and cities throughout Orange County, as well as Chicago, Las Vegas, Denver, Aspen, Colorado Springs, St. Louis, Tacoma, Sarasota and numerous cities across America.

Gary Tolar founded the company in 1991 after 20 years experience in the metal manufacturing industry. Upon graduation from Western High School in Anaheim, Tolar went to trade school to become a certified welder. Without benefit of a college education, he worked his way up from welder to vice president of manufacturing. When his employer went bankrupt, Tolar took out a second mortgage on his home and started Tolar Manufacturing as a small job shop in Anaheim.

Admitting he began by doing "anything for anybody," Tolar hand-welded grille work for home security, repaired fencing, and took whatever work he could find. He began bidding on his former company's jobs and landed a contract with Gannett Outdoor Transit to build bus shelters. As the market for transit shelters expanded, Tolar rode the boom, experiencing an average annual growth rate of 20-30 percent. To handle the workload, his facility expanded from the original 5,100-square-foot shop to its current 40,000-square-foot, three-building complex.

Revenue-sharing between advertising companies and municipalities drives the market for transit shelters. As more cities pass ordinances limiting or eliminating billboards, advertisers seek new ways of getting their message to consumers. Transit shelters provide one of the few venues left to reach the public in a cost-effective way. In exchange for the right to display advertising posters on each shelter, outdoor media companies purchase, install and maintain the units and then provide cities with a percentage of the revenue generated. Cities not only save the cost of purchasing and maintaining public amenities, the money earned funds other civic projects.

Tolar Manufacturing supplies the nation's top out-of-home media corporations. Eller Media, Outdoor Systems Advertising, Triumph Outdoor, Wall USA, Clear Channel Communications and LaMar Transit Advertising are some of the companies that have bid cities and won their franchises featuring Tolar shelters. Tolar also provides nonadvertising shelters and street furniture directly to those cities that choose to forego advertising. Gary Tolar employs no salespeople, successfully relying on his reputation, word of mouth and repeat customers to continue the company's growth.

In addition to its extensive product line, Tolar Manufacturing offers custom design and fabrication. Its in-house engineering department boasts more than 35 years of experience and state-of-the-art equipment. Utilizing AutoCAD software, it can easily and economically create custom designs or modify existing units to suit specific architectural styles, community character or local needs. For example, the city of Las Vegas found that transit benches grew exceedingly hot from direct sunlight and people burned themselves by sitting on them. Tolar Manufacturing designed a

Modular designs by Tolar Manufacturing Company, Inc. are used for train stations, major downtown transit centers, shopping malls, bus terminals and stops, college campuses and shuttle stops.

bench with seating made from open-wire mesh. The mesh cuts down on the actual seating surface so benches never get too hot, even in the city's 120 degree temperatures.

Many cities now request "anti-vagrant bars" on benches, raised pipes separating seating areas to prevent people from lying down on them. Colorado Springs wanted a bench adapted for its elderly, so Tolar raised the vagrant bars several inches to provide better leverage and support to help older residents stand. One of Tolar's bench designs received a patent.

The company receives metal pipes, mesh, glass and other raw materials at its Placentia headquarters and fabricates finished shelters on site. Buyers can choose from a variety of roof shapes, bench designs, wall materials and trash receptacle styles. Most shelters come with a choice of either fluorescent or solar lighting, and all the company's electrical work is UL-listed. The company uses a powder coating finish rather than paint, which complies with EPA and Air Quality Management District laws. The powder, which is baked onto the structure, looks like paint but is thicker, more durable and produces no polluting volatile organic compounds.

Shelters can be finished in over 100 different colors, but Gary Tolar always counsels against bright or light colors as those quickly attract graffiti. He most often recommends a flat shade of bronze, the color used for all Los Angeles shelters, because black spray paint doesn't show up well against it.

To reduce maintenance costs, Tolar Manufacturing frequently replaces the glass in the back of shelters with metal mesh. This design change offers protection from the elements and the safety of a see-through surface without the cost involved with repeatedly replacing large panels of glass.

In the wake of the Los Angeles riots, Gary Tolar worked with Mayor Richard Riordan to develop bus shelters for the L.A. Neighborhood Initiative (LANI) Project. The city designated eight community redevelopment areas to receive new custom-designed vandal-resistant shelters. Tolar attended meetings with community groups in churches and schools throughout South Central. Each community chose its own design, color and style of bench, and supplied its own labor force to clean and maintain them. Since installation in 1995, the shelters have remained remarkably well-kept and graffiti-free, and they serve as a symbol of community pride.

Tolar Manufacturing remains privately owned by Gary Tolar and his wife. They employ 30-45 people depending on the fluctuating workload. The company has its own delivery vehicles and ships directly within California, Arizona and Nevada, while a sister company begun by Tolar in 1995, Shelter Maintenance and Installation, Inc., installs Tolar shelters throughout Southern California.

Gary Tolar projects continuing expansion for his company well into the 21st century. "In Orange County alone," he says, "there is constant growth. OCTA ridership has risen dramatically over the past several years and this means more bus stops and more shelters. Increasing the use of public transportation and urban redevelopment are very important considerations for our cities these days. I don't see business slowing down — not in my lifetime."

One of the Tolar Manufacturing Company, Inc. advertising transit shelters currently in use in Orange County

TRU-TOP INC.

Photo by Lia Photography

Step up to an Orange County fast food restaurant counter, a corporate computer terminal, a teller at a recently merged bank or the kitchen of a refurbished RV, and chances are that you're encountering a laminated surface fabricated by Tru-Top Inc. Owned and run by Rob Foster, Tru-Top Inc. designs, forms and installs or ships high-pressure laminate for use in counters, cabinets, work stations and custom surfaces. From local shopping center checkout stands and school cafeterias to dormitories in Antarctica and surfaces in the earliest space shuttles, this Santa Ana company's products are in use on seven continents and in every major American city.

Tru-Top traces its origins to 1956, when Foster's father and eight partners began Alpine Materials, the first company in Orange County to utilize a new product: high-pressure laminate. Until that time, counters were generally made from tile or linoleum with metal trim. Alpine Materials incorporated high-pressure laminate into existing styles, postforming it to make counter tops for use in housing.

The company thrived, but Foster's father realized that owning only one ninth of a company didn't afford much of a financial future. He sold his Alpine stock and in 1962 opened his own firm, Tru-Top Inc.

In the beginning, Tru-Top consisted of Foster and his father, and the two began by doing strictly custom work and odd jobs. The company has since grown to be the largest independent, full-service laminate company in the western United States, if not the entire country, with more than 100 employees and a 35,000-square-foot manufacturing facility. The company offers customers a choice of over 5,000 laminate surfaces in a staggering array of finishes, colors and patterns, and will custom design work for individual home owners or major corporate customers.

The Santa Ana headquarters for Tru-Top Inc., one of the country's largest installers of high-pressure laminate
Photo by Lia Photography

The key to the company's success is versatility. Foster admits that for everything they do, a bigger company exists, but only Tru-Top Inc. offers such a wide range of services. While a home supply superstore might sell a kitchen, that company won't turn around and do custom cabinetry on a yacht. Tru-Top will. For pharmaceutical labs, the company built counters, walls and cabinetry that are antistatic, antibacterial and chemically resistant. For a ski resort, the company designed and installed tables with a special leg intended to withstand the weight of raucous revelers. They'll design and install a rec room or ship a thousand computer workstations to a corporation. Foster's philosophy is simple: never turn down work.

Tru-Top has never utilized a sales force. In the beginning, contacts made by Alpine Materials led to Tru-Top's first few jobs. Business grew through referrals from satisfied customers. The company's better known clients have included John Wayne, President Nixon's Western White House, and private homes for Orange County's Segerstrom and Irvine families.

The company rides out recessions because economic bad times for others create growth opportunities for them. When the recession of the late 1960s forced many mothers into the workplace, these women lacked the time to cook meals and demand for fast food exploded. While the country suffered through the recession,

Tru-Top ran shifts 24 hours a day, seven days a week producing product for McDonald's, Burger King and Taco Bell.

More recently, bank mergers have required the renovation of new branch offices to match the corporate color scheme, and the proliferation of HMOs have forced doctors to leave individual practices for combined medical offices. In both instances, Tru-Top gets the call to install new counters and cabinets and business booms.

During the economic downturn of the early 1990s, Tru-Top entered the systems furniture recycling market. Companies seeking to reconfigure their offices often balked at the average $3,000 per workstation quoted for new cubicles. Tru-Top offered an alternative: strip the company's existing units or provide salvaged merchandise and add new laminate of the customer's choice. The resulting modules look brand new, but cost approximately 60 percent less than new products.

From private custom kitchens to science laboratories to corporate offices, Tru-Top Inc. designs, manufactures and installs or ships its products throughout Orange County and around the world.
Photo by Lia Photography

Tru-Top stays atop its field by continually updating its equipment and training employees in new techniques. With no trade schools left to teach laminating skills, the company trains all of its own people, a process which takes up to five years. According to Foster, a top college graduate is no more qualified to work for the company than a motivated high school dropout. To that end, every year he hires at least six young people who have either dropped out of high school or shown no interest in attending college. According to Foster, "All they have to do is want to work." Each year, two or three of these young workers remain, and Tru-Top's employees stay with the company an average of six years as opposed to the national average of 19 months.

Tru-Top's future continues to expand into finished products for retail trade, such as high-end shelving units. And as one of the last independents in the country capable of handling large projects, Foster continually fields offers from laminate manufacturers who want to secure his exclusive services. He explains that with all the innovations in materials, nobody's advancing the fabrication side. End users find it progressively more difficult to find shops that can work with these materials, which makes Tru-Top a resource to be courted.

Photo by Lia Photography

Foster relishes his independent status and the freedom it gives him to bid to multiple manufacturers. And he has no fear of competition. To open a new laminate fabrication shop on par with Tru-Top, Foster estimates startup at $10-12 million, including equipment, facilities, training and salaries — but without his 35 years of experience, contacts and good will.

All of which bodes well for the continuing success of Tru-Top Inc. According to Foster, "Every year is a record year from the previous year, simply because we're not limited to any field. I can't think of anything we're not in, and I will always be filling the gap between everything you put in the catalogues and exactly what the customer wants."

CumminsAerospace.com

CumminsAerospace.com began in the early 1930s as Brown Machine Shop, providing mainly blacksmith work for the local community and performing other rough machine work that included repairing Wagon Wheels. It later underwent a name change to Yeager Manufacturing Corp., outlining its transformation from a mechanical machining approach to the fully computerized, automated equipment capable of manufacturing everything from simple bushings to the complex, large, multi-component assemblies that have made CumminsAerospace.com what it is today.

The facility currently occupies a 35,000-square-foot facility located in Anaheim, California, under the direction of current President Sean Cummins. The company is outfitted with state-of-the-art equipment allowing for in-house precision machining and inspection for all the products produced.

To further ensure and monitor this vital process, CumminsAerospace.com follows the Total Quality Management (TQM) and Statistical Process Control (SPC) systems to measure continuous improvement. The company utilizes an accredited ISO-9002 quality system to demonstrate to its customers the importance of quality and its dedication to delivering a quality product on time the first time.

"The company has developed a unique Manufacturing Outline, which has greatly assisted our development of products manufactured," says Cummins. This detailed document provides the written operation instructions, which include detailed drawings of each operation/task completed that is unparalleled in any other company. It is often a common comment from visiting customers and quality representatives, who, after reviewing these documents, to say that they have never seen anything as comprehensive.

Few companies match the credentialed staff of CumminsAerospace.com, its track record, and dedication in successfully providing specialized purchasing, manufacturing and logistic support services to its customer. The company has built an impeccable record in industry leadership, quality and delivery performance, and providing total customer satisfaction. And because of this, the future looks bright as the company moves

Few companies match the credentialed staff of CumminsAerospace.com, its track record, and dedication in successfully providing specialized purchasing, manufacturing and logistic support services to its customer. The company has built an impeccable record in industry leadership, quality and delivery performance, and providing total customer satisfaction.

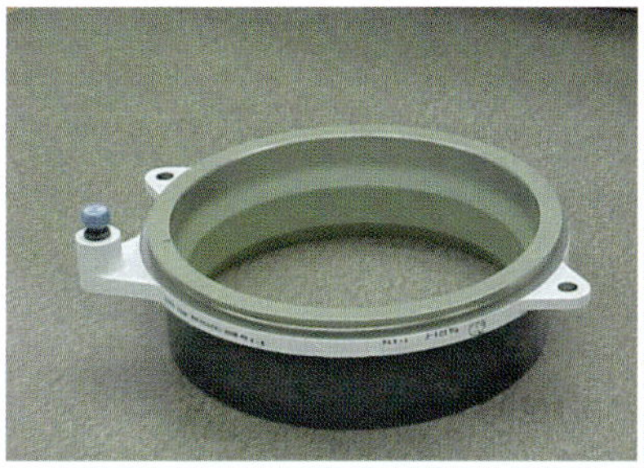

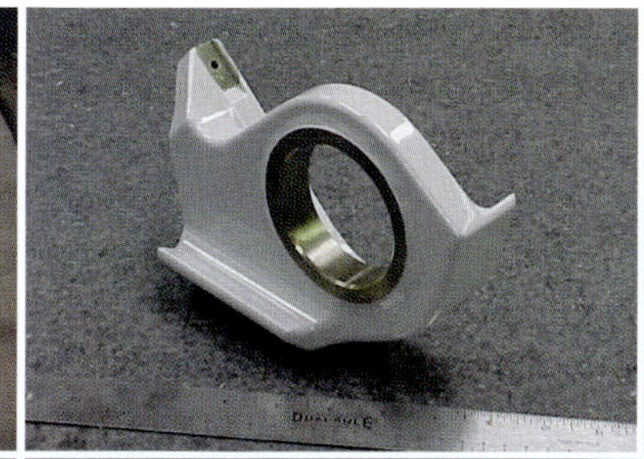

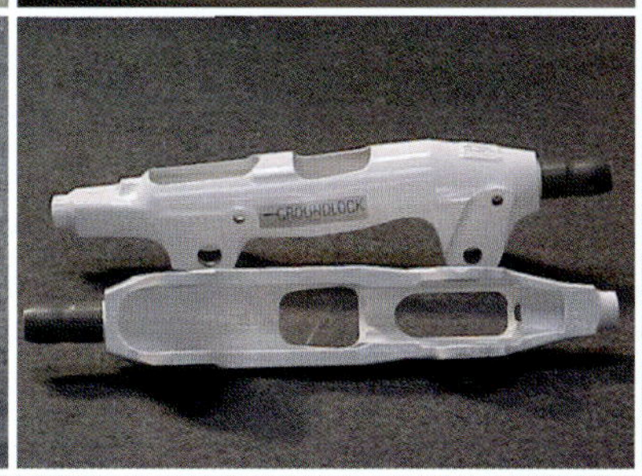

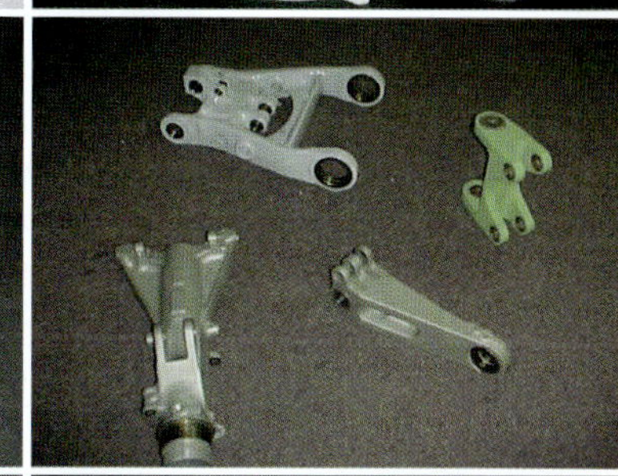
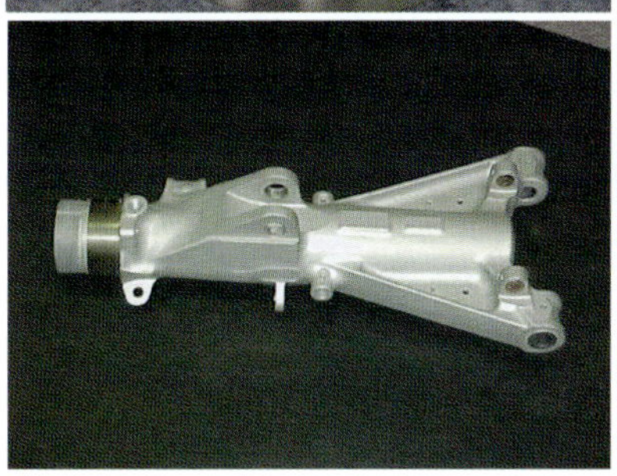

forward and toward more high-tech milling in the company's future, as well as an expanded employee base. Modern facilities, technical expertise and a management team that knows about the business from the bottom up all converge to make CumminsAerospace.com a leader in its field now and in the future.

CumminsAerospace.com has built its outstanding reputation as a quality supplier to the aerospace industry for over 50 years. Modern facilities and state-of-the-art equipment provide precision CNC Turning and 5-axis Milling of aerospace alloys, including beryllium copper, steels through 300 Kpsi, nylon and Thermo Plastic, titanium and other modern composites.

Specializing within the aerospace industry and aircraft landing gear field, the company's product line includes zero-gap bearings, centering cams, spherical bearings, as well as numerous assemblies, struts, braces, cylinders, pistons, tracks and structural frame components.

Prompt attention is given to all inquires and every effort is made to ensure that the customer's machining needs are met. CumminsAerospace.com is positioned to be the perfect choice for precision products.

Quality control begins with inspection of incoming raw material and continues through all phases of manufacturing, outside processing, packaging for shipment and delivery to the customer's facility. Quality is an ongoing process of review and analysis that does not end when a job is complete but is continuously evaluated to be sure that today's lessons are passed along for tomorrow's production.

MODERN FACILITIES, TECHNICAL EXPERTISE AND A MANAGEMENT TEAM THAT KNOWS ABOUT THE BUSINESS FROM THE BOTTOM UP ALL CONVERGE TO MAKE CUMMINS-AEROSPACE.COM A LEADER IN ITS FIELD NOW AND IN THE FUTURE.

ORCO BLOCK COMPANY

ORCO Block Company has helped lay the foundation and build the future of Orange County. Established in Santa Ana by Pete Muth and Arvid Johnson in 1946, ORCO has grown to become one of the country's top 10 concrete masonry producers. Pete Muth, chairman of the board, became sole owner of the family company in 1971. His son Rick joined ORCO in 1975 as assistant office manager and is now the firm's president. Mary Muth, Pete's wife and partner since 1939, serves as ORCO's secretary. Pete's son Lynn Muth is vice president. The company is now headquartered in Stanton, with locations in Riverside, Banning, Romoland and Oceanside. It is one of Southern California's leading providers of concrete block.

The first manufacturer of slump block in Orange County, ORCO was a pioneer in the research and development of color and texture. As styles of concrete block have improved, its applications as an alternative to other building materials have steadily increased. Block offers architects a broad palette of possibilities. They can easily incorporate diverse design elements in walls and paved surfaces. ORCO constantly strives to conceive new and beautiful products. It uses 500 molds to produce more than 8,000 different items.

Rick Muth, president

ORCO formulated a special color and block for Leisure World at Seal Beach and El Toro, now the city of Laguna Woods. The color and texture it created for the walls around Mission Viejo became the construction standard for that city. ORCO Block has helped build many of Orange County's most imposing structures. It supplied the block for Edison Field and the Ronald Reagan Courthouse. Its original ORCOBURST block added beauty and atmosphere to the Irvine Spectrum.

The company has contributed to Orange County's stability, not only with the quality products it produces, but also as a stalwart supporter of many charitable and civic organizations. ORCO and its principals have given money, time and materials to the Orange County Performing Arts Center, Bower's Museum, Pacific Symphony, Stanton Boys and Girls Club, St. Joseph's Ballet and many more. In 1986, its 40th year, ORCO was honored for its contributions by the Sales and Marketing Executives of Orange County. *The Orange County Register* included ORCO in its list of Orange County's top 50 companies.

The beginning — 1946 — young Pete Muth at the hand-operated Flamm in the original Santa Ana Plant

Rick Muth, current president of the multimillion-dollar enterprise, is an Orange County native. Muth is a graduate of the University of Southern California, which he attended on a track scholarship. A long-distance record holder, he made the school's all-time list. Like the company he heads, Rick Muth is an industry leader. In 1995 he was elected chairman of the board of the National Concrete Masonry Association. He became the first son of a past chairman to lead the organization. His father, Pete, led the NCMA in 1966.

Rick and Pete Muth share more than leadership qualities. Having both worked for very large corporations early in their respective careers, father and son have an aversion to the impersonal structure of big organizations. ORCO is a progressive company that has pursued expansion aggressively, but it is also a family company. It is a place where employees come to work because they want to, a place where workers can grow along with their job responsibilities. As a result, many of the company's 150 dedicated employees have been at ORCO for more than 20 years. The Muths are rightfully proud of their family company — and company family.

PAC FOAM PRODUCTS CORPORATION

PAC Foam Products Corporation is an international fabricator of foam and related products. Since opening its doors in 1977 it has earned a reputation as a respected and innovative fabricator. Today it supplies 95 percent of the world market in reticulated urethanes, which are utilized in open heart and bypass surgery.

Richard Tunila, the president of PAC Foam, began his career in foam products, working for a Costa Mesa-based foam fabricator, while he was a student at Orange Coast College. He started at the bottom of the ladder as a production worker, and over a period of five years, he progressed from lead foreman to production foreman and then to vice president of the company. After 10 years, he approached the owners asking them to allow him to buy ownership in the company. Tunila was refused and left to start his own business, Precision Plastics.

Precision Plastics was a small company that produced foam products. Tunila did the design work as well as running the office. A real one-man show, he sold the product, then rushed back to the company to design and produce it. Approximately one year later, undercapitalized, he closed Precision Plastics with no debt and returned to his previous employer. Once again he offered to buy into ownership of the company, was refused, and this time Tunila left for good.

In February 1977 Richard Tunila started PAC Foam Products and shortly thereafter asked his brother Tim to join him in ownership. Their first facility was a 6,800-square-foot building located in Santa Ana. The wives maintained the office for the first five years, and Karen, Richard's wife, today continues as the secretary/treasurer of the corporation.

The Tunila families worked long and hard in the early days. As president, Richard handled sales and general manager responsibilities. Tim Tunila was in charge of manufacturing and Karen Tunila ran the office. The brothers' parents, Lorene and Tom Tunila, also participated by volunteering their services. That hard work has paid off in annual sales of $6 million.

By 1980 PAC had outgrown its location and moved to a 24,000-square-foot building in Tustin. In 1981 they had sufficient business to run two shifts, which increased the manufacturing and office staff by approximately 200 percent. Over the next 13 years the company made two more moves, eventually purchasing its current 24,000-square-foot building in Costa Mesa. Now, the company runs three shifts, 24 hours a day, six days a week. Tunila acknowledges that a business is no better than its staff and attributes much of the company's success to his past and current personnel — in particular operations manager Walt Nobrega, administration/accounting manager Susan Noble, and customer service/office manager Tina Balsamo.

PAC Foam Products began making medical products in 1983. The move into this market took it to the forefront of reticulated foam medical device manufacturing, with products such as blood oxygenators and cardiotomy reservoirs.

PAC Foam expects its growth to continue at the rate of five to 10 percent a year with a target goal of $10 million in sales. As Tunila points out, "We fully intend to continue distinguishing ourselves in customer commitment, extensive product knowledge, integrity, product quality and reliability, which has been the formula of our success."

PLASTICOLOR MOLDED PRODUCTS, INC.

Success for PlastiColor Molded Products, Inc., has been built on durability, flexibility and style in both products and the company itself. PlastiColor's first product, a gamble on a niche market, was a black plastic automobile floor mat with small color designs. At the time, only single-color floor mats were available to consumers. With that in mind and after many years building careers in the rubber industry, CEO Gordon Bagne and partner Robert Klinger put their savings on the line to cofound PlastiColor in 1971. The company began with a handful of employees working in a 3,500-square-foot facility with a single production line. Patterns were drafted and prototypes cut by hand. The process was painstaking and mistakes could cost days.

They started literally at the floorboards to build what has become a small empire of licensed design after-market products for cars and trucks, including floor mats, mud flaps, splash guards, keychains, spare tire covers, sunshades, air fresheners and antenna toppers. The ubiquitous little Volkswagen Bug was a springboard for PlastiColor, which in 1972 created the "Bug Mat," cut to a special shape exclusively for the popular, durable cars.

Popular licensed and proprietary character designs keep PlastiColor's products in demand.

Consumers may not recognize PlastiColor's name, but they instantly recognize the various sports franchise, car, truck and motorcycle logos and cartoon characters that build loyalty for the products. What motorist hasn't stared at Yosemite Sam's grim expression over the words "Back Off" on a truck's mud flaps? That image, under license from Warner Bros. since 1973, was a PlastiColor creation. It was built on a breakthrough discovery that Bagne and Klinger developed, a formula that could mold a single item using several distinct colors. The result lends itself to the clean lines of cartoon images and licensed logos. PlastiColor patented its processes, which also yield plastics so flexible they are mistaken for rubber. PlastiColor specializes in manufacturing products with world-class licensed logos, which included GM, Ford, Harley-Davidson and Warner Bros. at the time of publication.

The Yosemite Sam mud flap is one of PlastiColor's most recognized products.

Today the company employs more than 250 people at its 130,000-square-foot facility. It doubled its space with a new building in mid-1998 to accommodate five manufacturing lines running on three shifts. With its own in-house graphics department and state-of-the-art computer design equipment, the company confines mistakes to the computer screen. A design can go from concept to finished, custom prototype in hours.

Even though its products are available in most national variety and auto specialty stores in the United States, Canada and Europe, PlastiColor has kept the values upon which it was founded. Bagne and Klinger remain the company's sole shareholders today; a total of five Bagnes and three Klingers still work for the company.

Thankful for their success, the Bagnes and Klingers enjoy giving back to the community through service to the Soroptimist International, Rotary International, Boys and Girls Club of Fullerton, the Chamber of Commerce and St. Jude's Hospital.

Like its products, PlastiColor is an idea built on old-fashioned values. The founding families continue to look to new frontiers. For the foreseeable future that means opening new markets overseas and branching into plastic home products domestically. PlastiColor expects the same innovative, flexible style that has made it a standard in the automotive industry to usher the company into housewares and other industries.

PROLONG SUPER LUBRICANTS

From the diamond mines of South Africa to the race tracks of the Indianapolis 500, you'll find people using a product developed by an Orange County company that has grown from a small business with a handful of employees to a nearly $50 million a year enterprise.

Prolong International Corporation is a little more than a decade old, but its line of car-care products is well known to mechanics, machinists and motorists around the world who want their cars and equipment to run better and last longer.

The man behind Prolong is Elton Alderman, an avid motor sports fan and car enthusiast who grew up in Daytona Beach, Florida, home to fast driving and NASCAR races.

As a young man Alderman lived and breathed cars while working with Smokey Yunick, one of the country's top premiere racing engine builders and a legendary mechanical innovator who is now a technical advisor for Prolong.

Alderman's love of automobiles lasted beyond being drafted into the Army and doing a stint with the 82nd Airborne Division of paratroopers at Ft. Bragg, North Carolina. Three years and 49 jumps later, Alderman left the Army in 1964. He packed up his family and moved to Southern California, where over the years he managed and served as dealer principal at several car dealerships throughout Southern California.

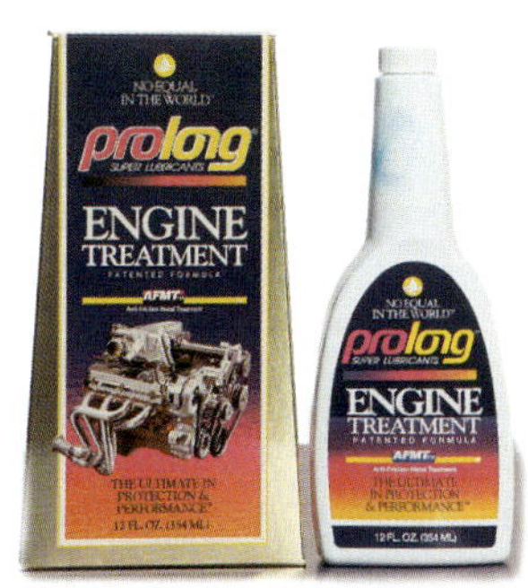

Prolong Super Lubricants' hallmark product is Prolong Engine Treatment, which comes in a 12-ounce bottle containing the patented Anti Friction Metal Treatment (AFMT) formula that bonds to moving metal parts.

Alderman was not only interested in selling cars, but in making them work better. He and his business partner, Ed Auld, were acquainted with the developing lubricant technology that would make car engines perform better.

In 1988 Alderman and Auld joined to invest in ownership of a company working to perfect extreme-pressure lubrication products.

Alderman and his team worked hard to develop an even better engine additive that would bond to metal and help machine parts run smoothly. A company milestone was reached on July 4, 1989, when Prolong was granted a U.S. patent for its specially formulated anti-friction metal treatment.

At first the product was used mostly by car enthusiasts in heavy-duty industrial applications. It was even used deep down in the diamond mines of South Africa where mechanics have to keep machinery operating efficiently if they don't want to haul it up for repair.

But in 1996 Alderman and Prolong decided to start mass marketing their product to the general public.

An enormously successful 30-minute infomercial was produced to run on television stations across the country. The advertisement helped quickly propel sales to $35 million in 1998.

Prolong utilizes motorsports as a tremendous catalyst and impression tool for its products, including sponsorship support of five-time NHRA world champion Kenny Bernstein's Top Fuel dragster, based in Lake Forest, California. This 6,000-plus-horsepower machine covers the quarter mile in 4.5 seconds at 320 mph — a true test of Prolong's protective lubrication properties.

With the success of Prolong Super Lubricants' consumer products, Alderman and his team launched a new product line. With the help of noted Orange County entrepreneur Alan Rypinski, who developed Armor All into a $200 million company, Prolong developed its own maintenance products for a car's exterior.

In November 1998 Prolong introduced Prolong Super Glass Cleaner, Prolong Super Protectant, Prolong Super Cleaner, Prolong Paint Sealant, and Prolong Waterless Wash and Shine.

That same year, the company moved from a small executive suite in Anaheim to its own spacious building near the Irvine Spectrum. The building is decorated in the company's trademark colors of navy blue, magenta and amber.

In the new century, Prolong expects to develop new automotive and commercial/industrial products aimed at bolstering its industry leadership in "No Equal In The World" technology.

When it comes to world-class events such as the Indianapolis 500, Prolong plays a significant role. In 1998 Prolong-sponsored driver Jeff Ward finished third in the world's single-largest sporting event, further bolstering the company's presence with proven results in the automotive aftermarket.

WESTERN MILL FABRICATORS, INC.

Western Mill Fabricators, Inc. is becoming increasingly well known throughout California and across the United States as a manufacturer and installer of restaurant seating and décor, commercial casework and contained play systems.

Kimball (Kim) Boyack founded Western Mill in 1980. Originally the company produced tabletops and other wood products for military bases throughout the United States. The original product line expanded quickly to commercial casework with AM-PM mini markets being the main customer. In 1983 Boyack began remodeling dining-room seating for Carl's Jr. In 1985 the company began building and installing seating for new Carl's stores. In addition Western Mill now supplies seating and décor to McDonald's in California.

(Right) McDonald's, Buttonwillow, California

(Far right) Carl's Jr., Bishop, California

Over the years Western Mill has built a variety cabinetry, ranging from complex concession stands for Edwards and other theaters to high-end architectural-style millwork for more than 100 Starbucks coffee stores. "Our focus has been to land large corporate accounts in order to limit overhead and eliminate a large sales force," says Boyack.

To maintain an efficient work force, the company has always looked toward more productive machinery as a way of keeping pace with the industry. In 1995 Western Mill purchased a computer-controlled routing-and-boring machine. Tabletops that used to take six machining operations to complete can now be produced in only two. Other benefits of this machine include reducing the amount of contact cement used in the products. This saves time and helps the company adhere to stricter Air Quality Control regulations.

Carl's Jr., Livermore, California

Western Mill Fabricators is heading in exciting new directions. In 1998 Gary Van Wagenen joined the company in order to increase its design and engineering capabilities. During that same year the company also decided to become a manufacturer of soft contained play systems for fast-food restaurants and the family-entertainment industry. The company has now designed a new system that will eliminate the maintenance problems associated with conventional play units.

Quality, value and experience are indeed the three principles that Boyack believes have fueled the growth of the company. "Supply your customers with a quality product that will give them years of service. This helps to ensure ongoing customers and gives you a feeling of pride and accomplishment when you see that product years later."

Boyack believes that experienced and reliable personnel are the backbone of his business. "The nature of the business often requires that employees work long days as well as varied shifts. But in spite of this," he notes, "they continue to have a great attitude and strive to please the customer." Many of the company's employees have been there for 10 years or more. Western Mill continues to be a family-owned business, with two of Kim's sons working as installers. His wife and daughter manage the office and the accounting functions.

Individualized design, legendary service and the highest-quality materials and workmanship are part of every product at Western Mill Fabricators. The company prides itself on its service, flexibility and ability to work with the customer.

Anaheim/Orange County Visitor & Convention Bureau

MARKETPLACE

Orange County retail establishments and service industries offer an impressive variety of choices for Orange County residents and visitors.

DRAPER'S & DAMON'S

Being one of Southern California's oldest family-run businesses is a distinction Draper's & Damon's can be proud of. The chain of 33 specialty retail stores — four in Orange County — celebrated its 73rd year in business in 2000 and shows little sign of slowing down.

This Irvine-based retailer caters to a steady and growing segment of the population — mature women — and has made a name for itself by offering classic, high-quality fashions and an almost old-fashioned level of customer service. For women who remember the days when service, selection and style were the hallmarks of fashion retailing, Draper's & Damon's can seem like a nostalgic breath of fresh air.

The senior-niche specialty store began humbly enough in 1927 as a small dress shop in Pasadena, California, catering exclusively to the close friends of its founder and namesake, Virginia Draper.

Draper started the store in the downstairs of her Colorado Boulevard home. Using her experience as a store buyer, she made frequent trips to New York where she purchased well-made, fashionable dresses to sell to her Bible-study group. As word of the dresses spread, so did the demand for them. The business grew, and Draper eventually expanded the shop by converting her upstairs living quarters into an alterations department. When "The Draper Studio of Modes," as it was then called, hosted its official grand opening fashion show, the who's who of 1920s Los Angeles were in attendance, eager to catch a glimpse of the chic and sophisticated ladies apparel and for a chance to see Draper, who was rapidly making a name for herself as a smart and savvy businesswoman.

The original home on Colorado Avenue in Pasadena, California, where Draper's & Damon's was born

With the incredible success of the flagship store, expansion was inevitable. In 1938 Draper partnered with her nephew, Simeon Draper, and in 1953 they opened a second store on Wilshire Boulevard in Los Angeles, California. In 1958 the pair purchased a couture dress shop called Damon's and decided to keep the name and concept and merge it with their own. The new boutique, catering to well-dressed society women throughout the Los Angeles area, offered moderate-to-better daywear and high-end evening wear.

In 1959 the third Draper's & Damon's store opened its doors in Orange County, in the small community of Tustin. Since then, 31 more stores have joined the Draper's & Damon's family in California, Arizona, Texas and Florida, including two new catalog outlet stores, which debuted in Laguna Hills, California, and Sun City, Arizona, in 1998. Store locations are strategic and well-planned, emphasizing convenience and easy access.

Draper's & Damon's customers are loyal, frequenting their favorite stores as much for the socializing as for the shopping. Indeed, the stores offer more than just fine clothing and accessories; complimentary coffee, cookies and affable salespeople are an equally big draw. Reminiscent of the quaint dress shops of decades past, Draper's & Damon's puts an emphasis on making customers feel at home. It's not uncommon for a manager to keep a store open late for a favorite customer, or to host a special evening for "husbands only," with preselected gift items already set aside for easy purchasing.

Customer loyalty is one thing, but employee loyalty in today's volatile job market is becoming increasingly rare. Draper's & Damon's remarkable family-like atmosphere and people-motivated management style allows them to boast employee retention numbers well above the norm — Irene Fish, a dedicated employee who started with the company's original alterations department, recently celebrated her 42nd year with the store. Employees with tenures of 10, 15 or 20 years are not uncommon in this close-knit company, which puts a high priority on recognition and communication.

Never content to rest on its laurels, Draper's & Damon's has evolved with the times. Though the merchandise has remained tried and true, bowing little to current trends, the method of distribution has expanded. In 1993 Draper's & Damon's launched its first mail-order catalog, and what began as a one-person operation in a back room is today a fully staffed division that produces as many as 10 glossy catalogs a year. And when looking at the average Draper's & Damon's customer, mail order makes perfect sense — it's a natural extension of the company's customer-service focus.

In 1975 Draper's & Damon's corporate headquarters relocated to Costa Mesa, California, closer to the homes of its then second-generation operators, Simeon Draper's sons-in-law Jack Bostwick and Steve Farmer. Today, the company is run by third-generation management and owned by family members Brad and Jeff Farmer and Brent Bostwick.

In 1998 after rapid growth of the retailing and catalog divisions caused it to outgrow its existing offices, Draper's & Damon's moved into an impressive new corporate headquarters near the Spectrum entertainment complex in Irvine, California.

Community involvement is an ongoing priority for Draper's & Damon's — the company actively supports a variety of local and national charities, including Children's Hospital of Orange County, Child Guidance Center and the American Cancer Society.

In the future, Draper's & Damon's plans to remain on the course that has kept it on the fashion forefront for the over-40 crowd. Buyers are bringing in more ageless styles to meet growing customer demand, and many younger women who frequent the stores with mothers or grandmothers are gradually becoming customers themselves. With its commitment to "service, selection and style," Draper's & Damon's seems destined to keep fashion-minded women well-dressed for generations to come.

The first "Draper Studio of Modes" fashion event in Los Angeles, California

Virginia and Simeon Draper in their Wilshire Boulevard Store

MON AMIE BRIDAL SALON

When brides-to-be walk through the doors of Mon Amie Bridal Salon, they begin to understand why their friends have said, "You just have to go to Mon Amie!" With this trust and assurance, no wonder Mon Amie is now happily celebrating its 25th anniversary!

Twenty-five years ago, when her daughter Diane was planning to get married, Verna Huson, owner of Mon Amie Bridal Salon, was surprised to learn that an elegant bridal salon did not exist in Orange County. In an effort to fulfill this need, Verna opened her first bridal boutique in Mesa Verde Center, Costa Mesa, in April 1976. That first 750-square-foot shop had two fitting-rooms and two full-time employees who catered to the needs of brides-to-be. In Verna's wildest dreams, she never imagined that the name Mon Amie would one day be acclaimed as one of the finest bridal salons in the nation.

Diane Flatten, Verna Huson, Joan Astle

Unique to Mon Amie, today's store, now located in the Countryside Center in Costa Mesa, is a magnificent 20,000-square-foot salon featuring individual departments devoted exclusively to the bride, her bridesmaids, mothers and special guests. Mon Amie offers one of the most exquisite collections of bridal gowns from leading American and international designers to be found on the West Coast. The finest selection of accessories, including beautiful headpieces, veils, jewelry, shoes and lingerie are available for the entire bridal party. Whatever the bride envisions for the happiest day of her life — sophisticated, classic, elegant or dramatic — Mon Amie offers every illusion.

While Mon Amie was a success from its inception as a charming bridal boutique, it is Verna Huson's personal background that laid the foundation for that success. During her third year of college at UCLA, Verna contracted polio. After undergoing months of therapy and rehabilitation, she was back in the swing of things. Due to the numerous stairs at UCLA, she transferred to a school of business where she finished her education. Verna's courses included advertising, public relations, personnel and general business, all of which would one day contribute to her success in the bridal industry.

In 1952 Verna married her sweetheart, Jim Huson, and worked with him in his real estate development company until their first daughter was born. Verna then spent the next 20 years devoting herself to her family and the raising of her two lovely children, Joan and Diane. It was during the empty-nest period, after Diane and Joan were married, that Verna focused on opening Mon Amie Bridal Salon, and the success story had its beginning.

Daughter Joan Astle joined Mon Amie in 1977 shortly after graduating from Chapman University. Because of her organizational skills and team-leading abilities as General Manager, she was most instrumental in propelling Mon Amie to a top-ranked store in just a few years. Today, although she and her family now reside in Park City, Utah, she holds the position of National Advertising and Public Relations Director and continues to be an integral part of the business. Verna's other daughter, Diane Flatten, lived in San Luis Obispo during Mon Amie's early years. In 1990, after moving to Newport Beach with her husband and children, she joined the company. Although her schooling was in Fine Arts, she soon adapted her artistic talents to the needs of Mon Amie. Diane now heads the Buying Office where she has taken the store in a more couture direction.

"Both daughters have been extremely valuable in building the business to what it is today, and I couldn't have done it without them," comments Verna with a proud smile. "The family not only loves the bridal business but thrives on the challenge of continually improving a good thing and keeping up with a changing market and all that it entails."

While Verna's daughters were an inherent part of the Mon Amie story, she believes that her excellent staff has been extremely

The Couture Salon at Mon Amie Bridal

vital to the success of the salon, and states, "Your company is only as good as the staff that represents you." From its early beginning with only two employees, Mon Amie now has a staff that ranges between 80 and 100 strong according to the season. These enthusiastic and knowledgeable employees are known for their expertise, sincere personalized service and unparalleled dedication to helping each and every bride make her wedding-day dreams a reality.

Every wedding is distinctive and every gown special to its bride. "It's important that a prospective bride leaves Mon Amie knowing that all of her questions have been answered and all of her needs have been met," offers Susan Bleckley, who has worked with Verna Huson as her Operations Manager for over 15 years. "The Mon Amie Experience" — so named by brides from all over the world — has established this beautiful salon as the most renowned in Southern California.

Always active in the Orange County community, Mon Amie has been pleased to contribute to the Orangewood Children's Home throughout the years for special events, and in particular, the prom season. In addition, Mon Amie has participated with City of Hope to raise funds for breast cancer research.

The Mon Amie story is definitely one of which Verna Huson and her daughters are very proud. Not only has Mon Amie Bridal Salon established itself as a leader in the industry, but it has grown to become one of the most famous and respected bridal salons in the country. As a result of providing brides-to-be with the highest levels of quality, service and selection, Verna Huson was inducted into the Bridal Hall of Fame and was also awarded *Bride's Magazine* Award of Excellence for Retailing. The salon was named California Bridal Retailer of the Year on several occasions, and has been voted the No. 1 Bridal Store in Orange County by *Orange County Register* readers for the past three years. With accolades like this, all roads definitely lead to Mon Amie Bridal Salon… for the ultimate expression of a bride.

Mon Amie Bridal Salon at Countryside Center

RANCHO LAS LOMAS

The beautifully landscaped grounds of Rancho Las Lomas, a special-events facility only 20 minutes away from Newport Beach

Nestled in foothills along the sycamore- and oak-shaded banks of the Aliso Creek lies a quiet Eden, one couple's testament to their love of the land and each other — Rancho Las Lomas. This sprawling, meticulously crafted 32-acre ranch, a short 20-minute drive above Newport Beach, serves as both a unique special-events facility and the private home of owners Rick and Jeannie Lawrence.

Weddings, corporate meetings, executive retreats, photo shoots, launch parties for new products — the Rancho has hosted memorable personal and professional events since 1983. Visitors are encouraged to wander the grounds of this whimsical, enchanted environment. Lush gardens and colorfully tiled pavilions wrap around clusters of white stucco, red-roofed buildings. Antique beams, fittings and fixtures grace each cottage and the large trellised dining room, and early California agricultural artifacts dot the property. Interiors are decorated in an eclectic mix of Spanish and Portuguese styles, creating a dramatic yet peaceful effect.

Rick Lawrence's stewardship of Rancho Las Lomas reads like a romance novel. In 1976, while on the Greek island of Santorini near the end of a round-the-world trip, he decided he wanted to buy a ranch close to his Newport Beach home. Shortly after his return, a friend told him of a rural property about to be placed on the market.

When he saw the land, Lawrence's response was instantaneous. "I don't fall in love with many things in my life," he says, "but when I do, that's it!" He purchased the land in 1977 and a friend named it Rancho Las Lomas, or ranch of rolling hills.

Rick's Cafe, a Casablanca-styled hillside villa and entertainment center, one of the many enticing environments available to guests during events at Rancho Las Lomas

The following Fourth of July, Rick chanced to meet Jeannie Sorrell on Balboa Pier. From Colorado, she came to Southern California to "be discovered," and she was — by Rick. He fell in love at first sight. Jeannie laughs as she recalls that their first "date" was at Rancho Las Lomas, where Rick walked her around the property and spelled out his dream of enhancing the land. Intrigued by the man and his vision, she never left, and the couple married in 1980.

Rick and Jeannie began building the ranch. With their love of antiques, they recycled salvage materials such as old doors, windows, brick and lumber into the Rancho's new buildings, which were built with the aid of master craftsmen. With no design background, Jeannie began creating fanciful interiors for the Rancho and their other projects, including the renovation of the McFadden Building and The Doryman's Inn Bed and Breakfast in Newport Beach.

Together, they created an environment filled with unexpected surprises: hand-painted Portuguese tile murals set into the white stucco building exteriors, wood beams with painted figures framing stained-glass windows, 100-year-old street lights,

Hand-painted Portuguese tile mural

an old-fashioned gumball machine that dispenses duck feed next to a tranquil pond, and everywhere walkways and fireplaces constructed with river rock "harvested" from the Aliso Creek. They planted thousands of trees and landscaped the hills with an artist's eye, all for their own enjoyment.

The Lawrences were raising their two sons and had no thought of making Rancho Las Lomas commercially available until one of their private parties, where a guest who worked as a caterer asked about renting the Rancho to stage special events. Rick and Jeannie agreed to let this caterer schedule two parties over the Thanksgiving weekend in 1984. When they returned from their vacation in Mexico, no trace of the parties remained. With this initial success, they decided to again permit a few more catered parties, and thanks to word-of-mouth praise, 1985 brought them 18 events.

After careful consideration, the Lawrences determined to commercially promote Rancho Las Lomas as a special-events facility. Jeannie wrote and designed the original brochure at their kitchen table, and in 1986 they printed and distributed 10,000 copies. Response proved immediate and overwhelming, with inquiries from private individuals, companies and event planners. Business grew rapidly, leading to their current schedule of over 100 events per year.

Rancho Las Lomas can handle groups of up to 500 guests or intimate parties of 25. The ever-evolving facilities include the Salon de Fiesta, a large rustic dining room that can seat 300; an outdoor pavilion that seats 360; private cottages for brides to dress and grooms to pace; and Rick's Cafe, a Casablanca-styled hillside villa with an oak bar, bay windows, an inviting fireplace and cozy conversation nooks. Many varieties of rare and unusual birds and animals fill its licensed semiprivate zoo and the cries of exotic birds decorate the air.

The Lawrences provide clients with a list of preferred vendors — special-events professionals familiar with the Rancho. Weddings provide the majority of bookings, but the corporate world is showing increased interest in the site for retreats, company parties and promotional events. The Rancho staff makes every attempt to accommodate the most creative wishes of its clients. At one party, the client turned cobblestone walkways into the Yellow Brick Road and dressed staff in costumes from The Wizard of Oz.

Today, Rick and Jeannie Lawrence live part time at Rancho Las Lomas, always tending to the property as instinctively as they breathe. Neither one ever walks the land without an eye to the needed repair or a clipper in their back pocket to trim a flower past bloom or remove a dead leaf. Under their steadfast care, the Rancho continues to evolve, never less beautiful than it is today, never as beautiful as it will be one day. Rancho Las Lomas is truly a monument to their dedication and commitment.

The beautiful, spacious interior of the Salon de Fiesta, a rustic banquet hall that can seat 300 guests

WOOLLEY'S PETITE SUITES

Successful enterprises are often built on a foundation of innovation and a customer-driven business approach. Each of entrepreneur Robert E. Woolley's ventures has exemplified these characteristics. But of all his corporate endeavors, it was Woolley's creation of the "all-suite hotel" concept that perhaps best illustrates his forward-thinking philosophy.

Woolley entered the real estate industry in 1969 by developing apartment complexes in Arizona. He soon recognized that a modified form of his apartment design would appeal to both business travelers and vacationers who wanted more space and comfort than typically found in a traditional hotel.

Using the burgeoning Phoenix building market as a laboratory, Woolley constructed a 75-room apartment building and turned it into what would eventually become the first in a chain of "Granada Royale Hometels." The fledgling project met with immediate success and served to introduce an exciting all-suite segment to the hotel industry.

Woolley ignored conventional hotel construction wisdom and opted instead to create a product based solely on the customer's needs. He bypassed costly public facilities, such as banquet rooms and retail shops, and focused attention on the suites themselves. Each spacious suite was designed to offer all the comforts of home, including such amenities as a king-size bed and separate living room with a sofa sleeper, remote-control cable TV and a kitchenette complete with wet bar, refrigerator, microwave and coffee maker.

From the onset, Woolley strove to strike a balance between "providing a comfortable and hassle-free stay without being overbearing and intrusive." To that end, he offered complimentary breakfast as well as evening cocktails in order to eliminate the service delays typically associated with traditional establishments. The no-tipping policy restored a "service for service's sake" attitude among employees while the express check-out expedited the process.

Woolley's Petite Suites offers something for everyone, from the corporate or business traveler to vacationing couples or families.

Despite the initial skepticism from financiers of this unique design style and business approach, guest acceptance of Woolley's innovative idea to offer "suites" instead of traditional hotel rooms has been overwhelmingly positive. The all-suite concept not only appealed to the commercial business traveler, but also created an environment in which the groundwork for a "weekend getaway" idea could be sold to the local family market.

Traditional commercial hotels, while busy during the work week, struggled for occupancy on weekends and holidays. Woolley's "all-suite" concept not only serves as a destination for discriminating business travelers, but also for vacationing families.

Woolley also believed the all-suites concept to be functionally superior to that of traditional hotels, and it wasn't long before corporate America caught on to the idea. To continue further expansion, Woolley sold his interests in all but one location to the Holiday Corporation and its all-suite operating entity, Embassy Suites.

That single, independently owned site, situated just off the 55 freeway between the Santa Ana and San Diego freeways in Santa Ana, is simply known as Woolley's Petite Suites.

(Far left)
The hotel's meeting rooms are the ideal location for virtually any type of corporate meeting or social gathering.

Guests enjoy the hotel's sparkling outdoor pool and spa.

The structure represents the culmination of this entrepreneur's original vision to feature "suites" rather than standard rooms. Constructed in 1985, it was also the Southern California prototype that would eventually come to be known as a pioneer in the industry.

As part of the largest hotel development project in the city of Santa Ana's history, Woolley's Petite Suites strives to meet the needs of every traveler. Executives enjoy easy access to the John Wayne Airport and nearby corporate offices, while vacationing families find themselves minutes away from some of Southern California's most popular theme parks, including Disneyland, Knott's Berry Farm and Wild Rivers Water Park and shopping destinations such as South Coast Plaza and Fashion Island.

Each of the 183 deluxe one-room suites is designed with the comfort of the corporate traveler in mind — telephones in each room offer computer dataports and voice mail — while a well-lit dining table does double-duty to provide ample work space. Five competitively priced meeting rooms are the ideal location for any type of corporate meeting or social gathering, from groups as small as five to as many as 80.

Each of the 184 deluxe one-room suites is designed with the comfort of its guests in mind.

Each morning, guests can catch up on the news with a free morning newspaper or chat with the chef while their complimentary cooked-to-order breakfast is prepared. After an afternoon of business meetings or sightseeing, guests can unwind during a complimentary two-hour manager's cocktail reception or swim in the outdoor heated pool and spa. Additional amenities range from courtesy airport and shopping mall shuttle service to complimentary on-site parking and valet laundry service.

Woolley's Petite Suites strives to not only meet, but also exceed the needs and expectations of business travelers and vacationing families. With everything under one roof, there's no need to leave. But guests who wish to explore Orange County at their leisure will find numerous recreational and fine dining opportunities all within easy access of the property.

BIG Y YARDAGE OUTLET

This is a love story. It is the story of how Larry and Norma Leifer's love for each other, and for people, built a business: the Big Y Yardage Outlet in Orange, California.

Larry and Norma Leifer in front of the new Big Y

When Larry and Norma Leifer started Big Y in 1964, neither knew much about the fabric business, but Larry did know fabric. He had worked for many years in the furniture trade, during which he had developed wonderful relationships with many fabric manufacturers and reps. With these friendships, Larry made fantastic buys and passed the savings along to Big Y's customers. Selling the finest fabrics at discount prices has distinguished Big Y as a unique store and formed the basis for its continued success.

The textiles at Big Y are all first quality — there are no seconds. Big Y buys directly from the nation's top mills. It offers a myriad of beautiful fabrics. The store's customers include top designers and decorators. Sophisticated customers from all over Southern California and beyond know that if you can't find it at Big Y, it probably can't be found.

Big Y, famous among fabric afficionados and bargain hunters alike, began life in a 4,520-square-foot space. Today, the beautiful new store, which encompasses more than 16,000 square feet, is packed to capacity with the very finest fabrics.

The superb fabrics, services and discount prices have attracted customers from as far away as Japan. The care, attention and love that Norma, Larry and their entire staff bestow upon the customers make it a very special store.

The well-trained staff at Big Y will always go the extra mile to insure customer satisfaction. Big Y employees give customers total attention and assistance; they will draw diagrams, show customers how to measure, and will explain everything to make sure customers understand what they need and get what they want — all at a great price.

Big Y discounts services, too; the drapery labor rate is half what others may charge. The store can make draperies, provide in-house design services, or it can recommend highly qualified outside upholsterers, designers, or drapery manufacturers. Big Y wants and gets nothing for providing this referral service — except total customer satisfaction.

Larry and Norma not only built a business, they created a Big Y family. Employees' birthdays, wedding showers, baby showers — Big Y celebrates them all.

Several employees have been with the firm for decades — Marrene Pacelli and Mary Ann Collins, Big Y's highly effective store administrators and astute buyers, since 1968 and 1969; John Mance, the talented in-house designer, since 1970; and Ruben Sanchez, affectionately nicknamed Big Y's "human computer," since 1989. Others who have also been an important part of the Big Y family for years include Mary Arteaga, Emmy Beuck, Georgette Brooks, Betsy Cunningham, Felipe Gonzales, Fidel Gonzales, Paula Green, Sylvia Orozco, Jenay Thalasinos, Elena Ward, Deborah Deeble, Bryan Gonzales, Barbara Monroe, Gina MacDonald and bookkeeper Sandy Miles.

Big Y Yardage Outlet, before the new store opened in October, 1998

Norma and Larry, now semiretired, depend on their trusted employees to continue the loving tradition of Big Y.

The Leifers' goal at Big Y Yardage Outlet has always been to create, as Norma says, "a wonderful store." And it is. Because love made it that way.

EL TORITO

When Larry Cano bought his first restaurant in 1954, who could have predicted it would become one of the largest casual dining Mexican chains in the nation? It wasn't easy, especially since Cano was operating on a shoestring budget when he rented the house-turned-restaurant in Encino. Add to that the fact that the 48-seat eatery offered Polynesian food, and the odds stacked even higher against him. Still, inspired by the tantalizing flavors and festive ambience of Mexico, he decided his restaurant would do better serving tacos. The concept was an immediate success and led to the opening of El Torito — the original Mexican dinnerhouse in America.

Since then, El Torito has become an authority on authentic Mexican cuisine and margaritas. Known for making its entire melt-in-your-mouth menu from scratch daily using only the finest fresh ingredients, El Torito also invented traditional favorites like edible tostada shells shaped like a bowl, fabulous guacamole made fresh at tableside, and the restaurant's signature cilantro pepita dressing. Always on the cutting edge of new cuisine, El Torito has also taken fajitas to a new level by forging an array of unique varieties and developing the XXL sizzling fajita skillet. And while margaritas are an old Mexican favorite, it was El Torito that made the Cadillac™ Margarita famous and pioneered blended margaritas in a variety of irresistible flavors. Another innovation brought to the highest level of excellence by El Torito is Sunday brunch — so much so that the most popular Sunday spread in Orange County can still be found there today.

Sizzling XXL Steak Fajita Platters are an El Torito favorite.

The Cadillac™ Margarita is an El Torito exclusive.

El Torito continues to blaze the trail with imaginative new dishes that take Mexican cooking into an exciting new arena. Tantalizing new chef's specials are introduced every three months, and for those who enjoy classic favorites, El Torito continues to tempt the appetite with favorites like its signature Mexican Caesar salad and tasty creations like rolled grilled tacos.

Innovative cuisine is not the only thing shaped by El Torito. Today, the El Torito family of restaurants includes exciting eateries like Who Song and Larry's Cantina, El Torito Grill, Casa Gallardo and the renowned Las Brisas overlooking the beautiful coastline in Laguna Beach — a landmark known for delicious seafood and specialties inspired by the Mexican Riviera. Also, El Torito has entered the fast-food arena with the opening of El Torito Express, the first "fast-casual" concept featuring the mesquite-grilled flavors of the Southwest. Ever intent on putting a new spin on a tried-and-true idea, the original El Torito restaurants will get a new look this year to celebrate their 45th anniversary. Using the most popular eateries in Baja California as inspiration, the new decor, dominated by lots of wood, bright colors, artifacts, and menus on surf boards, transports diners to a south-of-the-border beachside cantina.

So how to sum up all this success? El Torito attributes it to giving customers what they want. As a result, people go to El Torito to be satiated in every sense of the word. They go to enjoy fresh food, fabulous margaritas and the festive atmosphere that's perfect for celebrating everything from a special birthday to a wedding reception. There's no doubt about it. After 45 years, El Torito still knows how to throw a fabulous fiesta!

KNOWLWOOD

Home of The World's Best Hamburger

Back in the days before Imperial Highway ran through what is now Anaheim Hills, Fay Knowlton was serving hamburgers and making friends at a little fruit stand that stood in the midst of avocado and orange groves.

Soon she found a partner, Walter Wood, and in 1957 they bought the little stand, which grew into a chain of restaurants that now operate under the registered trademark of Knowlwood: Home of The World's Best Hamburger.

Fay Knowlton showing her million-dollar hamburger

"As a young woman I loved hamburgers," Knowlton says. "And I dreamed of owning my own hamburger restaurant so I could eat as many hamburgers as I wanted, whenever I wanted."

Knowlton cleaned up the fruit stand and started cooking food she would like to eat and treating people the way she would want to be treated. Quality food and good service remained consistent throughout the history of Knowlwood, and they were the keys to the success of the restaurant. Knowlwood became a local legend, a historical marker of sorts. "Back when Knowlwood was the only thing out here..." was a phrase used by many of the old-timers in the Liars Club, a group of ranchers who still met at Knowlwood every morning forty years after it first opened.

But back in 1957 the restaurant was still just a little stand, the kitchen scrubbed clean with bleach water each morning and the gravel surrounding the picnic tables raked clean each day. All the seating was outside, and when it rained, Knowlton brought her customers right into the kitchen.

In the beginning it was ranchers who stood in line for hamburgers, but when industry grew up around the orchards, men in suits and construction gear stood shoulder to shoulder with men in cowboy hats waiting for hamburgers, french fries, pies and other goodies made fresh from recipes developed under Knowlton's guidance.

Five years after the restaurant opened, Knowlton and Walter Wood named it Knowlwood. In the mid-1960s Wood sold his share back to Knowlton, and it was all hers. In November 1966 she moved out of the stand and built a restaurant with a patio and a fence. The new restaurant had six windows, five for food and one for beer, and it seated 500 people outside.

Knowlton's husband and sons worked alongside her, as did scores of other employees who became like family to her. "I always washed the dishes and scrubbed the floors," Knowlton says. "If you think you're too good to work in your business, you've got problems." Knowlton cleaned her restaurant the last day she worked there.

"I feel that I was a blessed woman," says Knowlton. "I had a high school education, but the knowledge within me is what we call common sense. And I loved people. I believe that if you give from your heart, God will give it back in other ways."

Over the years Knowlwood was often voted by the *Orange County Register's* readers as the Best of Orange County in the hamburger category.

In the late 1990s Dr. Thanh Nguyen became the new leader of Knowlwood. He preserved and further strengthened the original concept and philosophy of founder Fay Knowlton: large portions of fresh quality food, a family atmosphere and a fun environment where customers are treated as kings, queens, princes and princesses.

The fruit stand where the World's Best Hamburgers started

MORGAN MARKETING & PUBLIC RELATIONS

Some people are born with natural creative talent. Melinda Morgan is one of them. A dynamic individual with an effusive personality and a contagious smile, Melinda combines her in-depth knowledge of public relations with a brilliant marketing sense and clear vision of the qualities that distinguish extraordinary campaigns from those that are mediocre. And that's what makes Morgan Marketing & Public Relations so successful.

Founded in 1991, Morgan Marketing & Public Relations is a top-notch agency that provides creative communications programs to local, regional and national clients. The agency's stellar list of accounts has included such prominent names as El Torito, Hormel Foods, Denny's, King's Hawaiian, Marie Callender's, Winchell's, Sizzler and Wienerschnitzel. A generalist firm with a high concentration of clients in the food and restaurant industry, Morgan Marketing has also represented such golf field notables as Hyundai Golf Cars, U.S.A.; Grafalloy; Lyte Optronics; and Langert Golf Company. Additionally, the firm has represented clients in the high-tech field including Odetics, SOS Wireless Communications and AST. Other prestigious clients include Taylor Woodrow Homes, Club Med and Whittier Law School.

At Morgan Marketing and Public Relations the objective is the same for each and every client — to produce the results needed for the client to achieve their specific goals. Summing it up, Melinda says, "We use our creativity and expertise to assess each program with a fresh look, then we develop a high-caliber, creative program tailored to meet the client's needs. That's what sets us apart from other agencies."

Using new, precedent-setting creativity to deliver a comprehensive marketing program to clients is no small task, yet Morgan Marketing & Public Relations pulls it off with apparent ease. When a client in Omaha hired the agency as food, wine and special event consultant for a high-end networking party held in Rome, Italy, the elegant affair earned the highest accolades from the client. Morgan and her expert staff planned everything from stunning invitations that enticed company chief executive officers and senior staff members to attend, right down to a traditional Italian wine tasting. When Morgan Marketing launched a new cellular phone product, it dialed in to the senior market and wowed editors at the consumer electronics trade show with a memorable direct mail campaign. The campaign generated tremendous results in both print and broadcast media with sales leads pouring in to the client.

Creativity isn't the only thing that Morgan Marketing & Public Relations takes pride in. "We also focus on integrity and ethics," says Morgan, who hand-picks her clients just as surely as they pick her firm. "There has to be a chemistry in order to make it work, and above all the comfort to exchange ideas." But it's her staff that Melinda takes the most pride in. "We're a family-oriented group that works well together and really cares about each and every one of our clients," she says. That sense of caring — for both staff and client — is evident. And it's another reason why Morgan Marketing & Public Relations will continue to be so successful.

Melinda Morgan of Morgan Marketing & Public Relations

THE EARL'S PLUMBING, INC.

An old tin barn may seem a humble beginning for a nobleman, but Earl Nellesen and his wife Joyce used a fire hose to wash down just such a 40' X 80' wood-floor building, which would become The Earl of Plumbing store. The year was 1956, and this store in Anaheim was the couple's first.

Still a family company, The Earl's Plumbing now serves all of Orange County with full plumbing, heating, air-conditioning, water treatment and kitchen & bath remodeling departments.

Having served the region for almost half a century, The Earl's is a plumbing pioneer and has earned a place in Orange County history. The company can claim credit for many industry innovations. It led the way in the coordination of high visibility logos on trucks, uniforms and advertising and in the use of radio advertising. Earl himself sang his famous, "Never fear, The Earl is here" jingle. The first to develop an integrated computer system, The Earl's went "on line" in 1977.

Much of the company's success stems from the family's faith in God and deeply held values that underpin its business operations. Company employees reflect the family's dedication to service. "We want happy customers, and we've got that," says Earl Nellesen. "They all write us and tell us how happy they are."

The Earl's was one of the first discount plumbing shops to offer help and information on how to do-it-yourself. The personal help and service a customer receives still distinguish the company from the many large discount stores today. The Earl's Plumbing offers items other stores don't, such as hard-to-find parts and large specialty fixtures. Consumers can trust The Earl's to deliver the highest quality in service and materials. Often a fixture found at a huge discounter may have the same brand name and appearance but actually be an inferior model of lower quality than a similar fixture sold at The Earl's.

The Earl's headquarters — 1994-present
Photo by Lia Photography

The Earl's headquarters — 1969-1994

The company's special Maintenance Department offers low hourly rates for commercial customers. This provides businesses, such as hotels, motels and apartment buildings, an affordable solution for minor plumbing and drain problems.

Solving problems ethically and professionally has earned the company many honors, including the National Plumbing Contractor of the Year award presented by the National Association of Plumbing, Heating and Cooling Contractors (PHCC). In September 1999 the Orange, Riverside and San Bernadino Counties' local chapter of PHCC named Earl Nellesen the Contractor of the Century.

Grateful to God for his good fortune, Earl believes in giving back to the community. He was a founder and president of Aid for Baja and raised well over $50,000 a year to help the poor and hungry in Mexico. The National Conference of Christians and Jews named him Catholic Man of the Year. "The Earl of Good Works," as they have called him, has served the Catholic Big Brothers, Little League and many other community organizations. He had the distinct privilege in 1984 of carrying the Olympic torch through Anaheim on behalf of the YMCA.

After the long run from a tin barn to a chain of successful stores, Earl Nellesen has passed the torch of leadership to two of his sons and his daughter. Steve is now president and Kevin is vice president and head of the service department. Teresa serves as Customer Relations Representative. Earl has also passed along something far more precious. The values that have sustained his success and been a blessing to his family and the community.

THE GALARDI GROUP

When John Galardi came to California, he was 19 years old and had a dream: He wanted his own business, and he wanted to be a millionaire by the age of 30. What he didn't know was what business to pursue, so he went to work for the founder of Taco Bell, Glen Bell, and began to learn the fast-food business from the inside out. While searching for his own niche, he discarded the idea of selling tacos, hamburgers or chicken since these markets were already saturated. "Why not sell hot dogs?" Bell asked. At the time, no one else was doing it, so hot dogs it was.

The first Der Wienerschnitzel opened on Pacific Coast Highway in Wilmington in 1961. John sold hot dogs for 15 cents. He was the first in the fast-food business to give toys away to kids — "Oh Boy, Free Toy" was his debut advertising slogan — and he pioneered drive-thru technology by inventing the runner/charger system, a new concept whereby orders are taken at a speaker box, money is collected along the way and food is delivered to customers sometimes even before they arrive at the drive-up window.

(Left to right) For the past 18 years, Wienerschnitzel President and COO Dennis Tase and founder John Galardi have worked together to successfully carve out Wienerschnitzel's own niche in the fast food industry.

Business flourished at that first location, and two more walk-up/drive-thru stands opened in 1964. John was earning $52,000 a year — not bad for a kid from Kansas City. By 1965 Wienerschnitzel had expanded to include 20 Southern California locations, and earnings leapt to $250,000 a year. Thanks to the advent of franchising, great-tasting hot dogs and a famous chili recipe (it remains a secret even today), the chain continued to grow. By 1967, one year before he turned 30, John made his first million dollars. By 1972, there were more than 450 Wienerschnitzel stores in 20 states. Indeed, John Galardi's dream had come true.

Today, Wienerschnitzel (the Der was dropped in 1978) has over 300 stores in 10 states and sells more than 84 million hot dogs a year. The chain has also entered the international market with an opening in Guam. Since the early days of hot dogs and chili, the Wienerschnitzel menu has grown to include such sizzling specialty items as chili-cheese fries, bacon Western dogs, deluxe dogs and Polish sandwiches. The latest creation, named one of the most innovative products for 1998 by the *Orange County Register*, is the pretzel-bun dog, a soft, chewy pretzel-like bun woven around a tasty hot dog. Wienerschnitzel is also the official hot dog of the Anaheim Angels' Edison Field and ARCO Arena, home of the NBA Sacramento Kings.

But even more important than the stores opened and the delicious varieties of hot dogs turned out are the lives that Galardi's business has touched. "John's vision back in 61 was to start a company that would set him up for life," says Wienerschnitzel President Dennis Tase. "Over the years he built on that dream and brought entire families into the franchise business. He helped them get started and watched them grow with us. Today those people are bringing their families into the business. That really shows us their appreciation."

So with all this success, what's the Wienerschnitzel goal for the new millennium? Tase answers that with a smile. "When you think of hot dogs, we want you to think of us!"

NETWORKS

Orange County transportation, energy and other companies keep people, information and power circulating throughout the region.

SOUTHERN CALIFORNIA EDISON

Postwar Orange County was an explosion of people, industry and energy. Newcomers had discovered California during the war as military recruits or workers in war-related industries, and there was no turning back. They were hooked on the climate and the opportunities.

Southern California Edison, already more than 50 years old, was in place to anticipate energy needs for families, agriculture and industry, ensuring that the power infrastructure not only met the needs of the community, but also led to sustainable growth.

The 1950s and 1960s were happy days for providers and users of electrical power. Southern California Edison worked with builders to launch Gold Medallion all-electric communities across Southern California. In these communities, electricity was the sole energy source in homes and businesses.

Electricity was also powering agricultural irrigation and food processing, and it was driving the expansion of industry in Orange County. In 1951, after 65 years of service, Southern California Edison's one-millionth meter was placed. Only 13 years later it placed its two-millionth meter.

Electricity was inexpensive during that era, and the more you bought the less it cost.

But Edison was looking ahead, even during those early days of fast growth and inexpensive power. More than engineers with slide rules and crews of workers slinging cable, the company was, and still is, a vital part of the community. Success has only strengthened Edison's long-term commitments to local business, the environment and people.

More than two decades before the eco-movement of the 1970s, Edison was already concerned with the impact of growth on the environment. Before the word "smog" had even been coined, Edison was the first utility in the nation to begin a program of smoke abatement and air pollution control. Early in those post-war years, rapid population growth, industrial expansion, and the increase in usage of motor vehicles in the "South Coast Air Basin" caused a significant increase in air pollution.

At first, power plants and oil-burning industries were blamed for the smog. As early as 1947 the first smoke abatement laws and county smog ordinances had been passed — these were aimed at oil-burning facilities. At that time Edison plants burned oil because natural gas was only available on a short-term, interruptible basis. So Edison conducted research on how to reduce visible emissions and sulfur dioxide.

Using information in part from Edison's research, Dr. A.J. Haagen-Smit of Caltech identified conditions that caused photochemical smog. He also discovered that motor vehicles were the primary source of pollutants. But county agencies didn't want to go after motor vehicles. So in 1955 the Air Pollution Control District threatened to issue no further permits for power plant operation. But the continuing growth of the local economy and the increasing need for electricity prevented the district from acting on its threat.

Edison is a major supporter of Orange County business, sports, education and other organizations including the Orange County Performing Arts Center, Discovery Science Center, the Pacific Symphony and United Way.

Haagen-Smit was retained by Edison in 1956 to further research smog abatement, a pioneering effort in the industry. His research team developed a number of pollution control technologies that have since been adopted nationwide. As a result of this and other efforts, the South Coast Air Quality Management District estimates that Edison power plants produced less than 2 percent of the smog-forming air pollutants created in the air basin.

In the 1970s global issues changed the energy scene in the United States and around the world. The era of cheap, abundant foreign oil ended with the oil embargo.

Edison made history in the early 1970s as the first major utility in the nation to discontinue all marketing advertising and replace it with conservation messages aimed at reducing the overall consumption of electricity. Southern California's population was continuing to grow, and cost factors and regulatory approvals made new

For more than 90 years, Edison's home economists taught cooking tips to homemakers and professed the advantages of cooking electrically "without flame, without fumes and without byproducts of combustion."

power plant construction prohibitive. So Edison's plan to reduce per-capita consumption of electricity was both practical and environmentally sound.

By the time the California Public Utilities Commission ordered other utilities in the state to develop conservation programs, Edison had voluntarily launched its own successful programs and emerged as an industry role model. As a result of its foresight and leadership, Edison weathered the oil embargo of 1973. The company's campaign, "Make Every Kilowatt Count," was adopted throughout Southern California, as was the idea of "load management," or shifting electrical demand away from peak hours of usage. "Give Your Appliance the Afternoon Off," was Edison's load management slogan.

About 80 percent of Edison's electricity was generated by burning oil during the 1970s. During that decade the price of imported fuel oils increased by more than 1,200 percent, from $2.46 per barrel in 1970 to $32.16 in 1980. The nation's economy saw double-digit inflation, and the cost of electricity spiraled upward at an unprecedented rate. Because of Edison's education and information programs, its customers were ready for the company's double-barreled plan of energy conservation and load management.

By 1982 Edison had reduced its use of fuel oil to less than 4 percent. And its new plant construction was limited to completing San Onofre Nuclear Generating Station Units 2 and 3.

During these years Edison was also investigating alternative methods of generating electricity in the large quantities needed by the Southern Californian community. In 1980 Edison's chairman of the board, William R. Gould, announced that of the new generation capacity to be added by 1990, one-third, or about 1.9 million kilowatts, would be from plants using environmentally friendly and renewable technologies including wind power, geothermal, solar, fuel cells, cogeneration and hydroelectric generation. The nation's largest experimental wind turbine ever to be connected to a commercial power system went into operation on Edison's system in December 1980.

The winds of change hit Orange County's overall economy hard in the early 1990s. Rumors of improprieties by county officials were confirmed when Orange County declared bankruptcy in 1994. People and businesses began migrating out of Orange County, and property values fell. The county was losing up to 20,000 people a year.

Edison made a corporate-level commitment to help businesses remain profitable in Orange County by expanding and retaining companies and attracting new business. The company focused its attention on business-climate issues and increasing the competitiveness of the business community. The utility led in developing programs that would help businesses make money-saving decisions so they could meet competitive challenges and prosper.

While Edison had always offered these kinds of services to businesses, now their consultations were making a difference to the total business environment countywide. Edison's experts addressed energy, environmental and economic challenges facing companies in the post-bankruptcy climate.

Edison's Economic and Business Development Group estimates it helped save more than 127,000 jobs and assisted 570 companies within Edison's service area in the 1990s by providing customized information and services to assist in maintaining or relocating businesses in Orange County. Key in that effort were regional resources like TeamCalifornia, a collaborative partnership between the California Trade and Commerce Agency, local economic development organizations and communities, businesses, utilities and government agencies and Edison's own economic development services.

Edison also took TeamCalifornia online to link both the individual economic development practitioners and the public

Long before corporate America found it fashionable to be environmentally sensitive, Edison was on the cutting edge of environmental protection. The Alamitos Generating Station built an experimental bag filter house in the early 1960s to significantly reduce air emissions.

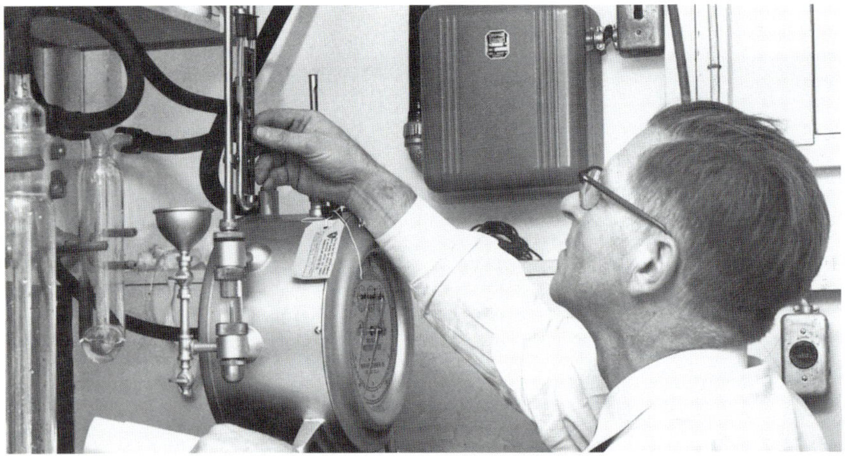

In the postwar years, the South Coast Air Basin found a direct correlation between population increases and industrial expansion and a brownish eye-stinging haze. Edison was the first utility in the nation to begin smoke abatement and air pollution controls. Dr. A.J. Haagen-Smit, a world authority on pollution control, headed Edison's "smog" prevention research in the early 1950s.

and private economic development agencies in the state. As a member of Team Irvine, Southern California Edison helped the city realize a 5.5 percent increase in the number of businesses in 1995.

Edison also focused on growing businesses in several critical sectors, including importing and exporting, the fashion and apparel industry, the food processing and manufacturing industry and motion picture production. It designed a Retention Economic Development Rate to encourage film companies to complete production in Southern California. To address the NAFTA-driven increase in competition between the United States, Mexico and Canada, Southern California Edison provided a $50,000 grant to the California Fashion Association-Technology & Education Council to help upgrade technology, equipment and workers' skills among regional apparel contractors and manufacturers.

The Food Industry Business Roundtable was created by Edison to bring together prominent Latino and Asian food-processing companies to address critical environmental and legislative issues that affected that industry.

Philanthropic activities also continued during this time. In the 1990s Edison provided nearly $6 million to charitable and nonprofit organizations in Orange County alone, in addition to donating more than $1.5 million in employee contributions to United Way and more than 40,000 employee volunteer hours throughout the county.

In 1999 Edison contributed more than $1 million toward the development of Orange County's community arts, including underwriting the Pacific Symphony Orchestra's free Summer Park Series and becoming the first corporate donor to the new symphony hall at the Orange County Performing Arts Center.

A major investor in the Orange County Business Council, Edison was one of only four corporations to contribute $500,000 over five years to sustain the organization and its emphasis on economic development and business vitality in Orange County.

Edison also was a major donor and supporter of the Huntington Beach Wetlands and Wildlife Care Center, located on the utility's property on Pacific Coast Highway. A joint venture with the Animal Alliance, the Huntington Beach Wetlands Conservancy, the State Department of Fish and Game and other contributing corporations, the center was developed primarily to mitigate oil-spill disasters by supporting the recovery, treatment and rehabilitation of animals and birds from Santa Barbara to San Diego.

Orange County recovered remarkably quickly from the financial woes of the early 1990s due in part to the efforts of Edison and other businesses and individuals committed to the health of Orange County. By the late 1990s the county had emerged as the new Silicon Valley of the world, with Edison helping to fuel that growth.

Edison supported the technology business in two ways: by encouraging businesses to come to Orange County through its Economic and Business Development Group, and by providing the high-tech industries with cleaner energy. The high-tech industry required a level of consistency of electrical delivery far beyond that necessary for homes and most other industries.

Edison's Customer Technology Application Center showcases the newest, most energy-efficient electrotechnologies available. With Edison's help, business customers are provided opportunities to find ways to improve productivity, increase energy efficiency and become more competitive.

As a part of Edison's service to the high-tech industry, it provided equipment on site to refine and purify electricity, giving it the stability necessary for quality production.

Another milestone in the history of the electricity industry came in 1998 when California restructured and partially deregulated the electricity market.

The regulatory environment of Orange County in the late 1990s posed as great a challenge to Edison as the oil embargo of the 1970s had. In 1996 the state of California enacted legislation to provide a transition to a competitive market structure. In 1998 Edison's traditional role as a generator and provider of electricity changed due to this new regulatory environment. The generation sector then had new competitors from non-utility power producers and regulators in California's restructured electric utility industry.

Customers could choose to remain utility customers with bundled electric service from Edison, or they could choose to buy electricity from other unregulated power suppliers. Southern California Edison continued to provide the core distribution service, delivering energy through its distribution system regardless of the customer's choice of electricity supplier. The California Public Utilities Commission continued to regulate the prices and service obligations related to distribution services.

Just as Edison anticipated the postwar boom and provided the innovative infrastructure for housing and business that grew Orange County at a critical point, Southern California Edison quickly embraced this new regulatory environment and adjusted to meet the needs of its community. It restructured its basic utility business in order to focus on transmission, distribution and customer service. It also expanded significantly into related non-utility businesses, particularly independent power generation and infrastructure finance.

Two of Edison International's non-utility businesses are headquartered in Orange County. Edison Mission Energy is one of the world's largest independent power producers with operations throughout the world. Edison Capital provides capital and financial services in energy/infrastructure and affordable housing.

Edison International, the parent company to Southern California Edison, also set its sights on growing globally. For example, Edison Mission Energy, an Irvine-based Edison International subsidiary, grew in the late 1990s from its initial roots in California to be one of the world's premiere private power companies. And Irvine-based Edison Capital, Edison International's capital and financial services subsidiary, became one of the largest investors in developing low-income housing in the United States.

Chairman and CEO John Bryson said no one should have been surprised at Southern California Edison and Edison International's success in the new market. "We have more than a century of experience in this industry. It's not as though somebody can just start up overnight and expect to compete with people who really know the business or who really care about their community the way we always have," he said. "We're experts at change. We can handle this."

From building Orange County after the war, to rebuilding it after the financial crisis of the early 1990s, to restructuring the company in light of the deregulated energy climate, Edison has consistently done whatever has been necessary to anticipate and serve the changing needs of Orange County. It has provided the county with much more than electricity. Edison's innovative practices have undergirded progress in Orange County, creating an energetic and prosperous community prepared to face whatever the future holds.

The depth and success of the Edison commitment to alternative and renewable energies can be traced back to the company's 1980 announcement to aggressively develop "clean" energy resources. Edison soon became the most energy diverse utility in the world by generating electricity from nine different energy sources like wind, solar and geothermal.

JOHN WAYNE AIRPORT

Thanks to the vision and ambition of an enterprising young man named Eddie Martin, Orange County's first airport was created in the middle of a bean field between Santa Ana and Costa Mesa. The year was 1923, and the land was owned by James Irvine of The Irvine Company. The Eddie Martin Airport began operations with an old Jenny that had been used as a training plane during World War I. It was a humble beginning of what is today the gateway to Orange County — John Wayne Airport.

Martin was an entrepreneur at heart. After signing a five-year lease with James Irvine for his airport, he opened a flying school called Martin Aviation, which remains one of the nation's oldest aviation firms. In 1939 the Airport became a publicly owned facility through a land swap between The Irvine Company and the county. After serving as a military base during World War II, it was returned by the federal government to the county with one stipulation: that it remain open to aviation uses.

Eddie Martin, founder of John Wayne Airport's original airfield, was issued his pilot's license by Orville Wright.

Over the years, the Airport has grown and evolved to meet the growing demands of the county. In 1967 a 22,000-square-foot Eddie Martin Terminal was built to accommodate 400,000 passengers annually. Over the next 15 years, remodeling brought the facility to 29,000 square feet.

The interior design of John Wayne Airport's baggage claim area was inspired by New York's Grand Central Station.

The Airport had a new look and as it evolved into a thriving aviation facility, it also adopted a new name. In 1979 the Eddie Martin Airport was renamed John Wayne Airport by the Orange County Board of Supervisors to honor the late Newport Beach resident.

In 1986 John Wayne Airport began a four-year major renovation known as the "Airport Improvement Project." At that time, it was the largest public works project in the county's history, and included expanded parking facilities and the construction of a new terminal, named after longtime Fifth District Supervisor Thomas F. Riley, in whose district the airport was located.

The long-awaited new terminal was opened to the public in September of 1990. The impressive 337,900-square-foot building features 14 loading bridges, four baggage carousals, two airline club lounges, and a variety of food and gift concessions. The state-of-the-art facility, resembling the interior of New York's Grand Central Station, is aesthetically beautiful. Many finishing touches, including rows of towering palm trees, 140-million-year-old marble containing millions of tiny sea shells, and a generous use of glass combine to create a bright and pleasing environment for air travelers. There are convenient separate arrival and departure levels, and the terminal offers travelers a short walk between ground transportation, baggage claim and aircraft gates.

To commemorate the Airport's namesake, the John Wayne Associates commissioned sculptor Robert Summers to create a bronze statue of "the Duke." It was dedicated to the county in 1982, and later refinished and restored prior to its placement in the lobby of the Thomas F. Riley Terminal in 1990. The nine-foot statue is located on the arrival level in the center of the terminal, and rests atop a pedestal covered in the same marble that graces the entire facility. Designed in two tiers to allow visitors to touch the statue, the pedestal provides an appropriate home for this tribute to one of the nation's most revered patriots and beloved actors.

Ease of use is cited by many as a benefit of flying in and out of John Wayne Airport. Centrally located, the Airport is easily accessed by major freeways. Four lots within walking distance of the terminal offer more than 5,700 public parking spaces. Off-airport parking is available in the Main Street Lot, which provides free shuttle service to the terminal every 15 minutes. Travelers short on time especially appreciate the Airport Valet Parking Service, just one more amenity that makes John Wayne Airport a favorite among air travelers.

The airport's rotated square is shown illuminated at dusk by light from the terminal.

John Wayne Airport is located in the heart of Orange County's thriving business community, and is recognized as one of its most important economic assets. It generates more than 57,000 jobs and contributes more than $3.5 billion annually to the county's economy — all without the use of taxpayer dollars. Managed by the County of Orange, the airport functions as a self-sustaining operation, much like a private business. Although the Airport has grown to accommodate nearly 8 million passengers annually, it employs a core team of only 133 people. This hard-working team oversees the day-to-day operations, while other services such as parking facility management and security are contracted out for cost-efficiency.

When it comes to being a good neighbor, John Wayne Airport serves as a national model — it enforces one of the most stringent aircraft access and noise programs in the United States. The regulations are the result of a 1985 federal court agreement that defined the operational and capacity limits at the Airport. Specifically, the agreement provides for a number of controls and limits, including a maximum of 8.4 million annual passengers to be served at John Wayne Airport through the year 2005; limits on the number of average daily commercial aircraft departures; a curfew restricting times of departures and arrivals; and noise level regulations for commercial and general aviation aircraft operations. In addition, under strict guidelines, all commercial aircraft flying out of the Airport are exclusively Stage Three, the quietest commercial aircraft in the nation. The Airport has also developed an Acoustical Insulation Program, which involves working with eligible local homeowners in the Airport's departure path to insulate homes from aircraft noise.

The Airport is further recognized for its award-winning Airport Community Relations program. To support the large artistic community, it sponsors regular art exhibitions featuring both local and world-renowned artists. Its Annual Student Art Contest has grown to nearly 3,500 entries from Orange County students. In addition, the Airport's Tour Program hosts over 6,500 visitors each year. The newest addition to Airport Community Relations is the Ambassador Program, which features trained volunteers wearing red blazers and "May I Help You?" buttons, who greet travelers throughout the terminal and offer assistance.

Over the years, John Wayne Airport has gone from a small local airfield to a respected, first-class aviation facility that balances the needs of the airline industry, the traveling public and the millions of people who call Orange County home. Ongoing passenger surveys show that an overwhelming majority — as many as 96 percent of survey participants — found Airport services good to excellent. And 95 percent of the survey participants gave the Airport overall marks of "A" and "B." With its strong focus on community involvement, economic growth and impeccable customer service, John Wayne Airport continues as a positive and influential force in Orange County, and a role model for other airports across the country.

The John Wayne statue on the airport's arrival level is 9 feet tall, weighs 1,100 pounds and is cast in bronze.

STEWART'S DATA SERVICE, INC.

Stewart's Data Service is an unsung hero in the business world. Although the Santa Ana-based business has but a handful of employees sharing a small office, it makes big things happen. The company offers data processing services for select customers throughout Southern California and the nation. Among the services offered by Stewart's Data Service are name and address database maintenance, seminar attendance tracking, statistics tracking and maintenance, payroll deduction and other data management services.

Owner Millie Stewart is modest about her accomplishments, but she's proud of her business ethics, which emphasize customer service and dedication to the job at hand. That's important for a service-oriented business like Stewart's Data Service, which receives most of its business through word-of-mouth referrals. Millie and her employees perform detail-oriented work that requires a high degree of efficiency, an essential ingredient in the recipe for Millie's success story.

With 15 years of experience and the urging of two mentors, Millie founded Stewart's Data Service in 1978, focusing on the accounting needs of the construction industry. Unlike most new companies, Stewart's suddenly found itself with 50 clients, including Ponderosa, Warmington Homes and many other leading builders.

The recession of 1982-83 caused Millie to briefly downsize her company and reassess her options, but the marketplace rebounded and Stewart's Data Service moved to a larger office in Costa Mesa to accommodate the three shifts of operators needed to meet the demand for services. Millie later moved her company to Santa Ana, where it remains to this day.

This chapter in the company's history also opened new sources of opportunity: animal tag registration for San Diego County, maintenance of name and address databases, inventory control for such companies as Millers Outpost, Bullocks, Sears and Robinsons-May, and Millie's most challenging assignment: income tax preparation data entry during the early phases of electronic filing.

"Most service bureaus won't and can't provide personalized service," says Millie. "Internal/departmental red tape inhibits quick changes in order to satisfy customer needs, and we are not like that. Our flexibility is a priority for superb customer service."

As with all businesses, new accounts are important — but not at the expense of sacrificing personal service for the sake of a few dollars. Indeed, it's that personal touch that makes Stewart's Data Service stand out from the crowd.

(Back row, left to right) Jorja Boyer, Paula Cottrill. (Front row, left to right) Margie Jones, holding Mandy; Millie Stewart, holding Ginger; and Lori Oakley
Photo by Lia Photography

Anaheim/Orange County Visitor & Convention Bureau

PROFESSIONAL SERVICES

Architects, engineers, photographers, accountants, advertising and other professionals provide essential services to the Orange County area.

BASSENIAN/LAGONI ARCHITECTS

Bassenian/Lagoni Architects, based in Newport Beach, is recognized nationally as a specialist in the design and land planning of residential communities. Its expertise encompasses a broad range, including single-family detached, high-density detached, patio homes, townhomes, condominiums, apartments, senior housing and resort communities. Recipient of more than 300 national and regional awards for design excellence, this innovative architectural firm reaches beyond Orange County to design homes for builders throughout North America and Southeast Asia.

Chairman and CEO Aram Bassenian, AIA, received his degree in architecture from the University of California at Berkeley in 1966. After internships with some noted architects and two early partnerships, he founded the firm of Aram Bassenian, AIA and Associates in 1979. That same year, Carl W. Lagoni joined the firm after receiving his bachelor's degree in architecture from California Polytechnic Institute. He rose quickly through the ranks to a partnership position in 1988, and to its presidency in 1994.

Bassenian/Lagoni specializes in the design of merchant-built housing for planned communities. The company's work shows a sophistication that is light years ahead of postwar tract housing.

Carl Lagoni, AIA, and Aram Bassenian, AIA, partners in Bassenian/Lagoni Architects
Photo by Smith Photography

Easily recognizable in white stucco and red tile roof, this Early California design by Bassenian/Lagoni Architects expertly reinterprets a familiar Southern California style in Coto de Caza, California, for Lennar Homes.
©John R. Bare

In the aftermath of the 1993 Laguna Beach fires, Bassenian/Lagoni Architects was involved with the design of the Bassenians' own private residence.
©John R. Bare

Those older developments consisted of little more than shelter, laid out by draftsmen, not architects, and they suffered from dreary sameness and limited amenities.

Bassenian/Lagoni's growth as a residential architectural firm parallels the growth of Orange County and has led to its involvement with most of the area's major developers. In the early 1980s, during the economic downturn, Mr. Bassenian researched and developed new ways to create affordability by building on smaller lots. At a time when the talk of the trade was building 400-square-foot condominiums, he offered clients a series of seminars on the virtues of small-lot detached housing, which was then a new concept. In addition, the firm demonstrated the ability to produce highly disciplined housing designs that could be built with control in construction costs. These ideas took hold in the building community, and Bassenian/Lagoni became positioned as a creative and cost-conscious design firm with new ideas and pragmatic solutions. Working with major builders such as Ponderosa Homes, the company designed some of the first small-lot detached homes in Orange County and Northern California. One of these designs won a Pacific Coast Builder's Conference Gold Nugget Grand Award for Best Detached (Small-Lot) Home of the Year.

Innovation in design and discipline in construction costs have become Bassenian/Lagoni trademarks. During each swing of the economy, the firm has adapted its designs to fit the demands of the marketplace. When the economy improved in the late 1980s, the firm became a leader in the move-up market. It designed increasingly sophisticated houses and became recognized for award-winning projects built by the J. M. Peters Company.

When the economy became difficult in the early 1990s, Bassenian/Lagoni helped clients such as Pardee Homes retool their products for maximum flexibility. Floor plans opened up and rooms became less defined by specific uses, and therefore, more adaptable to a homeowner's shifting needs.

According to Mr. Bassenian, "America has excelled in the art of home building and not always in neighborhood design." In the late 1990s, the firm placed major emphasis on creating variety in major developments for Standard Pacific, Warmington Homes, Shea Homes and others. It used changes in plan form, massing, styling and color to provide visual diversity.

Work stations at Bassenian/Lagoni headquarters spill over with subtly variegated samples of tile, stone, stucco, shingles and paint. Drawing on the firm's decades of experience, designers develop a palette of colors for each development. This affords the builders a dozen or more color combinations that add variations to each home.

Home building ranks second only to automobile manufacturing as a major industry — and Orange County is this industry's equivalent of Detroit. Given the number of homes designed and built since the 1970s, the art of residential development has

Fractured elevation, raised roof pitch, balconies and recessed windows that create shadow patterns add variety to this home designed by Bassenian/Lagoni Architects for Standard Pacific in Newport Beach, California. *©John R. Bare*

In the late 80s as the market demand skyrocketed in Orange County for move-up homes, Bassenian/Lagoni Architects designed this plan for J.M. Peters' Bryant Ranch in Yorba Linda to reflect a more current interpretation of Mediterranean styling. *©John R. Bare*

Tall, narrow openings and stone veneers accurately reflect the Tuscan Village theming in this Bassenian/Lagoni Architects-designed home built by Lennar Homes in Coto de Caza.
©John R. Bare

matured very rapidly. Southern California's housing boom sparked design innovations that have been exported around the world. The new California home is more open with vertical volume dominating its presence. Windows have increased in size, allowing natural light to flow and eliminating the distinction between indoor and outdoor space. The designs have evolved to separate the home's formal and informal zones. The kitchens have opened, the nook has become the central eating area, and the master bedroom suites have become more sophisticated. Many of these innovations have come from production housing designed by Bassenian/Lagoni in the past two decades.

The firm developed communities throughout California — from San Diego County up through Orange County, the Los Angeles area through the Central Valley to the San Francisco Bay area. Outside the state, it has designed communities in Arizona, Nevada, Illinois, Texas, Florida, North Carolina, and as far north as the state of Washington and Canada. Overseas their work appears in Japan, China and Indonesia. Foreign builders and government officials, seeking to learn the latest in housing design, regularly visit the company's offices and building sites.

In addition, Bassenian/Lagoni has excelled in creating housing solutions for urban in-fill locations. As cities have grown, land has become more scarce and in-fill projects take on greater importance. When the firm has worked within an existing neighborhood, it has taken pains to match the scale and general attributes of the surrounding community while making optimum use of modern design techniques. "We make a concerted effort to blend our in-fill projects into the fiber of established communities," states Carl Lagoni. Front porches, refined details, classic proportions and a variety of building materials help create a sense of continuity between the old housing and the new.

Its commitment to design excellence has earned Bassenian/Lagoni Architects more than 120 Gold Nugget Merit and Grand Awards. These are awarded annually to the best designs in the Western region, which stretches from Texas to Hawaii. In addition, the firm has garnered 109 MAME awards, 30 Best in American Living Awards, and two *Professional Builder* magazine's Smarter House for the Money selections. Aram Bassenian and Carl Lagoni participate regularly as guest speakers for numerous building industry organizations, including the annual PCBC Western Building Show and the National Association of Home Builders Convention. They have also served as judges for a number of building-industry award programs throughout the United States and Canada. In 1987 Mr. Bassenian was awarded *Professional Builder* magazine's Professional Achievement Award for consistent quality in the creation of exciting and highly marketable housing designs.

These awards line the entrance of Bassenian/Lagoni's 16,000-square-foot Newport Beach offices. The firm's offices are bright, with spacious work areas for its staff of 83. The company is known for a culture that cares about its people and provides ample opportunities to advance professionally.

As the population continues to grow in Orange County and throughout California, there will be a tremendous demand for housing. Bassenian/Lagoni is committed to taking a leadership position in the area's housing future, formulating new and exciting concepts for The Irvine Company, Talega Ranch in San Clemente, and the new city of Ladera, as well as in other growing areas in the Southwest.

Bassenian/Lagoni Architects remains committed to extending the hand of the designer to the masses by creating innovative, yet obtainable, housing. "There is a passion in this firm to design housing and to do it better than anyone else," Aram Bassenian states. "We enjoy being first in the field that we've selected, and we feel that we're making a valuable contribution when we house Americans better than people living anywhere else in the world. We take tremendous pride in that."

Bassenian/Lagoni Architects brought 1930s Craftsman styling into the 90s with the creation of this charming home designed for Pardee's Oakhurst neighborhood in Irvine.
©Keith A. Swan

GOUVIS ENGINEERING CALIFORNIA

In the same era President Lyndon B. Johnson was introducing his "Great Society," Gouvis Engineering was introducing an engineering discipline that would one day help create a "great new society" in Orange County.

Actually, President Johnson's plan debuted just a few short years after Nick Gouvis initiated his teaching of timber design at California State University, Long Beach. Gouvis' students would one day be at the forefront of today's structural engineering trade, and many of those students would eventually join Gouvis Engineering.

While Orange County was just that — a sea of orange groves — Nick Gouvis was sitting at his kitchen table preparing calculations for homes for $10 a sheet. He was often asked to write smaller to keep costs down. When the company began in 1960, architects were trained in basic engineering and were responsible for the structural design. Buildings that required more complex designs were sent to Gouvis, who has been referred to as the "Father of Modern Structural Engineering for Residential Housing."

But in 1973, as building codes became increasingly complex, full engineering plans were required in California and the structural engineer became responsible for the integrity of the design. With the preponderance of earthquakes and other natural disasters in recent times, building-code regulators are becoming even more cognizant of the need for structural engineering.

In fact, the field of structural engineering has proved its worth. A massive earthquake that hit Armenia in 1989 was approximately the same magnitude as the temblor that hit Northridge, California, in January 1994. Even though the region hit in California has a greater population, more people died in the Armenian quake — more than 10,000 compared to Northridge's 65 deaths. "This statistic illustrates what engineers have done; that the work we do pays off. After the Northridge quake, people really began to appreciate structural engineers. We became the unsung heroes," says Saeed Bekam, Gouvis' president and CEO.

Innovation Is a Gouvis Hallmark

What sets Gouvis apart from its competitors is its use of innovative techniques and technologies. The company was the first in the industry to embrace computerization. Back in 1976 Gouvis bought its first computers and developed its own programs long before similar types of programs were commercially available. The company has totally computerized all technical work, which increases efficiency and the ability to meet demanding schedules while maintaining competitive fees. Gouvis employs a staff of four full-time employees solely to write and update its in-house structural computer programs.

Another Gouvis innovation is providing a wider range of services than its competitors. The company has worked hard over the past 40 years to make its services as economical as possible to its clients. Because of this philosophy, the company provides a full range of structural engineering and drafting services, post-tension slab-on-grade design; roof- and floor-truss design and layouts; field observation and support; Title 24 energy calculations; structural investigation services; seismic retrofit, structural-integrity investigations; light-gauge steel design for housing; and expert witness services.

Gouvis provides full field quality control with signed certification of conformance, and it uses a unique system to ensure an instant response to field inquiries. Most of the many innovative structural details the company has developed and tested over the years have subsequently been adopted industrywide.

Gouvis holds itself to three main tenets. The first is safety. "That is our main concern because lives can be affected by what we do," adds Bekam. Second comes economy and third is creating a practical design. It has built a reputation for being able to handle the most complex jobs.

Growing Along With Orange County

Gouvis has played a big part in the housing community in Orange County. While Gouvis engineers aren't architects or planners and have no say as to the "look" of structures, they are responsible for the safety of the buildings they design. The company has partnered with developers for growth throughout Orange County. There has been an exodus from surrounding counties to Orange County over the years, and Gouvis has moved along with the developers to ensure the County's continual growth.

"A lot of architects and developers who do tract-type housing are located in Orange County. As more and more residential projects began to move to Orange County, so did the developers and so did we," explains Bekam. Gouvis first opened its Orange County office in 1986. "The years between 1986 and 1990 were a definite growth period for housing in California and specifically in Orange County. The early 1990s recession affected the market drastically. Ever since the recession our business has increased by at least 25 percent per year." But Orange County isn't the only area the company expanded to. It opened its first satellite office in Palm Springs in the late 1970s. Later, it opened offices in San Diego (1986), Las Vegas (1992) and Northern California (1994). The company is licensed to work in 14 states. In fact, Gouvis currently works with approximately 60 percent of all developers in California.

Gouvis has also branched out internationally with an office in Saigon, Vietnam (1999). Some of this international work involved single-family projects in Japan and Korea.

Streamlining With Computers

In its efforts to provide customers with quick, efficient and cost-effective plans, Gouvis has relied heavily on computers to streamline its operations. All administrative functions are computerized, such as tracking jobs, project histories, and costs. Additionally, the structural engineering calculations performed by Gouvis are fully computerized. As changes are made

to the UBC, company programmers immediately take on the task of updating the computer programs to reflect those changes. The technical aspect of the program, for instance, helps the engineer determine gravity loads, lateral loads and foundation systems. "The computer system enhances the engineer's work," explains Bekam. "Our programs make the job more efficient and accurate. It provides the most economical and practical solution, that meets code requirements.

"For instance, there are over 40 possible load combinations when engineering a beam. Finding the right load combination might take an engineer four to five hours of longhand calculations and there is a greater chance of error. The computer eliminates that error factor and can do the calculations in seconds. In addition, the computer determines the most economic design that meets current UBC. That is unique to our in-house programs," adds Bekam. "We

are always looking to make our programs better, easier to use, more effective and completely code compliant. Our in-house programs have been a great instrument for our success." In creating this computerized engineering system, Gouvis' goal is to avoid repetitious longhand calculations and devote more time to the thinking process required for design. "We are trying to come up with a bigger and better calculator."

Gouvis also utilizes the computer system to streamline job tracking. Everything is now computerized. Plans are scanned into the computer and updated as necessary. Instant access to plans allows the company to provide timely responses to questions raised in the field during construction. There is no longer a need to have a room stocked full of countless plan versions.

Gouvis Engineering has built its reputation on providing accurate analysis, superior service, and the ability to meet deadlines. It is committed to a tradition of quality engineering services of the highest caliber. The experienced team of engineers, principals and project managers takes a personal interest in the needs of its clients. Gouvis Engineering has committed the personnel and resources to be the leading source for structural engineering consulting.

VERMILLION & BESERLER, LLC

Vermillion & Beserler, LLC is building an electronic gateway to new homes by rendering the virtual doors that consumers beat down to buy them.

The company uses a dynamic blend of art and science to link homebuyers and builders of large tracts or individual custom homes and small and large commercial projects using a cutting-edge technique that will be increasingly important as the MTV generation comes of age.

The team of artists at Vermillion & Beserler, LLC relies on time-honored approaches to creating drawings, whether traditional or digital. They are professionals degreed in areas including interior design, graphic arts, commercial art, photographic engineering, information technology, multimedia, Web design, computer programming and kiosk solution technology. The variety of talents and approaches makes Vermillion & Beserler, LLC a full-service agency for any artwork a builder, architect or marketing agent might need.

Vermillion & Beserler, LLC offers a full range of traditional rendering, digital rendering and Web site services.

Founder Katherine Vermillion brought years of interior design and marketing experience to a new arena by using architectural software to literally build homes by computer. A solid foundation in architectural theory helps Vermillion and her staff to work with builders and architects, using the true house plans to reconstruct the home as a computer model so faithful, the renderings look almost better than photographs.

Vermillion & Beserler, LLC's computerized renderings give buyers not only a 360-degree view of a home's exterior design, but also fly-throughs and animated features that let shoppers open doors and peek into closets as they move through a home on the computer.

Vermillion & Beserler, LLC is able to reproduce not only the lines and features of a home, but also add details right down to matching the precise building and trim materials and colors. Homes can be individually decorated and landscaped to add a pastoral appeal. Models can include details all the way down to an animated change of shadow based on the sun's movement over a particular home, or even full sun studies that show where a shadow might fall at a specific time of day on any day of the year, based on the building 's latitude and longitude.

Sunset handcrafted renderings create a fantasy look that adds magic to images.

These artworks take hours of human and computer time to create. Artists use CAD software and must meet the construction specifications as painstakingly as the workers who put up the walls and install the utilities. Each detail is drawn into the model exactly the way it is built into the real home. The result has everything but weight.

The resulting renderings offer consumers a presentation not only packed with the information all buyers demand, but that also give the feel of a home by letting the visitor step right inside. For builders, this can open an untapped market of non-traditional consumers who don't approach transactions the way their parents did.

Before homes go up for sale, the computer models allow a builder to see exactly how blueprints will translate into a three-dimensional structure. Changes can be made on computer images and drawn into blueprints, particularly to builders of custom homes who often get just one chance to make the product perfect.

Vermillion & Beserler, LLC has a track record for delivering renderings, tract maps, computer models and floor plans to California builders including Taylor Woodrow Homes, Warmington Homes, Pacific Bay Homes and Sacramento-based Elliott Homes. As its reputation spreads, Vermillion & Beserler, LLC is gaining national interest as not only the builder's artist of choice, but as an indispensable sales tool.

Most builders are accustomed to building model homes on tract sites, then furnishing them invitingly to entice consumers to buy. Katherine Vermillion uses the same techniques and her design experience to incorporate subtle cues that help shoppers feel right at home. With a computer as her palette, she is now able to weave those subtle but crucial messages into an entire virtual presentation.

Whiz-bang technology alone does not a good presentation make. The amazing computer renderings are possible partly because Vermillion & Beserler, LLC artists are classically trained. Their diverse backgrounds in fine arts disciplines offer clients the benefit of renderings that are works of art in their own right, as well as advertising and sales tools. Vermillion & Beserler, LLC also provides one-stop shopping for a full range of media, each of which reaches viewers on a different level. These include:

Line illustrations faithfully recreate the appearance of a building with simple elegance. The effect is a traditional pen-and-ink quality. Images may be stark with no color, although watercolor may be added. These illustrations focus the viewer on the lines and angles of a subject.

Oils impart a stately, classical appearance to the rendering. Their weight and layerability allows for more texture in an image than other media. Oils can be thinned to create a more translucent and detailed look.

Gouache or tempera give the brightest, punchiest colors for the greatest impact. The vibrant colors give these images the inviting, magical feel of an oasis in the desert.

Watercolor provides that romantic, fantasy feel. Often the medium of choice for creating that warm, fuzzy feeling, watercolor uses no hard boundaries and presents an impressionistic, soft-focus look at the design. Ink Line Watercolors are a variation that includes hard lines, finely penned in.

Vermillion & Beserler, LLC artists can also create floor plans and site plans using state-of-the art technology. This allows them to produce digital images that are

Handcrafted Gouache Perspective Rendering

fully compatible with the graphic arts industry. This provides the highest resolution reproduction, whether it is used in a brochure, on a Web site or in a large display such as those found in model homes. This often makes the inevitable changes that builders require more manageable, without compromising the quality of the final presentation.

The expertise represented at Vermillion & Beserler, LLC includes interior design, so homes are sure to be represented in the most attractive settings and with the most striking appointments.

With this variety of techniques to offer, Vermillion & Beserler, LLC can help builders and architects choose the right medium, then create a professional presentation to fit any style and target audience. Renderings can be tailored for multiple uses throughout the sales life of a tract, from print and computer advertising to billboards and presentation visual aids. They also provide the pride of fine art for sales offices.

This combination of professionalism and art background means Vermillion & Beserler, LLC artists are prepared to do much more than just the artwork by crafting presentations that create advantages for builders.

- The fine art quality of the work invites consumers to stand and stare in the sales office the way they would at an art gallery. Renderings that succeed as art first draw viewers in, hold their interest and create the desire to share in the life inside the depicted home. They also keep the consumer's interest for those key extra moments that also mean they spend more time with sales representatives.
- The quality renderings instill in buyers a sense of confidence that the builder takes pride in every detail of a project. Consider the first impression one would get from a priceless work of art displayed in a

Classical art techniques like perspective help "bring viewers in" to Vermillion & Beserler, LLC renderings.

Computer renderings offer accuracy and flexibility not possible with manual techniques.

bargain basement frame. In the same way, quality renderings frame a product in consumers' minds before they ever see the genuine article. Renderings whet the buyer's appetite for the hands-on experience. Why should a builder or architect settle for less than the best when his or her reputation is at stake?

• The Vermillion & Beserler, LLC team brings design and marketing skills to each project. The appeal of any image is visceral and individual. Vermillion & Beserler, LLC employs perspective, composition, the psychology of color and tenets of advertising to create the inviting images that make buyers want to step in and stay a while.

• Presentations are packaged on CD-ROM or Zip disks, making it easier for the client to meet deadlines with images for printers, marketing agents or Web site developers. Packages can include slide and video presentations.

To expand the audience for any presentation, Vermillion & Beserler, LLC designs Web sites that entertain cyber visitors while giving them the information they want — fast. Sites can incorporate traditional and state-of-the art images to appeal to a variety of net shoppers.

Homes may be visible to passersby while they are under construction, but netizens will never see a Vermillion & Beserler, LLC Web site until it is complete. Modifications are tested and applied in a private environment and approved by the client before the public ever sees it. The company guarantees the Web site will be ready within 30 working days after the artwork is completed, and technicians will monitor each site to make sure it is functioning correctly. This prevents consumers from having a frustrating or negative first experience with a company.

An interactive Web site can generate excitement for a project well in advance, much the way Hollywood uses movie trailers to entice audiences into theaters. The techniques used to animate images and make them three-dimensional are adaptable to any product, so any firm that wants to show off all angles of its product can literally expand product exposure with a Vermillion & Beserler, LLC Web site. Presentations can include QuickTime virtual reality objects or movies or simple, computerized still images that avoid the inconsistency of scanned-in photos or artworks.

Savvy young consumers already shop for everything from automobiles to underwear by surfing the net. While they want interactive help, they won't waste time waiting for images to build or staring at information they can get from advertising messages. They want more: a real look at the product, a way to compare features and a look at the bottom line. And the remote control generation wants it the way they are used to getting things — instantly.

State-of-the-art equipment and education give Vermillion & Beserler, LLC artists an edge.

For homesellers, the benefits are countless. Relying on agents and model homes to sell a tract overlooks consumers who may not find it convenient to visit every tract that has beautiful homes, or who may want to shop while agents are sleeping.

Print and broadcast advertisements can show a general style and price range, but why would consumers settle for a few still images when they could visit a Web site that features a flythrough — a virtual magic carpet ride through the home or tract?

Open houses cast a wide net and often lure in shoppers who can't afford the homes they visit. With a Vermillion & Beserler, LLC Web site, busy people can shop at their leisure without pressure to disclose sensitive information. By the time this buyer drives to the tract, he or she knows whether the home is the right style, in the right area and in the right price range.

Animated renderings present a 360° view of the exterior and a walk-through of the interior.

For on-site presentations, an animated computer rendering at a sales office or model can capture shoppers' attention and give agents those extra precious minutes to seal a deal. Presentations can be packaged on CD-ROM for easy access and instant viewing.

The photographic accuracy of the renderings also creates a new opportunity to advertise projects well in advance of completion of the first real model home. Instead of using a logo or sketch to promote homes in print ads, Vermillion & Beserler, LLC computer renderings afford a true, three-dimensional view.

This full palette of approaches makes it possible for builders to reach multiple audiences with the media most appropriate for the target audience. Vermillion & Beserler, LLC can produce traditional materials for brochures and print ads, coupled with Internet and computer presentations to reach the maximum number of potential buyers.

Vermillion & Beserler, LLC has never missed a deadline. It manages and accepts only realistic deadlines to ensure that work is not only done right, but also done on time.

Vermillion & Beserler, LLC clients can expect to spend a little more for computer models than for two-dimensional renderings, but the accuracy with which the images can present their homes make them well worth the price. Combined with the classical techniques of focus and composition that bring an image to life and create desire in the viewer, these technological marvels sell more than just buildings. They sell lifestyles. More importantly, the demanding buyers of the next generation won't settle for less.

A finished rendering of above 3D model

FBA ENGINEERING

FBA Engineering has not only played a major role in the growth and development of Orange County — it has helped the region shine more brightly. Founded in Newport Beach in 1968, the consulting electrical engineering and lighting design firm has grown to be one of the largest and most respected in Southern California.

The hands-on engineering firm's exceptional designs and strict control of project budgets and schedules have won it a loyal following. Consummate professionals, FBA Engineering enjoys long-term working relationships with many satisfied clients; most new clients are the result of referrals. The firm's stellar reputation and impressive accomplishments are more than enough to recommend it for the most difficult electrical engineering tasks.

Architects, contractors, developers, government agencies, schools and universities rely upon FBA to provide cost-effective solutions for complex problems. Its original, high-quality designs have garnered worldwide attention and won numerous awards.

FBA's work on the Orange County Performing Arts Center received the National Electrical Contractor's Award for Electrical Excellence. In fact, the firm has won this award more than 30 times, for such diverse projects as the UCI Medical Center; the Richard Nixon Library and Birthplace; and the Oakley Technical Center. FBA has also been a winner, on numerous occasions, of Southern California Edison's Design for Excellence Awards Competition.

Many of FBA's landmark projects are also Orange County landmarks. The Ronald Reagan Federal Building and U.S. Courthouse, Irvine Civic Center and Police Facility, Irvine Meadows Amphitheater, Bower's Museum, Old Orange County Courthouse and the Santa Ana Law Library are some examples.

Ronald Reagan Courthouse and Federal Office Building, Santa Ana, California

(Front row left to right) Alan Bravo, Jeffrey Wolf, Darrel Peacock, Jim Proctor (Back row left to right) Steve Zajick, Bill Zavrsnick

From its earliest projects on, FBA has always been a leader in technological innovation. In its work for Orange Coast College's Environmental Center in the early 1970s, the firm became one of the first in California to use flexible plug-in wiring for lighting systems. The system is economical to produce and install, and it provides extra flexibility —lighting fixtures can be relocated by just unplugging and plugging in the cables.

FBA is proud of the work it has done for schools, colleges and universities. The firm has performed engineering services on projects in more than 40 of Southern California's school districts and on every college campus in Orange County. It engineered multimillion-dollar engineering laboratory buildings and the $14.5-million student recreation center at the University of California, Irvine, and has also completed projects for Golden West College, Cypress College, Saddleback College, Irvine Valley College, Fullerton College, Concordia University, Rancho Santiago College and many more. In any given month, FBA has staff working on more than 150 educational projects.

FBA established the design criteria for special outdoor lighting fixtures used by various school districts in the mid-70s. Designed to resist vandalism, the fixtures were later adopted by many cities for parks and other public places. The firm also designed audio/visual, data networking and telephone/intercom distribution systems, which allowed individual classrooms to originate programming for distribution to all other classrooms and students' residences throughout a school district.

The dedicated professionals at FBA have demonstrated the ability to design and engineer sophisticated systems required for the most complex applications. The Irvine Civic Center and Police Facility retained the firm to engineer the infrastructure for their state-of-the-art communication center that operates throughout the city and state. The web of systems includes 911 emergency services, computer traffic-control systems, California "ID," fingerprint identification system, and a traffic-control system with video cameras at intersections that monitor traffic flow and adjust signals to reduce congestion. An uninterruptable power system (UPS) with emergency generator backup supports all the critical equipment and devices in case of power failure.

The advent of centrally computerized SMART buildings has required increasingly sophisticated engineering to integrate disparate functions such as energy management and life safety systems. FBA has been called upon to handle these high-profile and challenging projects creatively and effectively.

Many office buildings designed by FBA represent some of the most effective SMART-building technology applications in Southern California. These building projects include a comprehensive Building Energy and Amenities Management computer program system to link advanced building automation, preventive maintenance and tenant billing systems. It accomplishes scheduled control of a multitude of lighting and air-conditioning points. The system efficiently provides tenant lighting, air conditioning and billing, on a suite-by-suite basis.

FBA has dealt with complexity in nearly all its forms. The Water Garden in Santa Monica, with over 1.5 million square feet of office space, required a parking structure of 45-acres below grade with a 2-acre lake located within the plaza area and over the parking structure; the Sunset Millennium, an office building, hotel, retail and restaurant project in design in 1999, comprises three entire city blocks on Sunset Boulevard in West Hollywood.

The firm's capacity to create the technological infrastructure necessary to achieve desired design effects is unsurpassed. For the Riverside County Courthouse restoration project, FBA was requested to design an indirect lighting system that would simulate natural sunlight coming through windows in the high-vaulted ceilings and rotunda. The firm was also involved in the design of custom lighting fixtures required to re-create the lighting ambience of 1903, while meeting today's standards by using modern, highly efficient components. FBA designed the lighting and electrical backbone system to complement the Mediterranean-village theme at the Promontory Point Apartment Complex in Newport Beach, an early project for the Irvine Company.

FBA's ability to meld technological and aesthetic elements was one reason it was selected to engineer a futuristic pedestrian bridge that joins both sides of the South Coast Plaza in Orange County.

Bridging FBA's past and future, the company has also proven adept at engineering its own evolution. A plan already in place provides for Vice President Darrel A. Peacock and senior associates William R. Zavrsnick, Stephen R. Zajicek, Jeffrey P. Wolf, James J. Proctor, Alan L. Bravo and others to acquire ownership in the firm.

The firm's entire staff celebrated its 30th anniversary in 1998 with a dinner cruise on the "Mojo," a resplendent yacht. At the occasion, the firm, originally founded by principals Frederick R. Brown, Melvin L. Harrier and Leslie K. McCrimmon as Frederick Brown Associates, was renamed FBA Engineering.

Since 1968 FBA Engineering has been using its amazing engineering acumen to help build Orange County. Now serving clients worldwide, the firm will continue to light the way to a brighter future for many years to come.

The Orange County Performing Arts Center, Costa Mesa, California

FBA Engineering Corporate Headquarters Office Building, Newport Beach, California

(Left to right) Leslie K. McCrimmon, Frederick R. Brown, Melvin L. Harrier

GLENN M. GELMAN & ASSOCIATES

Many times the pursuit of success has an ironic twist. Companies take care of their customers and grow. Growth becomes the ultimate reward at the expense of customer care, which in time erodes the success originally built by taking care of the customer.

Glenn M. Gelman & Associates is different. One of the largest CPA firms in Orange County and the only CPA firm named to *Inc.* magazine's 1989 list of the 500 fastest-growing privately held companies in America, the company has always been dedicated to providing its clients with old-fashioned, personal service.

Meticulous expertise in financial matters, superbly qualified personnel, an extensive range of professional services and an outstanding reputation are all essential elements in the firm's success, but its most prized attribute is an extraordinarily high level of genuine concern for the client.

The directors, managers and employees all empathize with the clients and manage accounts as though they were their own. It is this component of caring that truly distinguishes Glenn M. Gelman & Associates. It marks it as a service organization of the highest order and defines its commitment to quality.

The firm's founder, Glenn M. Gelman, had loved his chosen profession since his first accounting class in college. After graduating with honors from New York University, he went to work in New York City for one of the nation's largest CPA firms. Unfortunately, an eager Gelman watched his bright attitude quickly dim.

Glenn M. Gelman

A new and relatively inexperienced accountant, he found himself being assigned to tasks that at the time were beyond his capabilities. His training had been inadequate, and there was little, if any, concern for clients. Indeed, it was hard to find anything personal in a company comprising 35,000 employees. Gelman used to have to sign with his employee number, 0424, rather than his name. This accountant, with his prevailing sense of humanity, found himself trapped in a vast and impersonal corporate world.

Discouraged, Gelman resigned in 1981 and headed west. He came to Orange County and found employment with a much smaller firm. Freed at last from the robotic restraints of the massive organization, he relished working in the small CPA firm and excelled. In the two years he was there, Gelman's skills and dedication to spectacular service brought the small CPA company many new clients.

In 1983 Gelman established Glenn M. Gelman & Associates and opened his first office, a 100-square-foot executive suite, with a desk, a copy machine and one bookcase. His infant daughter used to sleep in her little bouncy seat on his desk while he worked.

Glenn M. Gelman dedicated himself to providing the old-fashioned service he knew clients wanted and deserved. Within the first few weeks the firm hired its first employee, Warren E. Hennagin, who, besides being an outstanding accountant, shared Glenn's attitude toward service. Warren is today one of the firm's directors.

Clients, impressed with the superb service, kept referring more clients. Sureties, banks and other financial institutions were also noticing the firm's excellent work. Although the new firm was small, its services were big on quality. Gelman had experience preparing financial statements at one of the world's largest accounting firms. He knew how to present banks and other institutions with the documentation they required in the format they desired. The phone wouldn't stop ringing.

Through the referrals of satisfied clients, Glenn M. Gelman & Associates began to carve out a niche as the CPA firm for the construction industry. Soon the firm's knowledge of software packages led it into consulting. It could set up the programs, maintain them, monitor them and support the client. Many clients for whom the company began as a consultant soon retained it as its CPA firm due to its high skill level and knowledge of the construction business.

The firm grew to nearly 25 employees completing $2 million in business in the first five years. A key employee, Larry M. Kane,

The entire staff at Glenn M. Gelman & Associates

joined Glenn M. Gelman & Associates in 1987. Larry Kane is now audit and accounting director. He has played an instrumental role in the firm's continued growth and success.

Concern for the client gave birth to innovation. Gelman & Associates offered many services that are usually only provided by much larger firms, and initiated services that even the larger ones didn't offer at the time. The firm's extensive experience and knowledge were the basis upon which services such as "loan packages" were built. Loan packages streamlined the process of applying for a loan or line of credit, making it less costly for the client. It made financial institutions happy by anticipating their questions and providing the right answers in the right format, reducing their analysis time.

Today, with more than 30 employees and a 10,000-square-foot office in its own building, Glenn M. Gelman & Associates provides accounting, auditing, tax services, computer consulting, management consulting, litigation support services, business operations evaluation and employment searches for the construction, manufacturing, distribution, health care, real estate and professional service industries throughout Southern California.

Three of the firm's directors hold master's degrees, have written articles for national publications, taught at the national and state levels and are frequent guest speakers for local business and civic organizations. *Construction Link* named Warren Hennagin "Best Accountant" in its first annual The Best of Southern California poll.

The firm lends vital support to its community, contributing to many worthwhile organizations. Warren Hennagin serves as president and chairman of several nonprofit agencies.

After serving as a volunteer cantor for an Irvine Synagogue, Glenn Gelman is now the official cantor of Temple Beth Shalom in Long Beach. Being a cantor brings this accomplished professional much joy. It fulfills a boyhood dream.

He has also realized his dream of providing clients with good old-fashioned CPA services. Glenn M. Gelman & Associates' main focus remains providing service that reflects the highest ethical standards and personal concern for the client's well being.

The laws affecting CPAs are changing. Safeguards are being eroded. Some see a potential loss of objectivity in what has always been regarded as the most trusted profession. CPAs will be allowed to accept commissions from referring agencies. Large financial-service companies, which are not CPA firms, are buying up CPA firms to gain access to their clients.

There have been a lot of changes at Glenn M. Gelman & Associates, too. Once a baby bounced on the single desk. Now the ambience in the office conveys world-class professionalism. But beneath these crisp executives' suits beat compassionate hearts.

Glenn M. Gelman knows what it feels like to be treated as a number — number 0424 to be exact. The masterful accomplishment of this organization is not just its resounding success, but that it has achieved the most sophisticated level of service while still caring for clients as though they were members of the family.

(Left to right) Larry M. Kane, Glenn M. Gelman, Warren E. Hennagin

LIA PHOTOGRAPHY

Photographer Lia Segerblom, camera in hand, wades back and forth in the Laguna Beach surf looking for the right angle from which to photograph a family perched atop a rock. She scrambles over the rocky cliffs of San Onofre in search of a rugged backdrop that will cradle an engaged couple. And in San Juan Capistrano, she plays make-believe with a child in a field of wild flowers until the child forgets the camera and focuses on the fantasy. For Lia, who specializes in creative portraiture, the setting and the light must be right and the emotion real to create art with her camera.

"When I'm looking through the lens, I'm creating a painting through the camera," says Lia.

Lia, as she is known professionally, has degrees in both fine art and photography and is the owner of Lia Photography in Dana Point. Her portfolio is full of paintings and photographs of a variety of subjects, including underwater scenes and equestrian events.

Yet the walls of her studio are covered with portraits — her passion. "I have a fascination with people and how they express themselves," she explains. "And when I'm able to show relationships — all that a person is, all that they are about — on film, that is very satisfying to me."

To Lia each portrait is as unique as the individuals in them. Some clients come to Lia knowing what they want; others ask for help. Often Lia brainstorms creative ideas with clients based on their lifestyles, interests and relationships.

As a fine artist, Lia also believes that presentation — the framing, the lighting and the placement of a work of art — is essential in completing a piece. She counsels clients to place a portrait where they will see it and enjoy it the most. Her studio includes a framing gallery for clients who want her to take their portrait from concept to completion.

Only after the discussion is over and the design elements are in place does Lia begin clicking away. She always includes a selection of traditional poses with people looking into the camera. Then she uses interactive poses — in which people are engaged with each other — to elicit storytelling images.

Some clients also request "photographic impressionism," a term Lia uses to describe her process of manipulating dyes on a Polaroid original so that the background looks like the work of an impressionistic painter.

"The final result is scanned into the computer and output on a canvas paper or watercolor paper," says Lia. "This gives people the opportunity to own fine art — and they're in it!"

But whether a client chooses photographic impressionism or a more traditional portrait, Lia's goal is the same: to create a unique work of art that evokes memories. These portraits become treasured family heirlooms.

"When I'm looking through the lens, I'm creating a painting through the camera," says Lia. "I know that every time people view their portraits, they are reminded of these people, places and special times. They relive the moment emotionally.

"That's why people love photography," she says. "And that's what I love about creating portraits for them. There is no greater gift to the heart than love. This is what is transferred from the artist to the viewer. And this gives me great satisfaction."

MESTRE GREVE ASSOCIATES

Noise is one of the unavoidable byproducts of the development and population of any area. Mestre Greve Associates is working to make not only the county, but also the world, a quieter place.

Because of an act of Congress in 1969, American communities began to pay more attention to noise levels. Shortly thereafter, demand for community standards led to the development of better methods for measuring and reducing noise.

Vince Mestre and Fred Greve met while studying civil and environmental engineering at the University of California, Irvine — one of the few colleges to offer the major at that time. While they studied air quality, water quality and noise pollution issues, they developed their interest in computer simulations of noise and air quality problems. Both earned master' s degrees.

Mestre formed Vince Mestre and Associates in 1978. The advent of compact personal computers helped the partners launch the company. The ability to maintain complex databases and to perform computer simulations on a personal computer allowed them to strike out on their own. The company incorporated as Mestre Greve Associates in 1981. The focus of the company was on engineering solutions to airport noise, community noise and air quality problems.

Mestre and Greve soon developed new techniques for measuring aircraft noise and calibrating effective models for noise projections. Some of their earliest noise studies were done for airports in Oklahoma. Once their work became known, public agencies and developers increasingly relied on Mestre Greve's expertise. The firm has since prepared airport noise studies as close to home as John Wayne Airport and as far away as New Zealand. The exciting takeoff that passengers experience when flying out of John Wayne Airport is a noise mitigation measure developed with the help of Mestre Greve. The concept of tailoring the departure procedures for airport noise mitigation was pioneered at John Wayne Airport. Mestre Greve also did the entire first round of noise and air quality studies in the planning process for the conversion of the El Toro Marine Corps Air Station to a commercial airport.

Mestre Greve experts were trailblazers in helping developers all over the world lay out sites and even entire communities with peace and quiet in mind. The firm now does more than 100 studies per year to determine the necessary sound walls and soundproofing for buildings to comply with state and local mandates. About 75 percent of the noise studies in Orange County carry the Mestre Greve stamp. But these noise consultants are also concerned with aesthetics. The relationship of structures, roads, open space and other facilities so influences the travel of noise that Mestre Greve's advice is most effective before a site is ever graded.

Mestre Greve Associates has prepared airport noise studies for John Wayne Airport and the El Toro Marine Corps Air Station, as well as other sites nationally and abroad. *Photo by Lawrence Crandall Photography*

When noise and air quality concerns are factored into the earliest stages of development, it can improve quality of life and prevent neighborhood disputes. Perhaps the most significant roadway projects in Orange County during the last 30 years have been the three toll roads. Mestre Greve Associates was involved in various aspects of the San Joaquin Hills, Eastern and Foothill Transportation Corridors. The involvement began with the earliest considerations of where the roads should be placed, through more detailed planning, environmental studies, final design and even measurement of noise and air quality once the toll roads began operating. Other major highway projects have included the confluence of Interstates 5 and 405; the addition of a High Occupancy Vehicle lane on the Costa Mesa (55) Freeway; and national Oklahoma State Highway 20. All of these studies were undertaken with the intent to minimize noise to the surrounding neighborhoods and to keep air quality levels within acceptable limits.

Mestre Greve Associates was involved in planning various aspects of Orange County's major transportation corridors, including the San Joaquin Hills Transportation Corridor.

Often the best examples of Mestre Greve's work are what people don't hear. Most homeowners are not even aware that Mestre Greve has made their neighborhoods quieter. But the firm did pre-development noise studies for planned communities produced by The Irvine Company, the Mission Viejo Company, and the communities of Rancho Santa Margarita and Portola Hills. Over 1,000 studies have been performed for developers including Shea Homes, Centex Homes, John Laing Homes, Presley Homes and Standard Pacific Homes to ensure that outdoor and indoor noise levels will meet city and state standards.

Though aircraft and roller coasters are obvious noise sources, Mestre Greve has been called upon to measure less obvious noise producers. In one study of noise generated by street performers, they discovered that crowd noise made mimes the noisiest of outdoor acts! Other facilities with outdoor entertainment — ranging from restaurants to amusement parks — also make sound waves in communities. Mestre Greve measured the noise levels at every concert held at Irvine Meadows Amphitheater in its first two years, helping to ensure compliance with community standards. Their expertise was also called upon during the planning process for the Anaheim Pond.

Mestre Greve Associates has helped set some of the noise standards that communities rely upon, creating noise elements for the General Plans of 40 California cities. As consultants, they have helped the Taiwanese government develop the noise standards applied by that nation's environmental protection agency. The company's consultants can help develop or revise noise level goals, standards and implementation programs for both public and private entities.

The measurement and computer simulation techniques developed for assessing airport noise and traffic noise are readily transferable to the assessment of air pollution for these sources. Mestre Greve Associates has also been a leader in evaluating airports and roadway projects for potential air quality impacts with advanced computer models. Air quality assessments have also been performed for residential and commercial developments, landfills, sports complexes, parking structures and industrial plants.

During the past 20 years, Mestre Greve's community commitment has extended to pro bono work done for numerous causes, some of which include Habitat For Humanity, the Discovery Science Center and a local AIDS hospice.

While Mestre Greve continues its trend of groundbreaking technical work, the company is also committed to growth and stability. New associates are steadily but carefully selected to join the firm to continuously increase personal service to clients. The company also plans to continue in its role as a pioneer in developing noise and air quality measurement techniques, computer simulations and mitigation strategies.

Fred Greve and Vince Mestre, founders of Mestre Greve Associates
Photo by Lia Photography

WAGNER PACIFIC

Now Known as WAGNER HALLADAY

The Wagner Pacific name has been known in the land development community, particularly developers in Orange County, as a reputable, professional name in civil engineering and land surveying. Founded in 1982 by President W. David Wagner, Wagner Pacific has seen substantial growth in Southern California and its principals feel fortunate to have been a part of it. Most often it is growing communities that create the need for civil engineering and surveying services. Long after their work is done, communities find they can continue to rely on the quality of the services upon which their homes, parks and workplaces are built. This has been the story of Wagner Pacific.

Wagner Pacific's prestigious corporate projects include the Kaiser Permanente Medical Centers in Fontana and Panorama City and the Home Savings of America headquarters in Irwindale (on the site of the former Irwindale Raceway grounds). The cities of Irvine, Mission Viejo, Orange and Santa Ana and the University of California, Irvine, have joined the ranks of public agencies and institutions in Orange and surrounding counties that have awarded projects to Wagner Pacific.

When Wagner opened the consulting civil engineering and surveying company, he brought with him many years of experience in the private sector and a successful career with the Los Angeles County Engineer's office, where he ran the Subdivision Section. Wagner struck out on his own with a desire to build a business on quality standards. With his wife Pat, the company's office administrator, Wagner has led the company to long-range growth and stability by assembling a staff brimming with talent and experience.

(Left to right) David Wagner, Dana Halladay, Robert Talafus and Robert Mim Mack *Photo by Lia Photography*

Engineers for Carmel, Aliso Viejo, the prestigious Gold Nugget Award-winning development

Executive Vice President Dana S. Halladay joined the company in 1982, bringing a new dimension in personal attention to the business. Halladay looks at every project with the aesthetics, as well as the functionality, of the end product in mind. He helps clients work through obstacles to projects whether they are technical or administrative. The extensive list of major public and private sector projects on which he has served as principal-in-charge includes numerous residential, health care and commercial projects.

Robert Mim Mack came on board in 1989 as vice president of surveying and mapping. Adding 10-plus years of field experience as a surveyor and construction inspector to his background in other aspects of engineering and mapping, Mim Mack took on responsibility for staffing, budgeting, preparing proposals, supervising field crews as well as interfacing with clients as principal-in-charge of all surveying projects.

Vice President Robert Talafus joined Wagner Pacific in 1987 as project manager and now, as a partner, serves as principal-in-charge on many projects. A veteran of the Orange County Environmental Management Agency, his civil engineering background emphasizes flood control facility, street and bridge design. Talafus' experience includes managing parks and recreation, hospital, commercial and industrial, residential and public works projects through planning, entitlements, design and construction administration.

The principals of Wagner Pacific are all family men who face the same needs and challenges as other families every day. Active family lives help the Wagner Pacific staff bring heart as well as professional skill to homes, schools, parks and offices.

The team brings out-of-the-box thinking to a rigid discipline to solve problems and generate the highest quality at the lowest cost to the client. In many cases, Wagner Pacific's eye for the bigger picture lets it utilize new approaches that save money not only on the project itself, but also on long-range operating costs.

On an Aliso Viejo hotel and golf course project undertaken

in the late 1990s, the team was able to save the developer $400,000 by evaluating a proposed sewer drainage system before it was installed. Wagner Pacific engineers proposed replacing the pump system with a gravity system that saved on up-front costs and long-term operating and maintenance costs.

The Wagner Pacific approach works because the company's employees treat clients as they like to be treated: reaching out to help solve problems and save clients time, money and hassles. They look not only to deliver quality in their own work, but also to spare clients from potential liability in many aspects of their projects.

Another creative example is Wagner Pacific's pioneering work to meet the challenge of land scarcity with "cluster homes." As land gets increasingly expensive in California and especially the Southland, families are looking for ways to feel at home in less space. This lot design allows full-size homes on small properties, so buyers may have a feeling of seclusion in an affordable environment.

Wagner Pacific is equally respected for its work on luxury home tracts such as Muirfield, overlooking the Dove Canyon Golf Course, for John Laing Homes. Other housing projects for Laing Homes have included the award-winning developments Carmel in Aliso Viejo, Santa Fe and Fiesta in Rancho Santa Margarita and Brittany in Foothill Ranch.

The company's services have become recognized as a standard for quality to homebuilders and developers like John Laing Homes, Ahmanson Development, Kaufman & Broad Homes, Inc., Robert P. Warmington homes and Sunrise Assisted Living, as well as companies including Kmart, Wells Fargo Bank, Mervyn's and Marriott Corporation.

Perhaps the crowning glory of Wagner Pacific's work is its ongoing involvement in the Kenneth Hahn State Recreation Area in Baldwin Hills. As the only civil engineer on the project since its inception in 1979, Wagner Pacific has guided development of 130 acres of the park — once an eroding oil field — through nine phases of construction. As the state acquires more land, the park will ultimately span 1,300 acres and be the largest urban park in the nation.

Howie Brashear, senior chairman, Wagner Pacific's first employee
Photo by Lia Photography

The family commitment that pervades Wagner Pacific also shows in its community service. Wagner Pacific donates in-kind services to local charities including Eli Home and Interval House, both shelters for domestic violence victims; Emmanuel House, a transitional living center for AIDS patients; and the Newport Aquatics Center expansion that will accommodate the Olympic Rowing Team.

Despite offers of purchase from public companies and merger offers from others, Wagner, Halladay and the other partners have opted to remain small and private to retain strict quality control and offer personal service. The company remains in the hands of its principals today.

As Wagner Pacific enters the new millennium, the four partners will focus on continuing to provide the same professional quality service that has earned them the respect of the development community. Their goals are simple: continue to grow, but not at the expense of the client, the company or its employees.

In keeping with its tradition of growth and progress, the company has another big change planned: from this time forward, it will be known as **Wagner Halladay**.

Brittany cluster development in Foothill Ranch

McCORMICK, KIDMAN & BEHRENS

Old-time feuds over water rights that eventually made orange growers wealthy overnight...gun battles over taking water to deprive down-river owners...a dispute over a vintage LaSalle. While it sounds like the stuff good movies are made of, it's the story of the start of McCormick, Kidman & Behrens, one of Orange County's most respected law firms.

Before World War II Merwin Wagner, an orange grower on the south side of the Santa Ana River, was aligned with the Santa Ana Valley Irrigation Company (SAVI). Clem McCullough, another grower north of the river, was the chief proponent behind the Anaheim Union Water Company. Both old-timers frequented a coffee shop where growers swapped stories. On the eve of World War II, when Wagner told his buddies about his plans to buy the last new LaSalle in town, McCullough was quick to buy the car first, aggravating the old-time feud between the north and south side interests on the Santa Ana River.

"This firm was formed out of a healthy respect for one another," say the partners.

Roger Howell, an Orange County water lawyer, also happened to be the Scout Master of a young boy named Russ Behrens, whose father was a country lawyer. Through his father's guidance, Russ graduated from law school.

In San Francisco, Mike McCormick began law practice after flying fighter jets in Korea. Mike's area of expertise was eminent domain, and he ultimately moved his practice to Orange County as a specialist in that area and as a member of Roger Howell's law firm; that firm represented landowners, including Merwin Wagner, and water districts on the south side of the Santa Ana River. A short time later, Roger Howell took on a young water lawyer understudy named Art Kidman. Art was raised in the Yakima Valley, Washington State, where water was also a precious commodity.

The LaSalle incident was never forgotten. Old passions of the fight between north and south of the river, influenced by the LaSalle incident, merged into later issues over who should pay for groundwater supplies and imported supplemental water. When Russ Behrens agreed to take on representation of the Municipal Water District of Orange County, headed up by Clem McCullough, he was pitted against none other than his old scout master, Roger Howell, and McCormick and Kidman at Rodger Howell's firm. Several years later, when Behrens' client wanted to build a pipeline from Yorba Linda to Mission Viejo, they decided to have Mike McCormick represent them to acquire the necessary right-of-way, and Behrens started working with McCormick and Kidman. An instant friendship was formed.

In 1988 McCormick and Kidman started their own firm, with many of the water districts historically represented by their former firm as their clients. They were joined in 1989 by Russ Behrens, who closed his own practice, bringing partners Suzanne Tague and Janet Morningstar along with him. Keith McCullough became a partner in 1996. Today the respected boutique law firm represents private parties and public agencies throughout the state in matters concerning business, corporations, succession and estate planning, real property litigation, condemnation/eminent domain proceedings, water rights, public utility services, facility construction, rate-setting, environmental regulation and compliance.

"This firm was formed out of a healthy respect for one another," say the partners, "and our mutual desire to provide high-quality legal services to the people of Orange County. As we expand, we are continuing to do the same thing for people in other areas." It does, indeed, sound like the stuff good movies are made of.

Russell G. Behrens, Arthur G. Kidman, H. L. Mike McCormick

PERLMAN ARCHITECTS, INC.

Howard Perlman's philosophy is simple: "Do whatever it takes to make our clients successful, and, in turn, this will make the firm successful." To achieve this philosophy, Perlman Architects prides itself in providing professionalism with a strong commitment to comprehensive service, cost control and effective on-time performance. Combined with innovative ideas and an overall understanding of the Orange County market, Perlman Architects assures the success of its clients' projects.

SINCE OPENING THE ORANGE COUNTY OFFICE, THEY HAVE BROUGHT A FRESH LOOK TO THE MARKET WITH NEW IDEAS IN DESIGN, COST EFFICIENCY AND AN INCREDIBLE UNDERSTANDING OF THE HOUSING MARKET FROM ENTRY LEVEL TO CUSTOM HOMES.

Howard Perlman began his architectural practice in 1977. Located in Phoenix, Arizona, it offered a full range of services in all aspects of housing. Now, celebrating nearly 25 years of experience, Perlman Architects' client base has grown to include all of the western United States as well as several Midwestern states, with both residential and commercial projects. Based in Las Vegas, Nevada, Perlman Architects has a new office in Irvine to meet the demands of Orange County's rapidly expanding industry.

Perlman Architects' Orange County office is led by the team of Michael Rupard, A.I.A., Douglas Ahlstrom, John Lazootin, A.I.A., Michael Ball, and Jim Naven, bringing many years of combined experience in the Orange County market to the table. With a full technical support staff, this team brings a higher level of design expertise and a core of highly specialized, synergistic, talented individuals licensed in several states, thereby enabling the firm to serve the sophisticated needs of its clients.

To keep up-to-date on the cutting edge of information that will better serve its clients' innovative design needs, Perlman Architects currently holds many affiliations in the building industry. Those affiliations include the National Association of Home Builders (NAHB) and Senior's Housing Council (SHC). Among the firm's notable clients are K. Hovnanian, the Bedford Group, Presley Homes, Olen, Western National and Triple Five. Local projects include Habitat for Humanity, Orangewood Children's Home and Four Seasons. Perlman Architects' designers also hold many national awards including the Gold Nugget, MAME, Homer, ELAN and the Best in Senior's Housing.

While the Southern California market is especially competitive in Orange County, Perlman Architects believes that the employees of the firm are its greatest asset. Since opening the Orange County office, they have brought a fresh look to the market with new ideas in design, cost efficiency and an incredible understanding of the housing market from entry level to custom homes. But above all, the firm is dedicated to providing the highest-quality service and superior design to develop marketable homes that will house the families of the new millennium.

(Left to right)
John Lazootin, Michael Rupard, Howard Perlman, Douglas Ahlstrom

THE ROXBURGH AGENCY, INC.

Creative professionals. Disciplined freethinkers. Those seeming opposites might best describe the uncommon marriage of artistic acumen and sound business sense that characterizes the creative vitality and focused clarity of The Roxburgh Agency.

Founded in 1980 by its president, Claudia Roxburgh, The Roxburgh Agency has grown to become one of the leading integrated communications companies in Southern California. The firm's ability to create results-oriented campaigns has earned it more than 150 major awards.

Playa Vista, California. Logo design, corporate identity, brochures, annual report

The Roxburgh Agency's awards result from ideas, strategies and solutions that rise to the top, but more important to this agency than winning awards is producing results that help its clients reach the top. The Roxburgh Agency packs the creative muscle to conceive fresh ideas that integrate advertising, marketing and public relations, which establish image, fortify reputation, support sales and reassure customers.

The Roxburgh Agency specializes in residential and commercial real estate marketing and is highly respected for its insight and understanding of the field. The firm's president and senior staff have extensive experience in this area. Beyond experience, the team shares a true affinity for the real estate industry. Roxburgh is proud to have played a part in building Orange County. Tens of thousands of Orange County's citizens live in homes marketed by The Roxburgh Agency. Though primarily involved with residential and commercial real estate, the firm now serves clients in a variety of fields, including architecture, land planning, finance, engineering, research, trade associations, automotive, manufacturing and interior design.

Brookfield Homes, Wyeth and Sarasota communities: logo design, ID package, brochure

Monierlifetile. Consumer ad, brochure, direct mail series. Mame winner: best marketing promotion

For the real estate and development industry, The Roxburgh Agency serves as a primary consultant. Roxburgh provides market consultation to help fashion an image and identity opportunities targeted at specific markets. The agency provides clients with ongoing market strategy, graphic identity, advertisements and public relations. Drawing on varied backgrounds, abundant talents, stable, long-term relationships and extensive marketing tools, the creative and account teams work together to maximize both cost efficiency and public impact.

Over the years, Roxburgh has developed strong relationships with the business trade, national, regional and local media. Among the firm's PR capabilities are strategic counseling, issues management and news and feature writing. Roxburgh also provides multimedia services including digital imaging, Web site design and maintenance, CD-ROMs and slide presentations.

The firm approaches its mission with the utmost integrity. It is committed to producing campaigns that improve a client's business and are beneficial to the community. Roxburgh further demonstrates its concern for the community in the pro bono work it has done for many worthy organizations, such as the Balboa Performing Arts Theatre Foundation, Home Aid and Project Playhouse.

The Roxburgh Agency possesses a positive attitude, exuberant spirit and creative passion, coupled with business awareness, cognizance of budgetary realities and market savvy.

Roxburgh is a multifaceted yet focused agency. It can create the freest and freshest campaigns, and manage their functionality. Creative professionals. Disciplined freethinkers — it makes sense.

Anaheim/Orange County Visitor & Convention Bureau

QUALITY OF LIFE

Educational, religious, arts, historical and service organizations, as well as health-related companies, all contribute to the quality of life enjoyed by Orange County residents and visitors.

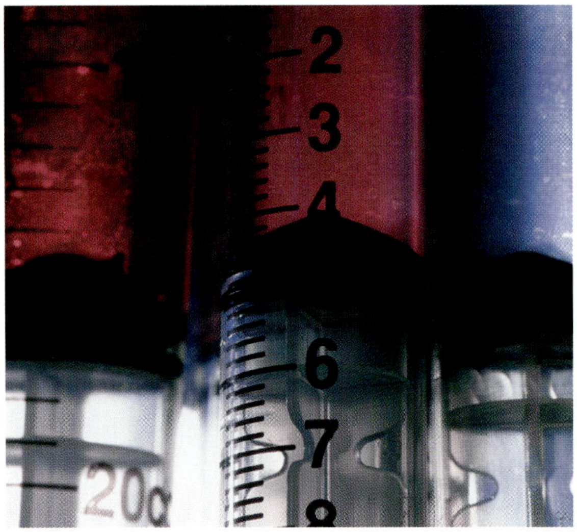

THE CRYSTAL CATHEDRAL

It was a love of the sky and a passion for pursuing the impossible that prompted Dr. Robert Schuller to build a church made almost entirely of glass. The pastor and founder of the world-famous Crystal Cathedral has dedicated his life to teaching life-success techniques based on the principle "if you believe it you can achieve it." And nowhere is that principle more dynamically illustrated than in the story of the building of the Crystal Cathedral.

The dream to build a sanctuary of light, space and grandeur was born in 1955, when Schuller and his wife Arvella arrived in Southern California with $500 to their name and a simple desire in their hearts: "To build a great church for God."

The church they would eventually build would defy convention and logic and come to symbolize the vision of a ministry which has become known for its many remarkable firsts — a ministry which has flourished under the leadership of a man known throughout the world as "the possibility preacher."

Robert Harold Schuller discovered his calling to preach at the age of four, and as a young Iowa farm boy, he got his early pulpit training by preaching to the cows in the woods behind his family's home. Schuller fulfilled his dream of entering the ministry in 1950, when he was ordained by the Reformed Church in America after receiving a bachelor's degree from Hope College and a master's of divinity from Western Theological Seminary, both in Holland, Michigan.

After ordination, Schuller pastored the Ivanhoe Reformed Church in Chicago for five years, but a bigger destiny was calling. An RCA committee, chaired by Mrs. Norman Vincent Peale, called on Schuller to take the church's message to the far west — a move that would lead Schuller and his young family to Garden Grove, California.

After arriving in Garden Grove, Schuller's first challenge was to find a meeting place for his new church. His initial list of possibilities included such unlikely venues as a mortuary chapel and a Masonic Temple. But it was possibility number 10 — the most outlandish on the list — that eventually became home to the Garden Grove Community Church. In an exercise of early "possibility-thinking," Schuller rented the Orange drive-in theater for $10 a month, and the world's first

The Crystal Cathedral
Photo by Ken Duncan

drive-in church was born. The young man who had once preached to cows would soon find himself preaching to cars.

With Arvella as organist, Schuller began conducting Sunday services from the tar-papered roof of the snack bar. To advertise, the Schullers distributed flyers that said "Come as you are in the family car." That first Sunday, a crowd of 100 showed up to hear the Dutch preacher from Iowa teach from the Gospel of Mark about the kind of faith that moves mountains.

There would be many more mountains to move as Schuller's ministry grew. The young pastor eventually found his niche preaching positive, guilt-free messages of inspiration and hope, messages that seemed intuitively in sync with the free-thinking California culture. Before long, the parking lot was overflowing, and in 1961, the ministry expanded to become the world's first walk-in, drive-in church. Their new building was designed by a visionary, modern architect named Richard Neutra. A sweeping glass, stone and wood-beamed structure, it allowed weekly Sunday services to be held both inside and out.

Over the years, the ministry celebrated many milestones. One of the most significant occurred in 1970 when it became the first and only one-hour, weekly, nationally televised church service. "The Hour of Power," as it was aptly called, is now an internationally televised program seen on seven continents that reaches a weekly worldwide audience of nearly 30 million people.

With a ministry of such far-reaching impact, it was only a matter of time before the walk-in, drive-in church outgrew its existing space. Operating on the principles of possibility-thinking he regularly espoused from the pulpit, Schuller hired renowned New York architect Philip Johnson to design a new building that would reflect the progressive vision of the ministry itself. Johnson's challenge, "To design the most beautiful church you can dream of," was complicated by one non-negotiable request by Schuller: the building was to be made entirely of glass.

Johnson met the challenge. His design, a stunning glass structure in the shape of a star, was absolutely breathtaking. The building he proposed featured more than 10,000 windows of silver-colored tempered glass held in place by a lace-like frame of white steel trusses, specifically fabricated for this phenomenal engineering feat. With an initial projected cost of nearly $7 million, the "Crystal Cathedral" seemed to be no more than an impossible dream. But to a man with Schuller's vision and tenacity, the price tag was just another mountain to be moved. Using the platform of his weekly "Hour of Power" television program, Schuller invited viewers across America to memorialize family, friends or loved ones by subscribing to personally inscribed windows for the structure. Each donation of $500 covered the cost of a window's installation. Response to his request was overwhelmingly positive, and letters — accompanied by donations — began pouring in, as many as 20,000 a week. The impossible dream was soon to become a reality.

On Sunday, September 14, 1980, the Crystal Cathedral opened its 90-foot doors for its first worship service. This architectural triumph stands 128 feet high, 207 feet wide, and 415 feet long, and has a sanctuary that seats nearly 3,000 people. On September 14, 1980, in an appropriate tribute, Schuller dedicated his dream building "To the greater glory of God."

The Crystal Cathedral, an Orange County landmark, welcomes thousands of visitors daily, including a congregation of more than 10,000 members. Its weekly services can be viewed on a giant indoor Sony Jumbotron television screen, or from a giant Nit-Star screen directly adjacent to the Cathedral, which displays each service for the many drive-in worshippers.

Congregation members and visitors alike enjoy weekly worship services that feature a diverse repertoire of musical selections resonating from the Cathedral's 16,000-pipe organ. The organ was made possible by a gift from the late Hazel Wright of Chicago and is world-renowned for its size and quality — it stands among the five largest church pipe organs in the world. And while its weekly worship services are impressive, the Crystal Cathedral enjoys even more pageantry and drama during the holiday season. Its annual pageants, "The Glory of Christmas" and "The Glory of Easter," are seasonal traditions for many who come to marvel and be inspired by the elaborate musical productions, replete with live flying angels. Engineered by Peter Foy, the mastermind who put Mary Martin to flight for the first time in the Broadway production of Peter Pan, the productions also feature a stable of live animals, including camels and horses.

In September of 1990 the Crystal Cathedral celebrated its 10th anniversary by dedicating a beautiful 236-foot spire and bell tower. One of Orange County's tallest structures, the tower is composed of expertly polished, mirrored stainless steel prisms that form a spectacular spire to catch light from all directions. Designed by Philip Johnson, this completion of the Crystal Cathedral houses a 52-bell carillon named in honor of Schuller's wife, Arvella, who has been the moving inspiration behind their music ministry.

The ministry which emanates from the Crystal Cathedral continues to grow and evolve. Its expansion plans include the addition of an International Hospitality and Visitor's Center, the first of its kind designed by world-famous architect Richard Meier. The center will contain exhibits, shops, a theater and a food court, and it will offer virtual reality experiences designed to teach positive-thinking techniques. It will be an exciting addition to an already impressive symbol of what the power of possibility-thinking can accomplish. For Schuller, it is yet another ministry tool to help people reach their full, God-given potential.

"I think religion in the next century is breaking loose," explains Schuller. "I know together we can create a community of people of faith who will get off their collision course into a coalition — working together to turn human beings into beautiful people."

ORANGE COUNTY BUSINESS COUNCIL

For more than 100 years, the Orange County Business Council and its predecessor organizations have promoted economic development countywide and served as the voice of business in America's fifth largest county. The Business Council is primed to lead Orange County business interests into even greater economic prosperity in the new century.

"Business cycles change over time," says Stan Oftelie, president and chief executive officer of the OCBC. "But there are two Orange County constants we can count on, year-in and year-out: Orange County needs a great business climate to thrive economically, and we need to safeguard our unparalleled quality of life to prosper as a community."

The Orange County Business Council's commitment to the economic development of Orange County can be traced to 1888, when the Orange County Board of Trade was organized to help promote the separation of Orange County from Los Angeles County. In 1893, the same year that a former Erie County Sheriff named Grover Cleveland was elected president of the United States, the county Board of Trade was reorganized into the pro-business Orange County Chamber of Commerce.

The county chamber evolved over the years into the Orange County Chamber of Commerce & Industry, which in 1995 merged with the influential Industrial League of Orange County and other business groups to form the Orange County Business Council, the county's most potent business organization.

Drawing on its pro-business reputation and long tradition of public involvement in civic affairs, the newly named Business

Council immediately involved itself in helping dig the county government out of the largest municipal bankruptcy in U.S. history.

The Business Council — led by George Argyros, Chairman and CEO of Arnel and Affiliates, Gary Hunt, executive vice president of the Irvine Company, and Thomas Sutton, CEO of

FOR BUSINESS DEVELOPMENT, THE OCBC IS THE BUSINESS POINT-OF-CONTACT FOR ECONOMIC DEVELOPMENT AND RELATED BUSINESS INFORMATION IN ORANGE COUNTY. THE ORGANIZATION IS ALSO IMPLEMENTING A MARKETING AND IMAGE PROGRAM TO PROMOTE ORANGE COUNTY AS A LEADING ECONOMIC REGION FOR THE INDUSTRIES OF THE 21ST CENTURY.

Pacific Mutual — brought together elected officials, lawyers, accountants, and representatives of more than 200 angry government agencies that were arguing over ways to move county government out of bankruptcy.

The Business Council convened top government leaders and created a constructive environment where a solution to the county government's bankruptcy could be developed. Today, county government's headline-grabbing bankruptcy is simply a bad memory, overwhelmed by the extraordinary growth of the county's powerhouse economy.

The Orange County Business Council, like its predecessor organizations and current partners in economic development, believes that an excellent business climate doesn't happen by accident. The county's business assets need to be nurtured and cultivated. To create an economic development strategy to nurture business in the future, the Business Council launched a detailed strategic planning process in late 1998 to sharpen efforts to improve Orange County's robust economy.

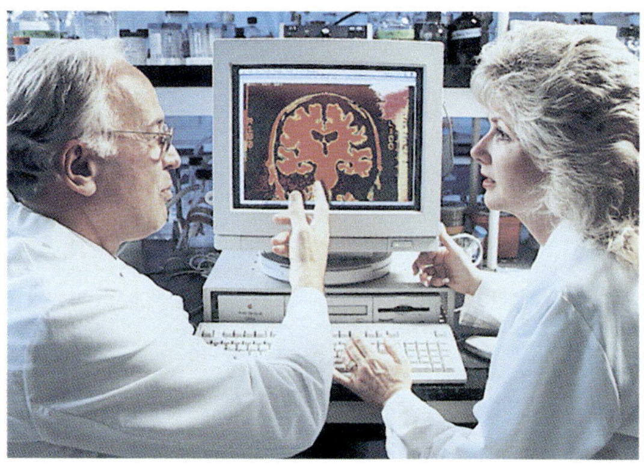

After reviewing the work of five special committees, more than 300 one-on-one interviews, dozens of workshops, more than 8,000 surveys, and detailed analytical work done pro bono by McKinsey & Company, the Business Council's board of directors zeroed in on three major strategic initiatives; business development, a pro-business legislative agenda, and workforce preparation.

For business development, the OCBC is the business point-of-contact for economic development and related business information in Orange County. The organization is also implementing a marketing and image program to highlight Orange County as a region with stable growth, a diverse economic base, strategic location and a high quality of life.

To boost workforce development, the OCBC is partnering with others to guarantee that the area has a high-quality, well-prepared workforce. It initiates and facilitates public policy and community-based partnerships between business leaders and educators to make sure that education/training programs meet the needs of area employers and will continue to do so in the future. OCBC helped bring down the cost of workers' compensation premiums and is dedicated to lowering taxes and making the area more business friendly. OCBC is also the united voice of Orange County business at local, regional, state and national legislative levels.

One major plus the OCBC has to offer businesses that are considering potential locations is the high quality of life offered here. Orange County was named by *Places Rated Almanac* as the No. 1 place to live, work and raise a family in North America in its latest edition. The Council does not want to jeopardize that high quality of life just to bring in jobs. "We are careful about the types of companies we are trying to attract due to the work environment we have to offer," explains Bill Carney, vice president of business development for OCBC. "We need to protect our quality of life while helping shape our economy."

The Council is partnering with government for good, long-term planning for the region, including upgrading the county's existing infrastructure. For example, recent studies conducted by the Orange County Business Council, several universities, the county of Orange and the Enterprise Foundation indicate that Orange County is on the verge of suffering a severe shortfall in the supply of quality housing for working families in the region. These studies have concluded that the cost of housing for employees is the number one barrier to business growth. In response to this potential economic growth barrier, the Orange County Business Council has entered into a partnership with Fannie Mae, the Building Industry Association of Southern California, Merrill Lynch and The Enterprise Foundation to launch the Orange County Affordable HomeOwnership Alliance (OCAHOA). OCAHOA is a collaborative effort dedicated to increasing the availability and affordability of quality housing for working families through proactive business-oriented solutions. The partnership with OCAHOA has been established to provide a framework around which the business community can take a leadership position in creating a comprehensive approach to housing issues that affect business interests in the area.

Another exciting new program for the OCBC is its Technology Small Business Development Center called Venture Point. This program, funded through a state grant with private matching funds, will act as an "incubator" and provide resources to help small entrepreneurs succeed.

With an illustrious history, focused strategic direction, strong input from Orange County's business leaders and other community partners, OCBC will lead the county as "The Voice of Business in Orange County for the 21st Century."

ORANGE COUNTY'S UNITED WAY

75 Years of Caring

No one is immune from a life-changing event. The loss of a job. A serious car accident. The birth of a child with special needs. When you or someone you know needs assistance, United Way is always there. It's a pretty safe bet that you, or someone you know, has benefited from services provided by one of the dozens of nonprofit organizations here in Orange County funded by United Way donations.

Living in Southern California, we know that disaster can strike at any time. Sandy Bush offers living proof. "We were living in Laguna when a flash flood hit. A river swept me away for two blocks. We lost everything. Help was there immediately, providing us with shelter, food and clothing. A United Way-supported agency saved our lives and our sanity."

History

Since the first Community Chest was established in Santa Ana in 1924, Orange County's United Way has been a catalyst for improving the quality of life for people in our community by focusing local fund-raising efforts to support health and human services for residents of virtually every walk of life.

Over the past 75 years the growth of United Way in Orange County has echoed the general pattern of change in this fast-growing community. What were once relatively isolated and independent small communities have become highly

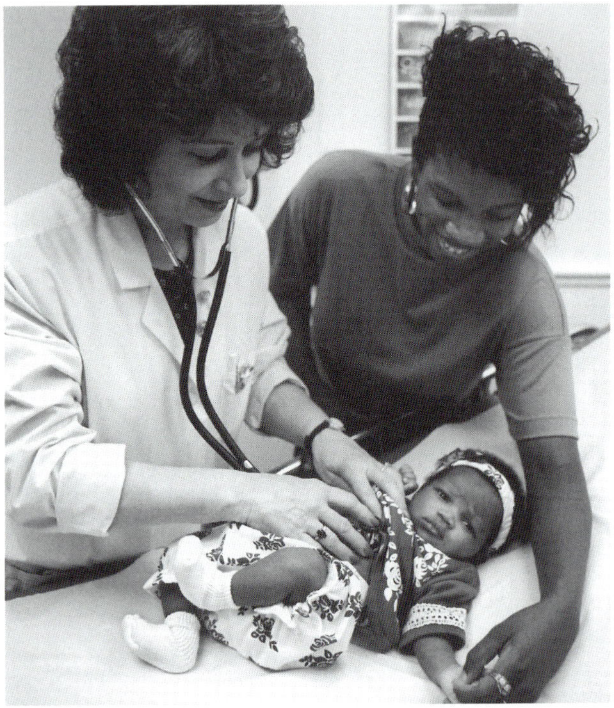

interdependent, metropolitan and suburban areas whose strongest identity often lies with the county. By the mid-1960s local Orange County United Funds and Community Chests began to respond to the changing growth patterns of the county by merging their operations.

In 1971 five funds merged to form Southern Orange County United Way. Three years later, seven funds combined to become North Orange County United Way. In 1975 those two offices joined forces to become United Way of Orange County North/South. In 1984 the North/South offices merged to form one United Way with three regional offices. Those operations were all consolidated into the local organization headquarters in Irvine in 1998.

Today's United Way

Today, Orange County's United Way is the largest non-governmental funder of health and human services in Orange County. It is affiliated with more than 100 local agencies that effectively address critical issues such as developing children and youth, promoting health, building stronger families and increasing independence. These charities have included local affiliates of well-known organizations like the American Cancer Society, Boy Scouts, Girl Scouts, Goodwill Industries, the American Red Cross and many more. In addition, local community organizations, including Acacia Adult Day Services, Community Day Nursery, Interval House and Lestonnac Free Clinic have received funding from United Way. By raising and distributing funds to these organizations, United Way has helped more than one million Orange County residents annually. And by working with such a diverse group of organizations, United Way makes it possible for donors' dollars to have a widespread impact in the community. For example, in 1998, a gift of $1,000 could fund 100 vision and hearing screenings for children and a hot meal for 95 homeless individuals and one week of well-balanced lunches for 35 low-income seniors.

Ralph Eure felt the impact in a very personal way. "I moved to California for a new life. Once I got here, the job I was promised fell through and I ended up on the streets. Luckily I found help. I was given food and shelter until I found a job. Now I'm healthy and productive, thanks to United Way."

The Impact of United Way

Orange County's United Way creates local results you can see. For a third of the county's population, this means directly benefiting from the programs and services funded by United Way. In 1998, for example, funding provided by Orange County's United Way gave 100,000 kids a safe place to go to get them off the streets; provided 42,400 nights of shelter to moms, dads and kids when they had none; helped 23,300 victims of domestic violence begin new lives; and provided affordable childcare for 9,000 kids.

Approximately 1,200 Orange County businesses participate in United Way workplace campaigns to raise money for the community. By sponsoring employee giving campaigns and making corporate gifts, these companies contribute 95 percent of all gifts to United Way. Individual community donors not involved in company campaigns also make substantial donations to United Way throughout the year. In fact, in 1999, United Way received its first two $1 million donations from two local entrepreneurs and their families. The remainder of donations comes from a growing variety of innovative programs.

During the past 10 years, Orange County's United Way has raised over $195 million to fund services and programs in the community. The 1998/99 fundraising campaign marked a new record of $21.5 million, representing a 10 percent increase over the previous year's total of $19.5 million.

While United Way is already one of Orange County's most efficient charitable organizations, the organization is committed to maximizing productivity by improving operational effectiveness and using the talents of over 200 volunteers — area professionals who serve on United Way's board of directors, committees, campaign cabinet and regional councils.

Addressing the Needs of Orange County

In 1999, United Way led Orange County in defining, reporting and impacting critical human needs for Orange County residents. A computer mapping system for Orange County has been developed to identify the unmet human needs within Orange County's various geographic and demographic areas. An unprecedented collaboration has been formed between Orange County's United Way, business, government agencies, funding entities, area universities and charitable organizations to develop the most effective health and human service delivery system possible to meet those identified needs.

Based on statistical information in the collaborative's initial report in May 1999, four areas were identified as critical health and human issues in Orange County. As a result, Orange County's United Way will direct applicable donor dollars to fund programs and services that address four "Targeted Community Investment" areas, which are:

- **Developing Children and Youth** — helps promote child development, after-school programs and mentoring programs through the teen years.
- **Building Stronger Families** — supports programs to prevent child abuse, provide transitional assistance for families in crisis and provide security for seniors.
- **Promoting Health** — helps improve health care access, link people to needed services and prevent illness through public education.
- **Increasing Independence** — helps the working poor, the transitionally homeless and people with disabilities to develop skills to prevent future crisis situations and live independently.

Tom Rogers, senior vice president and treasurer of the Irvine Company, and chairman of the United Way board of directors, sums it up best: "The need in our community is great, and the responsibility is ultimately ours as citizens of this community. A small investment can make a significant impact on the lives of Orange County residents."

PLANNED PARENTHOOD

Three Decades of Medical Care, Education and Advocacy

A group of Orange County citizens interested in bringing family planning services to those in need organized the Family Planning Council in 1965. One year later the council joined the Planned Parenthood Federation of America to become Planned Parenthood of Orange and San Bernardino counties. The organization now operates seven medical centers throughout the area, providing confidential, quality, and compassionate general reproductive health care, education and advocacy.

Planned Parenthood, a nonprofit organization, has been providing general medical and reproductive services nationwide for more than 80 years. Started by Margaret Sanger, a maternity nurse, the organization prides itself on helping people make informed, responsible decisions. Sanger, one of 11 children, saw her mother die young from tuberculosis caused by pregnancy-related hardships. As a result of this traumatic experience, she believed deeply in the right of every woman to choose when and whether to have children. She went to Europe to study advancements in women's health and contraception. Upon returning, she founded Planned Parenthood to help women and their families make informed decisions regarding reproductive health.

An early Planned Parenthood clinic
Planned Parenthood — World Population

Margaret Sanger, Planned Parenthood founder

While many were preaching the virtues of love and peace, Planned Parenthood was practicing them by opening its first medical center in Orange County. The Santa Ana center opened its doors in 1968, bringing quality reproductive health examinations and information on anatomy and birth control to women and men of all economic levels. By 1977 Planned Parenthood had opened a second center and hired an education coordinator. Ten years later, the organization had four medical centers in the county and was providing more than 20,000 women and men with quality medical services.

Similar to the franchise model of business, Planned Parenthood operates with a "think globally, act locally" philosophy. According to the organization's president/CEO, Planned Parenthood has a national protocol but allows affiliates certain freedoms in order to meet local needs.

One of those local needs was met by the formation of Education 2000 and its related services in 1990. Education 2000, a fund-raising support group of the Health Education Department of Planned Parenthood, aims to significantly reduce teen pregnancy in Orange County and the surrounding areas. The program trains high school students to provide accurate information to their peers at school and in the community. Special teen clinics are offered at each of Planned Parenthood's medical centers. The clinics offer walk-in hours for teens only. Medical personnel are on hand to provide a wide range of services to adolescents who may have no other way to obtain quality, confidential and low-cost care. Planned Parenthood's *Teens Ask Teens* hotline is staffed by teens who answer nonmedical questions, and provide factual information and connections so their peers can get the services they require. The overall goal of the Health Education Department is to teach teenagers the decision-making skills necessary to protect themselves and their communities.

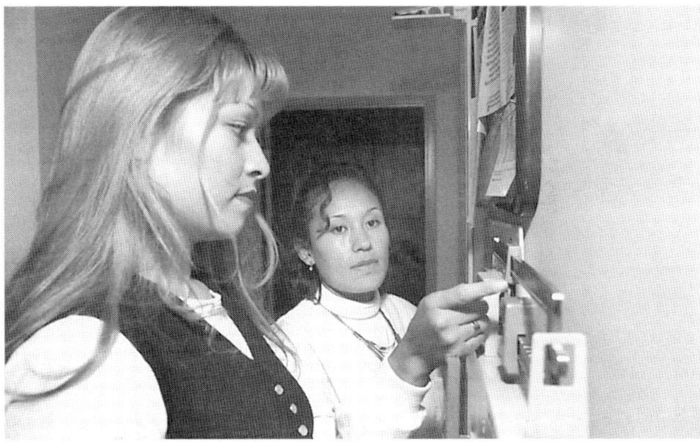

Orange County's Planned Parenthood medical centers provide prenatal healthcare to more than 4,000 women every year. These services include regular check-ups throughout pregnancy, educational classes, nutritional counseling and other medical services that may be required. The theory behind the program is that a healthy pregnancy leads to a healthy baby. In addition to enhancing the community, the prenatal program saves money. For every one dollar spent on prenatal services, the community saves three dollars in medical costs after the baby is born.

Women, infants and children (WIC) services are provided to women and their children who are determined to be nutritionally at risk. More than 22,000 clients have participated in the program since 1995, when Planned Parenthood began providing the service. WIC provides healthcare referrals, supplemental food and nutritional information, as well as nutritionally balanced menus and recipes. More than 75 percent of the services are provided to infants and children. A life that begins healthy has a better chance to remain healthy, and Planned Parenthood believes that this benefits the entire community.

In addition to operating its own programs, Planned Parenthood also provides family planning services to patients of local hospitals including Western Medical Center, Fountain Valley Medical Center and other regional hospitals. This allows the hospitals to save money while allowing patients to receive quality health care.

Essential community services, including low-cost and confidential HIV/AIDS testing and counseling, are provided by Planned Parenthood. Breast examinations and Pap tests are also available as part of its cancer screening program. Detection and treatment of cervical cancer and related disorders are provided at all seven Orange County area medical centers. Sometimes people prefer not to go to the family doctor for certain tests and procedures. The confidential and caring service is why many people choose Planned Parenthood clinics.

What the organization is best known for, however, is family planning. Whether the services are provided by Planned Parenthood at one of its medical centers or at another hospital, all forms of family planning services can be obtained from the organization.

Planned Parenthood provides all federally approved birth control methods, including emergency contraception. Although approximately 95 percent of patients are women, men can also receive birth control information, supplies and services at any of the medical centers. In fact, more than 65 percent of the patients visiting Planned Parenthood come for birth control-related services. That's more than 30,000 visitors in 1997 alone. Valuecare, a program for working women, provides affordable birth control packages that help a growing number of women determine and direct their own destiny. Sterilization counseling and referrals are available for men and women. For the woman that chooses to have a baby, excellent prenatal care, pregnancy options and adoption referrals are available from Planned Parenthood.

For more than three decades of service in Orange County, Planned Parenthood has provided quality, affordable medical care, education and advocacy to thousands of people. Planned Parenthood of Orange and San Bernardino counties: Responsible Voices for Responsible Choices.

Providing quality reproductive health care, education and advocacy

Planned Parenthood has served the local community for more than 30 years.

UNIVERSITY OF CALIFORNIA, IRVINE

Through a powerful blend of research, educational innovation, first-rate students and faculty and community service, the University of California, Irvine has become one of the nation's leading research universities. UCI's ascension into the ranks of the top universities is all the more impressive given that it is now in only its fourth decade.

The university is recognized for its academic excellence in diverse academic subjects, including the physical and biological sciences, medicine, information technology, the social sciences and the arts and humanities. In an achievement that brought the campus international attention, UCI in 1995 became the first public university with faculty awarded Nobel Prizes in two different fields — chemistry and physics — in the same year.

The university and its individual schools, departments and programs are consistently ranked among the nation's finest. For example, the prestigious ranking of graduate programs published by the National Research Council ranks UCI 11th among U.S. public universities and 27th overall. In other national rankings, UCI scores consistently in the top 50 for its quality programs.

In 1996 UCI was elected to the prestigious Association of American Universities — yet another indicator of UCI's status among the nation's foremost research institutions.

A key factor in this steady rise has been UCI's strong connection to the community. The university has developed along with Orange County, forging dynamic partnerships that form the cornerstone of the region's economic and cultural vitality. The campus opened in 1965 with key support from county leadership as well as The Irvine Company, which donated 1,000 acres on which to build the ninth campus in the prestigious University of California system.

The School of the Arts' acclaimed "ArtsBridge" program is helping to restore comprehensive arts education to Orange County's public schools.

Today UCI has approximately 18,000 students and is the county's third-largest employer. Among the faculty are many of the nation's elite researchers and educators. Each year, greater numbers of the highest-achieving high school students are attracted by UCI's academic quality, enriched by the campus' intellectual and cultural diversity.

Graduates of UCI number about 60,000, half of whom have remained in the area to contribute to a sophisticated workforce of entrepreneurs, managers and employees critical to the area's progress. In addition, UCI has an annual economic impact of more than $1 billion on the local economy.

UCI approaches the discovery and dissemination of knowledge and the solving of today's pressing issues through collaborations that cross disciplines and reach out to local, national and international partners. Among these areas of collaboration are information technology, energy and the environment, the health sciences, arts and humanities and educational outreach to the community.

In an innovative blend of art and technology, for instance, the Donald R. and Joan F. Beall Center for Art and Technology at the UCI School of the Arts — made possible with support from Rockwell International — will enable computer science and arts students to create digital arts projects, sharing their results online and in exhibits open to the public.

With intentionally small classes and an emphasis on teamwork, the Graduate School of Management has been recognized by the National Science Foundation as a leader in information technology. The management school prepares individuals to adapt in a global and changing marketplace through programs for part-time and fully employed students.

In a major partnership forged to advance medical research, the National Cancer Institute has established one of eight Cancer Genetics Research Centers at UCI's College of Medicine. The center at UCI is the only one in California. Faculty in epidemiology also manage a comprehensive cancer genetics database that forms the information hub of the network. As a cancer research and informatics center, UCI is a force in designing new strategies to attack cancer at the genetic level.

Alliances are crucial, as well, to addressing the world's environmental and energy issues. UCI faculty have long been involved in combustion research, transportation studies and identifying the causes of pollution. Their expertise helped bring about the establishment of the National Fuel Cell Research Center in UCI's School of Engineering, where government, private business and UCI researchers collaborate on developing clean, efficient power generation for the future.

The ability to think critically and creatively, and to work with others toward an objective, is much in demand in today's workplace, or any area of human endeavor. Providing the base for

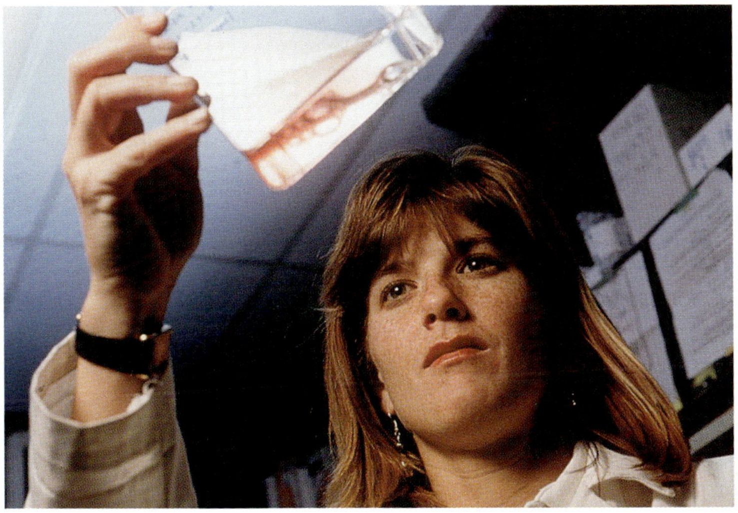

UCI's scientists and their pursuit of knowledge and discoveries have helped establish the university as one of the nation's top research institutions.

a comprehensive education are the humanities, the arts and social sciences at UCI. The Humanities Core Course, for example, is taught by a team of faculty from a wide range of disciplines who guide students through a rigorous immersion in reading, writing and analysis of issues affecting society.

In the schools of social sciences and social ecology, students and faculty explore diverse realms of understanding, from three-dimensional computer environments in the Center for Virtual Reality to working with law enforcement in computer tracking of gang violence.

A strong university relies on a strong educational foundation throughout the K-12 experience. Through the Center for Educational Partnerships, UCI prepares children for the challenges and opportunities that await them in college.

UCI faculty and students go out to schools and bring school children to the campus in more than 50 math, science, reading and other projects. One of these projects — Digital ArtsBridge — introduces children to the possibilities of combining their natural artistic talent with computer technology.

Education, ideas and a sophisticated workforce are elements fueling the economic engine known as Southern California's Technology Coast, which has become a mecca for high-tech and international business. The core of any such enterprise is the strong connection between university and community that nurtures growth and quality of life.

The UC tradition of learning for a lifetime is such a connection. UCI Extension offers more than 1,800 courses and 40 certificate programs at the Irvine campus and the UCI Learning Center in Orange. Whether it's a career change or maintaining a competitive edge in international business, UCI Extension responds to the needs of individuals and businesses for community-based education.

Bringing academic and corporate minds together creates many new opportunities. With an extensive database of faculty and available technology, the UCI Office of Technology Alliances works with corporate partners to encourage technology transfer, licensing and other avenues to productive affiliations. UCI also maintains close ties to the business community through a network of support groups, including the UCI Foundation and Chief Executive Roundtable.

Looking toward the future, another focal point for university-industry partnerships is the west campus, where University Research Park is being developed on 185 acres next to the UCI College of Medicine. The project is designed to attract companies, such as current tenants Canon and America Online, that will work closely with the university's faculty and students on research, internships and technology transfer.

Also on the west campus, the university is building on its strengths in biomedicine with a world-class research complex — the UCI Biomedical Research Center. The center will concentrate on neuroscience, genetics, cancer, infectious diseases and aging, increasing the possibility of finding new solutions to the health problems that plague millions of families. Work there will complement the clinical research and full range of quality patient services at the UCI Medical Center site in Orange, which includes the UCI Neuropsychiatric Center and the Chao Family Comprehensive Cancer Center — the county's only center awarded the National Cancer Institute's prestigious comprehensive designation.

The campus is preparing to meet projected enrollment of 30,000 students by the year 2015. A new student recreation center, a music building and arts complex renovation, and a new earth system science building are among the projects planned,under way or recently completed.

In these and many other ways, UCI is building strong minds that are building a strong future for Orange County.

A commitment to compassion and the use of new medical technology are at the core of patient care at UCI Medical Center.

YMCA OF ORANGE COUNTY

The Young Men's Christian Association (YMCA) was founded in London in 1844 in response to the unhealthy social conditions in large cities at the end of the Industrial Revolution. The organization's lofty goal of improving the spiritual, mental, social and physical conditions of young men proved popular in big cities everywhere as did the fact that the YMCA crossed all race, religion and nationality lines. So it wasn't long before a worldwide movement began, with groups sprouting up around the world. In 1854 the first international convention was held in Paris. In 1851 the movement reached local shores when Thomas Sullivan, a retired sea captain and lay missionary in Boston, began the first branch in the United States.

The genesis of the Orange County YMCA was in the 1880s when a group of Santa Ana community leaders met for Bible study and began searching for ways to better their community. Those men were so successful that in the early 1900s the Santa Ana YMCA grew from being the smallest branch in California to serving 1,100 boys and girls in 1912.

YMCAs (colloquially known as the Y) quickly spread throughout Orange County. In 1909 the Garden Grove building was completed, and a year later Fullerton had its own site. In 1912 the formation of the Triangle League, a group activity for young people, helped spur growth in Orange County. To sign up as part of the league, young people pledged to do their best to build "...a strong body, a clear mind, and an upright moral character..." Members also promised to abstain from alcohol or tobacco before age 18 and discourage the use of profanity among schoolmates. Values such as personal responsibility and trying to better the community were ideas taught at the YMCA from its inception.

By 1919 the organization was in full swing, expanding services to include swimming and counseling. And by 1965 Santa Ana had more than 800 active adult members and 1,300 children involved in youth groups. The Orange County branches have been steadily growing ever since, serving the entire county with programs for family, young people and adults that further the YMCA's goal of growing strong kids, strong families and strong communities.

Over the years many groups originally launched under the umbrella of the YMCA eventually became independent organizations as well. Toastmasters, for example, was founded in 1924 by Ralph C. Smedley. The club was originally part of the Santa Ana YMCA, and it was so successful that it became an international association in the 1930s. Boy Scouts and Campfire Girls were fostered by the YMCA as well.

The YMCA was also one of the six original agencies that together formed the USO centers, clubs devoted to providing wartime support to the military. During Word War II, YMCA facilities in Orange County were recruited for this purpose, broadening the concept of community to include soldiers from throughout the United States. It was also about this time that women and girls became part of the official organizational structure.

Today there are eight branches of the YMCA within Orange County that offer a variety of services and programs aimed at furthering the goal of building strong kids, strong families and strong communities. A popular activity that serves to strengthen families is the Y-Indian groups. This parent-child program encourages parents to spend time with their children camping, fishing and hiking or engaged in arts and crafts projects. The emphasis is on quality time spent as a family.

The concept of an Indian program was developed because according to YMCA literature, "The past and present culture of American Indians challenges parents in two ways: to be aware of their roles as parent, guide, friend, and example for their children; and to develop

(Far right) El Centro Club members playing chess, Willard Intermediate School, Santa Ana, CA

(Right and opposite page) YMCA Day Campers

young boys' and girls' natural curiosity and enthusiasm for life." Nearly 7,000 families participate in the Indian Guides, Princesses, Braves, Maidens and Trailblazers to build lifelong values and strengthen the bond between parent and child.

The YMCA of Orange County is also the largest provider of after-school childcare and offers a safe, structured place where children become involved in activities and learn the value of good citizenship. House rules emphasize that children are responsible for their own actions, and character development is an important part of the program. The YMCA also runs one of the largest camping programs in the county through which children and teens learn new skills, meet new friends and most of all enjoy nature and each other.

Though children are the main beneficiaries of the YMCA's efforts, there are many programs for adults as well. A variety of classes, including extensive fitness activities, are offered at many branches. And, of course, swimming is always popular with all ages, including senior citizens. Families can also take advantage of counseling services offered at the YMCA. Other programs offered at various branches include tutoring, mentoring and programs addressing drugs and alcohol problems, abused children and gang prevention.

There are also special programs for the developmentally disabled. The New Horizons program, founded in 1974, offers year-round excursions of one to five days that teach the disabled important life skills and appropriate social interactions. Of course, recreational activities such as sightseeing, attending baseball games and cultural events are also included.

Though the children's activities at the YMCA are always enjoyable and interesting, a primary goal of all activities at the Orange County YMCA is to build character. Increasing awareness of moral obligations and the moral significance of choices means strengthening the desire to do the right thing, YMCA leaders believe. To achieve this goal, teachers at the facilities model appropriate behavior and stress the Six Pillars of character development: trustworthiness, respect, responsibility, fairness, caring and citizenship.

Arthur L. Wannlund, hired as president/CEO of the YMCA in 1994, has a unique way of describing the organization. He calls it a "character factory." And indeed it is. The emphasis on teaching values and responsibility to children is something sorely needed in today's world and is seen by leadership as an "investment in tomorrow." But the YMCA of Orange County is also a place where people of all ages, ethnic, socio-economic and religious backgrounds unite in a common effort to enrich the quality of life for everyone in the community.

(Far left)
YMCA Indian Princesses, Dana Point, California

CALIFORNIA STATE UNIVERSITY, FULLERTON

Six leased rooms at Sunny Hills High School were the genesis of what today is a bustling 225-acre campus in north Orange County. An initial enrollment of 452 has risen to more than 27,000 students, making California State University, Fullerton the fastest-growing campus in the 23-campus Cal State system.

With 99 degree programs offered in seven colleges, plus numerous certificate programs available through University Extended Education, Cal State Fullerton aspires to combine the best qualities of teaching and research universities.

To enhance service to Orange County residents, the university opened satellites in Garden Grove, Irvine, Mission Viejo and Santa Ana, where Cal State Fullerton's Grand Central Art Center is part of that city's emerging Artists Village.

A chronicle of successes is being recognized this year as part of the university's 40th anniversary: "Celebrating 40 Years of Excellence."

From its first days as Orange County State College, the campus and its students have been thinking big ... which is why the elephant is the university's mascot. The choice of the elephant as mascot, dubbed Tuffy Titan, dates to the early 1960s when the campus hosted "The First Intercollegiate Elephant Race in Human History." The event attracted 10,000 spectators, 15 pachyderms, one tortoise and international media attention. It also ranked among Associated Press' top 10 stories for 1962. Day of the Titan was born.

Cal State Fullerton has continued to make history. Its undergraduate degree program in business has grown to be the nation's fifth largest. Its communications department has become the nation's second largest. And its athletic teams have collected an array of national championships in women's gymnastics, women's softball and baseball. In fact, the Titans are three-time College World Series champions.

The university's impact extends to Orange County's schoolchildren, as Cal State Fullerton has trained a majority of their teachers. And as part of a statewide effort to alleviate a growing teacher shortage, the university is home to a regional center for CalStateTEACH, which offers an intensive 18-month credential program to holders of emergency permits for teaching.

Photo by Phil Channing

Future teachers and other students find that the university offers programs designed to fire the imagination. Examples abound. With the aid of a $1 million National Science Foundation grant, the university recently refashioned one floor of a building into an Anthropology Research and Teaching Facility, which includes a museum with student-curated exhibits.

Another recent addition, the W.M. Keck Foundation Center for Molecular Structure, houses the nation's first comprehensive X-ray crystallography facility located at a predominately undergraduate institution.

Majoring in biology and chemistry can lead a Cal State Fullerton student to a medical career. Over the past two decades, the university's Health Professions Advisement Committee has built an enviable placement record: 85 percent of its recommended students have been accepted to medical and other health professions schools across the country. That rate soars well beyond the national average.

Cal State Fullerton's alumni ranks of more than 125,000 include Academy Award-winner Kevin Costner; Gold Medal-winning Olympian Leon Wood; best-selling novelist Elizabeth George; screenwriter Linda Woolverton, whose hits include *Beauty and the Beast* and *The Lion King*; retired Perrier chairman Ron Davis; and NASA's youngest astronaut, Dr. Tracy Caldwell. She returned to her alma mater in the fall to help launch Cal State Fullerton's 40th anniversary celebration, praising the institution for having "the right stuff."

GOODWILL INDUSTRIES OF ORANGE COUNTY

While many American organizations proudly trace their roots as far back as the turn of the 20th century, few have impacted the country's human landscape as profoundly as has Goodwill Industries. Founded in 1902 by the Rev. Edgar Helms, a Methodist minister, and anchored in Wesleyan tradition, Goodwill Industries continues its mission to ameliorate the quality of people's lives. What began as missionary work and providing for poor people has evolved into empowering people to "provide for themselves" through education, training and employment services.

Faustino Ambrocio, a Goodwill graduate, takes a moment from his work with assistive technology to strike a friendly pose.

Goodwill Industries of Orange County, one of the 186 Goodwill entities throughout North America, dates back to 1924. Established as a small venture to further the humanitarian goals of the organization as it expanded westward, Goodwill continues to adapt to the region's dynamic economy. Much more than a place to drop off unwanted clothes, the nonprofit organization also provides job training for people with disabilities and other barriers to employment, and it features a used computer store and retail stores that sell clothing, furniture, and other items. Revenues for programs are generated through these retail operations. Other funding sources include industrial subcontract services performed by Goodwill trainees and workers, as well as contributions from the state of California and private sources.

Less a charity than a business capable of competing with for-profit companies, Goodwill Industries effectively pairs market synergies with its underlying theme of helping people improve their own lives. Among a host of innovative training, employment and community-integration services offered is the ATEC program (Assistive Technology Exchange Center), which assists "clients" in determining the best technological solutions for overcoming their physical limitations. ATEC offers assessment, augmentative and alternative communication, training and installation, assistive listening devices for the hearing-impaired, an equipment loan program and job development for individuals using assistive technology. Project SCOP (Success Community Opportunity Program) and Multi-Cultural Options (MCO) provide physically and developmentally disabled clients with job training and placement services in an integrated-community environment, enabling them to lead independent lives and increase their ability to make life choices.

Recognizing the correlation between its mission to empower people and California's initiative to move people from welfare dependence to work fulfillment, Goodwill has entered into a partnership with the County of Orange Social Services Agency, ensuring employment readiness and providing support services for welfare recipients. DEAFinitely Jobs is a vocational program designed to assist the deaf and hearing-impaired. Keeping in stride with the emerging cyber-economy, Goodwill created *Kruzin Internet Services*, a unique service that provides competitive, high-quality, professional Web site development and hosting to individuals and companies. Revenues from *Kruzin* also support Goodwill's programs and services.

In 1974, Goodwill Industries of Orange County began its packaging and assembly enterprise, a business that has grown steadily through the years and realized annual revenue exceeding $1 million in 1996 and 1997. GIOC attributes the success of this enterprise to its competitive pricing, excellent quality and on-time delivery, as well as its method of tailoring services to the precise needs of its customers. These are but a few of the many innovative, client-focused services offered by the organization.

Thanks to its founding commitment to bettering the human condition by allowing people to help themselves, Goodwill Industries successfully differentiates itself from most other charitable organizations. A Goodwill spokesperson perhaps said it best: "We're a business that gives people an opportunity to work, to be productive for themselves."

One of Goodwill Industries' community-based groups working at Hurley International

JUNIOR LEAGUE OF ORANGE COUNTY

Orange County was a sleepy Los Angeles suburb in 1956 when a group of 44 young women, all Junior League members from other parts of the country, formed the Newport Harbor Service League. Its purpose was to train members for effective participation in the community through a focused program of education and volunteer service. From its inception, the league's goal was to become a member of the Association of Junior Leagues of America, an organization started in New York by Mary Harriman in 1901. Basing their philosophy on that of the original Junior League, these women formed a strong and progressive organization. The dream of the founding members became reality in 1971 when the league was officially accepted as the Junior League of Newport Harbor. In 1985, due to expansion and the scope of projects, it became the Junior League of Orange County, California Inc. (JLOCC).

The Junior League of Orange County, California Inc. in Newport Beach

Today's league is approximately 1,000 members strong, with a primary purpose of training women to become community leaders. Members share the vision of a community in which all children and adolescents are supported to flourish and realize their hopes and dreams. To support the JLOCC's projects and programs, two major fund-raisers are held each year: The Christmas Company, a multi-day shopping event held each October; and Monte Carlo Night, an elegant evening affair held each spring.

The league's first project in 1956 was to create the Volunteer Bureau (today's Volunteer Center of Orange County), which coordinated and encouraged volunteer work with agencies in the Newport Harbor area. The list of league projects developed since then is impressive and distinguished, and many of them have been turned over to the community to be continued as non-league projects after several years. Among those operated today as independent organizations are the Assessment and Treatment Services Center (ATSC), Court Appointed Special Advocates of Orange County (CASA) and the Child Abuse Services Team (CAST). It was the league's original challenge grant of $117,000 that helped to build the Orangewood Children's Home. In 1998 the league donated $100,000 of seed money to the Boys & Girls Club of Capistrano Valley to begin their capital campaign. A scholarship fund has also been set up for students who have participated in JLOCC projects and programs to continue their postsecondary education.

The league's newest project is a five-year partnership with the Girls & Boys Clubs of Garden Grove and The Boys and Girls Club of Capistrano Valley. This project will establish the nation's first Family Campus with the Garden Grove Clubs and provide funding for the ongoing development of the Capistrano Valley Club, with the ultimate goal being the creation of a second Family Campus in Capistrano Valley. The Family Campus will act as a center for adults and children of all ages that offers innovative programs and services for extended hours on a daily basis. This Family Campus will be a model for future centers developed in other communities.

The JLOCC is an exclusively educational and charitable organization for women committed to promoting volunteerism while improving the community through the effective actions and leadership of its trained volunteers. Membership comprises full-time professionals, stay-at-home mothers and students with various working conditions and scheduling availability. Information meetings for new members are held each spring.

ORANGE COUNTY HISTORICAL SOCIETY

The Orange County Historical Society was founded on June 26, 1919. The directors of the new Society were prominent leaders in the young county: Samuel Armor, author and educator; H. Clay Kellogg, engineer; Nellie P. Tedford, farm wife and town leader; Charles C. Chapman, educator, businessman and orchardist; Samuel M. Davis, civil servant; John L. Dryer; and Charles D. Ball, physician, taking the place of George W. Moore. At this first meeting, Dr. Charles Ball was elected president, a position he was to hold unopposed until he stepped down 15 years later in 1934. William McPherson and Terry E. Stephenson, Santa Ana postmaster, traded the presidency until 1946. Samuel M. Davis was elected secretary/treasurer at that 1919 meeting and served in that position as secretary until 1943 and treasurer until 1946.

This photo of a field trip for the Orange County Historical Society was taken on the porch of Yoch's Laguna Beach Hotel on October 29, 1921. Dr. C.D. Ball, OCHS's first president, is seated with cane; on his left, Judge J.E. Pleasants; next to him Laguna artist Anne Robinson. Directly behind Dr. Ball is William McPherson; two gentlemen to the right of McPherson is S.M. Davis, former district attorney.

The Society published several valuable volumes in the early years. *The Orange County Historical Series* contained some of the best papers presented to the Society in its decade. The 1931 and 1932 editions were printed by the now famous *Fine Arts Press.* In 1939 a third volume in this series (but smaller in size) was issued with more fine research papers read at society meetings.

The Society was re-established in 1961 with the Bowers Museum as its new home. The faces were new but the objectives had not changed: fostering and generating public interest in the history of California in general and Orange County in particular, and to collect and preserve historical material for the benefit of its members and the general public.

Since 1963 the Orange County Historical Society has published many works; the *Newsletter,* which became the *County Courier,* is perhaps the most interesting. Many fine volunteers have given hours of their time to produce this central publication. It has remained the single best tool for documenting the Society's history and its place in the county.

From 1963 to 1967 the society issued four pamphlets, three of which were labeled as part of the original *Orange County History Series* begun in 1931. It became a necessity, however, to publish separate works based on more detailed research. Leo J. Friis authored a history of the Bowers museum (1967); Ethel Jacobson issued several poems (1964 and 1969); Wayne Gibson profiled the Olive mill (1975); and Virginia Carpenter researched the Cañada de la Brea (1978). A new series based on writings by Society members rather than oral presentations was inaugurated. And there are now five volumes of *Orange Countiana* (1973, 1980, 1982, 1988, and 1992).

During the past several years, there has been much community involvement by the Society under numerous dedicated presidents. Members have represented the Society at festivals, Orange County Fairs, and numerous patriotic and social events. Since 1961 the Society has met at least 10 times a year to offer programs of interest and value. All of these have involved members in the enrichment of the community and the furtherance of the history of our county and its people.

There are more publications in the Society's future, and more programs and tours, as well as time to enlarge its local history holdings, photo archives and library. All will continue to be planned with the county and its increasingly multicultural people as the subject and producers of history.

This 1929 photo was taken at the Pleasants Ranch on the 90th anniversary of the Judge's birthday. Year of arrival in California follows each name. (Seated, left to right) J.P. Boyd, 1888; J.C. Joplin, 1877; J.E. Pleasants, 1849; James S. Rice, 1877; Jane Murdy, 1887; C.D. Ball, 1887. (Standing, left to right) T.E. Stephenson, 1884; E.L. Higgins, 1889; James Sleeper, 1888; W.L. Mitchell, 1889

ORANGE COUNTY PERFORMING ARTS CENTER

Segerstrom Hall

The Orange County Performing Arts Center is architecturally stunning and an acoustical marvel, absolutely one of the finest performing arts centers in the world.

With The Center's perfect acoustics, its meticulous upkeep and superb design, it is common for performing artists to feel as though it has been built just for them. Mikhail Baryshnikov declared The Center "a paradise" for artists. Beverly Sills called it an artist's "home away from home," and Rudolf Nureyev exclaimed, "Amazing, this is the first time a theater has been built and someone thought of the dancers."

The dramatic Fire Bird, by renowned sculptor Richard Lippold, dominates The Center's facade. *Photo by Jeffrey L. Brown*

The citizens of Orange County built The Center for the benefit of the entire community. They wanted a world-class performing arts center to serve as a cultural anchor for the people of this county; they paid for it and continue to do so. It is the nation's only performing arts center built and supported solely with private donations.

Orange County comprises more than 30 city governments, each with its own interests and needs. In many ways, The Center, without any government affiliation or support, is the de facto core of Orange County.

The Center has an amazingly loyal group of supporters. More than 4,000 Friends of The Center donate every year, because it is their center. There are more than 31 chapters of The Center's guilds. The ownership they have in The Center is genuinely heartfelt.

Since September 29, 1986, when the Orange County Performing Arts Center first opened its doors to the public, more than six million people have visited The Center to appreciate major ballet companies, top Broadway musicals and the finest in opera, jazz and chamber music — the most esteemed performing arts and the world's best performing artists — Russia's Kirov Ballet, the Bolshoi, the Paris Opera Ballet, Great Britain's Royal Ballet and the New York City Opera.

Audiences at The Center have thrilled to singers and musicians of the highest caliber, including Plácido Domingo, Dame Gwyneth Jones, Issac Stern and the Brodsky Quartet. They have been delighted by contemporary dance troupes such as the Martha Graham Dance Company, Paul Taylor Dance Company and Mikhail Baryshnikov's White Oak Dance Project. Top entertainers in jazz and popular music such as Ella Fitzgerald, Harry Belafonte, Tony Bennett, Bette Midler, Shirley Horn, Julio Iglesias and so many more have all ignited The Center with the soul-stirring sights and sounds of the performing arts.

The Center is also home to Orange County's leading regional groups, including Pacific Symphony Orchestra, the Philharmonic Society of Orange County, Opera Pacific, Pacific Chorale and the William Hall Master Chorale.

Most communities build arts centers once in a generation, or in a lifetime. After only 13 years, however, the Orange County Performing Arts Center began planning for a world-class concert hall and music hall. In the near future it will have four of the most superb theaters in the world.

The story of The Center itself is inspirational. There can be no greater monument to the spirit of Orange County than the magnificent home it has made for the performing arts.

Audiences enjoy the world's finest at the Orange County Performing Arts Center.

PACIFIC SYMPHONY ORCHESTRA

Drum rolls and flourishes should accompany the story of the Pacific Symphony Orchestra's meteoric rise, its sustained and successful community outreach efforts, world-class performances and innovative educational programs.

Founded in 1978 as the Pacific Chamber Orchestra, the Pacific Symphony Orchestra's ascendancy has been phenomenal. Its budget increased from just $13,000 its first season to more than $7 million by its 20th anniversary year. Now California's third largest orchestra, the Pacific Symphony Orchestra is frequently and favorably compared to orchestras more than five times its age and budget size.

The Pacific Symphony Orchestra, Carl St.Clair, Music Director

This accelerated momentum has coincided with the tenure of its esteemed music director and conductor, Carl St.Clair. Chosen in 1990 after an exhaustive national search, Maestro St.Clair, who had won the nation's most prestigious prize in conducting, the NEA/Seaver Conductors award, has brought dynamism, charm and a confident, adventurous spirit to the orchestra. His meticulous knowledge of music is awe-inspiring. Maestro St.Clair travels the globe as a sought-after guest conductor for the greatest orchestras in the world. He has been a magnet, attracting superb musicians who are eager to travel the path toward greatness with the Pacific Symphony Orchestra.

Carl St.Clair's magnetism was a major factor in attracting the Pacific Symphony Orchestra's president, John Forsyte, who credits the maestro with giving the orchestra its own sound. Under the musical direction of Maestro St.Clair, the Pacific Symphony Orchestra has joined the realm of unique and remarkable orchestras, distinguished by the imprint of its own voice. "It has a big, muscular sound, a vitality and style built by Carl," says Forsyte.

The Pacific Symphony Orchestra's prime concert venue is the acclaimed Orange County Performing Arts Center. It is the center's primary tenant, performing more than 50 concerts each season. In addition to its own concerts, it performs with the Pacific Chorale and serves as pit orchestra for the center's international ballet series.

The Pacific Symphony Orchestra's programs, tailored to different age and social groups, offer something of quality for everyone; every year, PSO's concerts and outreach programs allow more than 250,000 Orange County residents to enjoy soul-stirring live orchestral performances. Summer outdoor concerts at Irvine Meadows Amphitheatre, with preconcert picnicking and fireworks, thrill audiences of 10,000 to 12,000 per performance.

A prime example of PSO's educational efforts is its award-winning Class Act program. The American Symphony Orchestra League honored Class Act as one of three model music education programs, along with programs of the Boston Symphony Orchestra and the New York Philharmonic.

The program has been remarkably successful in involving parents as active volunteer participants, forming a lively partnership between the orchestra, elementary school students, teachers, administrators and parents throughout Orange County.

Class Act brings symphonic music into students' lives and brings the music to life. Each school gets an "adopted" musician who visits the schools regularly, conducting classroom lessons for each grade level. Students learn about a particular composer's music, country of origin and era. Students, faculty and parents all come together for a Family Night concert, and students and teachers attend free youth concerts at the Orange County Performing Arts Center. They conclude the year with a Bravo Assembly, at which the students thank the musicians and demonstrate what they have learned. It is a thoroughly enriching experience for all.

Carl St.Clair, Music Director

If a community has the wealth, it can import great culture. However, it usually takes tremendous dedication for long periods of time to build a great institution, such as the Pacific Symphony Orchestra, that can serve as a cultural ambassador to the world. The Pacific Symphony Orchestra — the touchstone of Orange County's cultural strength.

SADDLEBACK COLLEGE

California Governor Ronald Reagan stood in front of a handful of temporary college classrooms erected on a hillside in Mission Viejo and told the gathered throng of dignitaries and community members, "It is the function of education to help each individual grow to the maximum extent of his capabilities, to help him fulfill his great potential, and it is our job as responsible citizens to provide that opportunity. That this community has decided to move ahead in providing this opportunity is an action which I commend — and an action which will provide great rewards for the community." More than 30 years later, the community is still reaping the rewards of Saddleback College.

From the initial fall 1968 enrollment of several hundred students, Saddleback College has grown into one of the largest and most respected community colleges in California. More than 23,000 students attend classes on the sprawling 200-acre state-of-the-art campus that offers more than 240 certificate and degree programs for everything from computer science to radio/TV/film.

Saddleback students, teachers and administrators all share the vision expounded by Governor Reagan, but it is the O'Neill family that deserves credit for helping launch Saddleback College. In the mid-1960s, the O'Neills developed 10,000 acres of their ranch into the planned community of Mission Viejo and allowed the original Saddleback Junior College District to purchase 200 acres at $12,500 an acre.

As the college grew and expanded its curriculum, it earned a reputation for facilitating academic excellence in a dynamic and challenging learning environment. More importantly, Saddleback College has become an integral part of the south county landscape, linking education with community growth and vitality. More than half a million people have walked through

Members of the class of 1998 at Saddleback College

the school's doors since 1968, and many of those students have transferred to public and private universities. Saddleback alumni can be found in leadership positions in business, industry, athletics and the arts throughout the Southland and across the nation.

In addition to traditional academic classes, Saddleback College has become renowned for the caliber of its fine and performing arts programs, and the campus has become one of Orange County's premier cultural and entertainment sites. Thousands of people attend performances at the award-winning Saddleback Civic Light Opera, and music and dance fans enjoy concerts by resident and guest artists. The school also has its own radio station, KSBR-88.5 FM (the county's only jazz music station), which provides educational training for hundreds of students each year.

Intercollegiate sports teams for men and women provide Saddleback students with athletic and competitive opportunities. The school's athletic teams have a solid reputation for success, winning 109 conference titles, seven state championships and three national championships. That success is enhanced by an athletic program that encourages scholar-athletes.

The college offers comprehensive programs in occupational training and vocational education that rival and even exceed the quality of programs offered by specialty training schools, while the school's Emeritus Institute provides thousands of senior citizens with the opportunity to pursue lifelong learning. Cybercourses and distance education classes at dozens of off-campus sites help Saddleback College fulfill its mission of reaching out to the community.

In a world that's constantly changing, Saddleback has managed to stay one step ahead with innovative programs and teaching tools such as a virtual technology center, which teaches students skills used in everything from the dental technician field to construction design using a three-dimensional computer program. These and other cutting-edge programs are helping Saddleback College forge a bright path into the future of education.

SADDLEBACK MEMORIAL MEDICAL CENTER

Saddleback Memorial Medical Center, its carpeted hallways adorned with watercolor prints, feels more like a hotel than a hospital. It's hard to believe this beautiful facility got its start in the late 1960s when residents of Saddleback Valley and Leisure World went door to door with coffee cans asking for donations to build a hospital for their community.

The hospital's emphasis on community service — aided by an enthusiastic volunteer effort — has remained constant over the decades the hospital has served the local area.

As the community has grown and changed, so has the hospital — from a 146-bed hospital that specialized in the needs of senior citizens to a 220-bed hospital with a full obstetrics unit that offers labor, delivery, recovery and postpartum rooms as well as the highest level of intensive care for newborn babies.

But before the hospital was built, there was only the Leisure World Medical Center, a 24-hour medical care center staffed by one doctor and 12 nurses.

Twenty-five "pink ladies," named for the pink shirts they wore, started volunteering at the center in May 1965. By the end of the year, 130 volunteers had donated more than 7,000 hours of their time.

Soon the community had outgrown the medical center. With the help of the local community, Saddleback Community Hospital opened in 1974. A 20-bed medical-surgical wing was added in 1983, and the Breast Care Center debuted in 1985. In 1986 the Saddleback Heart Institute opened.

More young families started moving into south Orange County, and in 1988 the Saddleback Women's Hospital opened with the latest in labor, delivery and neonatal care.

Joining the MemorialCare network of hospitals in 1981, the hospital changed its name to Saddleback Memorial Medical Center in 1989, the same year it celebrated its 500th open-heart surgery. Along with its sister hospitals Anaheim Memorial Medical Center, Long Beach Memorial Medical Center and Orange Coast Memorial Medical Center, Saddleback Memorial Medical Center maintains a strong commitment to the standard of excellence in health care.

In 1995 the Saddleback Heart Institute and Wellness Center opened. This is one of the hospital's five centers of excellence, which include Saddleback Women's Hospital, Saddleback Heart Institute and Wellness Center, Saddleback Orthopedic Services, Saddleback Rehabilitation Center, Saddleback Cancer Services and Saddleback Home Care Services.

The hospital experienced tremendous technological and physical growth in the 1990s with the addition of a new dual linear accelerator to the oncology center, the installation of two state-of-the-art cardiac catheterization labs, the expansion of the Saddleback Heart Institute and Wellness Center, and the relocation of the MemorialCare Breast Center at Saddleback into an expanded space.

And the volunteer ladies in pink, now 350 in number, are still active. In 1998 they celebrated the milestone of two million hours of service. Four hundred fifty other volunteers donated time to other programs like the thrift shop, which had raised nearly $4.5 million for the hospital by 1998.

By the end of the 1990s, the hospital was admitting more than 10,000 inpatients and 200,000 outpatients each year. Current expansion efforts include building a new, state-of-the-art emergency department called the Meiklejohn Critical Care Pavilion and adding 15 beds to the Saddleback Women's Hospital.

But with all its growth and high-tech equipment, Saddleback Memorial Medical Center has maintained its vision for serving the community. While remaining committed to providing excellent medical care for seniors, the hospital has expanded its scope of services to meet the needs of the young families who are now a vital part of its community.

THE BLIND CHILDREN'S LEARNING CENTER

The history of the Blind Children's Learning Center can be described as the evolution of a miracle. It began in 1962 when six blind friends formed a support group to try and combat their feelings of isolation and dependence.

Virtually no services or transportation were available for the blind when the BCLC — originally called Services for the Blind — was established. It soon became a refuge of reassurance and began to teach braille and provide other services. Within two years it had incorporated as a nonprofit organization and moved into an old, Spanish-style house in Santa Ana.

As blind teens became involved with the organization, and more activities such as field trips were centered on youthful members, the founders —all mature adults who had all become blind in later life — realized the need to help children. Blindness can be a terribly isolating impairment. Society had always removed blind children from the mainstream of life and placed them in supposedly protective environments, isolating them even further, behind a wall of good intentions.

If it weren't for the white cane, one would never know this beautiful girl was blind. If it weren't for the Blind Children's Learning Center, it might not be that way.

The field of education was placing more emphasis on development in the first years of life, given that 80 percent of all knowledge is learned by age 5. This seemed especially important for blind children, since most early development is visually cued —even the way babies bond with their parents.

Blind and sighted children enjoy "circle time" together at the Early Childhood Center.

The Blind Children's Learning Center created a preschool based on the belief that blind children, given the proper training, could develop into independent, successful adults. Field trips and innovative practices, such as incorporating sighted children into classes as peer models, gave blind children an experiential link to the world.

It became apparent that to give the children the best chance for development, their families needed help, too. When their child is born blind, even exceptional parents have had their dreams dashed. They need to go through a grief process for their lost hopes, reach acceptance, and form new hopes based on the reality that their child can lead an independent, happy life.

Now, the Infant-Family Focus program sends professionals into the families' homes to provide counseling and experiential guidance. They help parents bond with the children and create an environment that stimulates pathways for alternative, sensory learning.

The BCLC's Early Childhood Center, for children from 6 months to 6 years of age, is an award-winning, comprehensive educational facility with a dedicated staff of accredited teachers, counselors and therapists. They teach blind children self-help, psychomotor, cognitive, socialization and language skills. About 90 percent of the Early Childhood Center's graduates gain the skills needed to enter mainstream kindergarten.

After having experienced the Early Childhood Center's supportive environment, families of children entering public school were horrified to find there was virtually no support available.

Today, the BCLC contracts with the school districts and is accountable for the education of blind students in public schools. Though heavily dependent on contributions, the non-profit BCLC raises some of its funds through these fee-based services. The Youth Outreach program offers a range of services that provide the advocacy, coaching and training to ensure the success of blind children in elementary and high school. Advances in technology have become the "white cane" of the future and are an integral part of BCLC's programs.

The Blind Children's Learning Center's mission is Destination Independence —helping blind and visually impaired children and youth reach the same destination as sighted children —an independent, happy life. The dream envisioned by six blind people in 1962 has evolved into a miraculous reality.

SANTA ANA HISTORICAL PRESERVATION SOCIETY

The Santa Ana walnut groves and sugar beet fields are gone, replaced by malls, theaters and office complexes. But look more closely at the city's varied architecture of local neighborhoods and the downtown buildings (now housing art galleries) and a rich history emerges.

Santa Ana, the county seat of Orange County, had its beginnings back in 1869, when William H. Spurgeon from Kentucky liked what he saw and paid $595 for the 74.2 acres where he built his city. The land was actually part of the Rancho Santiago de Santa Ana, an original Spanish land-use grant awarded back in 1810.The town started with 24 blocks of about 10 lots each.

Increasingly, the history of Orange County is being lost. One Santa Ana resident, Adeline Walker, had finally had enough of the plundering of historic neighborhoods back in the 1970s and decided to try to save this valued history. She saw old, historic homes being torn down and large apartment buildings going up in their place. But when the home originally built back in 1889 for Dr. Alvin and Dr. Willella Howe was being readied for the chopping block, Walker set her sights on saving it. This 12-room Queen Anne Victorian was set to be demolished in 1974 to make way for the widening of Civic Center Drive. Walker believed the house needed to be saved not only for its Victorian charms, but also as a tribute to Dr. Willella Howe-Waffle, a respected doctor who is best remembered for delivering more than 1,000 "Waffle babies."

The effort to save the Dr. Howe-Waffle House led to the formation of the Santa Ana Historical Preservation Society (SAHPS), which was able to save and restore the home that became its headquarters. The house is also home to a medical museum that pays tribute to Dr. Howe-Waffle.

Today the Society is busier than ever in its efforts to preserve local history and educate the community about the city's colorful heritage. It recently kicked off the "Making History Live!" sponsorship program, which supports numerous activities; holds classes on how to research the history of a home (in conjunction with the Santa Ana Public Library History Room); creates publications on research techniques and local history; salvages architectural elements from buildings slated for demolition; works with local developers on the impact to historic sites; and arranges special exhibits at the Dr. Howe-Waffle house, Cal State Fullerton and the Old Orange County Courthouse.

In 2000 SAHPS initiated a living history program that brings costumed actors to local schools to help illustrate local lore for the city's younger residents. Another highly acclaimed program is the Historical Cemetery Tour, which takes visitors through local historic cemeteries, again using costumed actors to help bring back memories. A new effort by the SAHPS is archiving the history of local families. The Society is reaching out to its older residents and trying to collect family documents and pictures before that part of the community is lost forever.

The Society also launched an Internet Web site that publishes information on early Santa Ana pioneers, buildings and history. The site is meant to be an online reference for residents, students and history buffs with worldwide accessibility.

Other activities of the SAHPS include: home and garden tours; seminars on local history and preservation; special events such as dedications, teas, boutiques and dinners; weddings and receptions; and allowing the Howe-Waffle house to be used as a movie location. This all-volunteer group has also increased the time the house is open to the public. The house, located on Civic Center Drive West, is now open for tours the first full weekend of every month.

The Dr. Willella Howe-Waffle House and Medical Museum *Photo by Tom Cohan, Cohan Graphics*

THE DISCOVERY MUSEUM OF ORANGE COUNTY

A visit to the Discovery Museum of Orange County is a unique experience, rather like being transported back in time to 19th-century Orange County. Located on 11 acres in Santa Ana adjacent to Centennial Regional Park, the museum consists of a five-acre nature center and several historic structures including two vintage houses, all open to the public.

Originally federal property, it was transferred to the Santa Ana Unified School District in 1967. By 1977 the school district had established it as an environmental learning center and by 1980, it had organized the Exploratory Learning Center. The property was used as a training site for high school students, and as a result, many Orange County students helped complete the grading, built the rock retaining wall, and did planting, masonry and foundation work for the houses. In 1981 the Exploratory Learning Center Foundation was created to raise money and maintain the site, which eventually became the Discovery Museum of Orange County.

The nature center features winding interpretive trails, riparian forests, freshwater marshes, coastal sage scrub and a small stream. A vegetable garden is maintained by volunteers, and the fruit of their labors is donated to homeless shelters.

The museum's center of activity is the fully restored Kellogg House, originally built in 1898 and moved to its present site in 1980. H.C. Kellogg, a prosperous civil engineer, served as Santa Ana's first city engineer. The house features a unique circular staircase. Visitors can play a pump organ, talk on a hand-cranked telephone, look through a stereoscope, try on Victorian clothing, wash clothes on a scrub board, and explore many other aspects of daily life in Orange County at the turn of the 19th century.

In addition to the Kellogg House, three other structures, moved from the orange groves originally owned by John Maag and converted to Fairhaven Cemetery, are located in the historic plaza of the museum. John Maag was an orange grower in Orange County and founded the Santiago Grower's Association, which later became Sunkist. The John Maag ranch house should be open for visitors to explore by the year 2002, but the carriage house and water tower are now open for exploration. The water tower functions as the museum's store, and the carriage house has been converted into the museum office and educational classroom.

Included in the historical plaza is the blacksmith shop and tool museum, which was built and is maintained by the Orange County Blacksmith's Guild. Another volunteer group, the Victorian Tea Society, actively supports the museum through theme teas it presents for holidays and special occasions. The profits from the teas are donated to the museum.

Field trips for school children are a significant feature of the museum. Tours last for either two or four hours. Some popular themes are "A Secret Garden," "Indians of California" and "Journey in Time."

The museum site is also available to private parties for events such as wedding ceremonies, receptions and corporate events.

Anaheim/Orange County Visitor & Convention Bureau

TECHNOLOGY

Diverse businesses have gathered to make Orange County one of the country's leading centers of technology innovation, development, manufacturing and employment.

INTERSTATE ELECTRONICS CORPORATION

Tucked away unobtrusively in Anaheim is Interstate Electronics Corporation (IEC), a company that for 40 years has played a key role in the most successful defense system of modern history — the U.S. Navy's Fleet Ballistic Missile Program. IEC comprises engineering, technical and manufacturing professionals and provides unique technical solutions for a broad spectrum of commercial, government and military customers. Its

THE BEDROCK OF THE COMPANY CONSISTS OF 40 YEARS DESIGNING AND MANUFACTURING HIGHLY SOPHISTICATED ELECTRONIC SYSTEMS.

portfolio of satellite-based signal processing products includes advanced global positioning system (GPS) solutions for sophisticated military applications for which positioning navigation and timing are critical. The company also provides test instrumentation support for the U.S. Navy's Fleet Ballistic Missile Program and is known for the advancement of technical solutions in the ruggedized display market.

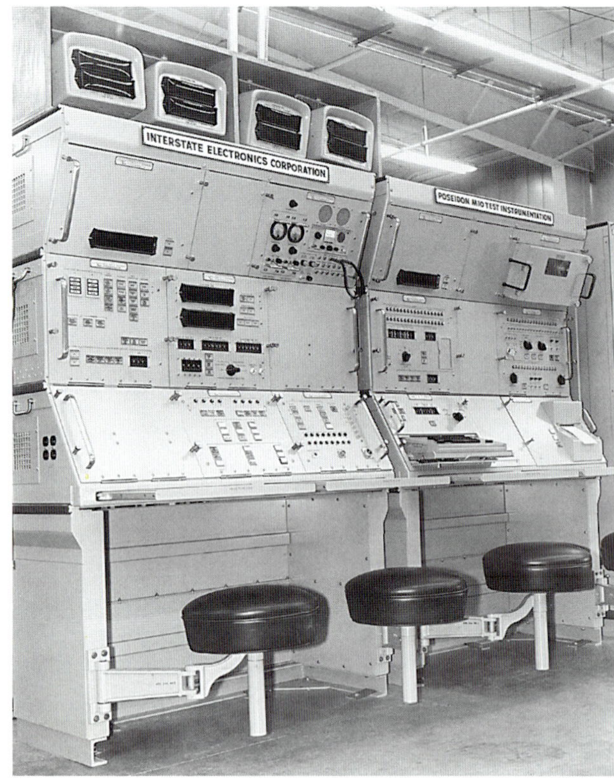

Early IEC test instrument system

In 1956 IEC was formed by a small group of experts in telemetry, navigation and control systems. That same year, IEC won a prime defense contract for the development of advanced test instrumentation and tracking systems for the U.S. Navy's Fleet Ballistic Missile Program, known as FBM. The company developed a complete range and instrumentation program designed for shipboard and submarine installation. Its contract with the U.S. Navy has been in existence for the past 40 years, and it is the only original contractor from the 1950s still involved in the program. The program includes the Polaris, the Poseidon and the Trident missile systems. These nuclear missiles ride on U.S. Navy submarines and are the greatest deterrent to any attack on the United States. IEC does not build the missiles, but it does build the instrumentation system that tracks the missiles.

Trident submarine

The bedrock of the company consists of 40 years designing and manufacturing highly sophisticated electronic systems. IEC's annual revenue is approximately $80 million — and still growing — with a work force of more than 500 people. The company employs hardware and software engineers, as well as production and support personnel. Although design and manufacturing take place in

(Far left)
Paul Reedy, founder of IEC

Seven generations of IEC GPS Receivers

Anaheim, IEC has field site-support facilities elsewhere on both coasts.

In addition to the FBM Strategic Instrumentation and Missile Tracking System, IEC designs and manufactures GPS receivers, satellite simulators and GPS flight management systems. Special understanding of GPS technology is the culmination of more than 20 years of development and use of GPS-based tracking systems. IEC's extensive involvement with GPS technology began in the early 1980s with the development of GPS tracking for the Navy's Trident Missile Program. Subsequently, IEC began providing GPS receiver-based systems for precise positioning information at Army, Navy and Air Force testing and evaluation ranges. IEC also provides GPS receiver technology for smart weapons, such as the conventional air-launched cruise missile and for the first precision-guided bomb in the U.S. Department of Defense inventory.

IEC is also a designer and manufacturer of flat-panel and high-resolution monitors for military and industrial applications. IEC displays are in use in such locations as Air Force One and the International Space Station. These rugged displays include smart-display systems, which are self-contained computers designed for harsh environments.

Interstate Electronics Corporation takes pride in the fact that during 40 years of growth and expansion it has been a stable icon in the local community. IEC is involved with a number of local charity organizations including the United Way of Orange County. IEC's facilities are located on East Vermont Street in Anaheim.

IEC corporate headquarters building

MICROSEPTEC

The numbers are eye-catching — population projections over the next 20 years in southern California indicate growth in the region shows no sign of slowing.

An additional one million people in San Diego County alone are projected by 2020. Orange County faces a similar situation, with its current rapid growth rate and escalating real estate costs pushing more and more of its population into continually expanding "edge" communities.

MicroSepTec Corporate Offices in Laguna Hills

The continuing growth and expansion predicted throughout the region presents a challenge to all existing and future infrastructures. Existing sewage treatment plants face particularly stringent regulatory and financial hurdles, and traditional septic systems utilizing leach fields are often an impractical alternative due to high system failure rates, geographical challenges to builders and rising maintenance costs for property owners.

MicroSepTec Inc. of Laguna Hills has recently stepped forward with an environmentally friendly alternative to traditional, archaic septic systems with its compact, "e-connected" computer-monitored and self-contained EnviroServer® appliance. Utilizing thermal degradation and fluid processing, the EnviroServer® Wastewater System reduces liquid and solid organic waste to recyclable water and harmless ash.

With more than one-third of the residences in the country currently relying on septic tanks, the introduction of MicroSepTec and its revolutionary EnviroServer® appliance has generated extensive interest from engineers involved in the design and installation of on-site treatment systems.

The cost-efficient system safely eliminates sludge and reduces harmful nitrates to an environmentally acceptable level while disinfecting all residual water. The dependence on percolation for wastewater purification is eliminated.

The odor-free water can then, depending upon the county or state, safely be used for landscape irrigation, re-piping into home or office toilets or for recycling into groundwater aquifers.

Golf courses, universities and other public institutions have long used reclaimed water to nurture their pastoral landscapes. Property owners can now do the same with the EnviroServer® system.

The patented thermal processor utilized by the EnviroServer® has been developed and refined over a four-year period, culminating in a revolutionary total waste water and reclamation process. The process is so unique that the company recently secured a process patent and has an additional component patent pending. In June 1998 a new management team was brought into the company and a commercial launch of the company's products occurred shortly thereafter.

The thermal processor technology is so advanced that new applications are consistently arising for it. MicroSepTec is developing a compact variation of the EnviroServer® system that will be used in vacuum-flush toilets for public transportation systems, starting with passenger trains in Europe. The same

The EnviroServer's® above-ground components are compact and can easily be hidden from view. Once installed, the EnviroServer's® above-ground components are out of the consumer's sight and mind.

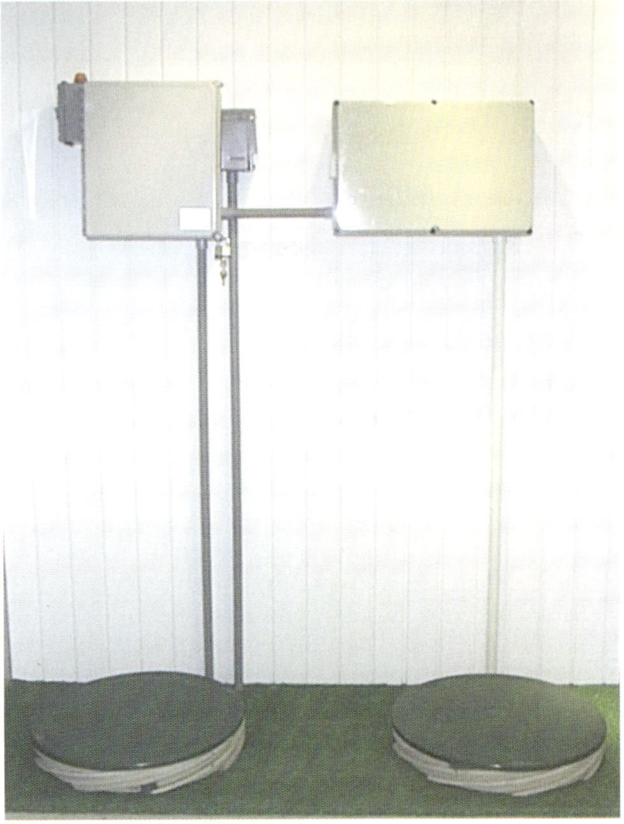

system that will be used in transit cars can be adapted for airlines and boats because of the elimination of the need for pumpout stations.

This cost-effective system requires no owner maintenance or monitoring. It monitors itself with an on-board, e-connected computer. Should a problem arise, the computer electronically notifies the company's Performance Assurance Center, and a certified technician is then dispatched to the property.

Orange County was a natural birthplace for such a product. The Southland's higher population density and recent drought-like conditions have created greater demand for water.

Residents in coastal areas of the county are also particularly sensitive to the way waste is disposed because of periodic beach closures due to contaminated water. Add those concerns to the county's high-tech environment and MicroSepTec, the EnviroServer® appliance and Orange County are a perfect fit.

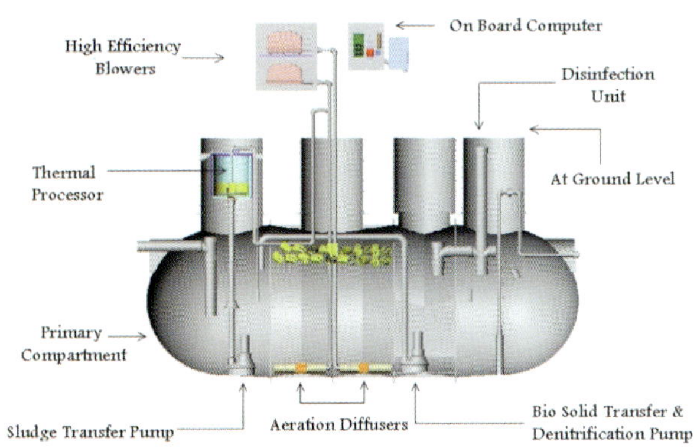

The MicroSepTec EnviroServer® appliance is an ideal solution for cases where the installation of septic tanks or sewers is impossible or impractical, or for structures in remote areas. It can be utilized in areas where soil has limited percolation; areas where strict environmental controls have been established; areas with high water tables; areas with existing ground water contamination; in-fill areas previously deemed unsuitable for building; and in situations where there is an acute need for water conservation and nitrogen-sensitive areas.

Communities with a large number of residents currently using traditional septic systems have embraced the EnviroServer®, including Malibu and Paradise Valley, a community north of Phoenix in the throes of the growing Arizona building boom. Ecologically minded communities such as Santa Fe, New Mexico and Rancho Santa Fe and Valley Center have also cleared the EnviroServer® for use. More communities are rapidly climbing on board. EnviroServer® systems will soon be in use in Santa Barbara, San Luis Obispo and northern California's Marin and Sonoma counties.

The MicroSepTec EnviroServer® system can be applied to a vast array of industries including existing single family homes, new home construction, manufactured homes, agriculture operations, shopping malls, commercial centers, land development, mining areas, military applications, light industrial, marine, hotels and restaurants.

MST engineers fine tune the computer-monitored components for EnviroServer®

MicroSepTec engineers engaged in R & D and continuous technology enhancement of EnviroServer®

PARAGON BIOMEDICAL, INC.

If you asked Nick Reed, CEO of Paragon Biomedical, Inc., what makes his company outstanding, his answer wouldn't be profits and revenue. He'd tell you about culture and the values that nurture a family-focused organization. Nick and his wife Gena Reed started Paragon in 1989 in a spare bedroom in their Irvine condo. Over the decade the business has grown rapidly but at its center has remained certain core values and commitments to both customers and associates. Says Nick, "I've always believed the key to business is essentially treating the customer — whether internal or external — better than they expect to be treated. We try to build relationships that endure, and we focus on the ideas that make any relationship strong: integrity, fairness, teamwork — and fun!"

Quality College graduates

Nick Reed, CEO, and Gena Reed, president

Paragon has a highly innovative approach to doing business. From the company's first days, Nick decided it could operate as a "network" model and built a decentralized organization with regional offices throughout the country. The decentralized structure ensures faster service and reduced costs for Paragon's customers. Associates benefit too — no relocation is required on employment.

Paragon is a service business that manages research studies in the rapidly growing pharmaceutical, biotech and medical device industries. Since many companies do not have the time or resources to adequately prepare, run and monitor clinical trials, Paragon provides them the means to establish proof that a particular drug or device works. While competition is strong in the research industry, Paragon has grown above the industry

Paragon's new office located at University Research Park

associates who feel ownership of the processes and services they provide."

Paragon's success and powerful model for growth and customer satisfaction has not gone unnoticed. In 1998 the Orange County Ernst and Young Entrepreneur of the Year Award (in the division of healthcare and life sciences) was awarded to Paragon Biomedical. In her acceptance speech, Gena Reed immediately shared the honor with all of Paragon's associates. Said Gena, "We've set our goals to be the best. Without our associates, Paragon might still be just another small business waiting for opportunity to knock. With them, there are no limits!"

Paula Brust, Susan Tate, Ken Hazelip, Monica Frey, Jeanette Walrath and Judy Swing celebrate their accomplishments at an all-associates meeting.

norm by focusing on two words: quality and value. Says Gena Reed, Paragon's president, "All companies in our field offer service — we work hard to find ways to add value to the service we give. And the best value is uncompromising quality." Over the past few years Paragon has emphasized improving the quality of their processes and systems. According to Gena, "We literally went to school last year on quality. We sent all of Paragon's managers and directors to Quality College. And today, we're beginning to see tremendous dividends on our quality investment."

While external customers have benefited, Paragon's greatest gains have come from within. Says Gena, "Rather than hiring external experts, our people were empowered to redesign what we do to make our service more efficient and powerful. We've seen that work on quality has created quality work — as well as

Tenley Koepnick, Monika Frey, Carol O'Brien and Patsy Trisler resting from the games at Mount Paragon event night

(Far left)
Steven Thayer, Susan Tate, Michele Doherty and Wendy Currlin take a picture at the 10 year celebration.

(Left)
Kim Mihalovich, Dawn Russell and Lynn White enjoy the 10th Anniversary celebration.

STARBASE

Science fiction is becoming science. People push buttons and seemingly magical things happen. Ideas traverse continents and oceans in seconds; in mere minutes computers accomplish tasks that once took years.

While some people may see technology as dehumanizing, technology comes from the human mind. It offers people the possibility of a different kind of progress, beyond making things easier and faster. It holds the promise of a new freedom.

The history of StarBase, one of the world's premier software developers, is a story of people — people's ideas and dreams and the hard work and dedication it took to carry them out. It is also about one man's spirit. A man who infused the company with his sense of intellectual honesty, and whose technical genius helped lay the foundation for StarBase.

The company took its name from a favorite phrase — "Establish a robust base, and then shoot for the stars" — of Mike Benson, one of the best software architects the world has ever known and the firm's co-founder.

The roots of StarBase stem from the early 90s, when company co-founder William R. Stow, III, the current chairman, CEO and president, was vice president of advanced development at Ashton-Tate.

Stow had hired Mike Benson as the chief architect for Ashton-Tate's replacement for dBASE IV. Code named Darwin, this next generation tool for programmers was used in 25 beta test sites and was called, at that time, "the most exciting product in the industry's history."

The combination of Stow's vision and Benson's technical genius were the guiding force behind Darwin, and eventually, StarBase. But shockingly, when Borland acquired Ashton-Tate it canceled Darwin without even reviewing the project.

Bill Stow realized that although Darwin was an exceptional and revolutionary tool, it was only part of what was needed. While its groundbreaking ease-of-use distinguished Darwin, it was still — like all development tools — meant to make the individual programmer more efficient and effective.

New and improved tools had succeeded in making programmers more productive but had failed to significantly improve the production of software. The twin bogeymen of being behind schedule and over budget had continued to plague software development.

Software applications may originate as one man's idea, but in reality they are built by large teams. It became apparent to Stow that part of the unique architectural brilliance of Darwin was its team environment. What the industry needed were not only improved tools for individual programmers, but a tool that would allow people to work together electronically on a project, as a team.

THE HISTORY OF STARBASE, ONE OF THE WORLD'S PREMIER SOFTWARE DEVELOPERS, IS A STORY OF PEOPLE — PEOPLE'S IDEAS AND DREAMS AND THE HARD WORK AND DEDICATION IT TOOK TO CARRY THEM OUT.

Stow and Benson envisioned a tool that would connect all the team members. Individuals could use their own development tools, all from different companies, and the team tool would integrate them. It would take all the code and store it in a common area. People could collaborate; they could look at code together, work on code together. The new tool would maintain an intricate history of the project, facilitating tracing and isolating any bugs.

The team that ultimately creates a software application comprises more that just programmers. It includes non-technical

Chairman/CEO/President William R. Stow, III, StarBase co-founder

Co-founder Michael Benson

people as well, many of whom know much about how the software should apply to the business, but can't translate it into technical language or code. Middle managers, people from the shop floor and many more — the tool has to be accessible and easy to use for these people as well.

SOFTWARE APPLICATIONS MAY ORIGINATE AS ONE MAN'S IDEA, BUT IN REALITY THEY ARE BUILT BY LARGE TEAMS.

The tool StarBase created, StarTeam, is revolutionizing the industry. Its foundation is SCM, software configuration management. While there are other SCM products, SCM is only the basis of StarTeam; the tool's unique aspects have won it vast respect. StarBase has more than 1,000 customers, among which are many of the world's largest companies, such as IBM, AT&T, Lucent Technologies, GTE, Boeing, Coca-Cola, Xerox and Dell Computer Corporation.

The company's first year revenues were $2 million. It hit $7 million in the second year and into its third year is approaching $18 million. The numbers are dramatic and the story is one of triumph, but there have been problems, too. Among the hardest was the death of co-founder Mike Benson.

Bill Stow calls Benson, "not only brilliant, but one of the finest human beings I've ever known." The privilege of working with Benson attracted many of the finest technical people to StarBase. His contribution to StarBase, however, goes deeper than his brilliance; the character of the man helped form the character of the company.

Mike never let his ego stand in the way of a project. His intellectual honesty and ethics were exceptional. He helped create an environment of trust, where it was safe to share ideas.

On the last day of Mike Benson's life, family and friends were gathered with him in the hospital for a happy occasion. It was his daughter's birthday, and there was a celebration taking place. Amidst all the festivities, Benson slipped into a coma.

Sometime later, as Mike Benson's wife, son, and father, along with Bill Stow, sat keeping vigil in Benson's room, Mike came to. He looked at his father, son and wife. As he said his last goodbyes, his eyes were shining as though he was filled with a bright light. Then he turned to his partner, Bill Stow. Taking Bill's hand, Mike looked into his eyes, the bright light shining from his own. "You're going to carry on my dream, aren't you?" he asked.

Stow's own eyes were now shining with emotion, as he answered with his whole heart — a simple "yes."

That promise goes deep into the heart of the company. Most firms could not withstand a complete change of direction such as StarBase undertook when it switched from making a programmer's tool to the StarTeam concept. The company had to start completely fresh in 1995. Stow had to seek entirely new financing, and often the road seemed lonely and bleak.

Still, that promise to Mike Benson held firm. And the promise Mike has returned to the company is to live on — with his ideas, his words, his intellect — flowing through the company's lifeblood and giving it inspiration and guidance to this day.

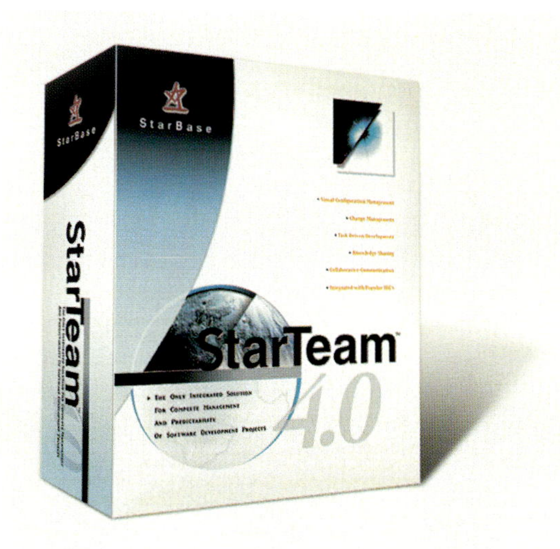

COTELLIGENT, INC.

Success in the ever-changing information technologies industry lies in the ability to forecast future trends. Specialists such as Ken Charlton, president of Cotelligent's Orange County operation, must be able to predict which cutting-edge computer concepts and systems software applications will be in demand long before clients even see the need for new technology.

Cotelligent's Orange County operation, formerly American Digital Technologies (ADT), was built upon this business philosophy. The firm provides business solutions for a wide spectrum of services, including systems analysis, design, implementation and training by application developers and systems engineers who are at the forefront of the software industry.

Ken Charlton, president of Cotelligent's Orange County operation

The key to its success has been in integrating quality products and services into complete customer solutions for Fortune 1000 clients, such as Intel, Cendant and First American Financial. Additionally, the firm is a certified training partner of Microsoft, Sybase, Rational Software and Platinum Technology.

As president and founder of ADT, Ken Charlton remained at its helm when the company merged with the San Francisco-based Cotelligent, Inc. in October of 1997.

A 1970 graduate of the University of California, Irvine, Charlton earned a degree in information and computer science when few of his fellow students even had an inkling of the impact information technologies would have on virtually every other industry.

As a programmer, systems analyst and consultant, Charlton charted a professional path that included various management positions in the information technologies divisions of several Fortune 500 companies, including Ford Aerospace, Unisys and PriceWaterhouse.

Then in 1986, Charlton made the fateful decision to accept a position as vice president for information technologies for American Diversified, a Southern California-based real estate developer.

When the company began downsizing, Charlton was retained to "keep the technologies department running" with a staff that shrank in number from 90 to 18 over the next two years.

It became evident that further cutbacks were merely a matter of time, so Charlton purchased what was left of the division in 1988 and outsourced its services to his previous employer.

Renamed American Digital Technologies, the fledgling firm quickly outgrew its 2,500-square-foot office space. Charlton relocated its operation into increasingly larger facilities before settling into its current location adjacent to the UC Irvine campus in the summer of 1999.

Cotelligent, Inc., a national supplier of IT consulting resources, recognized ADT as a firm with which it shared a common goal: to collaborate with clients to turn obstacles into opportunities.

As a pioneer consolidator in the software professional services industry, Cotelligent is structured to blend the scope, efficiency and resources of a national company with the flexibility and customized service capabilities of its locally managed constituent firms.

By building on the success of its existing subsidiaries, Cotelligent, Inc. creates a place where clients can be assured they are working with the best provider of implementation services and a company where employees are working at the most satisfying job possible.

"Simply put, we specialize in providing assistance in high-tech areas to corporations in virtually every industry to help them learn how to utilize current technology to run their businesses more efficiently," says Charlton. "The challenge lies in being able to read the future and anticipate where our clients will want to be two or three years down the road and invest today in the technology that will allow them to get there tomorrow."

Anaheim/Orange County Visitor & Convention Bureau

APPENDIX

TRANSPORTATION

By 1988, Orange County freeways accommodated the following volumes of traffic:

Freeway	Vehicles Per Day
I-5 n/o I-405	160,000
I-5 s/o E.T. Y	170,000
El Toro Y (Jct. I-5/I405)	260,000 (300,000 by 1994)
SR 55 (Costa Mesa Fwy)(n./o I-5)	180,000
(I-405/SR55 Xch = half billion by '94	500,000
SR 57 (Orange Fwy)	210,000
SR 91 (Riverside Fwy)	210,000

ECONOMICS

ECONOMIC DATA

This portion will focus on several key economic indicators that reflect the real growth of income and wealth in Orange County over the last 50 years.

On October 17, 1963, Orange County was recognized as a Standard Metropolitan Statistical Area by the federal government. This victory came at the end of a 14-year campaign to establish a separate economic entity. Prior to 1963, Orange County was part of the Los Angeles-Long Beach Metropolitan area. The advantages of establishing Orange County as a separate area were many. A Metropolitan District gave Orange County name recognition nationally, enhanced attention by firms seeking new industrial locations and summarization of data for comparison to other districts. In addition, more extensive data would be maintained. This data, commonly used by private market research firms, would enhance visibility. The first task was to set up census tracts, which was done in time for the 1960 Census.

The then current (1960) requirements were pale by today's standards. The county had to contain 10,000 nonagricultural workers, or 10 percent of the nonagricultural workers in the area, or have at least 50 percent of the population residing in contiguous area to the central city with a density of 150 per square mile. Finally 67 percent of all workers must be nonagricultural. Without this victory, the necessary economic data for this article would not have been compiled.

KEY INDICATORS

In order to display the growth in the county in the last 40-50 years, a few simple indicators were selected. These economic indicators were the Dow Jones Industrial Average, median family income, the consumer price index and the unemployment rate. While these fail to summarize the entire spectrum of economic activity, they give a reasonable picture in a simplified manner.

DJIA

The Dow Jones Industrial Average (DJIA) consists of a weighted index of the 30 leading stocks, on the New York Stock Exchange. The companies making up the DJIA reflect the changes and growth over time as the U. S. economy shifts away from a manufacturing base to a mix of manufacturing and service industries. Only six companies remain of the 30 on the 1950 index. The following table displays these changes from 1950 to the present:

1950 D. J. I.A. Components	1999 D.J.I.A. Components	*companies remaiming on index
Allied Chemical	3M	
American Can	ALCOA.	
American Smelting	Allied Signal	
American Tel. & Tel.	American Tel. & Tel.	*
American Tobacco	American Express	
Bethlehem Steel	Boeing	
Chrysler	Caterpillar	
Corn Products Refining	Chevron	
Du Pont	Du Pont	*
Eastman Kodak	Eastman Kodak	*
General Electric	General Electric	*
General Foods	Citigroup	
General Motors	General Motors	*
Goodyear	Goodyear	
International Harvester	Coca Cola	
International Nickel	Disney	
Johns-Manville	Hewlett - Packard	
Loew's	I. B. M.	
National Distillers	International Paper	
National Steel	J. P. Morgan	
Procter & Gamble	Procter & Gamble	*
Sears	Sears	
Standard Oil of Ca.	Exxon	
Standard Oil of N. J.	Johnson & Johnson	
Texas Corp	Mc Donalds	
U. S. Steel	Merck	
Union Carbide	Union Carbide	
United Aircraft	Philip Morris	
Westinghouse Electric	United Technologies	
Woolworth	Wal-Mart	

The securities markets have had three distinct eras. They can be described as the postwar boom from 1945 to 1964, then the Vietnam doldrums from 1965-1981, then the modern or Reagan market from 1981-present. Tax cuts, little inflation and better monetary policy have created the current market. In a public address early in his first term, President Reagan stated, "We will make America the investment capital of the world."

MEDIAN FAMILY INCOME

Median family income is that number at which half the families have incomes above and half the families have income below this level. Historically, median family income has been 80 percent of average income; however, in recent decades this percentage has fallen to 75 percent of average income. A cloud on the horizon of history is the increased share of GNP (Gross National Product) taxes at all levels, local, state and federal, consume. This trend is illustrated in the following table:

YEAR	PERCENTAGE
1944	48.8
1950	21.3
1960	26.6
1970	31.3
1980	32.6
1990	34.4
1999	38-40 (est.)

However, the effect of taxes on individuals or families is beyond our discussion. The rise in households consisting of single people and single parent families also clouds the issue of "family income."

UNEMPLOYMENT RATE

The unemployment rate gives an indication of job availability and overall employment. However, it does not address who is in the workforce and who is not? The issues preventing 0 percent unemployment are many.

The causes of unemployment are frictional, seasonal, technological and structural. Frictional is those people in transit from one job to another. Seasonal is the routine shut down of an industry due to recurring outside factors — particularly weather. Technological unemployment is when workers with obsolescent skills need and can benefit from retraining and upgrading their skills to current levels. Structural unemployment covers those in the workforce without current skills or without the physical, mental or emotional attributes to retain regular employment.

CONSUMER PRICE INDEX

The consumer price index is a weighted average of those items likely to be bought by the consumer. These indexes are changed on a regular basis. The items in the group are changed over time to reflect shifts in consumer preferences and the introduction of new products into the market place. The 1978 Consumer Price Index allocated the following weights to each group:

GROUPING	PERCENTAGE
Food	19
Shelter	44
Transportation	18
Apparel	6
Medical	5
Entertainment	4
Other	4

Obviously, the CPI does not reflect individuals' cost of living but the nation as a whole. Individuals' cost's of living may vary greatly with any index. To further complicate the issue, in 1978 the Bureau of Labor Statistics issued a new index for all Urban Consumers (CPI-U) and revised their index for urban wage earners and clerical workers (CPI-W). (CPI-U) is used in this study.

Also, only some taxes are covered, income taxes being an exception. Included in the index is the concept of substitution. Which items are similar and which are of either superior or inferior grade and how do we account for these? How do price changes in one grade of product effect the other grades or the entire product line?

Also missing is the change of product mix and the quality issues over the decades. Tires at any price did not last 40,000 to 60,000 miles in 1950. There were no personal computers, VCRs, CDs and the like in 1960. As we include these high-tech devices in the consumer market basket, the cost of living goes up but so does our quality of life. It is difficult to compare cost of living data over an extended period of time.

Orange County Economic Data 1949 - 1999
Boom Years

YEAR 12-31	DJIA	Inv. Index	Reagan Index	Median Family Income	CPI	Adj. Med. Family Income(1998)	Percent Unemp.	Unemp. Grade
1949	200	1.00						
1950	235	1.18		3,310	23.8	22,572	6.2	C
1951	269	1.35			25.8			
1952	292	1.46			26.5			
1953	281	1.41			26.7			
1954	404	2.02			26.7			
1955	488	2.44			26.7			
1956	499	2.50			27.1			
1957	436	2.18			28.0			
1958	584	2.92			28.8		7.2	D
1959	679	3.40			29.4		4.5	A
1960	616	3.08		7,219	30.0	39,055	5.8	B
1961	731	3.66			30.3		6.5	C
1962	652	3.26			30.7		4.8	A
1963	763	3.82			31.1		5.0	B
1964	874	4.37			31.7		5.1	B
1965	969	4.85			32.4		5.2	B
1966	786	3.93			33.0		4.0	A
1967	905	4.53		10,263	33.8	49,281	4.8	A
1968	941	4.71		11,012	35.2	50,774	4.2	A

Orange County Economic Data 1949 - 1999 The Doldrums								
YEAR 12-31	DJIA	Inv. Index	Reagan Index	Median Family Income	CPI	Adj. Med. Family Income(1998)	Percent Unemp.	Unemp. Grade
1969	800	4.00		11,695	36.8	51,579	4.4	A
1970	839	4.20		12,245	38.7	51,353	6.6	C
1971	889	4.45		12,955	40.1	52,434	7.8	D
1972	1020	5.10		13,688	41.4	53,661	6.2	C
1973	851	4.26		14,597	43.7	54,213	5.4	B
1974	616	3.08		15,371	48.2	51,758	6.6	C
1975	852	4.26		17,738	53.3	54,013	9.3	F
1976	1005	5.03		19,648	56.9	56,043	7.7	D
1977	831	4.16		20,731	60.8	55,339	5.8	B
1978	805	4.03		21,578	65.3	53,631	4.9	A
1979	839	4.20		24,081	72.3	54,057	4.2	A
1980	964	4.82		26,046	83.7	50,505	4.3	A

Orange County Economic Data 1949 - 1999 The Boom Resumes								
YEAR 12-31	DJIA	Inv. Index	Reagan Index	Median Family Income	CPI	Adj. Med. Family Income(1998)	Percent Unemp.	Unemp. Grade
1981	875	4.38	1.00	29,703	91.9	52,457	4.7	A
1982	1046	5.23	1.20	32,500	97.3	54,211	7.2	D
1983	1258	6.29	1.44	34,400	99.1	56,338	7.1	D
1984	1204	6.02	1.38	37,025	103.6	58,003	4.7	A
1985	1547	7.74	1.77	39,196	108.4	58,686	4.4	A
1986	1896	9.48	2.17	43,841	111.9	63,587	4.0	A
1987	1939	9.70	2.22	43,112	116.7	59,958	3.3	A
1988	2169	10.85	2.48	45,176	122.1	60,050	3.0	A
1989	2753	13.77	3.15	49,916	128.3	63,144	2.9	A
1990	2634	13.17	3.01	53,000	135.9	63,296	3.5	A
1991	3169	15.85	3.62	56,380	141.4	64,713	5.3	B
1992	3301	16.51	3.77	56,346	146.5	62,423	6.8	C
1993	3754	18.77	4.29	54,380	150.3	58,722	6.8	C
1994	3834	19.17	4.38	54,413	152.3	57,986	5.7	B
1995	5117	25.59	5.85	55,507	154.6	58,272	5.1	B
1996	6448	32.24	7.37	57,106	157.5	58,846	4.1	A
1997	7908	39.54	9.04	59,629	160.0	60,486	3.3	A
1998	9181	45.91	10.49	61,812	162.3	61,812	2.9	A
1999	11,497	57.49	13.14	63,478	166.1	62,025	2.7	A

The investors index (Inv. Index) is the relationship between the DJIA on 12-31-49 and the year in the left-hand column. By 1954 the DJIA had doubled.

The Reagan Index represents the growth in the DJIA in the current market era of low inflation.

The adjusted median family income adjusts current 1998 incomes for inflation back to 1950. In the postwar period 1945-1967, significant economic gains were made. Family income in 1998 dollars rose from $22,572 to $49,281. Adjusted family income peaked at $64,713 in 1991. However, the changes in the composition and quality issues in the cost of living index from 1970 onward understate the gains in terms of the quality of life.

The unemployment grade is a method of rating the degree of unemployment in the economy in a given year. A report card grade is given: an A = < 5.0 percent, B = 5.0-5.9 percent, C= 6.0 – 6.9 percent D = 7.0 – 7.9 percent, F = 8.0 percent >.

SOUTH COUNTY

The capsulated chronology of the 250-acre Marblehead Coastal parcel in San Clemente at the northern approach of the downtown area displays the dramatic give and take of participating entities.

1977: The city's Specific Plan for the Lusk Company's Marblehead Coast allowed 2,245 houses, 13 acres of commercial and 28 acres of industrial development.

1981: A revised Specific Plan with 1,576 homes and 21 acres commercial was proposed, then withdrawn.

1982: A plan was adopted with up to 2,353 residences and land set aside for the Nixon Library.

1985: A new Specific Plan showed 1,506 homes, 70 acres of commercial, 10 acres for a hotel and the Nixon Library.

1987: The number of housing units was cut to 1,198. However, the library was established outside the parcel, nullifying the city-approved plan.

1989: The General Plan was updated and The Lusk Company reoriented its development around a hotel, a golf course and homes.

1993: A new plan was approved by the city allowing 300 homes.

1995: Lusk resubmitted a plan for 600 homes, 60 acres of commercial and 15 acres of parks.

1998: The developer processed a plan for 434 homes, 61 acres of commercial and 19 acres of parks. The city approved the plan minus three major stores. A citizen's group initiated a voter initiative to overturn the council's approval.

1999: The petitions were declared invalid by the city... but the final word is still out on the sea-view bluffs whose view of San Clemente Island inspired city founder Ole Hanson to name his "Spanish Village by the Sea."

BIBLIOGRAPHY

ARTS

Arts Orange County. http://www.ocartsnet.org

Ballet Pacifica. http://www.ocartsnet.org/ballet_pacifica

Bowers Museum. http://www.bowers.org/splash.html

Discovery Science Center. http://www.go2disc.org

Fullerton Civic Light Opera. http://fclo.com

Irvine Barclay Theater. http://thebarclay.org

The Irvine Museum. http://www.irvinemuseum.org

Laguna Art Museum. http://www.lagunaartmuseum.org

Laguna Playhouse. http://www.lagunaplayhouse.com

Opera Pacific. http://www.operapacific.org

Orange County Museum of Art. http://www.ocma.net

Orange County Performing Arts Center. http://ocpac.org

Pacific Chorale. http://www.pacific-chorale.org

Pacific Symphony Orchestra. http://www.pso.org

"Season Preview — Arts in Orange County," Advertising Supplement, *Los Angeles Times, The Times Orange County*, September 9, 1998

South Coast Repertory. http://www.scr.org

William Hall Master Chorale. http://www.whmc.org

ARCHITECTURE

Emmons, Steve. *Orange County: A History and Celebration*. New York: Harry N. Abrams Inc., 1988.

Friis, Leo. *Orange County Through Four Centuries*. Anaheim: Pioneer Press, 1965.

Hallan-Gibson, Pamela. *The Golden Promise: An Illustrated History of Orange County*. Windsor Press, 1986.

Heyer, Paul. *American Architecture: Ideas and Ideologies in the Late Twentieth Century*. New York: Van Nostrand Reinhold, 1993.

Marsh, Diann. *Santa Ana: An Illustrated History*. Encinitas, California: Heritage Media Corp., 1994.

McAlester, Virginia and Lee. *A Field Guide to American Houses*. New York: Alfred Knopf, 1984.

Orange County Historical Commission. *One Hundred Years of Yesterdays: A Centennial History of Orange County and Their Communities*. Santa Ana: Orange County Register, 1989.

Reid, Richard. *The Book of Buildings*. New York: Rand McNally & Co., 1980.

Rifkind, Carole. *A Field Guide to American Architecture*. New York: Bonanza Books, 1980.

Winters, Robert. *A Compleat Guide to the Architecture of Los Angeles*. Los Angeles, 1984.

TRANSPORTATION

Donaldson, Stephen E. and William A. Myers. *Rails Through The Orange Groves, A Centennial Look at the Railroads of Orange County*. Interurban Press/Pentrex, 1989-90.

Smith, Vi. *From Jennies To Jets: The Aviation History of Orange County*. 1974.

Bail, Eli. *From Railway To Freeway (P.E. and the Motor Coach)*. Pentrex.

Thompson, Gregory Lee. *The Passenger Train In The Motor Age, California's Rail and Bus Industries*, 1910-1941. Ohio State, 1993.

Walker, Doris. *Orange County: A Centennial Celebration/ Slices Of Orange*. Pioneer Publications, 1989.

Orange County Airport. http://www.ocair.com

ECONOMICS

A. Gary Anderson Center For Economic Research. "Economic and Business Review." Chapman University, Volumes 1 to 17, two issues per year 1982-1998.

A. Gary Anderson Center For Economic Research. "Medium Family Income." Chapman University, Document Data \ Median Family Income — GCP. 1998.

Booth, Louise. *One to Twenty-eight — A History of the Anaheim Union High School District*. Anaheim Union High School District, 1980.

Burtt, Everett. *Labor Markets, Unions, and Government Policies*. St Martin's Press, 1963.

Dow Jones, "Current Components." http://averages.dowjones.com

Employment Development Department. "Civilian Labor Force, Employment, and Unemployment." State of California, http://calmis.cahwnet.gov/file//lfhis/oran$hlf.txt

Employment Development Department. *Annual Planning Information*. State of California, 1986.

Ford Motor Company. "1966 Mustang Manufacturers Suggested Retail Price List." — author's collection.

Lund, William S. *Orange County: Its Economic Growth 1940-1980*. Stanford Research Institute, 1959.

Mc Carthy, James H. *Orange County: Its Economic Growth 1940-1980 (Supplement)*. Stanford Research Institute, 1962.

Orange County Board of Supervisors. *Orange County Progress Reports*, Orange County, volumes and issues from 1954 to 1994. 1994 issues contain consumer price index (CPI) data.

Pierce, Phyllis S. *The Dow Jones Industrial Averages 1885-1990*. Dow Jones & Company, 1991.

Pulliam, Liz. "Questions Finance." *Orange County Register*, December 2, 1994.

Rawn, A. M. *Orange County Sewage Survey*. Edwards Brothers, 1947.

Travelodge Directory. 1959 — author's collection.

NORTH COUNTY

A SURGE TO THE NORTH

Architectural Forum Magazine, April, 1956, reprinted in the *Fullerton Daily News Tribune Newspaper*.

Butz, March. *Yorba Linda, A Child's History*.

Carpenter, Virginia L. *Placentia, A Pleasant Place*. Santa Ana, California: Friis-Pioneer Press, 1988.

Cramer, Esther R. *La Habra: The Pass Through the Hills*. Fullerton, California: Sultana Press, 1969.

Cramer, Esther Ridgway. *Brea: The City of Oil, Oranges and Opportunity*. Brea, California: Premier Printing Corporation, 1992.

Hampson, Teresa. *Brea: Celebration 75 Years, an illustrated history*. Placentia, California: Premier Editions 1993.

Ziebell, Robert E. *Fullerton*, a pictorial history. Virginia Beach, Virginia: The Donning Company/Publishers 1994.

Ziebell, Bob. *An Anniversary Album*, celebrating the 75th anniversary of the Daily Star Progress. Brea, California: Diversified Printing Co., 1991.

ANAHEIM

BOOKS

Ashley, Thomas J. *Power and Politics in Community Planning: an Empirical Analysis of Four Selected Policy Decisions Made in Anaheim, Calif., between 1945-60*. Ann Arbor, University Microfilms International, 1987. Thesis (Ph.D.) — Claremont Graduate School, 1962.

Black, Geoff and Bret Colson. *Dreams to Reality: A Profile of Modern Day Anaheim*. Houston: Pioneer Publications, Inc., 1993.

Booth, Louise. *One to Twenty-eight: A History of Anaheim Union High School District*. Anaheim: Anaheim Union High School District, 1980.

Friis, Leo J. *Anaheim's Cultural Heritage*. Santa Ana: Friis-Pioneer Press, 1975.

_______________. *Historic Buildings of Pioneer Anaheim*. Santa Ana: Friis-Pioneer Press, 1979.

_______________. *Orange County Through Four Centuries*. Santa Ana: Pioneer Press, 1965.

Hallan-Gibson, Pamela. *The Golden Promise: An Illustrated History of Orange County*. Northridge, Calif.: Windsor Publications, Inc., 1986.

Oral History Program at California State University, Fullerton. Anaheim Community History Project. Fullerton, 1978. 2 vols.

Orange County Centennial Inc. *A Hundred Years of Yesterday*. Santa Ana: Orange County Centennial Inc. and Orange County Register, 1988.

The Register. *Legacy: The Orange County Story*. The Register supplement, 1979.

Schultz, Elizabeth J. *Famous Firsts in Anaheim History*. Anaheim: Anaheim Public Library, 1983.

Walker, Doris. *Orange County: A Centennial Celebration*. Houston: Pioneer Publications, Inc., 1989.

Westcott, John. *Anaheim: City of Dreams*. Chatsworth: Windsor Publications, Inc., 1990.

ARTICLES

Bell, Joseph N. "The Big A." *Celebrate*! Vol. III, *Los Angeles Times* supplement, May 21, 1989: 24-25, 68-71.

Clements, Ken. "Anaheim Convention Center: A Fantastic Success Story." *Orange County Business*, Vol. 7, No. 2, (2nd Quarter 1973): 30-41, 43.

Davis, Kevin. "Hard times at Anaheim Plaza have OC's oldest shopping center trying to escape....Mall Malaise." *Orange County Register*, Jan. 16, 1992.

Diaz, Amy. "Anaheim releases terms of Sportstown lease." *Orange County Register*, Dec. 12, 1998.

Dodson, Marcida. "Anaheim: The Little Town that had Big Ideas." *Los Angeles Times*, July 6, 1982.

Fisher, Marla Jo. "Aging Anaheim longs for a face lift." *Orange County Register*, March 8, 1999.

_________________. "The ties that bind." *Orange County Register*, Jan. 31, 1999.

_________________. "You can imagine, too, at Disney Preview." *Orange County Register*, Oct. 19, 1998.

_________________. "Pond at 5: Popular Pauper." *Orange County Register*, June 19, 1998.

Gittelsohn, John. "District considers double sessions." *Orange County Register*, Nov. 18, 1997.

Himmelberg, Michele. "Mighty Ducks take the ice in Anaheim." *Orange County Register*, Oct. 9, 1993.

Kimler, Forest. "Downtown Is Not Where It's At." *The Register*, April 16, 1979.

Kingsley, Barbara. "Six-year lease agreement means forever for team." *Orange County Register*, April 18, 1998.

MacDonald, Brady. "Going Googie Gone: City cataloguing Googie art in Anaheim." *Anaheim Bulletin*, Nov. 21, 1996.

McLeod, Ramon G. "A Marriage of Convenience: For Better or For Worse, Anaheim and Disneyland Go Hand in Hand." *Orange County Register*, June 2, 1985.

Sharon, Clark. "Anaheim - The City of Muscle." *Orange County Illustrated*, April 1981: 43-55.

Sterling, Sally. "Festival Grew From Diversion to Major Celebration." *The Register*, October 23, 1984.

Villelabeitia, Ibon. "Anaheim grows up: Future holds promises, challenges as Anaheim enters new millennium." *Anaheim Bulletin*, April 23, 1998.

_______________. "Anaheim grows up: Growth to come to the Hills." *Anaheim Hills News*, April 23, 1998.

_______________. "Stuck in traffic: Construction turns Anaheim into maze for motorists." *Anaheim Bulletin*, Jan. 15, 1998.

_______________. "Dashing through the Plaza: Tis the season.... For shopping and Plaza merchants expect to be merry." *Anaheim Bulletin*, Dec. 4, 1997.

Woo, Louise. "Anaheim OKs 20,000-seat sports arena." *Orange County Register*, Dec. 28, 1989.

________________. "Still minus a team, Anaheim turns soil on arena." *Orange County Register*, Nov. 9, 1990.

Wroblewski, Annette M. "The Impact of World War II on Orange County." Proceedings of the Conference of Orange County History, 1988. Orange: Chapman College, 1988.

CENTRAL ORANGE COUNTY

BEACH CITIES

BOOKS

Cramer, Esther R., et al., eds. *A Hundred Years of Yesterdays: A Centennial History of the People of Orange County and their Communities*. Santa Ana, California: The Orange County Centennial, Inc. 1988.

Emmons, Steve. *Orange County: A History and Celebration*. New York: Harry N. Abrams, Inc., 1988.

Graebner, Janet E. *Orange County: An Economic Celebration*. Northridge, California: Windsor Publications, 1988.

Hallan-Gibson, Pamela. *The Golden Promise: An Illustrated History of Orange County*. Northridge, California: Windsor Publications, 1986.

Parker, C.E. and Marilyn. *Orange County: Indians to Industry*. Santa Ana, California: First American Title Insurance and Trust Company, 1963.

Reichman, Louis and Gary Cardinale. *The Orange County Experience*. Temple City, California: Pacific Shoreline Press, 1987.

ARTICLES

Blackburn, Cliff. "That Good Old Ground Covered With Houses." *Orange County Register*, March 10, 1969.

__________. "Preacher's Goal: To Start Model Christian Colony." *Orange County Register*, March 31, 1969.

Chappel, Paul. "Seal Beach Founding Tied to Liquor." *Orange County Register*, October 1, 1974.

Epstein, Benjamin. "Grounds for Spending Morning at Mile Square Park." *Los Angeles Times*, April 21, 1994.

Haldane, David. "The Sunset Strip of the Highway." *Los Angeles Times*, June 1, 1992.

Heffner, Kim. "Seal Beach Once Mecca to Gamblers." *Orange County Register*, March 26, 1998.

Kilroy, Mike. "Westminster Colony: Taming the Wild West." *Orange County Register*, May 1, 1997.

Michaud, Anne. "Little Saigon." *Los Angeles Times*, October 29, 1992.

Roberts, Jerry. "Still Crazy After All These Years." *Orange County Magazine*, September, 1998.

Rood, W. B. "Sunset Beach: A Small Town That Wants to Stay Small." *Los Angeles Times*, March 7, 1971.

Wallace, Susan Besze. "No New Wrinkles as Fountain Valley Turns 40." *Orange County Register*, June 12, 1997.

Taylor, Ruth Ellen. *Legacy: The Orange County Story*. Santa Ana, California: The Register, A Division of Freedom Newspapers, Inc., 1980.

SOUTH ORANGE COUNTY

IRVINE & SADDLEBACK VALLEY

"Acorn Day Organizers Plant Seeds of Hope." Ranchos and Canyons Supplement. *Saddleback Valley News: Orange County Register*, Oct. 23, 1998.

Berkman, Leslie. "The Irvine Saga." *Celebrate! Orange County's First 100 Years*. Costa Mesa, California: *Los Angeles Times*, Orange County. May 22, 1988, p. 102 ff.

Cramer, Esther, et. al., eds. *A Hundred Years of Yesterdays: A Centennial History of the People of Orange County and Their Communities*. Santa Ana, California: Orange County Centennial, Inc., Orange County Register, 1988.

Decker, Dr. Donald & Mary L. *Laguna Niguel: The Legacy and the Promise*. Laguna Niguel, California: Royal Literary Publications, 1990.

Fox, Clara Mason. *A History of El Toro*. El Toro, California: El Toro Women's Club, 1938.

"From Cattle to Concrete: Ranchos and Canyons." *Supplement to Saddleback Valley News*, Lake Forest, California: *Orange County Register*, Oct. 23, 1998.

"Irvine — An Emerging World Class High Technology Community." *Planning Ahead*. Irvine, California: The Irvine Company, Oct. 1997.

Jones, Lanie. "A Pitch Blossoms Into Art." *Celebrate! Orange County's First 100 Years*. Costa Mesa, California: *Los Angeles Times, Orange County*, pp. 72-75, 166-168, May 22, 1988.

Liebeck, Judy. *Irvine: A History of Innovation and Growth*. Houston, Texas: Pioneer Publications, Inc., 1990.

"Life With the Lakes." Lake Forest, California: *Saddleback Valley News, Mission Viejo Edition*, Nov. 11, 1998.

Loos, Charles H. "Irvine Was Born 20 Years Ago, But It Wasn't Easy." *Irvine World News*, Dec. 26, 1991.

Milkovich, Barbara, and Ester Cramer, eds. *Early Businesses in Orange County. Orange Countinan V*: Santa Ana, California: Orange County Historical Society, 1992.

Mission Viejo, City of. *Community Profile, Mission Viejo, California*. Mission Viejo, California, 1999.

Mott, Patrich. "Gun 'Em Down, String 'Em Up." *Celebrate! Orange County's First 100 Years*. Costa Mesa, California: *Los Angeles Times, Orange County*. pp. 76, 130-133. May 22, 1988.

Osterman, Joe. *50 Years In "Old" El Toro: A Family, A Time, A Place*. Fullerton, California: Sultana Press, 3d ed., 1992.

The "Old" El Toro Reader: A Guide to The Past."Old" Whittier, California: El Toro Press, 1992.

Parker, T. Jefferson. *Where Serpents Lie* (Fiction). New York City: Hyperion Press, 1998.

Sleeper, Jim. "Rancho Santa Margarita, Where History Found A Home." Trabuco Canyon, California: Trabuco Canyon News, Jan. 1990.

Smith, Joan Irvine. *The Irvine Muesum: A Description and a Statement of Goals*. Irvine, California, c. 1990.

"Story Behind Irvine's Excellent Schools, The." *Planning Ahead*. Irvine, California: Irvine Company, May 1998.

Walker, Doris. *The Key to Our New City*. Laguna Niguel, California: Monarch Bank 1989.

Weight, Harold O. *Twenty Mule Team Days In Death Valley*. Tewntynine Palms, California: The Calico Press, 1972.

SOUTH COAST

BOOKS:

Orton, Charles W. *The Colorful Coast: An Illustrated History of Newport Beach & Harbor*, Carlsbad, California: Heritage Media Corp., 1997.

Walker, I. Doris. *Dana Point Harbor/Capistrano Bay: Home Port for Romance*, 4th edition. Dana Point, California: To-the-Point Press, 1995.

____________. *Orange County, a Centennial Celebration: Sections of Orange*. Houston: Pioneer Publications, Inc., 1989.

PUBLICATIONS:

City of Dana Point. *Dana Point Headlands Specific Plans*, various dates.

City of San Clemente. *Marblehead Coastal Specific Plans*, various dates.

Selected articles from the *Orange County Register*, OCRegister.com and OCNow.com; *Times Orange County* and LATimes.com

Newport Beach Convention and Visitor's Bureau

INDEX

Photo by Shane Giblin

PARTNERS INDEX